THE VARIORUM WALDEN and THE VARIORUM CIVIL DISOBEDIENCE

W9-DGA-911

are the only editions that include comprehensive notes and introductions based on the research and criticism of the past century. The extensive annotations document Thoreau's sources and allusions, cite pertinent passages in his other works, and provide commentary from letters, diaries, reviews, articles, dissertations, biographies and notes by Thoreau's contemporaries and later scholars throughout the world.

The text of *Walden* reproduced here is the only text based on Thoreau's corrections and additions in his personal copy of the first edition.

Walter Harding has devoted the past twenty-five years to research on Thoreau. He has been the Secretary of the Thoreau Society and Editor of its quarterly *Bulletin* and annual *Booklets* since the Society's founding in 1941. The author of eight books about Thoreau and his associates, he has also published numerous articles in leading scholarly journals in this country and abroad.

The Variorum Walden *and* The Variorum Civil Disobedience *were originally published in hardcover editions by Twayne Publishers.*

HENRY DAVID THOREAU

THE VARIORUM
WALDEN AND
THE VARIORUM
CIVIL
DISOBEDIENCE

Annotated and with Introductions
by WALTER HARDING

WASHINGTON SQUARE PRESS
POCKET BOOKS • NEW YORK

THE VARIORUM WALDEN and
THE VARIORUM CIVIL DISOBEDIENCE

WASHINGTON SQUARE PRESS edition published December, 1968
6th printing.........................July, 1973

Published by
POCKET BOOKS, a division of Simon & Schuster, Inc.,
630 Fifth Avenue, New York, N.Y.

L

WASHINGTON SQUARE PRESS editions are distributed by
Simon & Schuster, Inc., 630 Fifth Avenue, New York, N.Y. 10020
and in Canada by Simon & Schuster of Canada, Ltd., Richmond
Hill, Ontario, Canada.

Standard Book Number: 671-47887-7.

ACKNOWLEDGMENTS

I wish to acknowledge my debt to the Research Foundation of the State University of New York for granting me a fellowship which enabled me to put this edition into its final form. I am also indebted to Mrs. Alleta French of Concord, Massachusetts, for passing on to me the notes her husband, the late Allen French, had gathered when he had planned to compile a similar annotated edition of *Walden,* and to Professor John Crossett of Clinton, New York, Mrs. Herbert Hosmer of Concord, Massachusetts, Mr. G. R. Rady of Montreal, Quebec, and Mr. Laurence Richardson and Mrs. Caleb Wheeler of Concord, Massachusetts—all of whom contributed or checked background information for me. And I wish to express my particular appreciation to Professor J. Lyndon Shanley of Northwestern University, who very carefully checked through the entire manuscript and added a wealth of invaluable material from his knowledge of the Walden Manuscripts in the Henry Huntington Library.

CONTENTS

The Variorum WALDEN

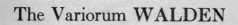

I DO NOT PROPOSE TO WRITE AN ODE TO DEJEC-
TION, BUT TO BRAG AS LUSTILY AS CHANTI-
CLEER IN THE MORNING, STANDING ON HIS
ROOST, IF ONLY TO WAKE MY NEIGHBORS UP.

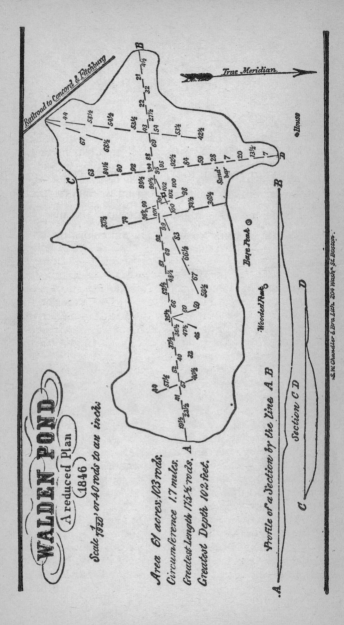

WALDEN POND

A reduced Plan

(1846)

Scale 1/1920, or 40 rods to an inch.

Area 61 acres, 103 rods.
Circumference 1.7 miles;
Greatest Length 175½ rods, A
Greatest Depth 102 feet.

Profile of a Section by the Line A B

Section C D

Railroad to Concord & Fitchburg

True Meridian.

House

Bare Peak

Wooded Peak

Sand-bar

S.W. Chandler & Bro. Lith. 204 Wash'n St. Boston.

INTRODUCTION

HENRY DAVID THOREAU was a few days short of his twenty-eighth birthday when he moved into his cabin on Walden Pond in Concord, Massachusetts, on July 4, 1845, and began what was to become one of the most famous experiments in living in American history. Thoreau was born in Concord on July 12, 1817. Graduating from Harvard in 1837, he turned to teaching, first for a few weeks in the Concord public schools, and then in a highly successful private school which he and his brother John maintained for three years and in which they anticipated many of the techniques of twentieth-century education. But his brother's illness in 1841 forced abandonment of the school, and Thoreau's interest turned toward writing. With John's death in 1842, Thoreau determined to write a memorial tribute, an account of an excursion the two brothers had taken on the Concord and Merrimack rivers in 1839. But the necessity of earning a living kept Thoreau from accomplishing his task until he moved out to Walden with the avowed purpose of writing the book.

It is impossible to pinpoint exactly when Thoreau determined to adopt the simple life and live by himself. He tells us that at the age of five, when he first visited Walden Pond, he had told others he wanted to live on its shores. While he was a student at Harvard, his friend and classmate Charles Stearns Wheeler spent a vacation living in a cabin on Flint's Pond, only a few miles from Walden, and Thoreau, according to tradition, spent several weeks visiting with him there. Another close friend, Ellery Channing, spent some time living in a cabin alone on the Illinois prairies. So there was ample precedent for Thoreau's experiment.

In 1841 there was a special surge of interest on Thoreau's part in such a project. On April 5th, he wrote in his *Journal* (I, 244), "I will build my lodge on the southern slope of some hill, and take there the life the gods send me. Will it not be employment enough to accept gratefully all that is yielded me between sun and sun?" On October 18th, Margaret Fuller wrote him, "Let me know whether you go to the lonely hut." And on December 24th, he wrote again in his *Journal* (I, 299), "I want to go soon and live away by the pond, where I shall hear only the wind whispering among the reeds. It will be success if I shall have left myself behind. But my friends ask what I will do when I get there. Will it not be employment enough to watch the progress of the seasons?" It is quite possible that Thoreau was not thinking of Walden Pond specifically that early, but of Flint's Pond where Stearns Wheeler had lived, or the Hollowell Farm, which Thoreau tells us in *Walden* he once nearly purchased.

But in the fall of 1844 his neighbor and mentor Ralph Waldo Emerson purchased several woodlots on the shores of Walden Pond to preserve them from the axe. On March 5, 1845, Ellery Channing wrote to Thoreau, "I see nothing for you in this earth but that field [at Walden] which I once christened 'Briars'; go out upon that, build yourself a hut, & there begin the grand process of devouring yourself alive." By the end of the month Thoreau had worked out an agreement with Emerson for the use of his land and started construction of his cabin.

The writing of *Walden* was apparently not among Thoreau's original plans when he went to live at the pond. *A Week on the Concord and Merrimack Rivers* was the book he proposed to write (and did write) there. But from the very beginning of his stay at the pond he was noting his impressions in his *Journal* and most of these notes he eventually worked into the text of *Walden*. By February of 1847 he was delivering lectures to his fellow townsmen on his experience at Walden—lectures that, too, eventually became a part of the text. And by 1849 he had sufficiently worked out the first draft of the book so that he was able to announce its publication "soon" in the back pages of the first edition of *A Week*. It is true the announcement proved to be premature, for the failure of *A Week* (only slightly more than two hundred copies were sold in the first four years) frightened publishers away from *Walden*, but *Walden* was eventually published in August of 1854. What happened to the book in those intervening years, how it was reworked, revamped, revised, reworded, and polished through at least seven distinct versions, has been told so well by J. Lyndon Shanley in *The Making of Walden*

(Chicago, 1957) that I shall not attempt to retell it here. The important fact is that out of all Thoreau's labor the masterpiece that is *Walden* was developed.

*   *   *

Thoreau is one of the major American prose stylists, and through an analysis of his style the student becomes more fully aware of just what Thoreau was trying to accomplish in *Walden*, and why *Walden* is considered a masterpiece.

Walden, like Thoreau's cabin, is tightly constructed. Each sentence, each paragraph, and each chapter is in its carefully chosen niche and cannot be moved or removed without severe damage to the artistry of the whole. The basic unifying device of the book is the year. Although Thoreau spent two years, two months, and two days at Walden Pond, in writing the book he compressed his adventures into the cycle of one year. *Walden* opens with the cutting down of the pine trees in March and the construction of the cabin through the spring. In summer he moves into the cabin and tends his beanfield. In the autumn he builds his fireplace and warms his house. In the winter he observes his neighbors—human, animal, and inanimate. Then with the breaking up of the ice on the pond and the renascence of spring he brings his book to a close. One of the most interesting facets of Lyndon Shanley's *The Making of Walden* is his revelation of how carefully Thoreau reworked and transposed his sentences to better carry out this theme of the cycle of the year.

Each individual chapter has its set place in the book as a whole. There is a careful alternation of the spiritual and the mundane ("Higher Laws" is followed by "Brute Neighbors"), the practical and the philosophical ("Economy" is followed by "Where I Lived, and What I Lived For"), the human and the animal ("Winter Visitors" is followed by "Winter Animals"). Adjacent chapters are tied together by contrast (as "Solitude" and "Visitors"), by chronology (as "The Pond in Winter" and "Spring"), or by carefully worded connective phrases (as after "Reading" he begins "Sounds" with, "But while we are confined to books . . ." or after "The Bean-Field" he begins "The Village" with, "After hoeing . . ."). And the three major expository chapters ("Economy," "Higher Laws," and "Conclusion") are placed strategically at the beginning, middle, and end of the book.

Within the individual chapters the details of construction are just as carefully worked out. In "The Ponds" he starts with Walden and then takes a southwestern sweep (his favorite direction for hiking according to his essay on "Walking") across Concord from Flint's Pond to Goose Pond to Fairhaven Bay, to White Pond. In "Former Inhabitants; and Winter Visitors," he starts with the residents of the days of the Revolution, works up through the most recent resident of the area —Hugh Quoil, who died the first autumn Thoreau was at the pond—and ends with those who visited him throughout his stay at the pond. Similar patterns can be worked out for each chapter.

Carefulness of construction continues into the individual paragraph. Although the average reader is not usually aware of it, Thoreau's paragraphs are unusually long. *Walden* contains only 423 paragraphs, an average of only slightly more than one a page in the typical edition. But so carefully developed are they that one does not ordinarily notice their length. Their structure is so varied that there is little point in attempting to pick out typical examples. However one of his favorite devices is at least worth mentioning—his use of the climax ending. Notice how frequently the final sentence in his paragraphs not only neatly sums up the paragraph as a whole, but usually carries it one step beyond, with an added thrust if the paragraph is satirical, with a broader concept if the paragraph is philosophical. Just as with his chapters, many of Thoreau's paragraphs are independent essays in themselves and can stand alone (See, for example, Charles R. Murphy, ed., *Little Essays from the Works of Henry David Thoreau*, Boston, 1931). But they cannot be moved from their specific niche within the book as a whole without damage to its structure.

Thoreau's sentences, too, are often unusually long. It takes very little search to find one half a page in length, and more than one runs on for a full page and more. But again so carefully constructed are they that the average reader has no difficulty with their syntax and is hardly aware of their complexity. Let me take just one serpentine example:

> I sometimes dream of a larger and more populous house, standing in a golden age, of enduring materials, and without gingerbread work, which shall still consist of only

one room, a vast, rude, substantial primitive hall, without ceiling or plastering, with bare rafters and purlins supporting a sort of lower heaven over one's head,—useful to keep off rain and snow, where the king and queen posts stand out to receive your homage, when you have done reverence to the prostrate Saturn of an older dynasty on stepping over the sill; a cavernous house, wherein you must reach up a torch upon a pole to see the roof; where some may live in the fireplace, some in the recess of a window, and some on settles, some at one end of the hall, some at another, and some aloft on rafters with the spiders, if they choose; a house which you have got into when you have opened the outside door, and the ceremony is over; where the weary traveler may wash, and eat, and converse, and sleep, without further journey; such a shelter as you would be glad to reach in a tempestuous night, containing all the essentials of a house, and nothing for housekeeping; where you can see all the treasures of the house at one view, and everything hangs upon its peg that a man should use; at once kitchen, pantry, parlor, chamber, storehouse, and garret; where you can see so necessary a thing as a barrel or a ladder, so convenient a thing as a cupboard, and hear the pot boil, and pay your respects to the fire that cooks your dinner, and the oven that bakes your bread, and the necessary furniture and utensils are the chief ornaments; where the washing is not put out, nor the fire, nor the mistress, and perhaps you are sometimes requested to move from off the trap-door, when the cook would descend into the cellar, and so learn whether the ground is solid or hollow beneath without stamping.

Three hundred and fifty-one words—and yet I doubt if any attentive student has any difficulty with its meaning. I do not, however, want to give the impression that all of Thoreau's sentences are grammatical leviathans. There are sentences in *Walden* only five words in length. One extreme is as frequent as the other and the majority are of more moderate length. Thoreau understood fully the necessity of variety in sentence structure and length. The point is that he could handle the sentence well no matter what its length.

Perhaps the most noticeable characteristic of Thoreau's word choice is the size of his vocabulary. *Walden* is guaranteed to send the conscientious student to the dictionary. In a random sampling we find such words as *integument, umbrageous, deliquium, aliment, fluviatile,* and *periplus.* Yet Thoreau cannot be termed ostentatious in his word-usage. He simply searches for and uses the best possible word for each situation.

A second characteristic is his allusiveness. It is precisely this characteristic of Thoreau's writing that makes an annotated edition of *Walden* so essential. On a typical page he may echo a biblical phrase, quote from a metaphysical poet, translate a few words from an ancient classic, make an allusion to a Greek god, cite an authority on early American history, and toss in a metaphor from a Hindu "Bible." It is true that he is usually careful to make his allusions in such a way that knowledge of the work alluded to is not essential to an understanding of Thoreau's meaning. But the serious reader has his curiosity aroused and wants his questions answered.

A third characteristic is his constant use of figurative speech. Skimming through *Walden,* I have found allusions ("twelve labors of Hercules"), metaphors ("No time to be anything but a machine"), rhetorical questions ("Does any divinity stir within him?"), alliteration ("fetch fresh fuel"), analogy ("Man's body is a stove"), puns ("cooked . . . *à la mode*"), epanorthosis ("more and richer food, larger and more splendid houses, fine and more abundant clothing"), archaisms ("vert"), parables (about the Indian selling his basket), similes ("grew like exogenous plants"), meiosis ("not being the owner, but merely a squatter"), anti-strophe ("Men are not so much the keepers of herds as herds are the keepers of men"), oxymoron ("pious slave-breeder"), epizeuxis ("Simplicity, simplicity, simplicity"), anaphora ("one man . . . one house . . . one vessel"), litotes ("Yet not a few . . ."), antithesis ("Why so seeming fast, but deadly slow?"), portmanteau words ("realometer"), metonymy ("My head is hands and feet"), contrast ("Their train of clouds . . . going to heaven while the cars are going to Boston"), onomatopoeia ("tr-r-r-oonk"), paradox ("I have a great deal of company in my house; especially in the morning, when nobody calls"), personification ("an elderly dame [nature], too, dwells in my neighborhood"), epistrophe ("This is the house that I built; this is the man that lives in the house that I built"), synecdoche ("asks the black bonnet of the gray coat"), irony ("I felt proud to know that the liberties of Massachusetts and of our fatherland were in such safe keeping"), apostrophe ("Walden, is it you?"), and hyperbole ("I could sometimes eat a fried rat with a good relish"). And this list could be extended almost indefinitely. There is hardly a trick of the writing trade that Thoreau does not use.

But the most important characteristic of Thoreau's word choice is its vividness. Emerson once said of Thoreau, "In reading him, I find the same thought, the same spirit that is in me, but he takes a step beyond, and illustrates by excellent images that which I should have conveyed in a sleepy generality" (*Journal*, IX, 522). Thoreau's words are primarily sensory. He makes you hear, see, taste, feel, and smell what he is writing about. He is particularly noted for his brilliant description of the world of nature around him. Take for example this account of the pickerel caught in Walden Pond:

When I see them lying on the ice, or in the well which the fisherman cuts in the ice, making a little hole to admit the water, I am always surprised by their rare beauty, as if they were fabulous fishes, they are so foreign to the streets, even to the woods, foreign as Arabia to our Concord life. They possess a quite dazzling and transcendent beauty which separates them by a wide interval from the cadaverous cod and haddock whose fame is trumpeted in our streets. They are not green like the pines, nor gray like the stones, nor blue like the sky; but they have, to my eyes, if possible, yet rarer colors, like flowers and precious stones, as if they were the pearls, the animalized *nuclei* or crystals of the Walden water.

Note also his descriptions of people, for example that of Mrs. Field:

She too was brave to cook so many successive dinners in the recesses of that lofty stove; with round greasy face and bare breast, still thinking to improve her condition one day; with the never absent mop in one hand, and yet no effects of it visible anywhere.

Even the abstract he is able to express in concrete terms:

Time is but the stream I go a-fishing in. I drink at it; but while I drink I see the sandy bottom and detect how

shallow it is. Its thin current slides away, but eternity
remains. I would drink deeper; fish in the sky, whose
bottom is pebbly with stars.

It has been said of Thoreau that he was the first American to
write a modern prose. One need only place *Walden* alongside
the work of his contemporaries to recognize how much most
prose of a century ago has dated and yet how modern, how
up-to-date is *his* style. There is little wonder that such authors
as Ernest Hemingway, Sinclair Lewis, Willa Cather, Ellen
Glasgow, E. B. White, Robert Frost, Marcel Proust, and even
Henry Miller have paid their tributes to Thoreau's style.

✲   ✲   ✲

But important as is Thoreau's style, it is his thought that has
won him his rank among America's literary greats. In content,
as Reginald Lansing Cook has pointed out ("This Side of
Walden," *English Leaflet*, LIII, 1954, 2), *Walden* has three
literary archetypes—*Robinson Crusoe, Gulliver's Travels,* and
Pilgrim's Progress. I would add a fourth—the *Natural History
of Selbourne.*

To the man in the street, Thoreau is primarily a naturalist,
and a large percentage of the readers of *Walden,* particularly
in the years shortly after its publication, read the book as they
did White's *Selbourne,* primarily for its natural history. Nineteenth-century readers were often advised to ignore the more
philosophical chapters such as "Economy" and "Higher Laws"
as transcendentalist nonsense and to concentrate on the nature
writing in "Sounds," "Brute Neighbors," and "The Pond in
Winter." And as a nature writer, Thoreau has few if any peers.
He is a master of the art of descriptive writing. The loons, the
frogs, the ants, and the mice of *Walden* not only come alive,
they become almost human to the reader. So long as man continues an interest in the world of nature around him, *Walden*
seems assured of readers.

To another large group of readers, *Walden,* like *Robinson
Crusoe,* is escape literature. Thoreau, like Crusoe, was able to
get away from it all, to shed the cares and tribulations of
modern civilization. No more alarm clocks, time schedules, dinner jackets, or headache powders. The reader can vicariously
enjoy the pleasures of the simple life, and at the same time just
as vicariously meet the challenge of pitting himself against his

environment, finding food, clothing, shelter, and fuel, living as his pioneer ancestors did a century or more ago—and never move from his comfortable armchair in front of his thermopane picture window.

Walden can be read in an armchair, but it is not likely that it will be. The reader may start it as escape literature, but almost inevitably he becomes involved. He begins to think, not in terms of escape, but in terms of reform, and particularly of reform of himself. *Walden* is a book that impels its readers to action. In his chapter on "Reading," Thoreau says, "How many a man has dated a new era in his life from the reading of a book." *Walden* has been just such a book for countless readers.

For some strange reason it is not obvious to all of Thoreau's readers that *Walden*, like *Gulliver's Travels*, is a subtle—and often not-too-subtle—satire on contemporary civilization. Even so eminent a critic as James Russell Lowell missed that side of *Walden* and so was able to come to the astounding conclusion that Thoreau lacked a sense of humor. It is true that often Thoreau's humor is, for the so-called "man in the street," a "topsy-turvy" humor. Thoreau laughs at what "John and Jonathan" take seriously, and takes seriously what they tend to laugh at. But there isn't a page of *Walden* without its satirical humor and anyone who cannot see humor in the book may be assured that he is missing the whole point of it. Thoreau announced on his title page that he is bragging as loudly as chanticleer if only to wake up his neighbors. And most of that bragging is satire. Once the reader begins to view the world through Thoreau's eyes, it becomes a very different world.

But *Walden* reaches its highest levels as a spiritual autobiography, a *Pilgrim's Progress* to the good life. I would not denigrate the other levels of appeal. It is one of the book's claims to greatness that it can be appreciated on so many different levels. But to Thoreau and to the perceptive reader *Walden* is as much a religious document as any collection of sermons. It is not concerned with theological technicalities. "Metaphysics," said his good friend Ellery Channing of Thoreau, "was his aversion." But he is concerned with spiritual values throughout *Walden* and particularly in those very chapters "Economy," "Higher Laws," and "Conclusion," that some of his early readers tended to ignore.

To fully appreciate Thoreau's spiritual progress, one must understand at least the basic precepts of transcendentalism.

Transcendentalism was primarily a revolt against the "cold intellectualism" of early nineteenth-century New England Unitarianism. The Unitarians had based their philosophy on the empiricism of John Locke (1632-1704) and his *Essay on Human Understanding,* whose fundamental principle was that all knowledge is sensual knowledge and thus only that which can be made evident to the senses is valid. The transcendentalists did not reject Locke's theories; they went beyond them. They agreed that mundane knowledge is acquired through the senses, but that a far more important body of knowledge— spiritual knowledge, moral judgment, conscience—call it what you will—was innate within man. This common core of knowledge within man was divinely inspired. The infant was born with it, but unfortunately he tended to be corrupted by society as he grew older and to become calloused to this voice within him, until finally he was no longer able to hear it. Therefore it was the good man's obligation to society, to self, and to God, to overcome this callousness, to return to a childish innocence, and to let this inner light be his guide. Such a return, however, was more easily talked about than attained. "The world is too much with us," or, as Thoreau rephrased Wordsworth, "We are too much with the world." We are altogether too willing to sacrifice the spiritual to the material. But try to return we must. And, Thoreau assures us:

> If one advances confidently in the direction of his dreams, and endeavors to live the life which he has imagined, he will meet with a success unexpected in common hours. He will put some things behind, will pass an invisible boundary; new, universal, and more liberal laws will begin to establish themselves around and within him; or the old laws be expanded, and interpreted in his favor in a more liberal sense, and he will live with the license of a higher order of beings.

It is true his success may only be momentary, but it is worth the effort, for in those moments he achieves a higher plane of life; he achieves what more theological writers than Thoreau would call the mystical experience. And one of the most vivid descriptions in our literature of the mystical experience is that recorded by Thoreau in the second paragraph of his chapter on "Sounds." *Walden,* then, is above all a spiritual autobiography and guide book. On the *Robinson Crusoe* level it may at times appear to be escapist, on the *Gulliver's Travels* level, carping and negative; but on its highest level it is dynamic and positive and above all, optimistic. To see that this was the final impression Thoreau wished to leave with his reader, one need only turn to the final paragraph of *Walden:*

> I do not say that John or Jonathan will realize all this; but such is the character of that morrow which mere lapse of time can never make to dawn. The light which puts out our eyes is darkness to us. Only that day dawns to which we are awake. There is more day to dawn. The sun is but a morning star.

Nor is this theme relegated to the final paragraph alone. The predominant images throughout the book—starting with the epigraph on the title page—are those of rebirth, of morning, of spring, of the new life that is ahead. The whole book is shaped around the cycle of the seasons, beginning with spring, passing along through summer, autumn, and winter, and ending with the rebirth of spring. The chapter on "Sounds" follows the same cycle in miniature for the day, beginning with the morning, progressing through the afternoon, the evening, the night, and ending with the sounds of the reawakening of the world at dawn. We read of the purification ceremonies of the Indians and the Mexicans. We learn of the rebirth of a marvelous insect buried for sixty years in the wood of an apple-tree table. We see even Thoreau's beloved Walden Pond become torpid with the ice of winter, only to revive once more with the coming of spring. Thoreau's *Walden* is fundamentally an optimistic book. He feels no need of waiting to attain heaven in another world. He has high hopes of attaining his heaven right here on earth and he does his level best to do so.

—*Walter Harding*

A Note on the Text

The text of this edition is based on the first edition published by Ticknor & Fields in Boston in 1854. It is the first edition of *Walden* to incorporate all the corrections Thoreau made in his personal copy.

A Note on the Annotations

The annotations in this edition are based on (1) Thoreau's own corrections of his copy of *Walden* (This copy is now in the Abernethy Library of Middlebury College, Middlebury, Vermont.); (2) a collation of the notes contained in some of the more than 130 editions of *Walden* that have been printed over the past century; (3) a collation of Thoreau's published *Journal* (Houghton Mifflin, 1906, 14 vols.); (4) a collation of several hundred reviews and critical articles on *Walden*; (5) a reading of every published biography of Thoreau; (6) a search through Thoreau's unpublished "commonplace books" now in the Harvard Library, the Morgan Library, the Berg Collection of the New York Public Library, the Library of Congress, and the Huntington Library; (7) a reading of every American doctoral dissertation on Thoreau, published or unpublished; and (8) reading of the autobiographies, diaries, letters, and other memoirs of his friends and contemporaries.

Abbreviations for periodical titles are those used by the Modern Language Association in *PMLA*.

ECONOMY[1]

WHEN I wrote the following pages, or rather the bulk of them, I lived alone, in the woods, a mile from any neighbor, in a house which I had built myself, on the shore of Walden Pond, in Concord, Massachusetts, and earned my living by the labor of my hands only. I lived there two years and two months. At present I am a sojourner in civilized life again.

I should not obtrude my affairs so much on the notice of my readers if very particular inquiries[2] had not been made by my townsmen concerning my mode of life, which some would call impertinent, though they do not appear to me at all impertinent, but, considering the circumstances, very natural and pertinent. Some have asked what I got to eat; if I did not feel lonesome; if I was not afraid; and the like. Others have been curious to learn what portion of my income I devoted to charitable purposes; and some, who have large families, how many poor children I maintained. I will therefore ask those of my readers who feel no particular interest in me to pardon me if I undertake to answer some of these questions in this book. In most books, the *I*, or first person, is omitted; in this it will be retained; that, in respect to egotism, is the main difference. We commonly do not remember that it is, after all, always the first person that is speaking. I should not talk so much about myself if there were any body else whom I knew as well. Unfortunately, I am confined to this theme by the narrowness of my experience. Moreover, I, or my side, require of every writer, first or last, a simple and sincere account of his own life, and not merely what he has heard of other men's lives; some such account as he would send to his kindred from a distant land; for if he has lived sincerely, it must have been in a distant land to me. Perhaps these pages are more particularly addressed to poor students.[3] As for the rest of my readers, they will accept such portions as apply to them. I trust that none will stretch the seams in putting on the coat, for it may do good service to him whom it fits.

I would fain say something, not so much concerning the Chinese and Sandwich Islanders⁴ as you who read these pages, who are said to live in New England; something about your condition, especially your outward condition or circumstances in this world, in this town, what it is, whether it is necessary that it be as bad as it is, whether it cannot be improved as well as not. I have travelled a good deal in Concord; and every where, in shops, and offices, and fields, the inhabitants have appeared to me to be doing penance in a thousand remarkable ways. What I have heard of Bramins⁵ sitting exposed to four fires and looking in the face of the sun⁶; or hanging suspended, with their heads downward, over flames; or looking at the heavens over their shoulders "until it becomes impossible for them to resume their natural position, while from the twist of the neck nothing but liquids can pass into the stomach;" or dwelling, chained for life, at the foot of a tree; or measuring with their bodies, like caterpillars, the breadth of vast empires; or standing on one leg on the tops of pillars,—even these forms of conscious penance are hardly more incredible and astonishing than the scenes which I daily witness. The twelve labors of Hercules⁷ were trifling in comparison with those which my neighbors have undertaken; for they were only twelve, and had an end; but I could never see that these men slew or captured any monster or finished any labor. They have no friend Iolas⁸ to burn with a hot iron the root of the hydra's head, but as soon as one head is crushed, two spring up.

I see young men, my townsmen, whose misfortune it is to have inherited farms, houses, barns, cattle, and farming tools; for these are more easily acquired than got rid of. Better if they had been born in the open pasture and suckled by a wolf,⁹ that they might have seen with clearer eyes what field they were called to labor in. Who made them serfs of the soil? Why should they eat their sixty acres, when man is condemned to eat only his peck of dirt?¹⁰ Why should they begin digging their graves as soon as they are born? They have got to live a man's life, pushing all these things before them, and get on as well as they can. How many a poor immortal soul have I met well nigh crushed and smothered under its load, creeping down the road of life, pushing before it a barn seventy-five feet by forty, its Augean stables[11] never cleansed, and one hundred acres of land, tillage, mowing, pasture, and wood-lot! The portionless, who struggle with no such unnecessary inherited encumbrances, find it labor enough to subdue and cultivate a few cubic feet of flesh.

But men labor under a mistake. The better part of the man is soon ploughed into the soil for compost. By a seeming fate, commonly called necessity, they are employed, as it says in an old book,[12] laying up treasures which moth and rust will corrupt and thieves break through and steal. It is a fool's life, as they will find when they get to the end of it, if not before. It is said that Deucalion and Pyrrha[13] created men by throwing stones over their heads behind them:—

> Inde genus durum sumus, experiensque laborum,
> Et documenta damus quâ simus origine nati.[14]

Or, as Raleigh rhymes it in his sonorous way,—

"From thence our kind hard-hearted is, enduring pain and care,
  Approving that our bodies of a stony nature are."[15]

So much for a blind obedience to a blundering oracle, throwing the stones over their heads behind them, and not seeing where they fell.

Most men, even in this comparatively free country, through mere ignorance and mistake, are so occupied with the factitious cares and superfluously coarse labors of life that its finer fruits cannot be plucked by them. Their fingers, from excessive toil, are too clumsy and tremble too much for that. Actually, the laboring man has not leisure for a true integrity day by day; he cannot afford to sustain the manliest relations to men; his labor would be depreciated in the market. He has no time to be any thing but a machine. How can he remember well his ignorance—which his growth requires—who has so often to use his knowledge? We should feed and clothe him gratuitously sometimes, and recruit him with our cordials, before we judge of him. The finest qualities of our nature, like the bloom on fruits, can be preserved only by the most delicate handling. Yet we do not treat ourselves nor one another thus tenderly.

Some of you, we all know, are poor, find it hard to live, are sometimes, as it were, gasping for breath. I have no doubt that some of you who read this book are unable to pay for all the dinners which you have actually eaten, or for the coats and shoes which are fast wearing or are already worn out, and have come to this page to spend borrowed or stolen time, robbing your creditors of an hour. It is very evident what mean and sneaking lives many of you live, for my sight has been whetted by experience; always on the limits,[16] trying to get into business and trying to get out of debt, a very ancient slough, called by the Latins *aes alienum*, another's brass, for some of their coins were made of brass; still living, and dying, and buried by this other's brass; always promising to pay, promising to pay, to-morrow, and dying to-day, insolvent; seeking to curry favor, to get custom, by how many modes, only not state-prison offences; lying, flattering, voting, contracting yourselves into a nutshell[17] of civility, or dilating into an atmosphere of thin and vaporous generosity, that you may persuade your neighbor to let you make his shoes, or his hat, or his coat, or his carriage, or import his groceries for him; making yourselves sick, that you may lay up something against a sick day, something to be tucked away in an old chest, or in a stocking behind the plastering, or, more safely, in the brick bank; no matter where, no matter how much or how little.

I sometimes wonder that we can be so frivolous, I may almost say, as to attend to the gross but somewhat foreign form of servitude called Negro Slavery, there are so many keen and subtle masters that enslave both north and south. It is hard to have a southern overseer; it is worse to have a northern one;[18] but worst of all when you are the slave-driver of yourself. Talk of a divinity in man![19] Look at the teamster on the highway, wending to market by day or night; does any divinity stir within him?[20] His highest duty to fodder and water his horses! What is his destiny to him compared with the shipping interests? Does not he drive for Squire Make-a-stir?[21] How god-like, how immortal, is he? See how he cowers and sneaks, how vaguely all the day he fears, not being immortal nor divine, but the slave and prisoner of his own opinion of himself, a fame won by his own deeds. Public opinion is a weak tyrant compared with our own private opinion. What a man thinks of himself, that it is which determines, or rather indicates, his fate. Self-emancipation even in the West Indian provinces of the fancy and imagination,—what Wilberforce[22] is there to bring that about? Think, also, of the ladies of the land weaving toilet cushions[23] against the last day, not to betray too green an interest in their fates! As if you could kill time without injuring eternity.

The mass of men lead lives of quiet desperation. What is called resignation is confirmed desperation. From the desperate city you go into the desperate country, and have to console yourself with the bravery of minks and muskrats. A stereotyped but unconscious despair is concealed even under what are called the games and amusements of mankind. There is no play in them, for this comes after work. But it is a characteristic of wisdom not to do desperate things.

When we consider what, to use the catechism, is the chief end of man,[24] and what are the true necessaries and means of life, it appears as if men had deliberately chosen the common mode of living because they preferred it to any other. Yet they honestly think there is no choice left. But alert and healthy natures remember that the sun rose clear. It is never too late to give up our prejudices. No way of thinking or doing, however ancient, can be trusted without proof. What every body echoes or in silence passes by as true to-day may turn out to be falsehood to-morrow, mere smoke of opinion, which some had trusted for a cloud that would sprinkle fertilizing rain on their fields. What old people say you cannot do you try and find that you can. Old deeds for old people, and new deeds for new. Old people did not know enough once, perchance, to fetch fresh fuel to keep the fire a-going; new people put a little dry wood under a pot,[25] and are whirled round the globe with the speed of birds, in a way to kill old people, as the phrase is. Age is no better, hardly so well, qualified for an instructor as youth, for it has not profited so much as it has lost. One may almost doubt if the wisest man has learned any thing of absolute value by living. Practically, the old have no very important advice to give the young, their own experience has been so partial, and their lives have been such miserable failures, for private reasons, as they must believe; and it may be that they have some faith left which belies that experience, and they are only less young than they were. I have lived some thirty years[26] on this planet, and I have yet to hear the first syllable of valuable or even earnest advice from my seniors. They have told me nothing, and probably cannot tell me any thing, to the purpose. Here is life, an experiment to a great extent untried by me; but it does not avail me that they have tried it. If I have any experience which I think valuable, I am sure to reflect that this my Mentors said nothing about.

One farmer says to me, "You cannot live on vegetable food[27] solely, for it furnishes nothing to make bones with;" and so he religiously devotes a part of his day to supplying his system with the raw material of bones; walking all the while he talks behind his oxen, which, with vegetable-made bones, jerk him and his lumbering plough along in spite of every obstacle. Some things are really necessaries of life in some circles, the most helpless and diseased, which in others are luxuries merely, and in others still are entirely unknown.

The whole ground of human life seems to some to have been gone over by their predecessors, both the heights and the valleys, and all things to have been cared for. According to Evelyn, "the wise Solomon prescribed ordinances for the very distances of trees; and the Roman praetors have decided how often you may go into your neighbor's land to gather the acorns which fall on it without trespass, and what share belongs to that neighbor."[28] Hippocrates[29] has even left directions how we should cut our nails; that is, even with the ends of the fingers, neither shorter nor longer. Undoubtedly the very tedium and ennui which presume to have exhausted the variety and the joys of life are as old as Adam. But man's capacities have never been measured; nor are we to judge of what he can do by any precedents, so little has been tried. Whatever have been thy failures hitherto, "be not afflicted, my child, for who shall assign to thee what thou hast left undone?"[30]

We might try our lives by a thousand simple tests; as, for instance, that the same sun which ripens my beans illumines at once a system of earths like ours. If I had remembered this it would have prevented some mistakes. This was not the light in which I hoed them. The stars are the apexes of what wonderful triangles! What distant and different beings in the various mansions of the universe are contemplating the same one at the same moment! Nature and human life are as various as our several constitutions. Who shall say what prospect life offers to another? Could a greater miracle take place than for us to look through each other's eyes for an instant? We should live in all the ages of the world in an hour; ay, in all the worlds of the ages. History, Poetry, Mythology!—I know of no reading of another's experience so startling and informing as this would be.

The greater part of what my neighbors call good I believe in my soul to be bad, and if I repent of any thing, it is very likely to be my good behavior. What demon possessed me that I behaved so well? You may say the wisest thing you can, old man, —you who have lived seventy years,[31] not without honor of a kind,—I hear an irresistible voice which invites me away from all that. One generation abandons the enterprises of another like stranded vessels.

I think that we may safely trust a good deal more than we do. We may waive just so much care of ourselves as we honestly bestow elsewhere. Nature is as well adapted to our weakness as to our strength. The incessant anxiety and strain of some is a well nigh incurable form of disease. We are made to exaggerate the importance of what work we do; and yet how much is not done by us! or, what if we had been taken sick? How vigilant we are! determined not to live by faith if we can avoid it; all the day long on the alert, at night we unwillingly say our prayers and commit ourselves to uncertainties. So thoroughly and sincerely are we compelled to live, reverencing our life, and denying the possibility of change. This is the only way, we say; but there are as many ways as there can be drawn radii from one centre. All change is a miracle to contemplate; but it is a miracle which is taking place every instant. Confucius said, "To know that we know what we know, and that we do not know what we do not know, that is true knowledge."[32] When one man has reduced a fact of the imagination to be a fact to his understanding, I foresee that all men will at length establish their lives on that basis.

Let us consider for a moment what most of the trouble and anxiety which I have referred to is about, and how much it is necessary that we be troubled, or, at least, careful. It would be some advantage to live a primitive and frontier life, though in the midst of an outward civilization, if only to learn what are the gross necessaries of life and what methods have been taken to obtain them; or even to look over the old day-books[33] of the merchants, to see what it was that men most commonly bought at the stores, what they stored, that is, what are the grossest groceries.[34] For the improvements of ages have had but little influence on the essential laws of man's existence; as our skeletons, probably, are not to be distinguished from those of our ancestors.

By the words, *necessary of life*, I mean whatever, of all that man obtains by his own exertions, has been from the first, or from long use has become, so important to human life that few, if any, whether from savageness, or poverty, or philosophy, ever attempt to do without it. To many creatures there is in this sense but one necessary of life, Food. To the bison of the prairie it is a few inches of palatable grass, with water to drink; unless he seeks the Shelter of the forest or the mountain's shadow. None of the brute creation requires more than Food and Shelter. The necessaries of life for man in this climate may, accurately enough, be distributed under the several heads of Food, Shelter, Clothing, and Fuel; for not till we have secured these are we prepared to entertain the true problems of life with freedom and a prospect of success. Man has invented, not only houses, but clothes and cooked food; and possibly from the accidental discovery of the warmth of fire, and the consequent use of it, at first a luxury, arose the present necessity to sit by it. We observe cats and dogs acquiring the same second nature. By proper Shelter and Clothing we legitimately retain our own internal heat; but with an excess of these, or of Fuel, that is, with an external heat greater than our own internal, may not cookery properly be said to begin? Darwin, the naturalist, says of the inhabitants of Tierra del Fuego, that while his own party, who were well clothed and sitting close to a fire, were far from too warm, these naked savages, who were farther off, were observed, to his great surprise, "to be streaming with perspiration at undergoing such a roasting."[35] So, we are told, the New Hollander[36] goes naked with impunity, while the European shivers in his clothes. Is it impossible to combine the hardiness of these savages with the intellectualness of the civilized man? According to Liebig,[37] man's body is a stove, and food the fuel which keeps up the internal combustion in the lungs. In cold weather we eat more, in warm less. The animal heat is the result of a slow combustion, and disease and death take place when this is too rapid; or for want of fuel, or from some defect in the draught, the fire goes out. Of course the vital heat is not to be confounded with fire; but so much for analogy. It appears, therefore, from the above list, that the expression, *animal life*, is nearly synonymous with the expression, *animal heat*; for while

Food may be regarded as the Fuel which keeps up the fire within us,—and Fuel serves only to prepare that Food or to increase the warmth of our bodies by addition from without,— Shelter and Clothing also serve only to retain the *heat* thus generated and absorbed.

The grand necessity, then, for our bodies, is to keep warm, to keep the vital heat in us. What pains we accordingly take, not only with our Food, and Clothing, and Shelter, but with our beds, which are our night-clothes, robbing the nests and breasts of birds to prepare this shelter within a shelter, as the mole has its bed of grass and leaves at the end of its burrow! The poor man is wont to complain that this is a cold world; and to cold, no less physical than social, we refer directly a great part of our ails. The summer, in some climates, makes possible to man a sort of Elysian life.[38] Fuel, except to cook his Food, is then unnecessary; the sun is his fire, and many of the fruits are sufficiently cooked by its rays; while Food generally is more various, and more easily obtained, and Clothing and Shelter are wholly or half unnecessary. At the present day, and in this country, as I find by my own experience, a few implements, a knife, an axe, a spade, a wheelbarrow, &c., and for the studious, lamplight, stationery, and access to a few books, rank next to necessaries, and can all be obtained at a trifling cost. Yet some, not wise, go to the other side of the globe,[39] to barbarous and unhealthy regions, and devote themselves to trade for ten or twenty years, in order that they may live,— that is, keep comfortably warm,—and die in New England at last. The luxuriously rich are not simply kept comfortably warm, but unnaturally hot; as I implied before, they are cooked, of course *à la mode*.

Most of the luxuries, and many of the so called comforts of life, are not only not indispensable, but positive hinderances to the elevation of mankind. With respect to luxuries and comforts, the wisest have ever lived a more simple and meagre life than the poor. The ancient philosophers, Chinese, Hindoo, Persian, and Greek, were a class than which none has been poorer in outward riches, none so rich in inward. We know not much about them. It is remarkable that *we* know so much of them as we do. The same is true of the more modern reformers and benefactors of their race. None can be an impartial or wise observer of human life but from the vantage ground of what *we* should call voluntary poverty. Of a life of luxury the fruit

is luxury, whether in agriculture, or commerce, or literature,
or art. There are nowadays professors of philosophy, but not
philosophers. Yet it is admirable to profess because it was once
admirable to live. To be a philosopher is not merely to have
subtle thoughts, nor even to found a school, but so to love
wisdom as to live according to its dictates, a life of simplicity,
independence, magnanimity, and trust. It is to solve some of
the problems of life, not only theoretically, but practically.
The success of great scholars and thinkers is commonly a
courtier-like success, not kingly, not manly. They make shift to
live merely by conformity, practically as their fathers did, and
are in no sense the progenitors of a nobler race of men. But
why do men degenerate ever? What makes families run out?
What is the nature of the luxury which enervates and destroys
nations? Are we sure that there is none of it in our own lives?
The philosopher is in advance of his age even in the outward
form of his life. He is not fed, sheltered, clothed, warmed, like
his contemporaries. How can a man be a philosopher and not
maintain his vital heat by better methods than other men?

When a man is warmed by the several modes which I have
described, what does he want next? Surely not more warmth of
the same kind, as more and richer food, larger and more
splendid houses, finer and more abundant clothing, more
numerous incessant and hotter fires, and the like. When he has
obtained those things which are necessary to life, there is another alternative than to obtain the superfluities; and that is, to
adventure on life now, his vacation from humbler toil having
commenced. The soil, it appears, is suited to the seed, for it has
sent its radicle downward, and it may now send its shoot upward also with confidence. Why has man rooted himself thus
firmly in the earth, but that he may rise in the same proportion
into the heavens above?—for the nobler plants[40] are valued for
the fruit they bear at last in the air and light, far from the
ground, and are not treated like the humbler esculents, which,
though they may be biennials, are cultivated only till they have
perfected their root, and often cut down at top for this purpose, so that most would not know them in their flowering
season.

I do not mean to prescribe rules to strong and valiant
natures, who will mind their own affairs whether in heaven or
hell, and perchance build more magnificently and spend more
lavishly than the richest, without ever impoverishing them-

selves, not knowing how they live,—if, indeed, there are any such, as has been dreamed; nor to those who find their encouragement and inspiration in precisely the present condition of things, and cherish it with the fondness and enthusiasm of lovers,—and, to some extent, I reckon myself in this number; I do not speak to those who are well employed, in whatever circumstances, and they know whether they are well employed or not;—but mainly to the mass of men who are discontented,[41] and idly complaining of the hardness of their lot or of the times, when they might improve them. There are some who complain most energetically and inconsolably of any, because they are, as they say, doing their duty. I also have in my mind that seemingly wealthy, but most terribly impoverished class of all, who have accumulated dross, but know not how to use it, or get rid of it, and thus have forged their own golden or silver fetters.

If I should attempt to tell how I have desired to spend my life in years past, it would probably surprise those of my readers who are somewhat acquainted with its actual history; it would certainly astonish those who know nothing about it. I will only hint at some of the enterprises which I have cherished.

In any weather, at any hour of the day or night, I have been anxious to improve the nick of time, and notch it on my stick too;[42] to stand on the meeting of two eternities,[43] the past and future, which is precisely the present moment; to toe that line. You will pardon some obscurities, for there are more secrets in my trade than in most men's, and yet not voluntarily kept, but inseparable from its very nature. I would gladly tell all that I know about it, and never paint "No Admittance" on my gate.

I long ago lost a hound, a bay horse, and a turtle-dove,[44] and am still on their trail. Many are the travellers I have spoken concerning them, describing their tracks and what calls they answered to. I have met one or two who had heard the hound, and the tramp of the horse, and even seen the dove disappear behind a cloud, and they seemed as anxious to recover them as if they had lost them themselves.

To anticipate, not the sunrise and the dawn merely, but, if possible, Nature herself! How many mornings, summer and winter, before yet any neighbor was stirring about his business, have I been about mine! No doubt, many of my townsmen

have met me returning from this enterprise, farmers starting
for Boston in the twilight, or woodchoppers going to their
work. It is true, I never assisted the sun materially in his rising,
but, doubt not, it was of the last importance only to be present
at it.

So many autumn, ay, and winter days, spent outside the
town, trying to hear what was in the wind, to hear and carry
it express! I well-nigh sunk all my capital in it, and lost my
own breath into the bargain, running in the face of it. If it had
concerned either of the political parties, depend upon it, it
would have appeared in the Gazette⁴⁵ with the earliest intelligence. At other times watching from the observatory of some
cliff or tree, to telegraph any new arrival; or waiting at evening
on the hill-tops for the sky to fall, that I might catch something, though I never caught much, and that, manna-wise,⁴⁶
would dissolve again in the sun.

For a long time I was reporter to a journal,⁴⁷ of no very wide
circulation, whose editor has never yet seen fit to print the bulk
of my contributions, and, as is too common with writers, I got
only my labor for my pains. However, in this case my pains
were their own reward.

For many years I was self-appointed inspector⁴⁸ of snow
storms and rain storms, and did my duty faithfully; surveyor,⁴⁹
if not of highways, then of forest paths and all across-lot
routes, keeping them open, and ravines bridged and passable
at all seasons, where the public heel had testified to their
utility.

I have looked after the wild stock of the town, which give a
faithful herdsman a good deal of trouble by leaping fences;
and I have had an eye to the unfrequented nooks and corners
of the farm; though I did not always know whether Jonas or
Solomon worked in a particular field to-day; that was none of
my business. I have watered the red huckleberry, the sand
cherry and the nettle tree, the red pine and the black ash, the
white grape and the yellow violet,⁵⁰ which might have withered
else in dry seasons.

In short, I went on thus for a long time, I may say it without
boasting, faithfully minding my business, till it became more
and more evident that my townsmen would not after all admit
me into the list of town officers, nor make my place a sinecure
with a moderate allowance. My accounts, which I can swear
to have kept faithfully, I have, indeed, never got audited, still

less accepted, still less paid and settled. However, I have not set my heart on that.

Not long since, a strolling Indian went to sell baskets at the house of a well-known lawyer[51] in my neighborhood. "Do you wish to buy any baskets?"[52] he asked. "No, we do not want any," was the reply. "What!" exclaimed the Indian as he went out the gate, "do you mean to starve us?" Having seen his industrious white neighbors so well off,—that the lawyer had only to weave arguments, and by some magic wealth and standing followed, he had said to himself: I will go into business; I will weave baskets; it is a thing which I can do. Thinking that when he had made the baskets he would have done his part, and then it would be the white man's to buy them. He had not discovered that it was necessary for him to make it worth the other's while to buy them, or at least make him think that it was so, or to make something else which it would be worth his while to buy. I too had woven a kind of basket of a delicate texture, but I had not made it worth any one's while to buy them. Yet not the less, in my case, did I think it worth my while to weave them, and instead of studying how to make it worth men's while to buy my baskets, I studied rather how to avoid the necessity of selling them. The life which men praise and regard as successful is but one kind. Why should we exaggerate any one kind at the expense of the others?

Finding that my fellow-citizens were not likely to offer me any room in the court house, or any curacy or living any where else, but I must shift for myself, I turned my face more exclusively than ever to the woods, where I was better known. I determined to go into business at once, and not wait to acquire the usual capital, using such slender means as I had already got. My purpose in going to Walden Pond was not to live cheaply nor to live dearly there, but to transact some private business[53] with the fewest obstacles; to be hindered from accomplishing which for want of a little common sense, a little enterprise and business talent, appeared not so sad as foolish.

I have always endeavored to acquire strict business habits; they are indispensable to every man. If your trade is with the Celestial Empire,[54] then some small counting house on the coast, in some Salem harbor, will be fixture enough. You will export such articles as the country affords, purely native products, much ice and pine timber and a little granite, always in native bottoms. These will be good ventures. To oversee all the details yourself in person; to be at once pilot and captain, and owner and underwriter; to buy and sell and keep the accounts; to read every letter received, and write or read every letter sent; to superintend the discharge of imports night and day; to be upon many parts of the coast almost at the same time;—often the richest freight will be discharged upon a Jersey shore;[55]—to be your own telegraph, unweariedly sweeping the horizon, speaking all passing vessels bound coastwise; to keep up a steady despatch of commodities, for the supply of such a distant and exorbitant market; to keep yourself informed of the state of the markets, prospects of war and peace every where, and anticipate the tendencies of trade and civilization,—taking advantage of the results of all exploring expeditions, using new passages and all improvements in navigation;—charts to be studied, the position of reefs and new lights and buoys to be ascertained, and ever, and ever, the logarithmic tables to be corrected, for by the error of some calculator the vessel often splits upon a rock that should have reached a friendly pier,—there is the untold fate of La Perouse;[56]—universal science to be kept pace with, studying the lives of all great discoverers and navigators, great adventurers and merchants, from Hanno[57] and the Phoenicians down to our day; in fine, account of stock to be taken from time to time, to know how you stand. It is a labor to task the faculties of a man,—such problems of profit and loss, of interest, of tare and tret,[58] and gauging of all kinds in it, as demand a universal knowledge.

I have thought that Walden Pond would be a good place for business, not solely on account of the railroad and the ice trade; it offers advantages which it may not be good policy to divulge; it is a good post[59] and a good foundation. No Neva marshes[60] to be filled; though you must every where build on piles of your own driving. It is said that a flood-tide, with a westerly wind, and ice in the Neva, would sweep St. Petersburg from the face of the earth.

As this business was to be entered into without the usual capital, it may not be easy to conjecture where those means, that will still be indispensable to every such undertaking, were to be obtained. As for Clothing,[61] to come at once to the practical part of the question, perhaps we are led oftener by the love of novelty, and a regard for the opinions of men, in procuring it, than by a true utility. Let him who has work to do recollect that the object of clothing is, first to retain the vital heat, and secondly, in this state of society,[62] to cover nakedness, and he may judge how much of any necessary or important work may be accomplished without adding to his wardrobe. Kings and queens who wear a suit but once, though made by some tailor or dress-maker to their majesties, cannot know the comfort of wearing a suit that fits. They are no better than wooden horses to hang the clean clothes on. Every day our garments become more assimilated to ourselves, receiving the impress of the wearer's character, until we hesitate to lay them aside, without such delay and medical appliances and some such solemnity even as our bodies. No man ever stood the lower in my estimation for having a patch in his clothes; yet I am sure that there is greater anxiety, commonly, to have fashionable, or at least clean and unpatched clothes, than to have a sound conscience. But even if the rent is not mended, perhaps the worst vice betrayed is improvidence. I sometimes try my acquaintances by such tests as this;—who could wear a patch, or two extra seams only, over the knee? Most behave as if they believed that their prospects for life would be ruined if they should do it. It would be easier for them to hobble to town with a broken leg than with a broken pantaloon. Often if an accident happens to a gentleman's legs, they can be mended; but if a similar accident happens to the legs of his pantaloons, there is no help for it; for he considers, not what is truly respectable, but what is respected. We know but few men, a great many coats and breeches. Dress a scarecrow in your last shift, you standing shiftless by, who would not soonest salute the scarecrow? Passing a cornfield the other day, close by a hat and coat on a stake, I recognized the owner of the farm. He was only a little more weather-beaten than when I saw him last. I have heard of a dog that barked at every stranger who approached his master's premises with clothes on, but was easily quieted by a naked thief. It is an interesting question how far men would retain their relative rank if they were divested of their clothes. Could you, in such a case, tell surely of any company of civilized men, which belonged to the most respected class? When Madam Pfeiffer, in her adventurous travels round the world, from east to west, had got so near home as Asiatic Russia, she says that she felt the necessity of wearing other than a travelling dress, when she went to meet the authorities, for she "was now in a civilized country, where —people are judged of by their clothes."[63] Even in our democratic New England towns the accidental possession of wealth, and its manifestation in dress and equipage alone, obtain for the possessor almost universal respect. But they who yield such respect, numerous as they are, are so far heathen, and need to have a missionary sent to them. Beside, clothes introduced sewing, a kind of work which you may call endless; a woman's dress, at least, is never done.

A man who has at length found something to do will not need to get a new suit to do it in; for him the old will do, that has lain dusty in the garret for an indeterminate period. Old shoes will serve a hero longer than they have served his valet, —if a hero ever has a valet,—bare feet are older than shoes, and he can make them do. Only they who go to soirées and legislative halls must have new coats, coats to change as often as the man changes in them. But if my jacket and trousers, my hat and shoes, are fit to worship God in, they will do; will they not? Who ever saw his old clothes,—his old coat, actually worn out, resolved into its primitive elements, so that it was not a deed of charity to bestow it on some poor boy, by him perchance to be bestowed on some poorer still, or shall we say richer, who could do with less? I say, beware of all enterprises that require new clothes, and not rather a new wearer of clothes. If there is not a new man, how can the new clothes be made to fit? If you have any enterprise before you, try it in your old clothes. All men want, not something to *do with*, but something to *do*, or rather something to *be*. Perhaps we should never procure a new suit, however ragged or dirty the old, until we have so conducted, so enterprised or sailed in some way, that we feel like new men in the old, and that to retain it would be like keeping new wine in old bottles.[64] Our moulting season, like that of the fowls, must be a crisis in our lives. The loon retires to solitary ponds to spend it. Thus also the snake casts its slough, and the caterpillar its wormy coat, by an internal industry and expansion; for clothes are but outmost cuticle and mortal coil.[65] Otherwise we shall be found sailing under false colors, and be inevitably cashiered at last by our own opinion, as well as that of mankind.

We don garment after garment, as if we grew like exogenous plants by addition without. Our outside and often thin and fanciful clothes are our epidermis or false skin, which partakes not of our life, and may be stripped off here and there without fatal injury; our thicker garments, constantly worn, are our cellular integument, or cortex; but our shirts are our liber or true bark, which cannot be removed without girdling and so destroying the man. I believe that all races at some seasons wear something equivalent to the shirt. It is desirable that a man be clad so simply that he can lay his hands on himself in the dark, and that he live in all respects so compactly and preparedly, that, if an enemy take the town, he can, like the old philosopher,[66] walk out the gate empty-handed without anxiety. While one thick garment is, for most purposes, as good as three thin ones, and cheap clothing can be obtained at prices really to suit customers; while a thick coat can be bought for five dollars, which will last as many years, thick pantaloons for two dollars, cowhide boots for a dollar and a half a pair, a summer hat for a quarter of a dollar, and a winter cap for sixty-two and a half cents, or a better be made at home at a nominal cost, where is he so poor that, clad in such a suit, *of his own earning,* there will not be found wise men to do him reverence?

When I ask for a garment of a particular form, my tailoress[67] tells me gravely, "They do not make them so now," not emphasizing the "They" at all, as if she quoted an authority as impersonal as the Fates, and I find it difficult to get made what I want, simply because she cannot believe that I mean what I say, that I am so rash. When I hear this sentence, I am for a moment absorbed in thought, emphasizing to myself each word separately that I may come at the meaning of it, that I may find out by what degree of consanguinity *They* are related to *me,* and what authority they may have in an affair which affects me so nearly; and, finally, I am inclined to answer her with equal mystery, and without any more emphasis of the "they,"—"It is true, they did not make them so recently, but they do now." Of what use this measuring of me if she does not measure my character, but only the breadth of my shoulders, as it were a peg to hang the coat on? We worship not the Graces,[68] nor the Parcae,[69] but Fashion. She spins and weaves and cuts with full authority. The head monkey at Paris puts on a traveller's cap, and all the monkeys in America do the same. I sometimes despair of getting any thing quite simple and honest done in this world by the help of men. They would have to be passed through a powerful press first,

to squeeze their old notions out of them, so that they would
not soon get upon their legs again, and then there would be
some one in the company with a maggot in his head, hatched
from an egg deposited there nobody knows when, for not even
fire kills these things, and you would have lost your labor.
Nevertheless, we will not forget that some Egyptian wheat[10]
was handed down to us by a mummy.

On the whole, I think that it cannot be maintained that
dressing has in this or any country risen to the dignity of an
art. At present men make shift to wear what they can get.
Like shipwrecked sailors, they put on what they can find on
the beach, and at a little distance, whether of space or time,
laugh at each other's masquerade. Every generation laughs
at the old fashions, but follows religiously the new. We are
amused at beholding the costume[11] of Henry VIII., or Queen
Elizabeth, as much as if it was that of the King and Queen of
the Cannibal Islands. All costume off a man is pitiful or grotesque. It is only the serious eye peering from and the sincere
life passed within it, which restrain laughter and consecrate
the costume of any people. Let Harlequin[12] be taken with a
fit of the colic and his trappings will have to serve that mood
too. When the soldier is hit by a cannon ball rags are as becoming as purple.

The childish and savage taste of men and women for new
patterns keeps how many shaking and squinting through kalei-
doscopes that they may discover the particular figure which
this generation requires today. The manufacturers have
learned that this taste is merely whimsical. Of two patterns
which differ only by a few threads more or less of a particular
color, the one will be sold readily, the other lie on the shelf,
though it frequently happens that after the lapse of a season
the latter becomes the most[13] fashionable. Comparatively, tat-
tooing is not the hideous custom which it is called. It is not
barbarous merely because the printing is skin-deep and un-
alterable.

I cannot believe that our factory system[14] is the best mode
by which men may get clothing. The condition of the operatives is becoming every day more like that of the English;
and it cannot be wondered at, since, as far as I have heard or
observed, the principal object is, not that mankind may be
well and honestly clad, but, unquestionably, that the corporations may be enriched. In the long run men hit only what they

aim at. Therefore, though they should fail immediately, they had better aim at something high.

As for a Shelter, I will not deny that this is now a necessary of life, though there are instances of men having done without it for long periods in colder countries than this. Samuel Laing says that "The Laplander in his skin dress, and in a skin bag which he puts over his head and shoulders, will sleep night after night on the snow—in a degree of cold which would extinguish the life of one exposed to it in any woollen clothing."⁵ He had seen them asleep thus. Yet he adds, "They are not hardier than other people." But, probably, man did not live long on the earth without discovering the convenience which there is in a house, the domestic comforts, which phrase may have originally signified the satisfactions of the house more than of the family; though these must be extremely partial and occasional in those climates where the house is associated in our thoughts with winter or the rainy season chiefly, and two thirds of the year, except for a parasol, is unnecessary. In our climate, in the summer, it was formerly almost solely a covering at night. In the Indian gazettes a wigwam was the symbol of a day's march, and a row of them cut or painted on the bark of a tree signified that so many times they had camped. Man was not made so large limbed and robust but that he must seek to narrow his world, and wall in a space such as fitted him. He was at first bare and out of doors; but though this was pleasant enough in serene and warm weather, by daylight, the rainy season and the winter, to say nothing of the torrid sun, would perhaps have nipped his race in the bud if he had not made haste to clothe himself with the shelter of a house. Adam and Eve, according to the fable,⁶ wore the bower before other clothes. Man wanted a home, a place of warmth, or comfort, first of physical warmth, then the warmth of the affections.

We may imagine a time when, in the infancy of the human race, some enterprising mortal crept into a hollow in a rock for shelter. Every child begins the world again, to some extent, and loves to stay out doors, even in wet and cold. It plays house, as well as horse, having an instinct for it. Who does not remember the interest with which when young he looked at shelving rocks, or any approach to a cave? It was the natural yearning of that portion of our most primitive ancestor which still survived in us. From the cave we have advanced to roofs of palm leaves, of bark and boughs, of linen woven and stretched, of grass and straw, of boards and shingles, of stones and tiles. At last, we know not what it is to live in the open air, and our lives are domestic in more senses than we think. From the hearth to the field is a great distance. It would be well perhaps if we were to spend more of our days and nights without any obstruction between us and the celestial bodies, if the poet did not speak so much from under a roof, or the saint dwell there so long. Birds do not sing in caves, nor do doves cherish their innocence in dovecots.

However, if one designs to construct a dwelling house, it behooves him to exercise a little Yankee shrewdness, lest after all he find himself in a workhouse, a labyrinth[77] without a clew, a museum, an almshouse, a prison, or a splendid mausoleum instead. Consider first how slight a shelter is absolutely necessary. I have seen Penobscot Indians,[78] in this town, living in tents of thin cotton cloth, while the snow was nearly a foot deep around them, and I thought that they would be glad to have it deeper to keep out the wind. Formerly, when how to get my living honestly, with freedom left for my proper pursuits, was a question which vexed me even more than it does now, for unfortunately I am become somewhat callous, I used to see a large box by the railroad, six feet long by three wide, in which the laborers locked up their tools at night, and it suggested to me that every man who was hard pushed might get such a one for a dollar, and, having bored a few auger holes in it, to admit the air at least, get into it when it rained and at night, and hook down the lid, and so have freedom in his love,[79] and in his soul be free. This did not appear the worst, nor by any means a despicable alternative. You could sit up as late as you pleased, and, whenever you got up, go abroad without any landlord or house-lord dogging you for rent. Many a man is harassed to death to pay the rent of a larger and more luxurious box who would not have frozen to death in such a box as this. I am far from jesting. Economy is a subject which admits of being treated with levity, but it cannot so be disposed of. A comfortable house for a rude and hardy race, that lived mostly out of doors, was once made here almost entirely of such materials as Nature furnished ready to their hands. Gookin, who was superintendent of the

Indians subject to the Massachusetts Colony, writing in 1674, says, "The best of their houses are covered very neatly, tight and warm, with barks of trees, slipped from their bodies at those seasons when the sap is up, and made into great flakes, with pressure of weighty timber, when they are green. . . . The meaner sort are covered with mats which they make of a kind of bulrush, and are also indifferently tight and warm, but not so good as the former. . . . Some I have seen, sixty or a hundred feet long and thirty feet broad. . . . I have often lodged in their wigwams, and found them as warm as the best English houses."[80] He adds, that they were commonly carpeted and lined within with well-wrought embroidered mats, and were furnished with various utensils. The Indians had advanced so far as to regulate the effect of the wind by a mat suspended over the hole in the roof and moved by a string. Such a lodge was in the first instance constructed in a day or two at most, and taken down and put up in a few hours; and every family owned one, or its apartment in one.

In the savage state every family owns a shelter as good as the best, and sufficient for its coarser and simpler wants; but I think that I speak within bounds when I say that, though the birds of the air[81] have their nests, and the foxes their holes, and the savages their wigwams, in modern civilized society not more than one half the families own a shelter. In the large towns and cities, where civilization especially prevails, the number of those who own a shelter is a very small fraction of the whole. The rest pay an annual tax for this outside garment of all, become indispensable summer and winter, which would buy a village of Indian wigwams, but now helps to keep them poor as long as they live. I do not mean to insist here on the disadvantage of hiring compared with owning, but it is evident that the savage owns his shelter because it costs so little, while the civilized man hires his commonly because he cannot afford to own it; nor can he, in the long run, any better afford to hire. But, answers one, by merely paying this tax the poor civilized man secures an abode which is a palace compared with the savage's. An annual rent of from twenty-five to a hundred dollars, these are the country rates, entitles him to the benefit of the improvements of centuries, spacious apartments, clean paint and paper. Rumford fireplace,[82] back plastering,[83] Venetian blinds, copper pump, spring lock, a commodious cellar, and many other things. But how happens it that he who is said to enjoy these things is so commonly a *poor* civilized man, while the savage, who has them not, is rich as a savage? If it is asserted that civilization is a real advance in the condition of man,—and I think that it is, though only the wise improve their advantages,—it must be shown that it has produced better dwellings without making them more costly; and the cost of a thing is the amount of what I will call life which is required to be exchanged for it, immediately or in the long run. An average house in this neighborhood costs perhaps eight hundred dollars, and to lay up this sum will take from ten to fifteen years of the laborer's life, even if he is not encumbered with a family;— estimating the pecuniary value of every man's labor at one dollar a day, for if some receive more, others receive less;—so that he must have spent more than half his life commonly before *his* wigwam will be earned. If we suppose him to pay a rent instead, this is but a doubtful choice of evils. Would the savage have been wise to exchange his wigwam for a palace on these terms?

It may be guessed that I reduce almost the whole advantage of holding this superfluous property as a fund in store against the future, so far as the individual is concerned, mainly to the defraying of funeral expenses. But perhaps a man is not required to bury himself. Nevertheless this points to an important distinction between the civilized man and the savage; and, no doubt, they have designs on us for our benefit, in making the life of a civilized people an *institution*, in which the life of the individual is to a great extent absorbed, in order to preserve and perfect that of the race. But I wish to show at what a sacrifice this advantage is at present obtained, and to suggest that we may possibly so live as to secure all the advantage without suffering any of the disadvantage. What mean ye by saying that the poor ye have always with you,[84] or that the fathers have eaten sour grapes,[85] and the children's teeth are set on edge?

"As I live, saith the Lord God, ye shall not have occasion any more to use this proverb in Israel."

"Behold all souls are mine; as the soul of the father, so also the soul of the son is mine: the soul that sinneth it shall die."[86]

When I consider my neighbors, the farmers of Concord, who are at least as well off as the other classes, I find that for the most part they have been toiling twenty, thirty, or forty years, that they may become the real owners of their farms, which commonly they have inherited with encumbrances, or else bought with hired money,—and we may regard one third of that toil as the cost of their houses,—but commonly they have not paid for them yet. It is true, the encumbrances sometimes outweigh the value of the farm, so that the farm itself becomes one great encumbrance, and still a man is found to inherit it, being well acquainted with it, as he says. On applying to the assessors, I am surprised to learn that they cannot at once name a dozen in the town who own their farms free and clear. If you would know the history of these homesteads, inquire at the bank where they are mortgaged. The man who has actually paid for his farm with labor on it is so rare that every neighbor can point to him. I doubt if there are three such men in Concord. What has been said of the merchants, that a very large majority, even ninety-seven in a hundred, are sure to fail, is equally true of the farmers. With regard to the merchants, however, one of them says pertinently that a great part of their failures are not genuine pecuniary failures, but merely failures to fulfil their engagements, because it is inconvenient; that is, it is the moral character that breaks down. But this puts an infinitely worse face on the matter, and suggests, beside, that probably not even the other three succeed in saving their souls, but are perchance bankrupt in a worse sense than they who fail honestly. Bankruptcy and repudiation are the spring-boards from which much of our civilization vaults and turns its somersets, but the savage stands on the unelastic plank of famine. Yet the Middlesex Cattle Show[87] goes off here with *éclat* annually, as if all the joints of the agricultural machine were suent.[88]

The farmer is endeavoring to solve the problem of a livelihood by a formula more complicated than the problem itself. To get his shoestrings he speculates in herds of cattle. With consummate skill he has set his trap with a hair spring[89] to catch comfort and independence, and then, as he turned away, got his own leg into it. This is the reason he is poor; and for a similar reason we are all poor in respect to a thousand savage comforts, though surrounded by luxuries. As Chapman sings,—

"The false society of men—
—for earthly greatness
All heavenly comforts rarefies to air."[90]

And when the farmer has got his house, he may not be the
richer but the poorer for it, and it be the house that has got
him. As I understand it, that was a valid objection urged by
Momus[91] against the house which Minerva made, that she
"had not made it movable, by which means a bad neighborhood might be avoided;" and it may still be urged, for our
houses are such unwieldy property that we are often imprisoned rather than housed in them; and the bad neighborhood
to be avoided is our own scurvy selves. I know one or two
families, at least, in this town, who, for nearly a generation,
have been wishing to sell their houses in the outskirts and
move into the village, but have not been able to accomplish
it, and only death will set them free.

Granted that the *majority* are able at last either to own or
hire the modern house with all its improvements. While civilization has been improving our houses, it has not equally
improved the men who are to inhabit them. It has created
palaces, but it was not so easy to create noblemen and kings.
And *if the civilized man's pursuits are no worthier than the
savage's, if he is employed the greater part of his life in obtaining gross necessaries and comforts merely, why should
he have a better dwelling than the former?*

But how do the poor *minority* fare? Perhaps it will be
found, that just in proportion as some have been placed in
outward circumstances above the savage, others have been
degraded below him. The luxury of one class is counterbalanced by the indigence of another. On the one side is the
palace, on the other are the almshouse and "silent poor."[92]
The myriads who built the pyramids to be the tombs of the
Pharaohs were fed on garlic,[93] and it may be were not decently buried themselves. The mason who finishes the cornice
of the palace returns at night perchance to a hut not so good
as a wigwam. It is a mistake to suppose that, in a country
where the usual evidences of civilization exist, the condition
of a very large body of the inhabitants may not be as degraded as that of savages. I refer to the degraded poor, not
now to the degraded rich. To know this I should not need to
look farther than to the shanties which every where border

our railroads, that last improvement in civilization; where I see in my daily walks human beings living in sties, and all winter with an open door, for the sake of light, without any visible, often imaginable, wood pile, and the forms of both old and young are permanently contracted by the long habit of shrinking from cold and misery, and the development of all their limbs and faculties is checked. It certainly is fair to look at that class by whose labor the works which distinguish this generation are accomplished. Such too, to a greater or less extent, is the condition of the operatives of every denomination in England, which is the great workhouse of the world. Or I could refer you to Ireland, which is marked as one of the white or enlightened spots on the map.[94] Contrast the physical condition of the Irish with that of the North American Indian, or the South Sea Islander, or any other savage race before it was degraded by contact with the civilized man. Yet I have no doubt that that people's rulers are as wise as the average of civilized rulers. Their condition only proves what squalidness may consist with civilization. I hardly need refer now to the laborers[95] in our Southern States who produce the staple exports of this country, and are themselves a staple production of the South. But to confine myself to those who are said to be in *moderate*[96] circumstances.

Most men appear never to have considered what a house is, and are actually though needlessly poor all their lives because they think that they must have such a one as their neighbors have. As if one were to wear any sort of coat which the tailor might cut out for him, or gradually leaving off palmleaf hat or cap of woodchuck skin, complain of hard times because he could not afford to buy him a crown! It is possible to invent a house still more convenient and luxurious than we have, which yet all would admit that man could not afford to pay for. Shall we always study to obtain more of these things, and not sometimes to be content with less? Shall the respectable citizen thus gravely teach, by precept and example, the necessity of the young man's providing a certain number of superfluous glowshoes,[97] and umbrellas, and empty guest chambers for empty guests, before he dies? Why should not our furniture be as simple as the Arab's or the Indian's? When I think of the benefactors of the race, whom we have apotheosized as messengers from heaven, bearers of divine gifts to man, I do not see in my mind any retinue at their heels, any car-load of fashionable furniture. Or what if I were to allow—would it not be a singular allowance?—that our furniture should be more complex than the Arab's, in proportion as we are morally and intellectually his superiors! At present our houses are cluttered and defiled with it, and a good house-wife would sweep out the greater part into the dust hole, and not leave her morning's work undone. Morning work! By the blushes of Aurora[98] and the music of Memnon,[99] what should be man's *morning work* in this world? I had three pieces of limestone on my desk, but I was terrified to find that they required to be dusted daily, when the furniture of my mind was all undusted still, and I threw them out the window in disgust. How, then, could I have a furnished house? I would rather sit in the open air, for no dust gathers on the grass, unless where man has broken ground.

It is the luxurious and dissipated who set the fashions which the herd so diligently follow. The traveller who stops at the best houses, so called, soon discovers this, for the publicans presume him to be a Sardanapalus,[100] and if he resigned himself to their tender mercies he would soon be completely emasculated. I think that in the railroad car we are inclined to spend more on luxury than on safety and convenience, and it threatens without attaining these to become no better than a modern drawing room, with its divans, and ottomans, and sunshades, and a hundred other oriental[101] things, which we are taking west with us, invented for the ladies of the harem and the effeminate natives of the Celestial Empire, which Jonathan[102] should be ashamed to know the names of. I would rather sit on a pumpkin and have it all to myself, than be crowded on a velvet cushion. I would rather ride on earth in an ox cart with a free circulation, than go to heaven in the fancy car of an excursion train[103] and breathe a *malaria* all the way.

The very simplicity and nakedness of man's life in the primitive ages imply this advantage at least, that they left him still but a sojourner in nature. When he was refreshed with food and sleep he contemplated his journey again. He dwelt, as it were, in a tent in this world, and was either threading the valleys, or crossing the plains, or climbing the mountain tops. But lo! men have become the tools of their tools. The man who independently plucked the fruits when he was hungry is become a farmer; and he who stood under a tree for shelter, a housekeeper. We now no longer camp as for a night, but have settled down on earth and forgotten heaven. We have adopted Christianity merely as an improved method of *agri-*culture.[104] We have built for this world a family mansion, and for the next a family tomb. The best works of art are the expression of man's struggle to free himself from this condition, but the effect of our art is merely to make this low state comfortable and that higher state to be forgotten. There is actually no place in this village for a work of *fine* art, if any had come down to us, to stand, for our lives, our houses and streets, furnish no proper pedestal for it. There is not a nail to hang a picture on, nor a shelf to receive the bust of a hero or a saint. When I consider how our houses are built and paid for, or not paid for, and their internal economy managed and sustained, I wonder that the floor does not give way under the visitor while he is admiring the gewgaws[105] upon the mantel-piece, and let him through into the cellar, to some solid and honest though earthy foundation. I cannot but perceive that this so called rich and refined life is a thing jumped at, and I do not get on in the enjoyment of the *fine arts* which adorn it, my attention being wholly occupied with the jump; for I remember that the greatest genuine leap, due to human muscles alone, on record, is that of certain wandering Arabs, who are said to have cleared twenty-five feet on level ground. Without factitious support, man is sure to come to earth again beyond that distance. The first question which I am tempted to put to the proprietor of such impropriety is, Who bolsters you? Are you one of the ninety-seven who fail, or the three who succeed? Answer me these questions, and then perhaps I may look at your baubles and find them ornamental. The cart before the horse is neither beautiful nor useful. Before we can adorn our houses with beautiful objects the walls must be stripped, and our lives must be stripped, and beautiful housekeeping and beautiful living be laid for a foundation: now, a taste for the beautiful is most cultivated out of doors, where there is no house and no housekeeper.

Old Johnson, in his "Wonder-Working Providence," speaking of the first settlers of this town, with whom he was contemporary, tells us that "they burrow themselves in the earth for their first shelter under some hillside, and, casting the soil aloft upon timber, they make a smoky fire against the earth, at the highest side."[106] They did not "provide them

houses," says he, "till the earth, by the Lord's blessing, brought
forth bread to feed them," and the first year's crop was so light
that "they were forced to cut their bread very thin for a long
season." The secretary of the Province of New Netherland,
writing in Dutch, in 1650, for the information of those who
wished to take up land there, states more particularly, that
"those in New Netherland, and especially in New England,
who have no means to build farm houses at first according
to their wishes, dig a square pit in the ground, cellar fashion,
six or seven feet deep, as long and as broad as they think
proper, case the earth inside with wood all round the wall,
and line the wood with the bark of trees or something else to
prevent the caving in of the earth; floor this cellar with plank,
and wainscot it overhead for a ceiling, raise a roof of spars
clear up, and cover the spars with bark or green sods, so that
they can live dry and warm in these houses with their entire
families for two, three, and four years, it being understood
that partitions are run through those cellars which are adapted
to the size of the family. The wealthy and principal men in
New England, in the beginning of the colonies, commenced
their first dwelling houses in this fashion for two reasons;
firstly, in order not to waste time in building, and not to want
food the next season; secondly, in order not to discourage
poor laboring people whom they brought over in numbers
from Fatherland. In the course of three or four years, when
the country became adapted to agriculture, they built themselves handsome houses, spending on them several thousands."[107]

In this course which our ancestors took there was a show
of prudence at least, as if their principle were to satisfy the
more pressing wants first. But are the more pressing wants
satisfied now? When I think of acquiring for myself one of
our luxurious dwellings, I am deterred, for, so to speak, the
country is not yet adapted to *human* culture,[108] and we are still
forced to cut our *spiritual* bread far thinner than our forefathers did their wheaten. Not that all architectural orna-
ment is to be neglected even in the rudest periods; but let our
houses first be lined with beauty, where they come in contact with our lives, like the tenement of the shellfish, and not
overlaid with it. But, alas! I have been inside one or two of
them, and know what they are lined with.

Though we are not so degenerate but that we might possibly live in a cave or a wigwam or wear skins today, it certainly is better to accept the advantages, though so dearly bought, which the invention and industry of mankind offer. In such a neighborhood as this, boards and shingles, lime and bricks, are cheaper and more easily obtained than suitable caves, or whole logs, or bark in sufficient quantities, or even well-tempered clay or flat stones. I speak understandingly on this subject, for I have made myself acquainted with it both theoretically and practically. With a little more wit we might use these materials so as to become richer than the richest now are, and make our civilization a blessing. The civilized man is a more experienced and wiser savage. But to make haste to my own experiment.

Near the end of March, 1845, I borrowed[109] an axe and went down to the woods by Walden Pond, nearest to where I intended to build my house, and began to cut down some tall arrowy white pines, still in their youth, for timber. It is difficult to begin without borrowing, but perhaps it is the most generous course thus to permit your fellow-men to have an interest in your enterprise. The owner of the axe, as he released his hold on it, said that it was the apple of his eye; but I returned it sharper than I received it. It was a pleasant hillside where I worked, covered with pine woods, through which I looked out on the pond, and a small open field in the woods where pines and hickories were springing up. The ice in the pond was not yet dissolved, though there were some open spaces, and it was all dark colored and saturated with water. There were some slight flurries of snow during the days that I worked there; but for the most part when I came out on to the railroad, on my way home, its yellow sand heap stretched away gleaming in the hazy atmosphere, and the rails shone in the spring sun, and I heard the lark and pewee[110] and other birds already come to commence another year with us. They were pleasant spring days, in which the winter of man's discontent[111] was thawing as well as the earth, and the life that had lain torpid began to stretch itself. One day, when my axe had come off and I had cut a green hickory for a wedge, driving it with a stone, and had placed the whole to soak in a pond hole in order to swell the wood, I saw a striped snake run into the water, and he lay on the bottom, apparently without inconvenience, as long as I staid there, or more than a quarter of an hour; perhaps because he had not yet fairly come out of the torpid state. It appeared to me that for a like reason men remain in their present low and primitive condition; but if they should feel the influence of the spring of springs arousing them, they would of necessity rise to a higher and more ethereal life. I had previously seen the snakes in frosty mornings in my path with portions of their bodies still numb and inflexible, waiting for the sun to thaw them. On the 1st of April it rained and melted the ice, and the early part of the day, which was very foggy, I heard a stray goose groping about over the pond and cackling as if lost, or like the spirit of the fog.

So I went on for some days cutting and hewing timber, and also studs and rafters, all with my narrow axe, not having many communicable or scholar-like thoughts, singing to myself,—

> Men say they know many things;
> But lo! they have taken wings,—
> The arts and sciences,
> And a thousand appliances;
> The wind that blows
> Is all that any body knows.[112]

I hewed the main timbers six inches square, most of the studs on two sides only, and the rafters and floor timbers on one side, leaving the rest of the bark on, so that they were just as straight and much stronger than sawed ones. Each stick was carefully mortised or tenoned by its stump, for I had borrowed other tools by this time. My days in the woods were not very long ones; yet I usually carried my dinner of bread and butter, and read the newspaper in which it was wrapped, at noon, sitting amid the green pine boughs which I had cut off, and to my bread was imparted some of their fragrance, for my hands were covered with a thick coat of pitch. Before I had done I was more the friend than the foe of the pine tree, though I had cut down some of them, having become better acquainted with it. Sometimes a rambler in the wood was attracted by the sound of my axe, and we chatted pleasantly over the chips which I had made.

By the middle of April, for I made no haste in my work, but rather made the most of it, my house was framed and ready for the raising. I had already bought the shanty of James Collins,[113] an Irishman who worked on the Fitchburg Railroad, for boards. James Collins' shanty was considered an uncommonly fine one. When I called to see it he was not at home. I walked about the outside, at first unobserved from within, the window was so deep and high. It was of small dimensions, with a peaked cottage roof, and not much else to be seen, the dirt being raised five feet all around as if it were a compost heap. The roof was the soundest part, though a good deal warped and made brittle by the sun. Doorsill there was none, but a perennial passage for the hens under the door board. Mrs. C. came to the door and asked me to view it from the inside. The hens were driven in by my approach. It was dark, and had a dirt floor for the most part, dank, clammy, and aguish, only here a board and there a board which would not bear removal. She lighted a lamp to show me the inside of the roof and the walls, and also that the board floor extended under the bed, warning me not to step into the cellar, a sort of dust hole two feet deep. In her own words, they were "good boards overhead, good boards all around, and a good window,"—of two whole squares originally, only the cat had passed out that way lately. There was a stove, a bed, and a place to sit, an infant in the house where it was born, a silk parasol, gilt-framed looking-glass, and a patent new coffee mill nailed to an oak sapling, all told. The bargain was soon concluded, for James had in the meanwhile returned. I to pay four dollars and twenty-five cents tonight, he to vacate at five tomorrow morning, selling to nobody else meanwhile: I to take possession at six. It were well, he said, to be there early, and anticipate certain indistinct but wholly unjust claims on the score of ground rent and fuel. This he assured me was the only encumbrance. At six I passed him and his family on the road. One large bundle held their all,—bed, coffee-mill, looking-glass, hens,—all but the cat, she took to the woods and became a wild cat, and, as I learned afterward, trod in a trap set for woodchucks, and so became a dead cat at last.

I took down this dwelling the same morning, drawing the nails, and removed it to the pond side by small cart-loads, spreading the boards on the grass there to bleach and warp back again in the sun. One early thrush gave me a note or two as I drove along the woodland path. I was informed treacherously by a young Patrick that neighbor Seeley,[114] an Irishman, in the intervals of the carting, transferred the still tolerable, straight, and drivable nails, staples, and spikes to his pocket, and then stood when I came back to pass the time of day, and look freshly up, unconcerned, with spring thoughts, at the devastation; there being a dearth of work, as he said. He was there to represent spectatordom, and help make this seemingly insignificant event one with the removal of the gods of Troy.[115]

I dug my cellar in the side of a hill[116] sloping to the south, where a woodchuck had formerly dug his burrow, down through sumach and blackberry roots, and the lowest stain of vegetation, six feet square by seven deep, to a fine sand where potatoes would not freeze in any winter. The sides were left shelving, and not stoned; but the sun having never shone on them, the sand still keeps its place. It was but two hours' work. I took particular pleasure in this breaking of ground, for in almost all latitudes men dig into the earth for an equable temperature. Under the most splendid house in the city is still to be found the cellar where they store their roots as of old, and long after the superstructure has disappeared posterity remark its dent in the earth.[117] The house is still but a sort of porch at the entrance of a burrow.

At length, in the beginning of May, with the help of some of my acquaintances,[118] rather to improve so good an occasion for neighborliness than from any necessity, I set up the frame of my house. No man was ever more honored in the character of his raisers than I. They are destined, I trust, to assist at the raising of loftier structures one day. I began to occupy my house on the 4th of July, as soon as it was boarded and roofed, for the boards were carefully feather-edged and lapped, so that it was perfectly impervious to rain; but before boarding I laid the foundation of a chimney at one end, bringing two cartloads of stones up the hill from the pond in my arms. I built the chimney after my hoeing in the fall, before a fire became necessary for warmth, doing my cooking in the mean while out of doors on the ground, early in the morning: which mode I still think is in some respects more convenient and agreeable than the usual one. When it stormed before my bread was baked, I fixed a few boards over the fire, and sat under them to watch my loaf, and passed some pleasant hours in that way. In those days, when my hands were much employed, I read but little, but the least scraps of paper which lay on the ground, my holder, or tablecloth, afforded me as much entertainment, in fact answered the same purpose as the Iliad.

It would be worth the while to build still more deliberately than I did, considering, for instance, what foundation a door, a window, a cellar, a garret, have in the nature of man, and perchance never raising any superstructure until we found a better reason for it than our temporal necessities even. There is some of the same fitness in a man's building his own house that there is in a bird's building its own nest. Who knows but if men constructed their dwellings with their own hands, and provided food for themselves and families simply and honestly enough, the poetic faculty would be universally developed, as birds universally sing when they are so engaged? But alas! we do like cowbirds and cuckoos,[119] which lay their eggs in nests which other birds have built, and cheer no traveller with their chattering and unmusical notes. Shall we forever resign the pleasure of construction to the carpenter? What does architecture amount to in the experience of the mass of men? I never in all my walks came across a man engaged in so simple and natural an occupation as building his house. We belong to the community. It is not the tailor alone who is the ninth part of a man,[120] it is as much the preacher, and the merchant, and the farmer. Where is this division of labor to end? and what object does it finally serve? No doubt another *may* also think for me; but it is not therefore desirable that he should do so to the exclusion of my thinking for myself.

True, there are architects so called in this country, and I have heard of one [121] at least possessed with the idea of making architectural ornaments have a core of truth, a necessity, and hence a beauty, as if it were a revelation to him. All very well perhaps from his point of view, but only a little better than the common dilettantism. A sentimental reformer in architecture, he began at the cornice, not at the foundation. It was only how to put a core of truth within the ornaments, that every sugar plum in fact might have an almond or caraway seed in it,—though I hold that almonds are most wholesome without the sugar,—and not how the inhabitant, the indweller, might build truly within and without, and let the ornaments take care of themselves. What reasonable man ever supposed that ornaments[122] were something outward and in the skin merely,—that the tortoise got his spotted shell, or the shellfish its mother-o'-pearl tints by such a contract as the inhabitants of Broadway their Trinity Church?[123] But a man has no more to do with the style of architecture of his house than a tortoise with that of its shell: nor need the soldier be so idle as to try to paint the precise *color* of his virtue on his standard. The enemy will find it out. He may turn pale when the trial comes. This man seemed to me to lean over the cornice, and timidly whisper his half truth to the rude occupants who really knew it better than he. What of architectural beauty I now see, I know has gradually grown from within outward, out of the necessities and character of the indweller, who is the only builder,—out of some unconscious truthfulness, and nobleness, without ever a thought for the appearance; and whatever additional beauty of this kind is destined to be produced will be preceded by a like unconscious beauty of life. The most interesting dwellings in this country, as the painter knows, are the most unpretending, humble log huts and cottages of the poor commonly; it is the life of the inhabitants whose shells they are, and not any peculiarity in their surfaces merely, which makes them *picturesque;*[124] and equally interesting will be the citizen's suburban box, when his life shall be as simple and as agreeable to the imagination, and there is as little straining after effect in the style of his dwelling. A great proportion of architectural ornaments are literally hollow, and a September gale would strip them off, like borrowed plumes, without injury to the substantials. They can do without *architecture* who have no olives nor wines[125] in the cellar. What if an equal ado were made about the ornaments of style in literature, and the architects of our bibles spent as much time about their cornices as the architects of our churches do? So are made the *belles-lettres* and the *beaux-arts* and their professors. Much it concerns a man, forsooth, how a few sticks are slanted over him or under him and what colors are daubed upon his box. It would signify somewhat, if, in any earnest sense, *he* slanted them and daubed it; but the spirit having departed out of the tenant, it is of a piece with constructing his own coffin,—the architecture of the grave, and "carpenter,"[126] is but another name for "coffin-maker." One man says, in his despair or indifference to life, take up a handful of the earth at your feet, and paint your house that color. Is he thinking of his last and narrow house?[127] Toss up a copper[128] for it as well. What an abundance of leisure he must have! Why do you take up a handful of dirt? Better paint your house your own complexion; let it turn pale or blush for you. An enterprise to improve the style of cottage architecture! When you have got my ornaments ready I will wear them.

Before winter I built a chimney,[129] and shingled the sides of my house, which were already impervious to rain, with imperfect and sappy shingles made of the first slice of the log, whose edges I was obliged to straighten with a plane.

I have thus a tight shingled and plastered[130] house, ten feet wide by fifteen long, and eight-feet posts, with a garret and a closet, a large window on each side, two trap doors, one door at the end, and a brick fireplace opposite. The exact cost of my house, paying the usual price for such materials as I used, but not counting the work, all of which was done by myself, was as follows; and I give the details because very few are able to tell exactly what their houses cost, and fewer still, if any, the separate cost of the various materials which compose them:—

Boards,	$8 03½,	mostly shanty boards.
Refuse shingles for roof and sides,	4 00	
Laths,	1 25	
Two second-hand windows with glass,	2 43	
One thousand old brick,	4 00	
Two casks of lime,	2 40	That was high.
Hair,	0 31	More than I needed.
Mantle-tree iron,	0 15	
Nails,[131]	3 90	
Hinges and screws,	0 14	
Latch,	0 10	
Chalk,	0 01	
Transportation,	1 40	} I carried a good part on my back.
In all,	$28 12½	

These are all the materials excepting the timber, stones and sand, which I claimed by squatter's right.[132] I have also a small wood-shed adjoining, made chiefly of the stuff which was left after building the house.

I intend to build me a house which will surpass any on the main street[133] in Concord in grandeur and luxury, as soon as it pleases me as much and will cost me no more than my present one.

I thus found that the student who wishes for a shelter can obtain one for a lifetime at an expense not greater than the rent which he now pays annually. If I seem to boast more than is becoming, my excuse is that I brag for humanity rather than for myself; and my shortcomings and inconsistencies do not affect the truth of my statement. Notwithstanding much cant and hypocrisy,—chaff[134] which I find it difficult to separate from my wheat, but for which I am as sorry as any man,—I will breathe freely and stretch myself in this respect, it is such a relief to both the moral and physical system; and I am resolved that I will not through humility become the devil's attorney.[135] I will endeavor to speak a good word for the truth. At Cambridge College[136] the mere rent of a student's room, which is only a little larger than my own, is thirty dollars each year, though the corporation had the advantage of building thirty-two side by side and under one roof, and the occupant suffers the inconvenience of many and noisy neighbors, and perhaps a residence in the fourth story.[137] I cannot but think that if we had more true wisdom in these respects, not only less education would be needed, because, forsooth, more would already have been acquired, but the pecuniary expense of getting an education would in a great measure vanish. Those conveniences which the student requires at Cambridge or elsewhere cost him or somebody else ten times as great a sacrifice of life as they would with proper management on both sides. Those things for which the most money is demanded are never the things which the student most wants. Tuition, for instance, is an important item in the term bill, while for the far more valuable education which he gets by associating with the most cultivated of his contemporaries no charge is made. The mode of founding a college is, commonly, to get up a subscription of dollars and cents, and then following blindly the principles of a division of labor to its extreme, a principle which should never be followed but with circumspection,—to call in a contractor who makes this a subject of speculation, and he employs Irishmen[138] or other opera-

tives actually to lay the foundation, while the students that
are to be are said to be fitting themselves for it; and for these
oversights successive generations have to pay. I think that it
would be *better than this*, for the students, or those who desire to be benefited by it, even to lay the foundation themselves. The student who secures his coveted leisure and retirement by systematically shirking any labor necessary to
man obtains but an ignoble and unprofitable leisure, defraud-
ing himself of the experience which alone can make leisure
fruitful. "But," says one, "you do not mean that the students
should go to work with their hands instead of their heads?"
I do not mean that exactly, but I mean something which he
might think a good deal like that; I mean that they should
not *play* life, or *study* it merely, while the community supports
them at this expensive game, but earnestly *live* it from beginning to end. How could youths better learn to live than by at
once trying the experiment of living? Methinks this would exercise their minds as much as mathematics. If I wished a boy
to know something about the arts and sciences, for instance, I
would not pursue the common course, which is merely to
send him into the neighborhood of some professor, where any
thing is professed and practised but the art of life;—to survey
the world through a telescope or a microscope, and never with
his natural eye; to study chemistry, and not learn how his
bread is made, or mechanics, and not learn how it is earned;
to discover new satellites to Neptune,[139] and not detect the
motes in his eyes,[140] or to what vagabond he is a satellite himself; or to be devoured by the monsters that swarm all around
him, while contemplating the monsters in a drop of vinegar.
Which would have advanced the most at the end of a month,—
the boy who had made his own jackknife from the ore which
he had dug and smelted, reading as much as would be necessary for this,—or the boy who had attended the lectures on
metallurgy at the Institute in the mean while, and had received a Rogers' penknife[141] from his father? Which would be
most likely to cut his fingers? . . . To my astonishment I was
informed on leaving college that I had studied navigation![142]—
why, if I had taken one turn down the harbor I should have
known more about it. Even the *poor* student studies and is
taught only *political* economy, while that economy of living
which is synonymous with philosophy is not even sincerely
professed in our colleges. The consequence is, that while he is

reading Adam Smith, Ricardo, and Say,[143] he runs his father in debt irretrievably.

As with our colleges, so with a hundred "modern improvements;" there is an illusion about them; there is not always a positive advance. The devil goes on exacting compound interest to the last for his early share and numerous succeeding investments in them. Our inventions are wont to be pretty toys, which distract our attention from serious things. They are but improved means to an unimproved end, an end which it was already but too easy to arrive at; as railroads lead to Boston or New York. We are in great haste to construct a magnetic telegraph from Maine to Texas; but Maine and Texas, it may be, have nothing important to communicate. Either is in such a predicament as the man who was earnest to be introduced to a distinguished deaf woman,[144] but when he was presented, and one end of her ear trumpet was put into his hand, had nothing to say. As if the main object were to talk fast and not to talk sensibly. We are eager to tunnel under the Atlantic and bring the old world some weeks nearer to the new; but perchance the first news that will leak through into the broad, flapping American ear will be that the Princess Adelaide[145] has the whooping cough. After all, the man whose horse trots a mile in a minute does not carry the most important messages; he is not an evangelist, nor does he come round eating locusts and wild honey.[146] I doubt if Flying Childers[147] ever carried a peck of corn to mill.

One says to me, "I wonder that you do not lay up money; you love to travel; you might take the cars and go to Fitchburg[148] to-day and see the country." But I am wiser than that. I have learned that the swiftest traveller is he that goes afoot. I say to my friend, Suppose we try who will get there first. The distance is thirty miles; the fare ninety cents.[149] That is almost a day's wages. I remember when wages were sixty cents a day for laborers on this very road. Well, I start now on foot, and get there before night; I have travelled at that rate by the week together. You will in the mean while have earned your fare, and arrive there some time to-morrow, or possibly this evening, if you are lucky enough to get a job in season. Instead of going to Fitchburg, you will be working here the greater part of the day. And so, if the railroad reached round the world, I think that I should keep ahead of you; and as for seeing the country and getting experience of that kind, I should have to cut your acquaintance altogether.

Such is the universal law, which no man can ever outwit, and with regard to the railroad even we may say it is as broad as it is long. To make a railroad round the world available to all mankind is equivalent to grading the whole surface of the planet. Men have an indistinct notion that if they keep up this activity of joint stocks and spades long enough all will at length ride somewhere, in next to no time, and for nothing; but though a crowd rushes to the depot, and the conductor shouts "All aboard!" when the smoke is blown away and the vapor condensed, it will be perceived that a few are riding, but the rest are run over,—and it will be called, and will be, "A melancholy accident."[150] No doubt they can ride at last who shall have earned their fare, that is, if they survive so long, but they will probably have lost their elasticity and desire to travel by that time. This spending of the best part of one's life earning money in order to enjoy a questionable liberty during the least valuable part of it, reminds me of the Englishman[151] who went to India to make a fortune first, in order that he might return to England and live the life of a poet. He should have gone up garret at once. "What!" exclaim a million Irishmen starting up from all the shanties in the land, "is not this railroad which we have built a good thing?" Yes, I answer, *comparatively* good, that is, you might have done worse; but I wish, as you are brothers of mine, that you should have spent your time better than digging in this dirt.

Before I finished my house, wishing to earn ten or twelve dollars by some honest and agreeable method, in order to meet my unusual expenses, I planted about two acres and a half of light and sandy soil near it chiefly with beans, but also a small part with potatoes, corn, peas, and turnips. The whole lot contains eleven acres, mostly growing up to pines and hickories, and was sold[152] the preceding season for eight dollars and eight cents an acre. One farmer said that it was "good for nothing but to raise cheeping squirrels on." I put no manure whatever on this land, not being the owner, but merely a squatter, and not expecting to cultivate so much again, and I did not quite hoe it all once. I got out several cords of stumps in ploughing, which supplied me with fuel for a long time, and left small circles of virgin mould, easily distinguishable through the summer by the greater luxuriance of the beans there. The dead and for the most part unmerchantable wood behind my house, and the driftwood from the pond, have supplied the remainder of my fuel. I was obliged to hire a team and a man for the ploughing, though I held the plough myself. My farm outgoes for the first season were, for implements, seed, work, &c., $14 72½. The seed corn was given me. This never costs any thing to speak of, unless you plant more than enough. I got twelve bushels of beans, and eighteen bushels of potatoes, beside some peas and sweet corn. The yellow corn and turnips were too late to come to any thing. My whole income from the farm was

		$23 44.
Deducting the outgoes, . . .		14 72½
There are left, ...		$8 71½,

beside produce consumed and on hand at the time this estimate was made of the value of $4 50,—the amount on hand much more than balancing a little grass which I did not raise. All things considered, that is, considering the importance of a man's soul and of to-day, notwithstanding the short time occupied by my experiment, nay, partly even because of its transient character, I believe that that was doing better than any farmer in Concord did that year.

The next year I did better still, for I spaded up all the land which I required, about a third of an acre, and I learned from the experience of both years, not being in the least awed by many celebrated works on husbandry, Arthur Young[153] among the rest, that if one would live simply and eat only the crop which he raised, and raise no more than he ate, and not exchange it for an insufficient quantity of more luxurious and expensive things, he would need to cultivate only a few rods of ground, and that it would be cheaper to spade up that than to use oxen to plough it, and to select a fresh spot from time to time than to manure the old, and he could do all his necessary farm work as it were with his left hand at odd hours in the summer; and thus he would not be tied to an ox, or horse, or cow, or pig, as at present. I desire to speak impartially on this point, and as one not interested in the success or failure of the present economical and social arrangements. I was more independent than any farmer in Concord, for I was not anchored to a house or farm, but could follow the bent of my genius, which

is a very crooked one, every moment. Beside being better off
than they already, if my house had been burned or my crops
had failed, I should have been nearly as well off as before.

I am wont to think that men are not so much the keepers of
herds as herds are the keepers of men,[154] the former are so
much the freer. Men and oxen exchange work; but if we consider necessary work only, the oxen will be seen to have greatly
the advantage, their farm is so much the larger. Man does
some of his part of the exchange work in his six weeks of haying, and it is no boy's play. Certainly no nation that lived
simply in all respects, that is, no nation of philosophers, would
commit so great a blunder as to use the labor of animals.[155]
True, there never was and is not likely soon to be a nation of
philosophers, nor am I certain it is desirable that there should
be. However, *I* should never have broken a horse or bull and
taken him to board for any work he might do for me, for fear
I should become a horse-man or a herds-man merely; and if
society seems to be the gainer by so doing, are we certain that
what is one man's gain is not another's loss,[156] and that the
stable-boy has equal cause with his master to be satisfied?
Granted that some public works would not have been constructed without this aid, and let man share the glory of such
with the ox and horse; does it follow that he could not have
accomplished works yet more worthy of himself in that case?
When men begin to do, not merely unnecessary or artistic, but
luxurious and idle work, with their assistance, it is inevitable
that a few do all the exchange work with the oxen, or, in other
words, become the slaves of the strongest. Man thus not only
works for the animal within him, but, for a symbol of this, he
works for the animal without him. Though we have many substantial houses of brick or stone, the prosperity of the farmer
is still measured by the degree to which the barn overshadows
the house. This town is said to have the largest houses for
oxen, cows, and horses hereabouts, and it is not behindhand
in its public buildings; but there are very few halls for free
worship or free speech[157] in this county. It should not be by
their architecture, but why not even by their power of abstract
thought, that nations should seek to commemorate themselves?
How much more admirable the Bhagvat-Geeta[158] than all the
ruins of the East! Towers and temples are the luxury of
princes. A simple and independent mind does not toil at the
bidding of any prince. Genius is not a retainer to any emperor,

nor is its material silver, or gold, or marble, except to a trifling extent. To what end, pray, is so much stone hammered? In Arcadia,[159] when I was there, I did not see any hammering stone. Nations are possessed with an insane ambition to perpetuate the memory of themselves by the amount of hammered stone they leave. What if equal pains were taken to smooth and polish their manners? One piece of good sense would be more memorable than a monument as high as the moon. I love better to see stones in place. The grandeur of Thebes[160] was a vulgar grandeur. More sensible is a rod of stone wall that bounds an honest man's field than a hundred-gated Thebes that has wandered farther from the true end of life. The religion and civilization which are barbaric and heathenish build splendid temples; but what you might call Christianity does not. Most of the stone a nation hammers goes toward its tomb only. It buries itself alive. As for the Pyramids,[161] there is nothing to wonder at in them so much as the fact that so many men could be found degraded enough to spend their lives constructing a tomb for some ambitious booby, whom it would have been wiser and manlier to have drowned in the Nile, and then given his body to the dogs. I might possibly invent some excuse for them and him, but I have no time for it. As for the religion and love of art of the builders, it is much the same all the world over, whether the building be an Egyptian temple or the United States Bank. It costs more than it comes to. The mainspring is vanity, assisted by the love of garlic and bread and butter. Mr. Balcom,[162] a promising young architect, designs it on the back of his Vitruvius,[163] with hard pencil and ruler, and the job is let out to Dobson & Sons,[164] stonecutters. When the thirty centuries[165] begin to look down on it, mankind begin to look up at it. As for your high towers and monuments, there was a crazy fellow[166] once in this town who undertook to dig through to China, and he got so far that, as he said, he heard the Chinese pots and kettles rattle; but I think that I shall not go out of my way to admire the hole which he made. Many are concerned about the monuments of the West and the East,— to know who built them. For my part, I should like to know who in those days did not build them,—who were above such trifling. But to proceed with my statistics.

By surveying, carpentry, and day-labor of various other kinds in the village in the mean while, for I have as many trades as fingers, I had earned $13 34. The expense of food for eight months, namely, from July 4 to March 1st, the time when these estimates were made, though I lived there more than two years,—not counting potatoes, a little green corn, and some peas, which I had raised, nor considering the value of what was on hand at the last date, was

Rice, ... $1 73½
Molasses, . . . 1 73   Cheapest form of the saccharine.
Rye meal, . . . 1 04¾
Indian meal, . . 0 99¾   Cheaper than rye.
Pork, ... 0 22

Flour, ... 0 88 } Costs more than Indian meal, both money and trouble.
Sugar, ... 0 80
Lard, ... 0 65
Apples, . . . 0 25
Dried apple, . . 0 22
Sweet potatoes, . 0 10
One pumpkin, . 0 6
One watermelon, 0 2

} All experiments which failed.

Salt,[167] 0 3

Yes, I did eat $8 74, all told; but I should not thus unblushingly publish my guilt, if I did not know that most of my readers were equally guilty with myself, and that their deeds would look no better in print. The next year I sometimes caught a mess of fish for my dinner, and once I went so far as to slaughter a woodchuck[168] which ravaged my bean-field,—effect his transmigration, as a Tartar[169] would say,—and devour him, partly for experiment's sake; but though it afforded me a momentary enjoyment, notwithstanding a musky flavor, I saw that the longest use would not make that a good practice, however it might seem to have your woodchucks ready dressed by the village butcher.

Clothing and some incidental expenses within the same dates, though little can be inferred from this item, amounted to

$8 40¾
Oil and some household utensils, . . . 2 00

So that all the pecuniary outgoes, excepting for washing and mending, which for the most part were done out of the house, and their bills[170] have not yet been received,—and these are all

and more than all the ways by which money necessarily goes
out in this part of the world,—were

House, ...	$28 12½ᵐ
Farm one year, ...	14 72½
Food eight months, ...	8 74
Clothing, &c., eight months, . . .	8 40¾
Oil, &c., eight months, ...	2 00
In all, ...	$61 99¾

I address myself now to those of my readers who have a living
to get. And to meet this I have for farm produce sold

	$23 44
Earned by day-labor, ...	13 34
In all, ...	$36 78,

which subtracted from the sum of the outgoes leaves a balance
of $25 21¾ on the one side,—this being very nearly the
means with which I started, and the measure of expenses to be
incurred,—and on the others, beside the leisure and independence and health thus secured, a comfortable house for
me as long as I choose to occupy it.

These statistics, however accidental and therefore uninstruc-
tive they may appear, as they have a certain completeness,
have a certain value also. Nothing was given me of which I
have not rendered some account. It appears from the above
estimate, that my food alone cost me in money about twenty-
seven cents a week. It was, for nearly two years after this, rye
and Indian meal without yeast, potatoes, rice, a very little salt
pork, molasses, and salt, and my drink water. It was fit that I
should live on rice, mainly, who loved so well the philosophy
of India. To meet the objections of some inveterate cavillers,[172]
I may as well state that if I dined out occasionally, as I always
had done, and I trust shall have opportunities to do again, it
was frequently to the detriment of my domestic arrangements.
But the dining out, being, as I have stated, a constant element,
does not in the least affect a comparative statement like this.

I learned from my two years' experience that it would cost
incredibly little trouble to obtain one's necessary food, even in
this latitude; that a man may use as simple a diet as the animals, and yet retain health and strength. I have made a satis-

factory dinner, satisfactory on several accounts, simply off a dish of purslane *(Portulaca oleracea)* which I gathered in my cornfield, boiled and salted. I give the Latin on account of the savoriness of the trivial name.[173] And pray what more can a reasonable man desire, in peaceful times, in ordinary noons, than a sufficient number of ears of green sweet-corn boiled, with the addition of salt? Even the little variety which I used was a yielding to the demands of appetite, and not of health. Yet men have come to such a pass that they frequently starve, not for want of necessaries; but for want of luxuries; and I know a good woman who thinks that her son lost his life because he took to drinking water only.

The reader will perceive that I am treating the subject rather from an economic than a dietetic point of view, and he will not venture to put my abstemiousness to the test unless he has a well-stocked larder.

Bread I at first made of pure Indian meal and salt, genuine hoe-cakes, which I baked before my fire out of doors on a shingle or the end of a stick of timber sawed off in building my house; but it was wont to get smoked and to have a piny flavor. I tried flour also; but have at last found a mixture of rye and Indian meal most convenient and agreeable. In cold weather it was no little amusement to bake several small loaves of this in succession, tending and turning them as carefully as an Egyptian his hatching eggs.[174] They were a real cereal fruit which I ripened, and they had to my senses a fragrance like that of other noble fruits, which I kept in as long as possible by wrapping them in cloths. I made a study of the ancient and indispensable art of bread-making, consulting such authorities as offered, going back to the primitive days and first invention of the unleavened kind, when from the wildness of nuts and meats men first reached the mildness and refinement of this diet, and travelling gradually down in my studies through that accidental souring of the dough which, it is supposed, taught the leavening process, and through the various fermentations thereafter, till I came to "good, sweet, wholesome bread," the staff of life. Leaven, which some deem the soul of bread, the *spiritus* which fills its cellular tissue, which is religiously preserved like the vestal fire,—some precious bottle-full, I suppose, first brought over in the Mayflower, did the business for America, and its influence is still rising, swelling, spreading, in cerealian[175] billows over the land,—this seed I regularly and faithfully procured from the village, till at length one morning I forgot the rules, and scalded my yeast; by which accident I discovered that even this was not indispensable,—for my discoveries were not by the synthetic but analytic process,—and I have gladly omitted it since, though most housewives earnestly assured me that safe and wholesome bread without yeast might not be, and elderly people prophesied a speedy decay of the vital forces. Yet I find it not to be an essential ingredient, and after going without it for a year am still in the land of the living; and I am glad to escape the trivialness of carrying a bottle-full in my pocket, which would sometimes pop and discharge its contents to my discomfiture. It is simpler and more respectable to omit it. Man is an animal who more than any other can adapt himself to all climates and circumstances. Neither did I put any sal soda, or other acid or alkali, into my bread. It would seem that I made it according to the recipe which Marcus Porcius Cato gave about two centuries before Christ. "Panem depsticium sic facito. Manus mortariumque bene lavato. Farinam in mortarium indito, aquae paulatim addito, subigitoque pulchre. Ubi bene subegeris, defingito, coquitoque sub testu."[176] Which I take to mean—"Make kneaded bread thus. Wash your hands and trough well. Put the meal into the trough, add water gradually, and knead it thoroughly. When you have kneaded it well, mould it, and bake it under a cover," that is, in a baking-kettle. Not a word about leaven. But I did not always use this staff of life. At one time, owing to the emptiness of my purse, I saw none of it for more than a month.

Every New Englander might easily raise all his own bread-stuffs in this land of rye and Indian corn, and not depend on distant and fluctuating markets for them. Yet so far are we from simplicity and independence that, in Concord, fresh and sweet meal is rarely sold in the shops, and hominy and corn in a still coarser form are hardly used by any. For the most part the farmer gives to his cattle and hogs the grain of his own producing, and buys flour, which is at least no more wholesome, at a greater cost, at the store. I saw that I could easily raise my bushel or two of rye and Indian corn, for the former will grow on the poorest land, and the latter does not require the best, and grind them in a hand-mill, and so do without rice and pork; and if I must have some concentrated sweet, I found by experiment that I could make a very good molasses either of pumpkins or beets, and I knew that I needed only to set out a few maples to obtain it more easily still, and while these were growing I could use various substitutes beside those which I have named. "For," as the Forefathers sang,—

> "we can make liquor to sweeten our lips
> Of pumpkins and parsnips and walnut-tree chips."[177]

Finally, as for salt, that grossest of groceries, to obtain this might be a fit occasion for a visit to the seashore, or, if I did without it altogether, I should probably drink the less water. I do not learn that the Indians ever troubled themselves to go after it.

Thus I could avoid all trade and barter, so far as my food was concerned, and having a shelter already, it would only remain to get clothing and fuel. The pantaloons which I now wear were woven in a farmer's family,—thank Heaven there is so much virtue still in man; for I think the fall from the farmer to the operative as great and memorable as that from the man to the farmer;—and in a new country fuel is an encumbrance. As for a habitat, if I were not permitted still to squat, I might purchase one acre at the same price for which the land I cultivated was sold—namely, eight dollars and eight cents. But as it was, I considered that I enhanced the value of the land by squatting on it.

There is a certain class of unbelievers who sometimes ask me such questions as, if I think that I can live on vegetable food alone; and to strike at the root of the matter at once,—for the root is faith,—I am accustomed to answer such, that I can live on board nails. If they cannot understand that, they cannot understand much that I have to say. For my part, I am glad to hear of experiments of this kind being tried; as that a young man[178] tried for a fortnight to live on hard, raw corn on the ear, using his teeth for all mortar. The squirrel tribe tried the same and succeeded. The human race is interested in these experiments, though a few old women who are incapacitated for them, or who own their thirds[179] in mills, may be alarmed.

My furniture,[180] part of which I made myself, and the rest cost me nothing of which I have not rendered an account, consisted of a bed, a table, a desk, three chairs, a looking-glass three inches in diameter, a pair of tongs and andirons, a kettle, a skillet, and a frying-pan, a dipper, a wash-bowl, two knives

and forks, three plates, one cup, one spoon, a jug for oil, a jug
for molasses, and a japanned lamp. None is so poor that he
need sit on a pumpkin. That is shiftlessness. There is a plenty
of such chairs as I like best in the village garrets to be had for
taking them away. Furniture! Thank God, I can sit and I can
stand without the aid of a furniture warehouse. What man but
a philosopher would not be ashamed to see his furniture
packed in a cart and going up country exposed to the light of
heaven and the eyes of men, a beggarly account of empty
boxes? That is Spaulding's[181] furniture. I could never tell from
inspecting such a load whether it belonged to a so called rich
man or a poor one; the owner always seemed poverty-stricken.
Indeed, the more you have of such things the poorer you are.
Each load looks as if it contained the contents of a dozen
shanties; and if one shanty is poor, this is a dozen times as
poor. Pray, for what do we *move* ever but to get rid of our
furniture, our *exuviae;*[182] at last to go from this world to another newly furnished, and leave this to be burned? It is the
same as if all these traps were buckled to a man's belt, and he
could not move over the rough country where our lines are cast
without dragging them,—dragging his trap. He was a lucky
fox[183] that left his tail in the trap. The muskrat will gnaw his
third leg off to be free. No wonder man has lost his elasticity.
How often he is at a dead set![184] "Sir, if I may be so bold, what
do you mean by a dead set?" If you are a seer, whenever you
meet a man you will see all that he owns, ay, and much that he
pretends to disown, behind him, even to his kitchen furniture
and all the trumpery which he saves and will not burn, and he
will appear to be harnessed to it and making what headway he
can. I think that the man is at a dead set who has got through
a knot hole or gateway where his sledge load of furniture cannot follow him. I cannot but feel compassion when I hear some
trig,[185] compact-looking man, seemingly free, all girded and
ready, speak of his "furniture," as whether it is insured or not.
"But what shall I do with my furniture?" My gay butterfly is
entangled in a spider's web then. Even those who seem for a
long while not to have any, if you inquire more narrowly you
will find have some stored in somebody's barn. I look upon
England to-day as an old gentleman who is travelling with a
great deal of baggage, trumpery which has accumulated from
long housekeeping, which he has not the courage to burn;
great trunk, little trunk, bandbox and bundle. Throw away the

first three at least. It would surpass the powers of a well man nowadays to take up his bed and walk,[186] and I should certainly advise a sick one to lay down his bed and run. When I have met an immigrant tottering under a bundle which contained his all—looking like an enormous wen which had grown out of the nape of his neck—I have pitied him, not because that was his all, but because he had all *that* to carry. If I have got to drag my trap, I will take care that it be a light one and do not nip me in a vital part. But perchance it would be wisest never to put one's paw into it.

I would observe, by the way, that it costs me nothing for curtains, for I have no gazers to shut out but the sun and moon, and I am willing that they should look in. The moon will not sour milk[187] nor taint meat of mine, nor will the sun injure my furniture or fade my carpet,[188] and if he is sometimes too warm a friend, I find it still better economy to retreat behind some curtain which nature has provided, than to add a single item to the details of housekeeping. A lady once offered me a mat, but as I had no room to spare within the house, nor time to spare within or without to shake it, I declined it, preferring to wipe my feet on the sod before my door. It is best to avoid the beginnings of evil.

Not long since I was present at the auction of a deacon's[189] effects, for his life had not been ineffectual:—

"The evil that men do lives after them."[190]

As usual, a great proportion was trumpery which had begun to accumulate in his father's day. Among the rest was a dried tapeworm. And now, after lying half a century in his garret and other dust holes, these things were not burned; instead of a *bonfire*,[191] or purifying destruction of them, there was an *auction*,[192] or increasing of them. The neighbors eagerly collected to view them, bought them all, and carefully transported them to their garrets and dust holes, to lie there till their estates are settled, when they will start again. When a man dies he kicks the dust.[193]

The customs of some savage nations might, perchance, be profitably imitated by us, for they at least go through the semblance of casting their slough annually; they have the idea of the thing, whether they have the reality or not. Would it not be well if we were to celebrate such a "busk,"[194] or "feast of first fruits," as Bartram describes to have been the custom of the Mucclasse Indians? "When a town celebrates the busk," says he, "having previously provided themselves with new clothes, new pots, pans, and other household utensils and furniture, they collect all their worn out clothes and other despicable things, sweep and cleanse their houses, squares, and the whole town, of their filth, which with all the remaining grain and other old provisions they cast together into one common heap, and consume it with fire. After having taken medicine, and fasted for three days, all the fire in the town is extinguished. During this fast they abstain from the gratification of every appetite and passion whatever. A general amnesty is proclaimed; all malefactors may return to their town.—

"On the fourth morning, the high priest, by rubbing dry wood together, produces new fire in the public square, from whence every habitation in the town is supplied with the new and pure flame."

They then feast on the new corn and fruits and dance and sing for three days, "and the four following days they receive visits and rejoice with their friends from neighboring towns who have in like manner purified and prepared themselves."[195]

The Mexicans[196] also practised a similar purification at the end of every fifty-two years, in the belief that it was time for the world to come to an end.

I have scarcely heard of a truer sacrament, that is, as the dictionary definies it, "outward and visible sign of an inward and spiritual grace,"[197] than this, and I have no doubt that they were originally inspired directly from Heaven to do thus, though they have no biblical record of the revelation.

For more than five years I maintained myself thus solely by the labor of my hands, and I found, that by working about six weeks[198] in a year, I could meet all the expenses of living. The whole of my winters, as well as most of my summers, I had free and clear for study. I have thoroughly tried school-keeping,[199] and found that my expenses were in proportion, or rather out of proportion, to my income, for I was obliged to dress and train, not to say think and believe, accordingly, and I lost my time into the bargain. As I did not teach for the good of my fellow-man, but simply for a livelihood, this was a failure. I have tried trade; but I found that it would take ten years to get under way in that, and that then I should probably be on my way to the devil. I was actually afraid that I might by that time be doing what is called a good business. When formerly I was looking about to see what I could do for a living, some sad experience in conforming to the wishes of friends being fresh in my mind to tax my ingenuity, I thought often and seriously of picking huckleberries; that surely I could do, and its small profits might suffice,—for my greatest skill has been to want but little,—so little capital it required, so little distraction from my wonted moods, I foolishly thought. While my acquaintances went unhesitatingly into trade or the professions, I contemplated this occupation as most like theirs; ranging the hills all summer to pick the berries which came in my way, and thereafter carelessly dispose of them; so, to keep the flocks of Admetus.[200] I also dreamed that I might gather the wild herbs, or carry evergreens to such villagers as loved to be reminded of the woods, even to the city, by hay-cart loads. But I have since learned that trade curses every thing it handles; and though you trade in messages from heaven, the whole curse of trade attaches to the business.

As I preferred some things to others, and specially valued my freedom, as I could fare hard and yet succeed well, I did not wish to spend my time in earning rich carpets or other fine furniture, or delicate cookery, or a house in the Grecian or the Gothic[201] style just yet. If there are any to whom it is no interruption to acquire these things, and who know how to use them when acquired, I relinquish to them the pursuit. Some are "industrious," and appear to love labor for its own sake, or perhaps because it keeps them out of worse mischief; to such I have at present nothing to say. Those who would not know what to do with more leisure than they now enjoy, I might advise to work twice as hard as they do,—work till they pay for themselves, and get their free papers.[202] For myself I found that the occupation of a day-laborer was the most independent of any, especially as it required only thirty or forty days in a year to support one. The laborer's day ends with the going down of the sun, and he is then free to devote himself to his chosen pursuit, independent of his labor; but his employer, who speculates from month to month, has no respite from one end of the year to the other.

In short, I am convinced, both by faith and experience, that to maintain one's self on this earth is not a hardship but a pastime, if we will live simply and wisely; as the pursuits of the simpler nations are still the sports of the more artificial. It is not necessary that a man should earn his living by the sweat of his brow, unless he sweats easier than I do.[203]

One young man[204] of my acquaintance, who has inherited some acres, told me that he thought he should live as I did, *if he had the means*. I would not have any one adopt *my* mode of living[205] on any account; for, beside that before he has fairly learned it I may have found out another for myself, I desire that there may be as many different persons in the world as possible; but I would have each one be very careful to find out and pursue *his own* way, and not his father's or his mother's or his neighbor's instead. The youth may build or plant or sail, only let him not be hindered from doing that which he tells me he would like to do. It is by a mathematical point only that we are wise, as the sailor or the fugitive slave keeps the polestar[206] in his eye; but that is sufficient guidance for all our life. We may not arrive at our port within a calculable period, but we would preserve the true course.

Undoubtedly, in this case, what is true for one is truer still for a thousand, as a large house[207] is not proportionately more expensive than a small one, since one roof may cover, one cellar underlie, and one wall separate several apartments. But for my part, I preferred the solitary dwelling. Moreover, it will commonly be cheaper to build the whole yourself than to convince another of the advantage of the common wall; and when you have done this, the common partition, to be much cheaper, must be a thin one, and that other may prove a bad neighbor, and also not keep his side in repair. The only coöperation which is commonly possible is exceedingly partial and superficial; and what little true coöperation there is, is as if it were not, being a harmony inaudible to men. If a man has faith he will coöperate with equal faith every where; if he has not faith, he will continue to live like the rest of the world, whatever company he is joined to. To coöperate, in the highest as well as the lowest sense, means to *get our living together*. I heard it proposed lately that two young men should travel together over the world, the one without money, earning his means as he went, before the mast and behind the plough, the other carrying a bill of exchange in his pocket. It was easy to see that they could not long be companions or coöperate, since one would not *operate* at all. They would part at the first interesting crisis in their adventures. Above all, as I have implied, the man who goes alone can start to-day; but he who travels with another must wait till that other is ready, and it may be a long time before they get off.

But all this is very selfish, I have heard some of my townsmen say. I confess that I have hitherto indulged very little in philanthropic enterprises.[208] I have made some sacrifices to a sense of duty, and among others have sacrificed this pleasure also. There are those who have used all their arts to persuade me to undertake the support of some poor family in the town; and if I had nothing to do,—for the devil finds employment[209] for the idle,—I might try my hand at some such pastime as that. However, when I have thought to indulge myself in this respect, and lay their Heaven under an obligation by maintaining certain poor persons in all respects as comfortably as I maintain myself, and have even ventured so far as to make them the offer, they have one and all unhesitatingly preferred to remain poor. While my townsmen and women are devoted in so many ways to the good of their fellows, I trust that one at least may be spared to other and less humane pursuits. You must have a genius for charity as well as for any thing else. As for Doing-good,[210] that is one of the professions which are full. Moreover, I have tried it fairly, and, strange as it may seem, am satisfied that it does not agree with my constitution. Probably I should not consciously and deliberately forsake my particular calling to do the good which society demands of me, to save the universe from annihilation; and I believe that a like but infinitely greater steadfastness elsewhere is all that now preserves it. But I would not stand between any man and his genius; and to him who does this work, which I decline, with his whole heart and soul and life, I would say, Persevere, even if the world call it doing evil, as it is most likely they will.

I am far from supposing that my case is a peculiar one; no doubt many of my readers would make a similar defence. At doing something,—I will not engage that my neighbors shall pronounce it good,—I do not hesitate to say that I should be a capital fellow to hire; but what that is, it is for my employer to find out. What *good* I do, in the common sense of that word, must be aside from my main path, and for the most part wholly unintended. Men say, practically, Begin where you are and such as you are, without aiming mainly to become of more worth, and with kindness aforethought go about doing good. If I were to preach at all in this strain, I should say rather, Set about being good. As if the sun should stop when he had kindled his fires up to the splendor of a moon or a star of the sixth magnitude, and go about like a Robin Goodfellow,[211] peeping in at every cottage window, inspiring lunatics, and tainting meats, and making darkness visible, instead of steadily increasing his genial heat and beneficence till he is of such brightness that no mortal can look him in the face, and then, and in the mean while too, going about the world in his own orbit, doing it good, or rather, as a truer philosophy has discovered, the world going about him getting good. When Phaeton,[212] wishing to prove his heavenly birth by his beneficence, had the sun's chariot but one day, and drove out of the beaten track, he burned several blocks of houses in the lower streets of heaven, and scorched the surface of the earth, and dried up every spring, and made the great desert of Sahara, till at length Jupiter hurled him headlong to the earth with a thunderbolt, and the sun, through grief at his death, did not shine for a year.

There is no odor so bad as that which arises from goodness tainted. It is human, it is divine, carrion. If I knew for a certainty that a man was coming to my house with the conscious design of doing me good, I should run for my life, as from that dry and parching wind of the African deserts called the simoom, which fills the mouth and nose and ears and eyes with dust till you are suffocated, for fear that I should get some of his good done to me,—some of its virus mingled with my blood. No,—in this case I would rather suffer evil the natural way. A man is not a good *man* to me because he will feed me if I should be starving, or warm me if I should be freezing, or pull me out of a ditch if I should ever fall into one. I can find you a Newfoundland dog that will do as much. Philanthropy is not love for one's fellow-man in the broadest sense. Howard[213] was no doubt an exceedingly kind and worthy man in his way, and has his reward; but, comparatively speaking, what are a hundred Howards to *us*, if their philanthropy do not help *us* in our best estate, when we are most worthy to be helped? I never heard of a philanthropic meeting in which it was sincerely proposed to do any good to me, or the like of me.

The Jesuits[214] were quite balked by those Indians who, being burned at the stake, suggested new modes of torture to their tormentors. Being superior to physical suffering, it sometimes chanced that they were superior to any consolation which the missionaries could offer; and the law to do as you would be done by[215] fell with less persuasiveness on the ears of those, who, for their part, did not care how they were done by, who loved their enemies[216] after a new fashion, and came very near freely forgiving them[217] all they did.

Be sure that you give the poor the aid they most need, though it be your example which leaves them far behind. If you give money, spend yourself with it, and do not merely abandon it to them. We make curious mistakes sometimes. Often the poor man is not so cold and hungry as he is dirty and ragged and gross. It is partly his taste, and not merely his misfortune. If you give him money, he will perhaps buy more rags with it. I was wont to pity the clumsy Irish laborers who cut ice on the pond, in such mean and ragged clothes, while I shivered in my more tidy and somewhat more fashionable garments, till, one bitter cold day, one who had slipped into the water came to my house to warm him, and I saw him strip off three pairs of pants and two pairs of stockings ere he got down to the skin, though they were dirty and ragged enough, it is true, and that he could afford to refuse the *extra* garments which I offered him, he had so many *intra*[218] ones. This ducking was the very thing he needed. Then I began to pity myself, and I saw that it would be a greater charity to bestow on me a flannel shirt than a whole slop-shop on him. There are a thousand hacking at the branches of evil to one who is striking at the root, and it may be that he who bestows the largest amount of time and money on the needy is doing the most by his mode of life to produce that misery which he strives in vain to relieve. It is the pious slavebreeder devoting the proceeds of every tenth slave[219] to buy a Sunday's liberty for the rest. Some show their kindness to the poor by employing them in their kitchens. Would they not be kinder if they employed themselves there? You boast of spending a tenth part of your income in charity; may be you should spend the nine tenths so, and done with it. Society recovers only a tenth part of the property then. Is this owing to the generosity of him in whose possession it is found, or to the remissness of the officers of justice?

Philanthropy is almost the only virtue which is sufficiently appreciated by mankind. Nay, it is greatly overrated; and it is our selfishness which overrates it. A robust poor man, one sunny day here in Concord, praised a fellow-townsman to me, because, as he said, he was kind to the poor; meaning himself. The kind uncles and aunts of the race are more esteemed than its true spiritual fathers and mothers. I once heard a reverend lecturer on England, a man of learning and intelligence, after enumerating her scientific, literary, and political worthies, Shakspeare, Bacon, Cromwell, Milton, Newton, and others, speak next of her Christian heroes, whom, as if his profession required it of him, he elevated to a place far above all the rest, as the greatest of the great. They were Penn, Howard, and Mrs. Fry.[220] Every one must feel the falsehood and cant of this. The last were not England's best men and women; only, perhaps, her best philanthropists.

I would not subtract any thing from the praise that is due to philanthropy, but merely demand justice for all who by their lives and works are a blessing to mankind. I do not value chiefly a man's uprightness and benevolence, which are, as it were, his stem and leaves. Those plants of whose greenness withered we make herb tea for the sick, serve but a humble use, and are most employed by quacks. I want the flower and fruit of a man; that some fragrance be wafted over from him to me, and some ripeness flavor our intercourse. His goodness must not be a partial and transitory act, but a constant superfluity, which costs him nothing and of which he is unconscious. This is a charity that hides a multitude of sins.[221] The philanthropist too often surrounds mankind with the remembrance of his own cast-off griefs as an atmosphere, and calls it sympathy. We should impart our courage, and not our despair, our health and ease, and not our disease, and take care that this does not spread by contagion. From what southern plains comes up the voice of wailing? Under what latitudes reside the heathen to whom we would send light? Who is that intemperate and brutal man whom we would redeem? If any thing ail a man, so that he does not perform his functions, if he have a pain in his bowels[222] even,—for that is the seat of sympathy,—he forthwith sets about reforming—the world. Being a microcosm himself, he discovers, and it is a true discovery, and he is the man to make it,—that the world has been eating green apples; to his eyes, in fact, the globe itself is a great green apple, which there is danger awful to think of that the children of men will nibble before it is ripe; and straightway his drastic philanthropy seeks out the Esquimaux and the Patagonian, and embraces the populous Indian and Chinese villages; and thus, by a few years of philanthropic activity, the powers in the mean while using him for their own ends, no doubt, he cures himself of his dyspepsia, the globe acquires a faint blush on one or both of its cheeks, as if it were beginning to be ripe, and life loses its crudity and is once more sweet and wholesome to live. I never dreamed of any enormity greater than I have committed. I never knew, and never shall know, a worse man than myself.

I believe that what so saddens the reformer is not his sympathy with his fellows in distress, but, though he be the holiest son of God, is his private ail. Let this be righted, let the spring come to him, the morning rise over his couch, and he will forsake his generous companions without apology. My excuse for not lecturing against the use of tobacco is, that I never chewed it; that is a penalty which reformed tobacco-chewers have to pay; though there are things enough I have chewed, which I could lecture against. If you should ever be betrayed into any of these philanthropies, do not let your left hand know[223] what your right hand does, for it is not worth knowing. Rescue the drowning and tie your shoe-strings. Take your time, and set about some free labor.

Our manners[224] have been corrupted by communication with the saints. Our hymn-books resound with a melodious cursing of God and enduring him forever.[225] One would say that even the prophets and redeemers had rather consoled the fears than confirmed the hopes of man. There is nowhere recorded a simple and irrepressible satisfaction with the gift of life, any memorable praise of God. All health and success does me good, however far off and withdrawn it may appear; all disease and failure helps to make me sad and does me evil, however much sympathy it may have with me or I with it. If, then, we would indeed restore mankind by truly Indian, botanic, magnetic,[226] or natural means, let us first be as simple and well as Nature ourselves, dispel the clouds which hang over our own brows, and take up a little life into our pores. Do not stay to be an overseer of the poor, but endeavor to become one of the worthies of the world.

I read in the Gulistan, or Flower Garden, of Sheik Sadi of Shiraz, that "They asked a wise man, saying; Of the many celebrated trees which the Most High God has created lofty and umbrageous, they call none azad, or free, excepting the cypress, which bears no fruit; what mystery is there in this? He replied; Each has its appropriate produce, and appointed season, during the continuance of which it is fresh and blooming, and during their absence dry and withered; to neither of which states is the cypress exposed, being always flourishing; and of this nature are the azads, or religious independents.—Fix not thy heart on that which is transitory; for the Dijlah,²²⁷ or Tigris, will continue to flow through Bagdad after the race of caliphs is extinct: if thy hand has plenty, be liberal as the date tree; but if it affords nothing to give away, be an azad, or free man, like the cypress."²²⁸

COMPLEMENTAL VERSES[229]

THE PRETENSIONS OF POVERTY.

"Thou dost presume too much, poor needy wretch,
To claim a station in the firmament,
Because thy humble cottage, or thy tub,
Nurses some lazy or pedantic virtue
In the cheap sunshine or by shady springs,
With roots and pot-herbs; where thy right hand,
Tearing those humane passions from the mind,
Upon whose stocks fair blooming virtues flourish,
Degradeth nature, and benumbeth sense,
And, Gorgon-like, turns active men to stone
We not require the dull society
Of your necessitated temperance,
Or that unnatural stupidity
That knows nor joy nor sorrow; nor your forc'd
Falsely exalted passive fortitude
Above the active. This low abject brood,
That fix their seats in mediocrity,
Become your servile minds; but we advance
Such virtues only as admit excess,
Brave, bounteous acts, regal magnificence,
All-seeing prudence, magnanimity
That knows no bound, and that heroic virtue
For which antiquity hath left no name,
But patterns only, such as Hercules,
Achilles, Theseus. Back to thy loath'd cell;
And when thou seest the new enlightened sphere,
Study to know but what those worthies were."

T. CAREW

II

WHERE I LIVED, AND WHAT I LIVED FOR

At a certain season of our life we are accustomed to consider every spot as the possible site of a house. I have thus surveyed the country on every side within a dozen miles of where I live. In imagination I have bought all the farms in succession, for all were to be bought, and I knew their price. I walked over each farmer's premises, tasted his wild apples, discoursed on husbandry with him, took his farm at his price, at any price, mortgaging it to him in my mind; even put a higher price on it,—took every thing but a deed of it,—took his word for his deed, for I dearly love to talk,—cultivated it, and him too to some extent, I trust, and withdrew when I had enjoyed it long enough, leaving him to carry it on. This experience entitled me to be regarded as a sort of real-estate broker by my friends. Wherever I sat, there I might live, and the landscape radiated from me accordingly. What is a house but a *sedes*, a seat?—better if a country seat. I discovered many a site for a house not likely to be soon improved, which some might have thought too far from the village, but to my eyes the village was too far from it. Well, there I might live, I said; and there I did live, for an hour, a summer and a winter life; saw how I could let the years run off, buffet the winter through, and see the spring come in. The future inhabitants of this region, wherever they may place their houses, may be sure that they have been anticipated. An afternoon sufficed to lay out the land into orchard, woodlot, and pasture, and to decide what fine oaks or pines should be left to stand before the door, and whence each blasted tree could be seen to the best advantage; and then I let it lie, fallow perchance, for a man is rich in proportion to the number of things which he can afford to let alone.[1]

My imagination carried me so far that I even had the refusal of several farms,—the refusal was all I wanted,—but I

never got my fingers burned by actual possession. The nearest
that I came to actual possession was when I bought the Hollowell place,² and had begun to sort my seeds, and collected
materials with which to make a wheelbarrow to carry it on
or off with; but before the owner gave me a deed of it, his
wife—every man has such a wife—changed her mind and
wished to keep it, and he offered me ten dollars to release
him. Now, to speak the truth, I had but ten cents in the
world, and it surpassed my arithmetic to tell, if I was that
man who had ten cents, or who had a farm, or ten dollars,
or all together. However, I let him keep the ten dollars and
the farm too, for I had carried it far enough; or rather, to be
generous, I sold him the farm for just what I gave for it, and,
as he was not a rich man, made him a present of ten dollars,
and still had my ten cents, and seeds, and materials for a
wheelbarrow left. I found thus that I had been a rich man
without any damage to my poverty. But I retained the landscape, and I have since annually carried off what it yielded
without a wheelbarrow. With respect to landscapes,—

> "I am monarch of all I *survey*,
> My right there is none to dispute."³

I have frequently seen a poet withdraw, having enjoyed the
most valuable part of a farm, while the crusty farmer supposed that he had got a few wild apples only. Why, the owner
does not know it for many years when a poet has put his farm
in rhyme, the most admirable kind of invisible fence, has
fairly impounded it, milked it, skimmed it, and got all the
cream, and left the farmer only the skimmed milk.

The real attractions of the Hollowell farm, to me, were;
its complete retirement, being about two miles from the village, half a mile from the nearest neighbor, and separated
from the highway by a broad field; its bounding on the river,
which the owner said protected it by its fogs from frosts in
the spring, though that was nothing to me; the gray color
and ruinous state of the house and barn, and the dilapidated
fences, which put such an interval between me and the last
occupant; the hollow and lichen-covered apple trees, gnawed
by rabbits, showing what kind of neighbors I should have;
but above all, the recollection I had of it from my earliest
voyages up the river, when the house was concealed behind a

dense grove of red maples, through which I heard the house-dog bark. I was in haste to buy it, before the proprietor finished getting out some rocks, cutting down the hollow apple trees, and grubbing up some young birches which had sprung up in the pasture, or, in short, had made any more of his improvements. To enjoy these advantages I was ready to carry it on; like Atlas,[4] to take the world on my shoulders,—I never heard what compensation he received for that,—and do all those things which had no other motive or excuse but that I might pay for it and be unmolested in my possession of it; for I knew all the while that it would yield the most abundant crop of the kind I wanted if I could only afford to let it alone. But it turned out as I have said.

All that I could say, then, with respect to farming on a large scale, (I have always cultivated a garden,) was, that I had had my seeds ready. Many think that seeds improve with age. I have no doubt that time discriminates between the good and the bad; and when at last I shall plant, I shall be less likely to be disappointed. But I would say to my fellows, once for all, As long as possible live free and uncommitted. It makes but little difference whether you are committed to a farm or the county jail.

Old Cato, whose "De Re Rusticâ" is my "Cultivator,"[5] says, and the only translation I have seen makes sheer nonsense of the passage, "When you think of getting a farm, turn it thus in your mind, not to buy greedily; nor spare your pains to look at it, and do not think it enough to go round it once. The oftener you go there the more it will please you, if it is good."[6] I think I shall not buy greedily, but go round and round it as long as I live, and be buried in it first, that it may please me the more at last.

The present was my next experiment of this kind, which I purpose to describe more at length, for convenience, putting the experience of two years[7] into one. As I have said,[8] I do not propose to write an ode to dejection, but to brag as lustily as chanticleer in the morning, standing on his roost, if only to wake my neighbors up.

When first I took up my abode in the woods, that is, began to spend my nights as well as days there, which, by accident, was on Independence day, or the fourth of July, 1845, my house was not finished for winter, but was merely a defence against the rain, without plastering or chimney, the walls being of rough weather-stained boards, with wide chinks, which made it cool at night. The upright white hewn studs and freshly planed door and window casings gave it a clean and airy look, especially in the morning, when its timbers were saturated with dew, so that I fancied that by noon some sweet gum would exude from them. To my imagination it retained throughout the day more or less of this auroral character, reminding me of a certain house[9] on a mountain which I had visited the year before. This was an airy and unplastered cabin, fit to entertain a travelling god, and where a goddess might trail her garments. The winds which passed over my dwelling were such as sweep over the the ridges of mountains, bearing the broken strains, or celestial parts only, of terrestrial music. The morning wind forever blows, the poem of creation is uninterrupted; but few are the ears that hear it. Olympus[10] is but the outside of the earth every where.

The only house I had been the owner of before, if I except a boat,[11] was a tent, which I used occasionally when making excursions in the summer, and this is still rolled up in my garret; but the boat, after passing from hand to hand, has gone down the stream of time. With this more substantial shelter about me, I had made some progress toward settling in the world. This frame, so slightly clad, was a sort of crystallization around me, and reacted on the builder. It was suggestive somewhat as a picture in outlines. I did not need to go out doors to take the air, for the atmosphere within had lost none of its freshness. It was not so much within doors as behind a door where I sat, even in the rainiest weather. The Harivansa says, "An abode without birds is like a meat without seasoning."[12] Such was not my abode, for I found myself suddenly neighbor to the birds; not by having imprisoned one, but having caged myself near them. I was not only nearer to some of those which commonly frequent the garden and the orchard, but to those wilder and more thrilling songsters of the forest which never, or rarely, serenade a villager, —the wood-thrush, the veery, the scarlet tanager, the field-sparrow, the whippoorwill, and many others.

I was seated by the shore of a small pond, about a mile and a half[13] south of the village of Concord and somewhat higher than it, in the midst of an extensive wood between that town and Lincoln, and about two miles south of that our only field known to fame, Concord Battle Ground;[14] but I was so low in the woods that the opposite shore, half a mile off, like the rest, covered with wood, was my most distant horizon. For the first week, whenever I looked out on the pond it impressed me like a tarn high up on the side of a mountain, its bottom far above the surface of other lakes, and, as the sun arose, I saw it throwing off its nightly clothing of mist, and here and there, by degrees, its soft ripples or its smooth reflecting surface was revealed, while the mists, like ghosts, were stealthily withdrawing in every direction into the woods, as at the breaking up of some nocturnal conventicle. The very dew seemed to hang upon the trees later into the day than usual, as on the sides of mountains.

This small lake was of most value as a neighbor in the intervals of a gentle rain storm in August, when, both air and water being perfectly still, but the sky overcast, mid-afternoon had all the serenity of evening, and the wood-thrush sang around, and was heard from shore to shore. A lake like this is never smoother than at such a time; and the clear portion of the air above it being shallow and darkened by clouds, the water, full of light and reflections, becomes a lower heaven itself so much the more important. From a hill top[15] near by, where the wood had been recently cut off, there was a pleasing vista southward across the pond, through a wide indentation in the hills which form the shore there, where their opposite sides sloping toward each other suggested a stream flowing out in that direction through a wooded valley, but stream there was none. That way I looked between and over the near green hills to some distant and higher ones in the horizon, tinged with blue. Indeed, by standing on tiptoe I could catch a glimpse of some of the peaks of the still bluer and more distant mountain ranges[16] in the northwest, those true-blue coins from heaven's own mint, and also of some portion of the village. But in other directions, even from this point, I could not see over or beyond the woods which surrounded me. It is well to have some water in your neighborhood, to give buoyancy to and float the earth. One value even of the smallest well is, that when you look into it you see that earth is not continent but insular. This is as important as that it keeps butter cool.[17] When I looked across the pond from this peak toward the Sudbury meadows, which in time of flood[18] I distinguished elevated perhaps by a mirage in their seething valley, like a coin in a basin, all the earth beyond the pond appeared like a thin crust insulated and floated even by this small sheet of intervening water, and I was reminded that this on which I dwelt was but *dry land*.

Though the view from my door was still more contracted, I did not feel crowded or confined in the least. There was pasture enough for my imagination. The low shrub-oak plateau to which the opposite shore arose, stretched away toward the prairies of the West and the steppes of Tartary,[19] affording ample room for all the roving families of men. "There are none happy in the world but beings who enjoy freely a vast horizon,"[20]—said Damodara, when his herds required new and larger pastures.

Both place and time were changed, and I dwelt nearer to those parts of the universe and to those eras in history which had most attracted me. Where I lived was as far off as many a region viewed nightly by astronomers. We are wont to imagine rare and delectable places in some remote and more celestial corner of the system, behind the constellation of Cassiopeia's Chair, far from noise and disturbance. I discovered that my house actually had its site in such a withdrawn, but forever new and unprofaned, part of the universe. If it were worth the while to settle in those parts near to the Pleiades or the Hyades, to Aldebaran or Altair,[21] then I was really there, or at an equal remoteness from the life which I had left behind, dwindled and twinkling with as fine a ray to my nearest neighbor, and to be seen only in moonless nights by him. Such was that part of creation where I had squatted;—

> "There was a shepherd that did live,
>   And held his thoughts as high
> As were the mounts whereon his flocks
>   Did hourly feed him by."[22]

What should we think of the shepherd's life if his flocks always wandered to higher pastures than his thoughts?

Every morning was a cheerful invitation to make my life of equal simplicity, and, I may say, innocence, with Nature herself. I have been as sincere a worshipper of Aurora[23] as the Greeks. I got up early and bathed in the pond; that was a religious exercise, and one of the best things which I did. They

say that characters were engraven on the bathing tub of king
Tchingthang to this effect: "Renew thyself completely each
day; do it again, and again, and forever again."²⁴ I can understand that. Morning brings back the heroic ages. I was as
much affected by the faint hum of a mosquito making its invisible and unimaginable tour through my apartment at earliest dawn, when I was sitting with door and windows open,
as I could be by any trumpet that ever sang of fame.²⁵ It was
Homer's requiem; itself an Iliad and Odyssey in the air, singing its own wrath and wanderings.²⁶ There was something
cosmical about it; a standing advertisement, till forbidden,²⁷ of
the everlasting vigor and fertility of the world. The morning,
which is the most memorable season of the day, is the awakening hour. Then there is least somnolence in us; and for an
hour, at least, some part of us awakes which slumbers all the
rest of the day and night. Little is to be expected of that day,
if it can be called a day, to which we are not awakened by
our Genius, but by the mechanical nudgings of some servitor,
are not awakened by our own newly-acquired force and
aspirations from within, accompanied by the undulations of
celestial music, instead of factory bells, and a fragrance filling
the air—to a higher life than we fell asleep from; and thus
the darkness bear its fruit, and prove itself to be good, no
less than the light. That man who does not believe that each
day contains an earlier, more sacred, and auroral hour than
he has yet profaned, has despaired of life, and is pursuing a
descending and darkening way. After a partial cessation of
his sensuous life, the soul of man, or its organs rather, are
reinvigorated each day, and his Genius tries again what noble
life it can make. All memorable events, I should say, trans-
pire in morning time and in a morning atmosphere. The
Vedas say, "All intelligences awake with the morning."²⁸ Poetry
and art, and the fairest and most memorable of the actions of
men, date from such an hour. All poets and heroes, like Memnon,²⁹ are the children of Aurora, and emit their music at
sunrise. To him whose elastic and vigorous thought keeps
pace with the sun, the day is a perpetual morning. It matters
not what the clocks say or the attitudes and labors of men.
Morning is when I am awake and there is a dawn in me.
Moral reform is the effort to throw off sleep. Why is it that
men give so poor an account of their day if they have not
been slumbering? They are not such poor calculators. If they

had not been overcome with drowsiness they would have performed something. The millions are awake enough for physical
labor; but only one in a million is awake enough for effective
intellectual exertion, only one in a hundred millions to a poetic
or divine life. To be awake is to be alive. I have never yet
met a man who was quite awake. How could I have looked
him in the face?

We must learn to reawaken and keep ourselves awake, not
by mechanical aids, but by an infinite expectation of the
dawn, which does not forsake us in our soundest sleep. I
know of no more encouraging fact than the unquestionable
ability of man to elevate his life by a conscious endeavor. It is
something to be able to paint a particular picture, or to carve
a statue, and so to make a few objects beautiful; but it is far
more glorious to carve and paint the very atmosphere and
medium through which we look, which morally we can do.
To affect the quality of the day, that is the highest of arts.
Every man is tasked to make his life, even in its details,
worthy of contemplation of his most elevated and critical
hour. If we refused, or rather used up, such paltry information as we get, the oracles would distinctly inform us how
this might be done.

I went to the woods because I wished to live deliberately,
to front only the essential facts of life, and see if I could not
learn what it had to teach, and not, when I came to die, discover that I had not lived. I did not wish to live what was not
life, living is so dear; nor did I wish to practise resignation,
unless it was quite necessary. I wanted to live deep and suck
out all the marrow of life, to live so sturdily and Spartan-
like[30] as to put to rout all that was not life, to cut a broad
swath and shave close, to drive life into a corner, and reduce
it to its lowest terms, and, if it proved to be mean, why then
to get the whole and genuine meanness of it, and publish its
meanness to the world; or if it were sublime, to know it by
experience, and be able to give a true account of it in my
next excursion.[31] For most men, it appears to me, are in a
strange uncertainty about it, whether it is of the devil or of
God, and have *somewhat hastily* concluded that it is the chief
end of man here to "glorify God and enjoy him forever."[32]

Still we live meanly, like ants; though the fable[33] tells us
that we were long ago changed into men; like pygmies[34] we
fight with cranes; it is error upon error, and clout upon clout,[35]

and our best virtue has for its occasion a superfluous and evitable wretchedness. Our life is frittered away by detail. An honest man has hardly need to count more than his ten fingers, or in extreme cases he may add his ten toes, and lump the rest. Simplicity, simplicity, simplicity! I say, let your affairs be as two or three, and not a hundred or a thousand; instead of a million count half a dozen, and keep your accounts on your thumb nail. In the midst of this chopping sea of civilized life, such are the clouds and storms and quicksands and thousand-and-one items to be allowed for, that a man has to live, if he would not founder and go to the bottom and not make his port at all, by dead reckoning and he must be a great calculator indeed who succeeds. Simplify, simplify. Instead of three meals a day, if it be necessary eat but one; instead of a hundred dishes, five; and reduce other things in proportion. Our life is like a German Confederacy,[36] made up of petty states, with its boundary forever fluctuating, so that even a German cannot tell you how it is bounded at any moment. The nation itself, with all its so called internal improvements, which, by the way, are all external and superficial, is just such an unwieldy and overgrown establishment, cluttered with furniture and tripped up by its own traps, ruined by luxury and heedless expense, by want of calculation and a worthy aim, as the million households in the land; and the only cure for it as for them is in a rigid economy, a stern and more than Spartan simplicity of life and elevation of purpose. It lives too fast. Men think that it is essential that the *Nation* have commerce, and export ice, and talk through a telegraph, and ride thirty miles an hour, without a doubt, whether *they* do or not; but whether we should live like baboons or like men, is a little uncertain. If we do not get out sleepers,[37] and forge rails, and devote days and nights to the work, but go to tinkering upon our *lives* to improve *them,* who will build railroads? And if railroads are not built, how shall we get to heaven[38] in season? But if we stay at home and mind our business, who will want railroads? We do not ride on the railroad; it rides upon us. Did you ever think what those sleepers are that underlie the railroad? Each one is a man, an Irishman, or a Yankee man. The rails are laid on them, and they are covered with sand, and the cars run smoothly over them. They are sound sleepers, I assure you. And every few years a new lot is laid down and run over; so that, if some have the pleasure of riding on a rail,[39] others have the misfortune to be ridden upon. And when they run over a man that is walking in his sleep, a supernumerary sleeper in the wrong position, and wake him up, they suddenly stop the cars, and make a hue and cry about it, as if this were an exception. I am glad to know that it takes a gang of men for every five miles to keep the sleepers down and level in their beds as it is, for this is a sign that they may sometime get up again.

Why should we live with such hurry and waste of life? We are determined to be starved before we are hungry. Men say that a stitch in time[40] saves nine, and so they take a thousand stitches to-day to save nine to-morrow. As for *work*, we haven't any of any consequence. We have the Saint Vitus' dance,[41] and cannot possibly keep our heads still. If I should only give a few pulls at the parish bell-rope, as for a fire, that is, without setting the bell,[42] there is hardly a man on his farm in the outskirts of Concord, notwithstanding that press of engagements which was his excuse so many times this morning, nor a boy, nor a woman, I might also say, but would forsake all and follow that sound, not mainly to save property from the flames, but, if we will confess the truth, much more to see it burn, since burn it must, and we, be it known, did not set it on fire,[43]—or to see it put out, and have a hand in it, if that is done as handsomely; yes, even if it were the parish church itself. Hardly a man takes a half hour's nap after dinner, but when he wakes he holds up his head and asks, "What's the news?" as if the rest of mankind had stood his sentinels. Some give directions to be waked every half hour, doubtless for no other purpose; and then, to pay for it, they tell what they have dreamed. After a night's sleep the news is as indispensable as the breakfast. "Pray tell me any thing new that has happened to a man any where on this globe,"—and he reads it over his coffee and rolls, that a man has had his eyes gouged out this morning on the Wachito River;[44] never dreaming the while that he lives in the dark unfathomed mammoth cave[45] of this world, and has but the rudiment of an eye himself.

For my part, I could easily do without the post-office. I think that there are very few important communications made through it. To speak critically, I never received more than one or two letters in my life—I wrote this some years ago—that

were worth the postage. The penny-post is, commonly, an
institution through which you seriously offer a man that penny
for his thoughts which is so often safely offered in jest. And
I am sure that I never read any memorable news in a newspaper. If we read of one man robbed, or murdered, or killed
by accident, or one house burned, or one vessel wrecked, or
one steamboat blown up, or one cow run over on the Western
Railroad,[46] or one mad dog killed, or one lot of grasshoppers
in the winter,—we never need read of another. One is enough.
If you are acquainted with the principle, what do you care
for a myriad instances and applications? To a philosopher all
news, as it is called, is gossip, and they who edit and read it
are old women over their tea. Yet not a few are greedy after
this gossip. There was such a rush, as I hear, the other day at
one of the offices to learn the foreign news by the last arrival, that several large squares of plate glass belonging to the
establishment were broken by the pressure,—news which I
seriously think a ready wit might write a twelve-month or
twelve years beforehand with sufficient accuracy. As for Spain,
for instance, if you know how to throw in Don Carlos and
the Infanta, and Don Pedro and Seville and Granada,[47] from
time to time in the right proportions,—they may have changed
the names a little since I saw the papers,—and serve up a
bull-fight when other entertainments fail, it will be true to
the letter, and give us as good an idea of the exact state or
ruin of things in Spain as the most succinct and lucid reports
under this head in the newspapers: and as for England, almost the last significant scrap of news from that quarter was
the revolution of 1649;[48] and if you have learned the history of
her crops for an average year, you never need attend to that
thing again, unless your speculations are of a merely pecuniary
character. If one may judge who rarely looks into the newspapers, nothing new does ever happen in foreign parts, a
French revolution not excepted.

What news! how much more important to know what that
is which was never old! "Kieou-he-yu (great dignitary of the
state of Wei) sent a man to Khoung-tseu to know his news.
Khoung-tseu caused the messenger to be seated near him,
and questioned him in these terms: What is your master doing? The messenger answered with respect: My master de-
sires to diminish the number of his faults, but he cannot come
to the end of them.[49] The messenger being gone, the philoso-

pher remarked: What a worthy messenger! What a worthy
messenger!"[50] The preacher, instead of vexing the ears of
drowsy farmers on their day of rest at the end of the week,—
for Sunday[51] is the fit conclusion of an ill-spent week, and
not the fresh and brave beginning of a new one,—with this
one other draggletail of a sermon, should shout with thundering voice,—"Pause! Avast![52] Why so seeming fast, but deadly
slow?"

Shams and delusions are esteemed for soundest truths,
while reality is fabulous. If men would steadily observe realities only, and not allow themselves to be deluded, life, to
compare it with such things as we know, would be like a
fairy tale and the Arabian Nights' Entertainments. If we respected only what is inevitable and has a right to be, music
and poetry would resound along the streets. When we are un-
hurried and wise, we perceive that only great and worthy
things have any permanent and absolute existence,—that
petty fears and petty pleasures are but the shadow of the
reality. This is always exhilarating and sublime. By closing
the eyes and slumbering, and consenting to be deceived by
shows, men establish and confirm their daily life of routine
and habit every where, which still is built on purely illusory
foundations. Children,[53] who play life, discern its true law
and relations more clearly than men, who fail to live it
worthily, but think that they are wiser by experience, that is,
by failure. I have read in a Hindoo book, that "there was a
king's son, who, being expelled in infancy from his native
city, was brought up by a forester, and, growing up to maturity in that state, imagined himself to belong to the barbarous race with which he lived. One of his father's ministers
having discovered him, revealed to him what he was, and the
misconception of his character was removed, and he knew
himself to be a prince. So soul," continues the Hindoo philosopher, "from the circumstances in which it is placed, mistakes
its own character, until the truth is revealed to it by some holy
teacher, and then it knows itself to be *Brahme*."[54] I perceive
that we inhabitants of New England live this mean life that
we do because our vision does not penetrate the surface of
things. We think that that *is* which *appears* to be. If a man
should walk through this town and see only the reality,
where, think you, would the "Mill-dam"[55] go to? If he should
give us an account of the realities he beheld there, we should

not recognize the place in his description. Look at a meeting-house, or a court-house, or a jail, or a shop, or a dwelling-house, and say what that thing really is before a true gaze, and they would all go to pieces in your account of them. Men esteem truth remote, in the outskirts of the system, behind the farthest star, before Adam and after the last man. In eternity there is indeed something true and sublime. But all these times and places and occasions are now and here. God himself culminates in the present moment, and will never be more divine in the lapse of all the ages. And we are enabled to apprehend at all what is sublime and noble only by the perpetual instilling and drenching of the reality that surrounds us. The universe constantly and obediently answers to our conceptions; whether we travel fast or slow, the track is laid for us. Let us spend our lives in conceiving then. The poet or the artist never yet had so fair and noble a design but some of his posterity at least could accomplish it.

Let us spend one day as deliberately as Nature, and not be thrown off the track[56] by every nutshell and mosquito's wing that falls on the rails. Let us rise early and fast, or break fast, gently and without perturbation; let company come and let company go, let the bells ring and the children cry,—determined to make a day of it. Why should we knock under and go with the stream? Let us not be upset and overwhelmed in that terrible rapid and whirlpool called a dinner, situated in the meridian shallows. Weather this danger and you are safe, for the rest of the way is down hill. With unrelaxed nerves, with morning vigor, sail by it, looking another way, tied to the mast like Ulysses.[57] If the engine whistles, let it whistle till it is hoarse for its pains. If the bell rings, why should we run? We will consider what kind of music they are like. Let us settle ourselves, and work and wedge our feet downward through the mud and slush of opinion, and prejudice, and tradition, and delusion, and appearance, that alluvion which covers the globe, through Paris and London, through New York and Boston and Concord, through church and state, through poetry and philosophy and religion, till we come to a hard bottom and rocks in place, which we can call *reality*, and say, This is, and no mistake; and then begin, having a *point d'appui*,[58] below freshet and frost and fire, a place where you might found a wall or a state, or set a lamp-post safely, or perhaps a gauge, not a Nilometer,[59] but a Realometer, that

future ages might know how deep a freshet of shams and ap-
pearances had gathered from time to time. If you stand right
fronting and face to face to a fact, you will see the sun glimmer
on both its surfaces, as if it were a cimeter, and feel its sweet
edge dividing you through the heart and marrow, and so you
will happily conclude your mortal career. Be it life or death,
we crave only reality. If we are really dying, let us hear the
rattle in our throats and feel cold in the extremities; if we are
alive, let us go about our business.

Time is but the stream I go a-fishing in. I drink at it; but
while I drink I see the sandy bottom and detect how shallow
it is. Its thin current slides away, but eternity remains. I
would drink deeper; fish in the sky, whose bottom is pebbly
with stars. I cannot count one. I know not the first letter of
the alphabet. I have always been regretting that I was not as
wise as the day I was born.[60] The intellect is a cleaver; it
discerns and rifts its way into the secret of things. I do not
wish to be any more busy with my hands than is necessary.
My head is hands and feet. I feel all my best faculties concentrated in it. My instinct tells me that my head is an organ for
burrowing, as some creatures use their snout and fore-paws,
and with it I would mine and burrow my way through these
hills. I think that the richest vein is somewhere hereabouts;
so by the divining rod and thin rising vapors I judge; and
here I will begin to mine.

III

READING

WITH a little more deliberation in the choice of their pursuits, all men would perhaps become essentially students and observers, for certainly their nature and destiny are interesting to all alike. In accumulating property for ourselves or our posterity, in founding a family or a state, or acquiring fame even, we are mortal; but in dealing with truth we are immortal, and need fear no change nor accident. The oldest Egyptian or Hindoo philosopher raised a corner of the veil from the statue of the divinity; and still the trembling robe remains raised, and I gaze upon as fresh a glory as he did, since it was I in him that was then so bold, and it is he in me that now reviews the vision. No dust has settled on that robe; no time has elapsed since that divinity was revealed. That time which we really improve, or which is improvable, is neither past, present, nor future.

My residence was more favorable, not only to thought, but to serious reading, than a university; and though I was beyond the range of the ordinary circulating library, I had more than ever come within the influence of those books which circulate round the world, whose sentences were first written on bark, and are now merely copied from time to time on to linen paper. Says the poet Mîr Camar Uddîn Mast, "Being seated to run through the region of the spiritual world; I have had this advantage in books. To be intoxicated by a single glass of wine; I have experienced this pleasure when I have drunk the liquor of the esoteric doctrines."[1] I kept Homer's[2] Iliad on my table through the summer, though I looked at his page only now and then. Incessant labor with my hands, at first, for I had my house to finish and my beans to hoe at the same time, made more study impossible. Yet I sustained myself by the prospect of such reading in future. I read one or two shallow books of travel in the intervals of my work, till that employment made me ashamed of myself, and I asked where it was then that *I* lived.

The student may read Homer or Æschylus in the Greek without danger of dissipation or luxuriousness, for it implies that he in some measure emulate their heroes, and consecrate morning hours to their pages. The heroic books, even if printed in the character of our mother tongue, will always be in a language dead to degenerate times; and we must laboriously seek the meaning of each word and line, conjecturing a larger sense than common use permits out of what wisdom and valor and generosity we have. The modern cheap and fertile press, with all its translations, has done little to bring us nearer to the heroic writers of antiquity. They seem as solitary, and the letter in which they are printed as rare and curious, as ever. It is worth the expense of youthful days and costly hours, if you learn only some words of an ancient language,³ which are raised out of the trivialness of the street, to be perpetual suggestions and provocations. It is not in vain that the farmer remembers and repeats the few Latin words which he has heard. Men sometimes speak as if the study of the classics would at length make way for more modern and practical studies; but the adventurous student will always study classics, in whatever language they may be written and however ancient they may be. For what are the classics but the noblest recorded thoughts of man? They are the only oracles which are not decayed, and there are such answers to the most modern inquiry in them as Delphi and Dondona⁴ never gave. We might as well omit to study Nature because she is old. To read well, that is, to read true books in a true spirit, is a noble exercise, and one that will task the reader more than any exercise which the customs of the day esteem. It requires a training such as the athletes underwent, the steady intention almost of the whole life to this object. Books must be read as deliberately and reservedly as they were written. It is not enough even to be able to speak the language of that nation by which they are written, for there is a memorable interval between the spoken and the written language, the language heard and the language read. The one is commonly transitory, a sound, a tongue, a dialect merely, almost brutish, and we learn it unconsciously, like the brutes, of our mothers. The other is the maturity and experience of that; if that is our mother tongue, this is our father tongue, a reserved and select expression, too significant to be heard by the ear, which we must be born again⁵ in order to speak. The crowds of men who merely *spoke* the Greek and Latin tongues in the middle ages were not entitled by the accident of birth to *read* the works of genius written in those languages; for these were not written in that Greek or Latin which they knew, but in the select language of literature. They had not learned the nobler dialects of Greece and Rome, but the very materials on which they were written were waste paper[6] to them, and they prized instead a cheap contemporary literature. But when the several nations of Europe had acquired distinct though rude written languages of their own, sufficient for the purposes of their rising literatures, then first learning revived, and scholars were enabled to discern from that remoteness the treasures of antiquity. What the Roman and Grecian multitude could not *hear,* after the lapse of ages a few scholars *read,* and a few scholars only are still reading it.

However much we may admire the orator's[7] occasional bursts of eloquence, the noblest written words are commonly as far behind or above the fleeting spoken language as the firmament with its stars is behind the clouds. *There* are the stars, and they who can may read them. The astronomers forever comment on and observe them. They are not exhalations like our daily colloquies and vaporous breath. What is called eloquence in the forum is commonly found to be rhetoric in the study. The o͞rator yields to the inspiration of a transient occasion, and speaks to the mob before him, to those who can *hear* him; but the writer, whose more equable life is his occasion, and who would be distracted by the event and the crowd which inspire the orator, speaks to the intellect and heart of mankind, to all in any age who can *understand* him.

No wonder that Alexander[8] carried the Iliad with him on his expeditions in a precious casket. A written word is the choicest of relics. It is something at once more intimate with us and more universal than any other work of art. It is the work of art nearest to life itself. It may be translated into every language, and not only be read but actually breathed from all human lips;—not be represented on canvas or in marble only, but be carved out of the breath of life itself. The symbol of an ancient man's thought becomes a modern man's speech. Two thousand summers have imparted to the monuments of Grecian literature, as to her marbles, only a maturer golden and autumnal tint, for they have carried their own serene and celestial atmosphere into all lands to protect them against the corrosion of time. Books are the treasured wealth of the world and the fit inheritance of generations and nations. Books, the oldest and the best, stand naturally and rightfully on the shelves of every cottage. They have no cause of their own to plead, but while they enlighten and sustain the reader his common sense will not refuse them. Their authors are a natural and irresistible aristocracy in every society, and, more than kings or emperors, exert an influence on mankind. When the illiterate and perhaps scornful trader has earned by enterprise and industry his coveted leisure and independence, and is admitted to the circles of wealth and fashion, he turns inevitably at last to those still higher but yet inaccessible circles of intellect and genius, and is sensible only of the imperfection of his culture and the vanity and insufficiency of all his riches, and further proves his good sense by the pains which he takes to secure for his children that intellectual culture whose want he so keenly feels; and thus it is that he becomes the founder of a family.

Those who have not learned to read the ancient classics in the language in which they were written must have a very imperfect knowledge of the history of the human race; for it is remarkable that no transcript of them has ever been made into any modern tongue, unless our civilization itself may be regarded as such a transcript. Homer[9] has never yet been printed in English, nor Æschylus, nor Virgil even,—works as refined, as solidly done, and as beautiful almost as the morning itself; for later writers, say what we will of their genius, have rarely, if ever, equalled the elaborate beauty and finish and the lifelong and heroic literary labors of the ancients. They only talk of forgetting them who never knew them. It will be soon enough to forget them when we have the learning and the genius which will enable us to attend to and appreciate them. That age will be rich indeed when those relics which we call Classics, and the still older and more than classic but even less known Scriptures of the nations, shall have still further accumulated, when the Vaticans[10] shall be filled with Vedas and Zendavestas[11] and Bibles with Homers and Dantes and Shakspeares, and all the centuries to come shall have successively deposited their trophies in the forum of the world. By such a pile[12] we may hope to scale heaven at last.

The works of the great poets have never yet been read by mankind, for only great poets can read them. They have only been read as the multitude read the stars, at most astrologically, not astronomically. Most men have learned to read to serve a paltry convenience, as they have learned to cipher in order to keep accounts and not be cheated in trade; but of reading as a noble intellectual exercise they know little or nothing; yet this only is reading, in a high sense, not that which lulls us as a luxury and suffers the nobler faculties to sleep the while, but what we have to stand on tiptoe to read and devote our most alert and wakeful hours to.

I think that having learned our letters we should read the best that is in literature, and not be forever repeating our a b abs,[13] and words of one syllable, in the fourth or fifth classes, sitting on the lowest and foremost form[14] all our lives. Most men are satisfied if they read or hear read, and perchance have been convicted by the wisdom of one good book, the Bible, and for the rest of their lives vegetate and dissipate their faculties in what is called easy reading. There is a work in several volumes in our Circulating Library entitled Little Reading,[15] which I thought referred to a town of that name which I had not been to. There are those who, like cormorants and ostriches,[16] can digest all sorts of this, even after the fullest dinner of meats and vegetables, for they suffer nothing to be wasted. If others are the machines to provide this provender, they are the machines to read it. They read the nine thousandth tale about Zebulon and Sephronia,[17] and how they loved as none had ever loved before, and neither did the course of their true love run smooth,[18]—at any rate, how it did run and stumble, and get up again and go on! how some poor unfortunate got up onto a steeple,[19] who had better never have gone up as far as the belfry; and then, having needlessly got him up there, the happy novelist rings the bell for all the world to come together and hear, O dear! how he did get down again! For my part, I think that they had better metamorphose all such aspiring heroes of universal noveldom into man weathercocks, as they used to put heroes among the constellations, and let them swing round there till they are rusty, and not come down at all to bother honest men with their pranks. The next time the novelist rings the bell I will not stir though the meeting-house burn down. "The Skip of the Tip-Toe-Hop,[20] a Romance of the Middle Ages, by the

celebrated author of "Tittle-Tol-Tan,"[21] to appear in monthly
parts;[22] a great rush; don't all come together." All this they
read with saucer eyes, and erect and primitive curiosity, and
with unwearied gizzard, whose corrugations even yet need no
sharpening, just as some little four-year-old bencher[23] his
two-cent gilt-covered edition of Cinderella,—without any
improvement, that I can see, in the pronunciation, or accent,
or emphasis, or any more skill in extracting or inserting the
moral. The result is dulness of sight, a stagnation of the vital
circulations, and a general deliquium and sloughing off of all
the intellectual faculties. This sort of gingerbread is baked
daily and more sedulously than pure wheat or rye-and-Indian[24]
in almost every oven, and finds a surer market.

The best books are not read even by those who are called
good readers. What does our Concord culture amount to?
There is in this town, with a very few exceptions, no taste for
the best or for very good books even in English literature,
whose words all can read and spell. Even the college-bred
and so called liberally educated men here and elsewhere have
really little or no acquaintance with the English classics; and
as for the recorded wisdom of mankind, the ancient classics
and Bibles, which are accessible to all who will know of
them, there are the feeblest efforts any where made to become
acquainted with them. I know a woodchopper,[25] of middle
age, who takes a French paper, not for news as he says, for
he is above that, but to "keep himself in practice," he being a Canadian by birth; and when I ask him what he considers the best thing he can do in this world, he says, beside
this, to keep up and add to his English. This is about as much
as the college bred generally do or aspire to do, and they
take an English paper for the purpose. One who has just come
from reading perhaps one of the best English books will find
how many with whom he can converse about it? Or suppose
he comes from reading a Greek or Latin classic in the original,
whose praises are familiar even to the so called illiterate; he
will find nobody at all to speak to, but must keep silence about
it. Indeed, there is hardly the professor in our colleges, who,
if he has mastered the difficulties of the language, has proportionally mastered the difficulties of the wit and poetry of a
Greek poet, and has any sympathy to impart to the alert and
heroic reader; and as for the sacred Scriptures, or Bibles of
mankind, who in this town can tell me even their titles? Most

men do not know that any nation but the Hebrews have had a scripture. A man, any man, will go considerably out of his way to pick up a silver dollar; but here are golden words, which the wisest men of antiquity have uttered, and whose worth the wise of every succeeding age have assured us of;— and yet we learn to read only as far as Easy Reading,²⁶ the primers and class-books, and when we leave school, the "Little Reading," and story books, which are for boys and beginners; and our reading, our conversation and thinking, are all on a very low level, worthy only of pygmies and manikins.

I aspire to be acquainted with wiser men than this our Concord soil has produced, whose names are hardly known here. Or shall I hear the name of Plato and never read his book? As if Plato were my townsman and I never saw him,— my next neighbor and I never heard him speak or attended to the wisdom of his words. But how actually is it? His Dialogues, which contain what was immortal in him, lie on the next shelf, and yet I never read them. We are under-bred and low-lived and illiterate; and in this respect I confess I do not make any very broad distinction between the illiterateness of my townsman who cannot read at all, and the illiterateness of him who has learned to read only what is for children and feeble intellects. We should be as good as the worthies of antiquity, but partly by first knowing how good they were. We are a race of tit-men,²⁷ and soar but little higher in our intellectual flights than the columns of the daily paper.

It is not all books that are as dull as their readers. There are probably words addressed to our condition exactly, which, if we could really hear and understand, would be more salutary than the morning or the spring to our lives, and possibly put a new aspect on the face of things for us. How many a man has dated a new era in his life from the reading of a book. The book exists for us perchance which will explain our miracles and reveal new ones. The at present unutterable things we may find somewhere uttered. These same questions that disturb and puzzle and confound us have in their turn occurred to all the wise men; not one has been omitted; and each has answered them, according to his ability, by his words and his life. Moreover, with wisdom we shall learn liberality. The solitary hired man on a farm in the outskirts of Concord, who has had his second birth²⁸ and peculiar religious experience, and is driven as he believes into silent

gravity and exclusiveness by his faith, may think it is not
true; but Zoroaster,[29] thousands of years ago, travelled the
same road and had the same experience; but he, being wise,
knew it to be universal, and treated his neighbors accordingly,
and is even said to have invented and established worship
among men. Let him humbly commune with Zoroaster then,
and through the liberalizing influence of all the worthies, with
Jesus Christ himself, and let "our church" go by the board.[30]

We boast that we belong to the nineteenth century and are
making the most rapid strides of any nation. But consider how
little this village does for its own culture. I do not wish to
flatter my townsmen, nor to be flattered by them, for that will
not advance either of us. We need to be provoked,—goaded
like oxen, as we are, into a trot. We have a comparatively decent system of common schools, schools for infants only; but
excepting the half-starved Lyceum in the winter, and latterly
the puny beginning of a library suggested by the state, no
school for ourselves. We spend more on almost any article of
bodily aliment or ailment than on our mental aliment. It is time
that we had uncommon schools, that we did not leave off our
education when we begin to be men and women. It is time that
villages were universities,[31] and their elder inhabitants the fellows of universities, with leisure—if they are indeed so well off
—to pursue liberal studies the rest of their lives. Shall the
world be confined to one Paris or one Oxford forever? Cannot
students be boarded here and get a liberal education under the
skies of Concord? Can we not hire some Abelard[32] to lecture to
us? Alas! what with foddering the cattle and tending the store,
we are kept from school too long, and our education is sadly
neglected. In this country, the village should in some respects
take the place of the nobleman of Europe. It should be the
patron of the fine arts. It is rich enough. It wants only the
magnanimity and refinement. It can spend money enough on
such things as farmers and traders value, but it is thought
Utopian to propose spending money for things which more
intelligent men know to be of far more worth. This town has
spent seventeen thousand dollars on a town-house, thank fortune or politics, but probably it will not spend so much on living wit, the true meat to put into that shell, in a hundred years.
The one hundred and twenty-five dollars annually subscribed
for a Lyceum[33] in the winter is better spent than any other
equal sum raised in the town. If we live in the nineteenth

century, why should we not enjoy the advantages which the nineteenth century offers? Why should our life be in any respect provincial? If we will read newspapers, why not skip the gossip of Boston and take the best newspaper in the world at once?—not be sucking the pap of "neutral family" papers,[34] or browsing "Olive-Branches"[35] here in New England. Let the reports of all the learned societies come to us, and we will see if they know any thing. Why should we leave it to Harper & Brothers and Redding & Co.[36] to select our reading? As the nobleman of cultivated taste surrounds himself with whatever conduces to his culture,—genius—learning—wit—books— paintings—statuary—music—philosophical instruments, and the like; so let the village do,—not stop short at a pedagogue, a parson, a sexton, a parish library, and three selectmen, be- cause our pilgrim forefathers got through a cold winter once on a bleak rock with these. To act collectively is according to the spirit of our institutions; and I am confident that, as our circumstances are more flourishing, our means are greater than the nobleman's. New England can hire all the wise men in the world to come and teach her, and board them round the while, and not be provincial at all. That is the *uncommon* school we want. Instead of noblemen, let us have noble villages of men. If it is necessary, omit one bridge over the river, go round a little there, and throw one arch at least over the darker gulf of ignorance which surrounds us.

IV

SOUNDS

But while we are confined to books,[1] though the most select and classic, and read only particular written languages, which are themselves but dialects and provincial, we are in danger of forgetting the language which all things and events speak without metaphor, which alone is copious and standard. Much is published, but little printed. The rays which stream through the shutter will be no longer remembered when the shutter is wholly removed. No method nor discipline can supersede the necessity of being forever on the alert. What is a course of history, or philosophy, or poetry, no matter how well selected, or the best society, or the most admirable routine of life, compared with the discipline of looking always at what is to be seen? Will you be a reader, a student merely, or a seer? Read your fate, see what is before you, and walk on into futurity.

I did not read books the first summer; I hoed beans. Nay, I often did better than this. There were times when I could not afford to sacrifice the bloom of the present moment to any work, whether of the head or hands. I love a broad margin to my life.[2] Sometimes, in a summer morning, having taken my accustomed bath,[3] I sat in my sunny doorway from sunrise till noon, rapt in a revery, amidst the pines and hickories and sumachs, in undisturbed solitude and stillness, while the birds sang around or flitted noiseless through the house, until by the sun falling in at my west window, or the noise of some traveller's wagon on the distant highway, I was reminded of the lapse of time. I grew in those seasons like corn in the night,[4] and they were far better than any work of the hands would have been. They were not time subtracted from my life, but so much over and above my usual allowance. I realized what the Orientals mean by contemplation and the forsaking of works. For the most part, I minded not how the hours went. The day advanced as if to light some work of mine; it was morning, and lo, now it is evening, and nothing memorable is accomplished. Instead of singing like the birds, I silently smiled at my incessant good fortune. As the sparrow had its trill, sitting on the hickory before my door, so had I my chuckle or suppressed warble which he might hear out of my nest. My days were not days of the week, bearing the stamp of any heathen deity,⁵ nor were they minced into hours and fretted by the ticking of a clock; for I lived like the Puri Indians, of whom it is said that "for yesterday, to-day, and to-morrow they have only one word, and they express the variety of meaning by pointing backward for yesterday, forward for to-morrow, and overhead for the passing day."⁶ This was sheer idleness to my fellow-townsmen, no doubt; but if the birds and flowers had tried me by their standard, I should not have been found wanting. A man must find his occasions in himself, it is true. The natural day is very calm, and will hardly reprove his indolence.

I had this advantage, at least, in my mode of life, over those who were obliged to look abroad for amusement, to society and the theatre, that my life itself was become my amusement and never ceased to be novel. It was a drama of many scenes and without an end. If we were always indeed getting our living, and regulating our lives according to the last and best mode we had learned, we should never be troubled with ennui. Follow your genius closely enough, and it will not fail to show you a fresh prospect every hour. Housework was a pleasant pastime. When my floor was dirty, I rose early, and, setting all my furniture out of doors on the grass, bed and bedstead making but one budget, dashed water on the floor, and sprinkled white sand from the pond on it, and then with a broom scrubbed it clean and white; and by the time the villagers had broken their fast the morning sun had dried my house sufficiently to allow me to move in again, and my meditations were almost uninterrupted. It was pleasant to see my whole household effects out on the grass, making a little pile like a gypsy's pack, and my three-legged table, from which I did not remove the books and pen and ink, standing amid the pines and hickories. They seemed glad to get out themselves, and as if unwilling to be brought in. I was sometimes tempted to stretch an awning over them and take my seat there. It was worth the while to see the sun shine on these things, and hear the free wind blow on them; so much more interesting most familiar objects look out of doors than in the house. A bird sits on the next bough, life-everlasting grows under the table, and blackberry vines run round its legs; pine cones, chestnut burs, and strawberry leaves are strewn about. It looked as if this was the way these forms came to be transferred to our furniture, to tables, chairs, and bedsteads,—because they once stood in their midst.

My house was on the side of a hill, immediately on the edge of the larger wood, in the midst of a young forest of pitch trees and hickories, and half a dozen rods[7] from the pond, to which a narrow footpath led down the hill. In my front yard grew the strawberry, blackberry, and life-everlasting, johnswort and goldenrod, shrub-oaks and sand-cherry, blueberry and ground-nut. Near the end of May, the sand-cherry, *(cerasus pumila,)* adorned the sides of the path with its delicate flowers arranged in umbels cylindrically about its short stems, which last, in the fall, weighed down with good sized and handsome cherries, fell over in wreaths like rays on every side. I tasted them out of compliment to Nature, though they were scarcely palatable. The sumach, *(rhus glabra,)* grew luxuriantly about the house, pushing up through the embankment which I had made, and growing five or six feet the first season. Its broad pinnate tropical leaf was pleasant though strange to look on. The large buds, suddenly pushing out late in the spring from dry sticks which had seemed to be dead, developed themselves as by magic into graceful green and tender boughs, an inch in diameter; and sometimes, as I sat at my window, so heedlessly did they grow and tax their weak joints, I heard a fresh and tender bough suddenly fall[8] like a fan to the ground, when there was not a breath of air stirring, broken off by its own weight. In August, the large masses of berries, which, when in flower, had attracted many wild bees, gradually assumed their bright velvety crimson hue, and by their weight again bent down and broke the tender limbs.

As I sit at my window this summer afternoon,[9] hawks are circling about my clearing; the tantivy[10] of wild pigeons,[11] flying by twos and threes athwart my view, or perching restless on the white-pine boughs behind my house, gives a voice to the air; a fishhawk dimples the glassy surface of the pond and brings up a fish; a mink[12] steals out of the marsh before my door and seizes a frog by the shore; the sedge is bending under the weight of the reed-birds[13] flitting hither and thither; and for the last half hour I have heard the rattle of railroad cars, now dying away and then reviving like the beat of a partridge,[14] conveying travellers from Boston to the country. For I did not live so out of the world as that boy, who, as I hear, was put out to a farmer in the east part of the town, but ere long ran away and came home again, quite down at the heel and homesick. He had never seen such a dull and out-of-the-way place; the folks were all gone off; why, you couldn't even hear the whistle! I doubt if there is such a place in Massachusetts now:—

> "In truth, our village has become a butt
> For one of those fleet railroad shafts, and o'er
> Our peaceful plain its soothing sound is—Concord"[15]

The Fitchburg Railroad[16] touches the pond about a hundred rods south of where I dwell. I usually go to the village along its causeway, and am, as it were, related to society by this link. The men on the freight trains, who go over the whole length of the road, bow to me as to an old acquaintance, they pass me so often, and apparently they take me for an employee; and so I am. I too would fain be a track-repairer somewhere in the orbit of the earth.

The whistle of the locomotive penetrates my woods summer and winter, sounding like the scream of a hawk sailing over some farmer's yard, informing me that many restless city merchants are arriving within the circle of the town, or adventurous country traders from the other side. As they come under one horizon, they shout their warning to get off the track to the other, heard sometimes through the circles of two towns. Here come your groceries, country; your rations, countrymen! Nor is there any man so independent on his farm that he can say them nay. And here's your pay for them! screams the countryman's whistle; timber like long battering rams going twenty miles an hour against the city's wall, and chairs enough to seat all the weary and heavy laden[17] that dwell within them. With such huge and lumbering civility the country hands a chair to the city. All the Indian huckleberry hills are stripped, all the cranberry meadows are raked into the city. Up comes the cotton, down goes the woven cloth; up comes the silk, down goes the woollen; up come the books, but down goes the wit that writes them.

When I meet the engine with its train of cars moving off with planetary motion,—or, rather, like a comet, for the beholder knows not if with that velocity and with that direction it will ever revisit this system, since its orbit does not look like a returning curve,—with its steam cloud like a banner streaming behind in golden and silver wreaths, like many a downy cloud which I have seen, high in the heavens, unfolding its masses to the light,—as if this travelling demigod, this cloud-compeller,[18] would ere long take the sunset sky for the livery of his train; when I hear the iron horse make the hills echo[19] with his snort like thunder, shaking the earth with his feet, and breathing fire and smoke from his nostrils, (what kind of winged horse or fiery dragon they will put into the new Mythology I don't know,) it seems as if the earth had got a race now worthy to inhabit it. If all were as it seems, and men made the elements their servants for noble ends! If the cloud that hangs over the engine were the perspiration of heroic deeds, or as beneficent as that which floats over the farmer's fields, then the elements and Nature herself would cheerfully accompany men on their errands and be their escort.

I watch the passage of the morning cars with the same feeling that I do the rising of the sun, which is hardly more regular. Their train of clouds stretching far behind and rising higher and higher, going to heaven while the cars are going to Boston,[20] conceals the sun for a minute and casts my distant field into the shade, a celestial train[21] beside which the petty train of cars which hugs the earth is but the barb of the spear. The stabler of the iron horse was up early this winter morning by the light of the stars amid the mountains, to fodder and harness his steed. Fire, too, was awakened thus early to put the vital heat in him and get him off. If the enterprise were as innocent as it is early! If the snow lies deep, they strap on his snow-shoes, and with the giant plough plough a furrow from the mountains to the seaboard, in which the cars, like a following drill-barrow,[22] sprinkle all the restless men and floating merchandise in the country for seed. All day the fire-steed flies over the country, stopping only that his master may rest, and I am awakened by his tramp and defiant snort at midnight, when in some remote glen in the woods he fronts the elements incased in ice and snow; and he will reach his stall only with the morning star, to start once more on his travels without rest or slumber. Or perchance, at evening, I hear him in his stable blowing off the superfluous energy of the day, that he may calm his nerves and cool his liver and brain for a few hours of

iron slumber. If the enterprise were as heroic and commanding
as it is protracted and unwearied!

Far through unfrequented woods on the confines of towns,
where once only the hunter penetrated by day, in the darkest
night dart these bright saloons without the knowledge of their
inhabitants; this moment stopping at some brilliant station-
house in town or city, where a social crowd is gathered, the
next in the Dismal Swamp,[23] scaring the owl and fox. The start-
ings and arrivals of the cars are now the epochs in the village
day. They go and come with such regularity and precision, and
their whistle can be heard so far, that the farmers set their
clocks by them, and thus one well conducted institution regu-
lates a whole country. Have not men improved somewhat in
punctuality since the railroad was invented? Do they not talk
and think faster in the depot than they did in the stage-office?
There is something electrifying in the atmosphere of the former
place. I have been astonished at the miracles it has wrought;
that some of my neighbors, who, I should have prophesied,
once for all, would never get to Boston by so prompt a conveyance, are on hand when the bell rings.[24] To do things "railroad fashion" is now the by-word; and it is worth the while to
be warned so often and so sincerely by any power to get off its
track. There is no stopping to read the riot act, no firing over
the heads of the mob, in this case. We have constructed a fate,
an *Atropos*,[25] that never turns aside. (Let that be the name of
your engine.) Men are advertised that at a certain hour and
minute these bolts will be shot toward particular points of the
compass; yet it interferes with no man's business, and the children go to school on the other track. We live the steadier for
it. We are all educated thus to be sons of Tell. The air is full of
invisible bolts. Every path but your own is the path of fate.
Keep on your own track, then.

What recommends commerce to me is its enterprise and
bravery. It does not clasp its hands and pray to Jupiter. I see
these men every day go about their business with more or less
courage and content, doing more even than they suspect, and
perchance better employed than they could have consciously
devised. I am less affected by their heroism who stood up for
half an hour in the front line at Buena Vista,[26] than by the
steady and cheerful valor of the men who inhabit the snow-
plough for their winter quarters; who have not merely the
three-o'-clock in the morning[27] courage, which Bonaparte

thought was the rarest, but whose courage does not go to rest so early, who go to sleep only when the storm sleeps or the sinews of their iron steed are frozen. On this morning of the Great Snow,[28] perchance, which is still raging and chilling men's blood, I hear the muffled tone of their engine bell from out the fog bank of their chilled breath, which announces that the cars *are coming*, without long delay, notwithstanding the veto of a New England north-east snow storm, and I behold the ploughmen covered with snow and rime, their heads peering above the mould-board which is turning down other than daisies and the nests of field-mice,[29] like bowlders of the Sierra Nevada, that occupy an outside place in the universe.

Commerce is unexpectedly confident and serene, alert, adventurous, and unwearied. It is very natural in its methods withal, far more so than many fantastic enterprises and sentimental experiments, and hence its singular success. I am refreshed and expanded when the freight train rattles past me, and I smell the stores which go dispensing their odors all the way from Long Wharf[30] to Lake Champlain, reminding me of foreign parts,[31] of coral reefs, and Indian oceans, and tropical climes, and the extent of the globe. I feel more like a citizen of the world at the sight of the palm-leaf[32] which will cover so many flaxen New England heads the next summer, the Manila hemp and cocoa-nut husks,[33] the old junk, gunny bags,[34] scrap iron, and rusty nails. This car-load of torn sails[35] is more legible and interesting now than if they should be wrought into paper and printed books. Who can write so graphically the history of the storms they have weathered as these rents have done? They are proof-sheets which need no correction. Here goes lumber from the Maine woods, which did not go out to sea in the last freshet,[36] risen four dollars on the thousand because of what did go out or was split up; pine, spruce, cedar,—first, second, third and fourth qualities, so lately all of one quality, to wave over the bear, and moose, and caribou. Next rolls Thomaston lime,[37] a prime lot, which will get far among the hills before it gets slacked. These rags in bales, of all hues and qualities, the lowest condition to which cotton and linen descend, the final result of dress,—of patterns which are now no longer cried up, unless it be in Milwaukie, as those splendid articles, English, French, or American prints, ginghams, muslins, &c., gathered from all quarters both of fashion and poverty, going to become paper of one color or a few shades only, on which forsooth will

be written tales of real life, high and low, and founded on fact!
This closed car smells of salt fish, the strong New England and
commercial scent, reminding me of the Grand Banks[38] and the
fisheries. Who has not seen a salt fish, thoroughly cured for this
world, so that nothing can spoil it, and putting the persever-
ance of the saints to the blush? with which you may sweep or
pave the streets, and split your kindlings, and the teamster
shelter himself and his lading against sun, wind and rain behind it,—and the trader, as a Concord trader[39] once did, hang
it up by his door for a sign when he commences business, until
at last his oldest customer cannot tell surely whether it be animal, vegetable, or mineral,[40] and yet it shall be as pure as a
snowflake, and if it be put into a pot and boiled, will come out
an excellent dun fish[41] for a Saturday's dinner. Next Spanish
hides, with the tails preserving their twist and the angle of elevation they had when the oxen that wore them were careering
over the pampas of the Spanish main,—a type of all obstinacy,
and evincing how almost hopeless and incurable are all con-
stitutional vices. I confess, that practically speaking, when I
have learned a man's real disposition, I have no hopes of
changing it for the better or worse in this state of existence. As
the Orientals say, "A cur's tail may be warmed, and pressed,
and bound round with ligatures, and after a twelve years' labor
bestowed upon it, still it will retain its natural form."[42] The
only effectual cure for such inveteracies as these tails exhibit is
to make glue of them, which I believe is what is usually done
with them, and then they will stay put and stick.[43] Here is a
hogshead of molasses or of brandy directed to John Smith,
Cuttingsville,[44] Vermont, some trader among the Green Mountains, who imports for the farmers near his clearing, and now
perchance stands over his bulk-head and thinks of the last arrivals on the coast, how they may affect the price for him,
telling his customers this moment, as he has told them twenty
times before this morning, that he expects some by the next
train of prime quality. It is advertised in the Cuttingsville
Times.

While these things go up other things come down. Warned
by the whizzing sound, I look up from my book and see some
tall pine, hewn on far northern hills, which has winged its way
over the Green Mountains and the Connecticut, shot like an
arrow through the township within ten minutes, and scarce
another eye beholds it; going

"to be the mast
Of some great ammiral."[45]

And hark! here comes the cattle-train bearing the cattle of a
thousand hills,[46] sheepcots, stables, and cow-yards in the air,
drovers with their sticks, and shepherd boys in the midst of
their flocks, all but the mountain pastures, whirled along like
leaves blown from the mountains by the September gales. The
air is filled with the bleating of calves and sheep, and the
hustling of oxen, as if a pastoral valley were going by. When
the old bell-weather at the head rattles his bell, the mountains
do indeed skip like rams[47] and the little hills like lambs. A car-
load of drovers, too, in the midst, on a level with their droves
now, their vocation gone, but still clinging to their useless sticks
as their badge of office. But their dogs, where are they? It is a
stampede to them; they are quite thrown out; they have lost
the scent. Methinks I hear them barking behind the Peterboro'
Hills,[48] or panting up the western slope of the Green Mountains. They will not be in at the death. Their vocation, too, is
gone. Their fidelity and sagacity are below par now. They will
sink back to their kennels in disgrace, or perchance run wild
and strike a league with the wolf and the fox. So is your
pastoral life whirled past and away. But the bell rings, and I
must get off the track and let the cars go by;—

What's the railroad to me?
I never go to see
Where it ends.
It fills a few hollows,
And makes banks for the swallows,
It sets the sand a-blowing,
And the blackberries a-growing,[49]

but I cross it like a cart-path in the woods. I will not have my
eyes put out and my ears spoiled by its smoke and steam and
hissing.

Now that the cars are gone by and all the restless world
with them, and the fishes in the pond no longer feel their
rumbling, I am more alone than ever. For the rest of the long
afternoon, perhaps, my meditations are interrupted only by the
faint rattle of a carriage or team along the distant highway.

Sometimes, on Sundays, I heard the bells, the Lincoln,

Acton, Bedford,[50] or Concord bell, when the wind was favorable, a faint, sweet, and, as it were, natural melody, worth importing into the wilderness. At a sufficient distance over the woods this sound acquires a certain vibratory hum, as if the pine needles in the horizon were the strings of a harp which it swept. All sound heard at the greatest possible distance produces one and the same effect, a vibration of the universal lyre, just as the intervening atmosphere makes a distant ridge of earth interesting to our eyes by the azure tint it imparts to it. There came to me in this case a melody which the air had strained, and which had conversed with every leaf and needle of the wood, that portion of the sound which the elements had taken up and modulated and echoed from vale to vale. The echo is, to some extent, an original sound, and therein is the magic and charm of it. It is not merely a repetition of what was worth repeating in the bell, but partly the voice of the wood; the same trivial words and notes sung by a wood-nymph.

At evening, the distant lowing of some cow in the horizon beyond the woods sounded sweet and melodious, and at first I would mistake it for the voices of certain minstrels by whom I was sometimes serenaded, who might be straying over hill and dale; but soon I was not unpleasantly disappointed when it was prolonged into the cheap and natural music of the cow. I do not mean to be satirical, but to express my appreciation of those youths' singing, when I state that I perceived clearly that it was akin to the music of the cow, and they were at length one articulation of Nature.

Regularly at half past seven, in one part of the summer, after the evening train had gone by, the whippoorwills chanted their vespers for half an hour, sitting on a stump by my door, or upon the ridge pole of the house. They would begin to sing almost with as much precision as a clock, within five minutes of a particular time, referred to the setting of the sun, every evening. I had a rare opportunity to become acquainted with their habits. Sometimes I heard four or five at once in different parts of the wood, by accident one a bar behind another, and so near me that I distinguished not only the cluck after each note, but often that singular buzzing sound like a fly in a spider's web, only proportionally louder. Sometimes one would circle round and round me in the woods a few feet distant as if tethered by a string, when probably I was near its eggs. They sang at intervals throughout the night, and were again as musical as ever just before and about dawn.

When other birds are still the screech owls take up the strain, like mourning women their ancient u-lu-lu.[51] Their dismal scream is truly Ben Jonsonian.[52] Wise midnight hags! It is no honest and blunt tu-whit tu-who[53] of the poets, but, without jesting, a most solemn graveyard ditty, the mutual consolations of suicide lovers remembering the pangs and the delights of supernal love in the infernal groves. Yet I love to hear their wailing, their doleful responses, trilled along the woodside; reminding me sometimes of music and singing birds; as if it were the dark and tearful side of music, the regrets and sighs that would fain be sung. They are the spirits, the low spirits and melancholy forebodings, of fallen souls that once in human shape night-walked the earth and did the deeds of darkness, now expiating their sins with their wailing hymns or threnodies in the scenery of their transgressions. They give me a new sense of the variety and capacity of that nature which is our common dwelling. *Oh-o-o-o-o that I never had been bor-r-r-r-n!*[54] sighs one on this side of the pond, and circles with the restlessness of despair to some new perch on the gray oaks. Then—*that I never had been bor-r-r-r-n!* echoes another on the farther side with tremulous sincerity and—*bor-r-r-r-n!* comes faintly from far in the Lincoln woods.

I was also serenaded by a hooting owl. Near at hand you could fancy it the most melancholy sound in Nature, as if she meant by this to stereotype and make permanent in her choir the dying moans of a human being,—some poor weak relic of mortality who has left hope behind,[55] and howls like an animal, yet with human sobs, on entering the dark valley, made more awful by a certain gurgling melodiousness,—I find myself beginning with the letters gl when I try to imitate it,—expressive of a mind which has reached the gelatinous mildewy stage in the mortification of all healthy and courageous thought. It reminded me of ghouls and idiots and insane howlings. But now one answers from far woods in a strain made really melodious by distance,—*Hoo hoo hoo, hoorer hoo;* and indeed for the most part it suggested only pleasing associations, whether heard by day or night, summer or winter.

I rejoice that there are owls. Let them do the idiotic and maniacal hooting for men. It is a sound admirably suited to

swamps and twilight woods which no day illustrates, suggest-
ing a vast and undeveloped nature which men have not recognized. They represent the stark twilight and unsatisfied
thoughts which all have. All day the sun has shone on the surface of some savage swamp, where the single spruce[56] stands
hung with usnea lichens, and small hawks circulate above, and
the chicadee lisps amid the evergreens, and the partridge and
rabbit skulk beneath; but now a more dismal and fitting day
dawns, and a different race of creatures awakes to express the
meaning of Nature there.

Late in the evening I heard the distant rumbling of wagons
over bridges,—a sound heard farther than almost any other at
night,—the baying of dogs, and sometimes again the lowing of
some disconsolate cow in a distant barn-yard. In the mean
while all the shore rang with the trump of bullfrogs, the sturdy
spirits of ancient winebibbers and wassailers, still unrepentant,
trying to sing a catch in their Stygian lake,[57]—if the Walden
nymphs will pardon the comparison, for though there are almost no weeds, there are frogs there,—who would fain keep up
the hilarious rules of their old festal tables, though their voices
have waxed hoarse and solemnly grave, mocking at mirth, and
the wine has lost its flavor, and become only liquor to distend
their paunches, and sweet intoxication never comes to drown
the memory of the past, but mere saturation and waterlogged-
ness and distention. The most aldermanic, with his chin upon
a heartleaf, which serves for a napkin to his drooling chaps,
under this northern shore quaffs a deep draught of the once
scorned water, and passes round the cup with the ejaculation
tr-r-r-oonk, tr-r-r-oonk, tr-r-r-oonk! and straightway comes over
the water from some distant cove the same password repeated,
where the next in seniority and girth has gulped down to his
mark;[58] and when this observance has made the circuit of the
shores, then ejaculates the master of ceremonies, with satisfaction, *tr-r-r-oonk!* and each in his turn repeats the same down to
the least distended, leakiest, and flabbiest paunched, that there
be no mistake; and then the bowl goes round again and again,
until the sun disperses the morning mist, and only the patriarch
is not under the pond,[59] but vainly bellowing *troonk* from time
to time, and pausing for a reply.

I am not sure that I ever heard the sound of cock-crowing
from my clearing, and I thought that it might be worth the

while to keep a cockerel for his music merely, as a singing bird. The note of this once wild Indian pheasant is certainly the most remarkable of any bird's, and if they could be naturalized without being domesticated, it would soon become the most famous sound in our woods, surpassing the clangor of the goose and the hooting of the owl; and then imagine the cackling of the hens to fill the pauses when their lords' clarions rested! No wonder that man added this bird to his tame stock,—to say nothing of the eggs and drumsticks. To walk in a winter morning in a wood where these birds abounded, their native woods, and hear the wild cockerel crow on the trees, clear and shrill for miles over the resounding earth, drowning the feebler notes of other birds,—think of it! It would put nations on the alert. Who would not be early to rise,[60] and rise earlier and earlier every successive day of his life, till he became unspeakably healthy, wealthy, and wise? This foreign bird's note is celebrated by the poets of all countries along with the notes of their native songsters. All climates agree with brave Chanticleer. He is more indigenous even than the natives. His health is ever good, his lungs are sound, his spirits never flag. Even the sailor[61] on the Atlantic and Pacific is awakened by his voice; but its shrill sound never roused me from my slumbers. I kept neither dog, cat, cow, pig, nor hens, so that you would have said there was a deficiency of domestic sounds; neither the churn, nor the spinning wheel, nor even the singing of the kettle, nor the hissing of the urn, nor children crying, to comfort one. An old-fashioned man would have lost his senses or died of ennui before this. Not even rats in the wall, for they were starved out, or rather were never baited in,—only squirrels on the roof and under the floor, a whippoorwill on the ridge pole, a blue-jay screaming beneath the window, a hare or woodchuck under the house, a screech-owl or a cat-owl behind it, a flock of wild geese or a laughing loon on the pond, and a fox to bark in the night. Not even a lark[62] or an oriole, those mild plantation birds, ever visited my clearing. No cockerels to crow nor hens to cackle in the yard. No yard! but unfenced Nature reaching up to your very sills. A young forest growing up under your windows, and wild sumach and blackberry vines breaking through into your cellar; sturdy pitch-pines rubbing and creaking against the shingles for want of room, their roots reaching quite under the house. Instead of a scuttle or a blind blown off in the gale,—a pine tree snapped off or torn up by the roots behind your house for fuel. Instead of no path to the front-yard gate in the Great Snow,[63] —no gate—no front-yard,—and no path to the civilized world!

V

SOLITUDE

THIS is a delicious evening, when the whole body is one sense, and imbibes delight through every pore. I go and come with a strange liberty in Nature, a part of herself. As I walk along the stony shore of the pond in my shirt sleeves, though it is cool as well as cloudy and windy, and I see nothing special to attract me, all the elements are unusually congenial to me. The bull frogs trump to usher in the night, and the note of the whip-poorwill is borne on the rippling wind from over the water. Sympathy with the fluttering alder and poplar leaves almost takes away my breath; yet, like the lake, my serenity is rippled but not ruffled. These small waves raised by the evening wind are as remote from storm as the smooth reflecting surface. Though it is now dark, the wind still blows and roars in the wood, the waves still dash, and some creatures lull the rest with their notes. The repose is never complete. The wildest animals do not repose, but seek their prey now; the fox, and skunk, and rabbit, now roam the fields and woods without fear. They are Nature's watchmen,—links which connect the days of animated life.

When I return to my house I find that visitors have been there and left their cards, either a bunch of flowers, or a wreath of evergreen, or a name in pencil on a yellow walnut leaf or a chip. They who come rarely to the woods take some little piece of the forest into their hands to play with by the way, which they leave, either intentionally or accidentally. One has peeled a willow wand, woven it into a ring, and dropped it on my table. I could always tell if visitors had called in my absence, either by the bended twigs or grass, or the print of their shoes, and generally of what sex or age or quality they were by some slight trace left, as a flower dropped, or a bunch of grass plucked and thrown away, even as far off as the railroad, half a mile distant, or by the lingering odor of a cigar or pipe. Nay, I was frequently notified of the passage of a traveller along the highway sixty rods off by the scent of his pipe.

There is commonly sufficient space about us. Our horizon is never quite at our elbows. The thick wood is not just at our door, nor the pond, but somewhat is always clearing, familiar and worn by us, appropriated and fenced in some way, and reclaimed from Nature. For what reason have I this vast range and circuit, some square miles of unfrequented forest, for my privacy, abandoned to me by men? My nearest neighbor is a mile distant, and no house is visible from any place but the hill-tops within half a mile of my own. I have my horizon bounded by woods all to myself; a distant view of the railroad where it touches the pond on the one hand, and of the fence which skirts the woodland road on the other. But for the most part it is as solitary where I live as on the prairies. It is as much Asia or Africa as New England. I have, as it were, my own sun and moon and stars, and a little world all to myself. At night there was never a traveller passed my house, or knocked at my door, more than if I were the first or last man; unless it were in the spring, when at long intervals some came from the village to fish for pouts,—they plainly fished much more in the Walden Pond of their own natures, and baited their hooks with darkness,—but they soon retreated, usually with light baskets, and left "the world to darkness and to me,"[1] and the black kernel of the night was never profaned by any human neighborhood. I believe that men are generally still a little afraid of the dark, though the witches are all hung, and Christianity and candles have been introduced.

Yet I experienced sometimes that the most sweet and tender, the most innocent and encouraging society may be found in any natural object, even for the poor misanthrope and most melancholy man. There can be no very black melancholy[2] to him who lives in the midst of Nature and has his senses still. There was never yet such a storm but it was Æolian music[3] to a healthy and innocent ear. Nothing can rightly compel a simple and brave man to a vulgar sadness. While I enjoy the friendship of the seasons I trust that nothing can make life a burden to me. The gentle rain which waters my beans and keeps me in the house to-day is not drear and melancholy, but good for me too. Though it prevents my hoeing them, it is of far more worth than my hoeing. If it should continue so long as to cause the seeds to rot in the ground and destroy the potatoes in the low lands, it would still be good for the grass on the uplands, and, being good for the grass, it would be good for me. Sometimes, when I compare myself with other men, it seems as if I were more favored by the gods than they, beyond any deserts that I am conscious of; as if I had a warrant and surety at their hands which my fellows have not, and were especially guided and guarded. I do not flatter myself, but if it be possible they flatter me. I have never felt lonesome, or in the least oppressed by a sense of solitude, but once, and that was a few weeks after I came to the woods, when, for an hour, I doubted if the near neighborhood of man was not essential to a serene and healthy life. To be alone was something unpleasant. But I was at the same time conscious of a slight insanity in my mood, and seemed to foresee my recovery. In the midst of a gentle rain while these thoughts prevailed, I was suddenly sensible of such sweet and beneficent society in Nature, in the very pattering of the drops, and in every sound and sight around my house, an infinite and unaccountable friendliness all at once like an atmosphere sustaining me, as made the fancied advantages of human neighborhood insignificant, and I have never thought of them since. Every little pine needle expanded and swelled with sympathy and befriended me. I was so distinctly made aware of the presence of something kindred to me, even in scenes which we are accustomed to call wild and dreary, and also that the nearest of blood to me and humanest was not a person nor a villager, that I thought no place could ever be strange to me again.—

> "Mourning untimely consumes the sad;
> Few are their days in the land of the living,
> Beautiful daughter of Toscar."⁴

Some of my pleasantest hours were during the long rain storms in the spring or fall, which confined me to the house for the afternoon as well as the forenoon, soothed by their ceaseless roar and pelting; when an early twilight ushered in a long evening in which many thoughts had time to take root and unfold themselves. In those driving north-east rains which tried the village houses so, when the maids stood ready with mop and pail in front entries to keep the deluge out, I sat behind my door in my little house, which was all entry, and thoroughly enjoyed its protection. In one heavy thunder shower the lightning struck a large pitch-pine across the pond, making a very conspicuous and perfectly regular spiral groove from top to bottom, an inch or more deep, and four or five inches wide, as you would groove a walking-stick. I passed it again the other day, and was struck with awe on looking up and beholding that mark, now more distinct than ever, where a terrific and resistless bolt came down out of the harmless sky eight years ago. Men frequently say to me, "I should think you would feel lonesome down there, and want to be nearer to folks, rainy and snowy days and nights especially." I am tempted to reply to such,—This whole earth which we inhabit is but a point in space. How far apart, think you, dwell the two most distant inhabitants of yonder star, the breadth of whose disk cannot be appreciated by our instruments? Why should I feel lonely? is not our planet in the Milky Way? This which you put seems to me not to be the most important question. What sort of space is that which separates a man from his fellows and makes him solitary? I have found that no exertion of the legs can bring two minds much nearer to one another. What do we want most to dwell near to? Not to many men surely, the depot, the post-office, the bar-room, the meeting-house, the school-house, the grocery, Beacon Hill, or the Five Points,⁵ where men most congregate, but to the perennial source of our life, whence in all our experience we have found that to issue, as the willow stands near the water and sends out its roots in that direction. This will vary with different natures, but this is the place where a wise man will dig his cellar. . . . I one evening overtook one of my townsmen, who has accumulated what is called "a handsome property,"—though I never got a fair view of it,—on the Walden road, driving a pair of cattle to market, who inquired of me how I could bring my mind to give up so many of the comforts of life. I answered that I was very sure I liked it passably well; I was not joking. And so I went home to my bed, and left him to pick his way through the darkness and the mud to Brighton,⁶—or Bright-town,⁷—which place he would reach some time in the morning.

Any prospect of awakening or coming to life to a dead man makes indifferent all times and places. The place where that may occur is always the same, and indescribably pleasant to all our senses. For the most part we allow only outlying and transient circumstances to make our occasions. They are, in fact, the cause of our distraction. Nearest to all things is that power which fashions their being. *Next* to us the grandest laws are continually being executed. *Next* to us is not the workman whom we have hired, with whom we love so well to talk, but the workman whose work we are.

"How vast and profound is the influence of the subtile powers of Heaven and of Earth!

"We seek to perceive them, and we do not see them; we seek to hear them, and we do not hear them; identified with the substance of things, they cannot be separated from them.

"They cause that in all the universe men purify and sanctify their hearts, and clothe themselves in their holiday garments to offer sacrifices and oblations to their ancestors. It is an ocean of subtile intelligences. They are every where, above us, on our left, on our right; they environ us on all sides."[8]

We are the subjects of an experiment which is not a little interesting to me. Can we not do without the society of our gossips a little while under these circumstances,—have our own thoughts to cheer us? Confucius says truly, "Virtue does not remain as an abandoned orphan; it must of necessity have neighbors."[9]

With thinking we may be beside ourselves in a sane sense. By a conscious effort of the mind we can stand aloof from actions and their consequences; and all things, good and bad, go by us like a torrent. We are not wholly involved in Nature. I may be either the driftwood in the stream, or Indra[10] in the sky looking down on it. I *may* be affected by a theatrical exhibition; on the other hand, I *may not* be affected by an actual event which appears to concern me much more. I only know myself as a human entity; the scene, so to speak, of thoughts and affections; and am sensible of a certain doubleness by which I can stand as remote from myself as from another. However intense my experience,[11] I am conscious of the presence and criticism of a part of me, which, as it were, is not a part of me, but spectator, sharing no experience, but taking note of it; and that is no more I than it is you. When the play, it may be the tragedy, of life is over, the spectator goes his way. It was a kind of fiction, a work of the imagination only, so far as he was concerned. This doubleness may easily make us poor neighbors and friends sometimes.

I find it wholesome to be alone the greater part of the time. To be in company, even with the best, is soon wearisome and dissipating. I love to be alone. I never found the companion that was so companionable as solitude. We are for the most part more lonely when we go abroad among men than when

we stay in our chambers. A man thinking or working is always alone, let him be where he will. Solitude is not measured by the miles of space that intervene between a man and
his fellows. The really diligent student in one of the crowded
hives of Cambridge College[12] is as solitary as a dervish in the
desert. The farmer can work alone in the field or the woods
all day, hoeing or chopping, and not feel lonesome, because
he is employed; but when he comes home at night he cannot
sit down in a room alone, at the mercy of his thoughts, but
must be where he can "see the folks," and recreate, and as he
thinks remunerate,[13] himself for his day's solitude; and hence
he wonders how the student can sit alone in the house all
night and most of the day without ennui and "the blues;"
but he does not realize that the student, though in the house,
is still at work in *his* field, and chopping in *his* woods, as the
farmer in his, and in turn seeks the same recreation and
society that the latter does, though it may be a more condensed form of it.

Society is commonly too cheap. We meet at very short intervals, not having had time to acquire any new value for
each other. We meet at meals three times a day, and give
each other a new taste of that old musty cheese that we are.
We have had to agree on a certain set of rules, called etiquette and politeness, to make this frequent meeting tolerable,
and that we need not come to open war. We meet at the
post-office, and at the sociable, and about the fireside every
night; we live thick and are in each other's way, and stumble over one another, and I think that we thus lose some
respect for one another. Certainly less frequency would
suffice for all important and hearty communications. Consider
the girls in a factory,[14]—never alone, hardly in their dreams.
It would be better if there were but one inhabitant to a square
mile, as where I live. The value of a man is not in his skin,
that we should touch him.

I have heard of a man lost[15] in the woods and dying of
famine and exhaustion at the foot of a tree, whose loneliness
was relieved by the grotesque visions with which, owing to
bodily weakness, his diseased imagination surrounded him,
and which he believed to be real. So also, owing to bodily and
mental health and strength, we may be continually cheered
by a like but more normal and natural society, and come to
know that we are never alone.

I have a great deal of company in my house; especially in the morning, when nobody calls. Let me suggest a few comparisons, that some one may convey an idea of my situation. I am no more lonely than the loon in the pond that laughs so loud, or than Walden Pond itself. What company has that lonely lake, I pray? And yet it has not the blue devils,[16] but the blue angels in it, in the azure tint of its waters. The sun is alone, except in thick weather, when there sometimes appear to be two, but one is a mock sun.[17] God is alone,—but the devil, he is far from being alone; he sees a great deal of company; he is legion.[18] I am no more lonely than a single mullein or dandelion in a pasture, or a bean leaf, or sorrel, or a horse-fly, or a humble-bee. I am no more lonely than the Mill Brook,[19] or a weathercock, or the north star, or the south wind, or an April shower, or a January thaw, or the first spider in a new house.

I have occasional visits in the long winter evenings, when the snow falls fast and the wind howls in the wood, from an old settler[20] and original proprietor, who is reported to have dug Walden Pond, and stoned it, and fringed it with pine woods; who tells me stories of old time and of new eternity; and between us we manage to pass a cheerful evening with social mirth and pleasant views of things, even without apples or cider,—a most wise and humorous friend, whom I love much, who keeps himself more secret than ever did Goffe or Whalley;[21] and though he is thought to be dead, none can show where he is buried. An elderly dame,[22] too, dwells in my neighborhood, invisible to most persons, in whose odorous herb garden I love to stroll sometimes, gathering simples and listening to her fables; for she has a genius of unequalled fertility, and her memory runs back farther than mythology, and she can tell me the original of every fable, and on what fact every one is founded, for the incidents occurred when she was young. A ruddy and lusty old dame, who delights in all weathers and seasons, and is likely to outlive all her children yet.

The indescribable innocence and beneficence of Nature,—of sun and wind and rain, of summer and winter,—such health, such cheer, they afford forever! and such sympathy have they ever with our race, that all Nature would be affected, and the sun's brightness fade, and the winds would sigh humanely, and the clouds rain tears, and the woods shed their leaves and put on mourning in midsummer, if any man should ever for a just cause grieve. Shall I not have intelligence with the earth? Am I not partly leaves and vegetable mould myself?

What is the pill[23] which will keep us well, serene, contented? Not my or thy great-grandfather's, but our great-grandmother Nature's universal, vegetable, botanic medicines, by which she has kept herself young always, outlived so many old Parrs[24] in her day, and fed her health with their decaying fatness. For my panacea, instead of one of those quack vials[25] of a mixture dipped from Acheron[26] and the Dead Sea, which come out of those long shallow black-schooner looking wagons which we sometimes see made to carry bottles, let me have a draught of undiluted morning air. Morning air! If men will not drink of this at the fountain-head of the day, why, then, we must even bottle up some and sell it in the shops, for the benefit of those who have lost their subscription ticket to morning time in this world. But remember, it will not keep quite till noon-day even in the coolest cellar, but drive out the stopples long ere that and follow westward the steps of Aurora.[27] I am no worshipper of Hygeia,[28] who was the daughter of that old herb-doctor Æsculapius,[29] and who is represented on monuments holding a serpent in one hand, and in the other a cup out of which the serpent sometimes drinks; but rather of Hebe,[30] cupbearer to Jupiter, who was the daughter of Juno and wild lettuce, and who had the power of restoring gods and men to the vigor of youth. She was probably the only thoroughly sound-conditioned, healthy, and robust young lady that ever walked the globe, and wherever she came it was spring.

VI

VISITORS

I THINK that I love society as much as most, and am ready enough to fasten myself like a bloodsucker for the time to any full-blooded man that comes in my way. I am naturally no hermit, but might possibly sit out the sturdiest frequenter of the bar-room, if my business called me thither.

I had three chairs in my house; one for solitude, two for friendship, three for society. When visitors came in larger and unexpected numbers there was but the third chair for them all, but they generally economized the room by standing up. It is surprising how many great men and women a small house will contain. I have had twenty-five or thirty souls, with their bodies, at once under my roof, and yet we often parted without being aware that we had come very near to one another. Many of our houses, both public and private, with their almost innumerable apartments, their huge halls and their cellars for the storage of wines and other munitions of peace, appear to me extravagantly large for their inhabitants. They are so vast and magnificent that the latter seem to be only vermin which infest them. I am surprised when the herald blows his summons before some Tremont or Astor or Middlesex House,[1] to see come creeping out over the piazza for all inhabitants a ridiculous mouse,[2] which soon again slinks into some hole in the pavement.

One inconvenience I sometimes experienced in so small a house, the difficulty of getting to a sufficient distance from my guest when we began to utter the big thoughts in big words. You want room for your thoughts to get into sailing trim and run a course or two before they make their port. The bullet of your thought must have overcome its lateral and ricochet motion and fallen into its last and steady course before it reaches the ear of the hearer, else it may plough out again through the side of his head. Also, our sentences wanted room to unfold and form their columns in the interval. Individuals, like nations, must have suitable broad and natural boundaries,

even a considerable neutral ground, between them. I have
found it a singular luxury to talk across the pond to a companion on the opposite side. In my house we were so near
that we could not begin to hear,—we could not speak low
enough to be heard; as when you throw two stones into calm
water so near that they break each other's undulations. If we
are merely loquacious and loud talkers, then we can afford to
stand very near together, cheek by jowl, and feel each other's
breath; but if we speak reservedly and thoughtfully, we want
to be farther apart, that all animal heat and moisture may
have a chance to evaporate. If we would enjoy the most intimate society with that in each of us which is without, or
above, being spoken to, we must not only be silent, but commonly so far apart bodily that we cannot possibly hear each
other's voice in any case. Referred to this standard, speech
is for the convenience of those who are hard of hearing; but
there are many fine things which we cannot say if we have to
shout. As the conversation began to assume a loftier and
grander tone, we gradually shoved our chairs farther apart till
they touched the wall in opposite corners, and then commonly there was not room enough.

My "best" room, however, my withdrawing room,[3] always
ready for company, on whose carpet the sun rarely fell,[4] was
the pine wood behind my house. Thither in summer days,
when distinguished guests came, I took them, and a priceless
domestic swept the floor and dusted the furniture and kept
the things in order.

If one guest came he sometimes partook of my frugal meal,
and it was no interruption to conversation to be stirring a
hasty-pudding,[5] or watching the rising and maturing of a loaf
of bread in the ashes, in the mean while. But if twenty came
and sat in my house there was nothing said about dinner,
though there might be bread enough for two, more than if
eating were a forsaken habit; but we naturally practised abstinence; and this was never felt to be an offence against hospitality, but the most proper and considerate course. The
waste and decay of physical life, which so often needs repair,
seemed miraculously retarded in such a case, and the vital
vigor stood its ground. I could entertain thus a thousand as
well as twenty; and if any ever went away disappointed or
hungry from my house when they found me at home, they
may depend upon it that I sympathized with them at least.

So easy is it, though many housekeepers doubt it, to establish
new and better customs in the place of the old. You need not
rest your reputation on the dinners you give. For my own
part, I was never so effectually deterred from frequenting
a man's house, by any kind of Cerberus[6] whatever, as by the
parade one made about dining me, which I took to be a very
polite and roundabout hint never to trouble him so again. I
think I shall never revisit those scenes. I should be proud to
have for the motto of my cabin those lines of Spenser which
one of my visitors inscribed on a yellow walnut leaf for a
card:—

> "Arrivéd there, the little house they fill,
>   Ne looke for entertainment where none was;
> Rest is their feast, and all things at their will:
>   The noblest mind the best contentment has."[7]

When Winslow, afterward governor of the Plymouth Colony, went with a companion on a visit of ceremony to Massassoit on foot through the woods, and arrived tired and
hungry at his lodge, they were well received by the king, but
nothing was said about eating that day. When the night arrived, to quote their own words,—"He laid us on the bed with
himself and his wife, they at the one end and we at the other,
it being only plank, laid a foot from the ground, and a thin
mat upon them. Two more of his chief men, for want of room,
pressed by and upon us; so that we were worse weary of our
lodging than of our journey." At one o'clock the next day
Massassoit "brought two fishes that he had shot," about thrice
as big as a bream; "these being boiled, there were at least
forty looked for a share in them. The most ate of them. This
meal only we had in two nights and a day; and had not one
of us bought a partridge, we had taken our journey fasting."
Fearing that they would be light-headed for want of food
and also sleep, owing to "the savages' barbarous singing (for
they used to sing themselves asleep,)"[8] and that they might get
home while they had strength to travel, they departed. As
for lodging, it is true they were but poorly entertained, though
what they found an inconvenience was no doubt intended for
an honor; but as far as eating was concerned, I do not see
how the Indians could have done better. They had nothing
to eat themselves, and they were wiser than to think that

apologies could supply the place of food to their guests; so they drew their belts tighter and said nothing about it. Another time when Winslow visited them, it being a season of plenty with them, there was no deficiency in this respect.

As for men, they will hardly fail one any where. I had more visitors while I lived in the woods than at any other period of my life; I mean that I had some. I met several there under more favorable circumstances than I could any where else. But fewer came to see me upon trivial business. In this respect, my company was winnowed by my mere distance from town. I had withdrawn so far within the great ocean of solitude, into which the rivers of society empty, that for the most part, so far as my needs were concerned, only the finest sediment was deposited around me. Beside, there were wafted to me evidences of unexplored and uncultivated continents on the other side.

Who should come to my lodge this morning but a true Homeric or Paphlagonian⁹ man,—he had so suitable and poetic a name that I am sorry I cannot print it here,—a Canadian, a wood-chopper and post-maker, who can hole fifty posts in a day, who made his last supper on a woodchuck which his dog caught. He, too, has heard of Homer, and, "if it were not for books," would "not know what to do rainy days," though perhaps he has not read one wholly through for many rainy seasons. Some priest who could pronounce the Greek itself taught him to read his verse in the testament in his native parish far away; and now I must translate to him, while he holds the book, Achilles' reproof to Patroclus for his sad countenance.—"Why are you in tears, Patroclus, like a young girl?"—

"Or have you alone heard some news from Phthia?
They say that Menœtius lives yet, son of Actor,
And Peleus lives, son of AEacus, among the Myrmidons,
Either of whom having died, we should greatly grieve."¹⁰

He says, "That's good." He has a great bundle of white-oak bark¹¹ under his arm for a sick man, gathered this Sunday morning. "I suppose there's no harm in going after such a thing to-day," says he. To him Homer was a great writer, though what his writing was about he did not know. A more simple and natural man it would be hard to find. Vice and disease, which cast such a sombre moral hue over the world, seemed to have hardly any existence for him. He was about twenty-eight years old, and had left Canada and his father's house a dozen years before to work in the States, and earn money to buy a farm with at last, perhaps in his native country. He was cast in the coarsest mould; a stout but sluggish body, yet gracefully carried, with a thick sunburnt neck, dark bushy hair, and dull sleepy blue eyes, which were occasionally lit up with expression. He wore a flat gray cloth cap, a dingy wool-colored greatcoat, and cowhide boots. He was a great consumer of meat, usually carrying his dinner to his work a couple of miles past my house,—for he chopped all summer, —in a tin pail; cold meats, often cold woodchucks, and coffee in a stone bottle which dangled by a string from his belt; and sometimes he offered me a drink. He came along early, crossing my bean-field, though without anxiety or haste to get to his work, such as Yankees exhibit. He wasn't a-going to hurt himself. He didn't care if he only earned his board. Frequently he would leave his dinner in the bushes, when his dog had caught a woodchuck by the way, and go back a mile and a half to dress it and leave it in the cellar of the house where he boarded, after deliberating first for half an hour whether he could not sink it in the pond safely till nightfall,—loving to dwell long upon these themes. He would say, as he went by in the morning, "How thick the pigeons¹² are! If working every day were not my trade, I could get all the meat I should want by hunting,—pigeons, woodchucks, rabbits, partridges,¹²—by gosh! I could get all I should want for a week in one day."

He was a skilful chopper, and indulged in some flourishes and ornaments in his art. He cut his trees level and close to the ground, that the sprouts which came up afterward might be more vigorous and a sled might slide over the stumps; and instead of leaving a whole tree to support his corded wood, he would pare it away to a slender stake or splinter which you could break off with your hand at last.

He interested me because he was so quiet and solitary and so happy withal; a well of good humor and contentment which overflowed at his eyes. His mirth was without alloy. Sometimes I saw him at his work in the woods, felling trees, and he would greet me with a laugh of inexpressible satisfaction, and a salutation in Canadian French, though he spoke

English as well. When I approached him he would suspend his work, and with half-suppressed mirth lie along the trunk of a pine which he had felled, and, peeling off the inner bark, roll it up into a ball and chew it while he laughed and talked. Such an exuberance of animal spirits had he that he sometimes tumbled down and rolled on the ground with laughter at any thing which made him think and tickled him. Looking round upon the trees he would exclaim,—"By George! I can enjoy myself well enough here chopping; I want no better sport." Sometimes, when at leisure, he amused himself all day in the woods with a pocket pistol, firing salutes to himself at regular intervals as he walked. In the winter he had a fire by which at noon he warmed his coffee in a kettle; and as he sat on a log to eat his dinner the chicadees would sometimes come round and alight on his arm and peck at the potato in his fingers; and he said that he "liked to have the little *fellers* about him."

In him the animal man chiefly was developed. In physical endurance and contentment he was cousin to the pine and the rock. I asked him once if he was not sometimes tired at night, after working all day; and he answered, with a sincere and serious look, "Gorrappit, I never was tired in my life." But the intellectual and what is called spiritual man in him were slumbering as in an infant. He had been instructed only in that innocent and ineffectual way in which the Catholic priests teach the aborigines, by which the pupil is never educated to the degree of consciousness, but only to the degree of trust and reverence, and a child is not made a man, but kept a child. When Nature made him, she gave him a strong body and contentment for his portion, and propped him on every side with reverence and reliance, that he might live out his threescore years and ten[14] a child. He was so genuine and unsophisticated that no introduction would serve to introduce him, more than if you introduced a woodchuck to your neighbor. He had got to find him out as you did. He would not play any part. Men paid him wages for work, and so helped to feed and clothe him; but he never exchanged opinions with them. He was so simply and naturally humble—if he can be called humble who never aspires—that humility was no distinct quality in him, nor could he conceive of it. Wiser men were demigods to him. If you told him that such a one was coming, he did as if he thought that any thing so grand would expect nothing of himself, but take all the responsibility on itself, and let him be forgotten still. He never heard the sound of praise. He particularly reverenced the writer and the preacher. Their performances were miracles. When I told him that I wrote considerably, he thought for a long time that it was merely the handwriting which I meant, for he could write a remarkably good hand himself. I sometimes found the name of his native parish handsomely written in the snow by the highway, with the proper French accent, and knew that he had passed. I asked him if he ever wished to write his thoughts. He said that he had read and written letters for those who could not, but he never tried to write thoughts,—no, he could not, he could not tell what to put first, it would kill him, and then there was spelling to be attended to at the same time!

I heard that a distinguished wise man and reformer asked him if he did not want the world to be changed; but he answered with a chuckle of surprise in his Canadian accent, not knowing that the question had ever been entertained before, "No, I like it well enough." It would have suggested many things to a philosopher to have dealings with him. To a stranger he appeared to know nothing of things in general; yet I sometimes saw in him a man whom I had not seen before, and I did not know whether he was as wise as Shakspeare or as simply ignorant as a child, whether to suspect him of a fine poetic consciousness or of stupidity. A townsman told me that when he met him sauntering through the village in his small close-fitting cap, and whistling to himself, he reminded him of a prince in disguise.

His only books were an almanac and an arithmetic, in which last he was considerably expert. The former was a sort of cyclopaedia to him, which he supposed to contain an abstract of human knowledge, as indeed it does to a considerable extent. I loved to sound him on the various reforms of the day, and he never failed to look at them in the most simple and practical light. He had never heard of such things before. Could he do without factories? I asked. He had worn the home-made Vermont gray,[15] he said, and that was good. Could he dispense with tea and coffee? Did this country afford any beverage beside water? He had soaked hemlock leaves in water and drank it, and thought that was better than water in warm weather. When I asked him if he could do without money, he showed the convenience of money in such a way as to suggest and coincide with the most philosophical accounts of the origin of this institution, and the very derivation of the word *pecunia*.¹⁶ If an ox were his property, and he wished to get needles and thread at the store, he thought it would be inconvenient and impossible soon to go on mortgaging some portion of the creature each time to that amount. He could defend many institutions better than any philosopher, because, in describing them as they concerned him, he gave the true reason for their prevalence, and speculation had not suggested to him any other. At another time, hearing Plato's definition of a man,—a biped¹⁷ without feathers,—and that one exhibited a cock plucked and called it Plato's man, he thought it an important difference that the *knees* bent the wrong way. He would sometimes exclaim, "How I love to talk! By George, I could talk all day!" I asked him once, when I had not seen him for many months, if he had got a new idea this summer. "Good Lord," said he, "a man that has to work as I do, if he does not forget the ideas he has had, he will do well. May be the man you hoe with is inclined to race; then, by gorry, your mind must be there; you think of weeds." He would sometimes ask me first on such occasions, if I had made any improvement. One winter day I asked him if he was always satisfied with himself, wishing to suggest a substitute within him for the priest without, and some higher motive for living. "Satisfied!" said he; "some men are satisfied with one thing, and some with another. One man, perhaps, if he has got enough, will be satisfied to sit all day with his back to the fire and his belly to the table, by George!" Yet I never, by any manoeuvring, could get him to take the spiritual view of things; the highest that he appeared to conceive of was a simple expediency, such as you might expect an animal to appreciate; and this, practically, is true of most men. If I suggested any improvement in his mode of life, he merely answered, without expressing any regret, that it was too late. Yet he thoroughly believed in honesty and the like virtues.

There was a certain positive originality, however slight, to be detected in him, and I occasionally observed that he was thinking for himself and expressing his own opinion, a phenomenon so rare that I would any day walk ten miles to observe it, and it amounted to the re-origination of many of the institutions of society. Though he hesitated, and perhaps failed to express himself distinctly, he always had a presentable thought behind. Yet his thinking was so primitive and immersed in his animal life, that, though more promising than a merely learned man's, it rarely ripened to any thing which can be reported. He suggested that there might be men of genius in the lowest grades of life, however permanently humble and illiterate, who take their own view always, or do not pretend to see at all; who are as bottomless even as Walden Pond was thought to be, though they may be dark and muddy.

Many a traveller came out of his way to see me and the inside of my house, and, as an excuse for calling, asked for a glass of water. I told them that I drank at the pond, and pointed thither, offering to lend them a dipper.[18] Far off as I lived, I was not exempted from that annual visitation which occurs, methinks, about the first of April, when every body is on the move; and I had my share of good luck, though there were some curious specimens among my visitors. Half-witted men from the almshouse[19] and elsewhere came to see me; but I endeavored to make them exercise all the wit they had, and make their confessions to me; in such cases making wit the theme of our conversation; and so was compensated. Indeed, I found some of them to be wiser than the so called *overseers* of the poor[20] and selectmen of the town, and thought it was time that the tables were turned. With respect to wit, I learned that there was not much difference between the half and the whole. One day, in particular, an inoffensive, simple-minded pauper,[21] whom with others I had often seen used as fencing stuff, standing or sitting on a bushel in the fields to keep cattle and himself from straying, visited me, and expressed a wish to live as I did. He told me, with the utmost simplicity and truth, quite superior, or rather *inferior*, to any thing that is called humility, that he was "deficient in intellect." These were his words. The Lord had made him so, yet he supposed the Lord cared as much for him as for another. "I have always been so," said he, "from my childhood; I never had much mind; I was not like other children; I am weak in the head. It was the Lord's will, I suppose." And there he was to prove the truth of his words. He was a metaphysical puzzle to me. I have rarely met a fellow-man on such promising ground,—it was so simple and sincere and so true all that he said. And, true enough, in proportion as he appeared to humble himself was he exalted.[22] I did not know at first but it was the result of a wise policy. It seemed that from such a basis of truth and frankness as the poor weak-headed pauper had laid, our intercourse might go forward to something better than the intercourse of sages.

I had some guests from those not reckoned commonly among the town's poor, but who should be; who are among the world's poor, at any rate; guests who appeal, not to your hospitality, but to your *hospitalality;* who earnestly wish to be helped, and preface their appeal with the information that they are resolved, for one thing, never to help themselves. I require of a visitor that he be not actually starving, though he may have the very best appetite in the world, however he got it. Objects of charity are not guests. Men who did not know when their visit had terminated, though I went about my business again, answering them from greater and greater remoteness. Men of almost every degree of wit called on me in the migrating season. Some who had more wits than they knew what to do with; runaway slaves[23] with plantation manners, who listened from time to time, like the fox[24] in the fable, as if they heard the hounds a-baying on their track, and looked at me beseechingly, as much as to say,—

"O Christian, will you send me back?"[25]

One real runaway slave, among the rest, whom I helped to forward toward the north star. Men of one idea, like a hen with one chicken, and that a duckling; men of a thousand ideas, and unkempt heads, like those hens which are made to take charge of a hundred chickens, all in pursuit of one bug, a score of them lost in every morning's dew,—and become frizzled and mangy in consequence; men of ideas instead of legs, a sort of intellectual centipede that made you crawl all over. One man proposed a book in which visitors should write their names, as at the White Mountains; but, alas! I have too good a memory to make that necessary.

I could not but notice some of the peculiarities of my visitors. Girls and boys and young women generally seemed glad to be in the woods. They looked in the pond and at the flowers, and improved their time. Men of business, even farmers, thought only of solitude and employment, and of the great distance at which I dwelt from something or other; and though they said that they loved a ramble in the woods occasionally, it was obvious that they did not. Restless, committed men, whose time was all taken up in getting a living or keeping it; ministers who spoke of God as if they enjoyed a monopoly of the subject, who could not bear all kinds of opinions; doctors, lawyers, uneasy housekeepers who pried into my cupboard and bed when I was out,—how came Mrs. — to know that my sheets were not as clean as hers?—young men who had ceased to be young, and had concluded that it was safest to follow the beaten track of the professions,—all these generally said that it was not possible to do so much good in my position. Ay! there was the rub.[26] The old and infirm and the timid, of whatever age or sex, thought most of sickness, and sudden accident and death; to them life seemed full of danger,—what danger is there if you don't think of any?—and they thought that a prudent man would carefully select the safest position, where Dr. B.[27] might be on hand at a moment's warning. To them the village was literally a *community*, a league for mutual defence, and you would suppose that they would not go a-huckleberrying without a medicine chest. The amount of it is, if a man is alive, there is always *danger* that he may die, though the danger must be allowed to be less in proportion as he is dead-and-alive to begin with. A man sits as many risks as he runs. Finally, there were the self-styled reformers,[28] the greatest bores of all, who thought that I was forever singing,—

> This is the house that I built;
> This is the man that lives in the house that I built;[29]

but they did not know that the third line was,—

> These are the folks that worry the man
> That lives in the house that I built.

I did not fear the hen-harriers,[30] for I kept no chickens; but I feared the men-harriers rather.

I had more cheering visitors than the last. Children come a-berrying, railroad men taking a Sunday morning walk in clean shirts, fishermen and hunters, poets and philosophers, in short, all honest pilgrims, who came out to the woods for freedom's sake, and really left the village behind, I was ready to greet with,—"Welcome, Englishmen! welcome, Englishmen!"[31] for I had had communication with that race.

VII

THE BEAN-FIELD

MEANWHILE my beans, the length of whose rows, added together, was seven miles[1] already planted, were impatient to be hoed, for the earliest had grown considerably before the latest were in the ground; indeed they were not easily to be put off. What was the meaning of this so steady and self-respecting, this small Herculean labor,[2] I knew not. I came to love my rows, my beans, though so many more than I wanted. They attached me to the earth, and so I got strength like Antaeus.[3] But why should I raise them? Only Heaven knows. This was my curious labor, all summer,—to make this portion of the earth's surface, which had yielded only cinquefoil, blackberries, johnswort, and the like, before, sweet wild fruits and pleasant flowers, produce instead this pulse. What shall I learn of beans or beans of me? I cherish them, I hoe them, early and late I have an eye to them; and this is my day's work. It is a fine broad leaf to look on. My auxiliaries are the dews and rains which water this dry soil, and what fertility is in the soil itself, which for the most part is lean and effete. My enemies are worms, cool days, and most of all woodchucks.[4] The last have nibbled for me a quarter of an acre clean. But what right had I to oust johnswort and the rest, and break up their ancient herb garden? Soon, however, the remaining beans will be too tough for them, and go forward to meet new foes.

When I was four years old,[5] as I well remember, I was brought from Boston[6] to this my native town, through these very woods and this field, to the pond. It is one of the oldest scenes stamped on my memory. And now to-night my flute[7] has waked the echoes over that very water. The pines still stand here older than I; or, if some have fallen, I have cooked my supper with their stumps, and a new growth is rising all around, preparing another aspect for new infant eyes. Almost the same johnswort springs from the same perennial root in this pasture, and even I have at length helped to clothe that fabulous landscape of my infant dreams, and one of the results of my presence and influence is seen in these bean leaves, corn blades, and potato vines.

I planted about two acres and a half of upland; and as it was only about fifteen years since the land was cleared, and I myself had got out two or three cords of stumps, I did not give it any manure; but in the course of the summer it appeared by the arrow-heads[8] which I turned up in hoeing, that an extinct nation had anciently dwelt here and planted corn and beans ere white men came to clear the land, and so, to some extent, had exhausted the soil for this very crop.

Before yet any woodchuck or squirrel had run across the road, or the sun had got above the shrub-oaks, while all the dew was on, though the farmers warned me against it,—I would advise you to do all your work if possible while the dew is on,—I began to level the ranks of haughty weeds in my bean-field and throw dust upon their heads.[9] Early in the morning I worked barefooted, dabbling like a plastic artist in the dewy and crumbling sand, but later in the day the sun blistered my feet. There the sun lighted me to hoe beans, pacing slowly backward and forward over that yellow gravelly upland, between the long green rows, fifteen rods, the one end terminating in a shrub oak copse where I could rest in the shade, the other in a blackberry field where the green berries deepened their tints by the time I had made another bout. Removing the weeds, putting fresh soil about the bean stems, and encouraging this weed which I had sown, making the yellow soil express its summer thought in bean leaves and blossoms rather than in wormwood and piper and millet grass, making the earth say beans instead of grass,—this was my daily work. As I had little aid from horses or cattle, or hired men or boys, or improved implements of husbandry, I was much slower, and became much more intimate with my beans than usual. But labor of the hands, even when pursued to the verge of drudgery, is perhaps never the worst form of idleness. It has a constant and imperishable moral, and to the scholar it yields a classic result. A very *agricola laboriosus* was I to travellers bound westward through Lincoln and Wayland[10] to nobody knows where; they sitting at their ease in gigs, with elbows on knees, and reins loosely hanging in festoons; I the home-staying, laborious native of the soil. But soon my homestead was out of their sight and thought. It was the only open and cultivated field for a great distance on either side of the road, so they made the most of it; and sometimes the man in the field heard more of travellers' gossip and comment than was meant for his ear: "Beans so late! peas so late!"—for I continued to plant when others had began to hoe,—the ministerial husbandman[11] had not suspected it. "Corn, my boy, for fodder; corn for fodder." "Does he *live* there?" asks the black bonnet of the gray coat; and the hard-featured farmer reins up his grateful dobbin to inquire what you are doing where he sees no manure in the furrow, and recommends a little chip dirt, or any little waste stuff, or it may be ashes or plaster. But here were two acres and a half of furrows, and only a hoe for cart and two hands to draw it,—there being an aversion to other carts and horses,—and chip dirt far away. Fellow-travellers as they rattled by compared it aloud with the fields which they had passed, so that I came to know how I stood in the agricultural world. This was one field not in Mr. Coleman's[12] report. And, by the way, who estimates the value of the crop which Nature yields in the still wilder fields unimproved by man? The crop of *English* hay[13] is carefully weighed, the moisture calculated, the silicates and the potash; but in all dells and pond holes in the woods and pastures and swamps grow a rich and various crop only unreaped by man. Mine was, as it were, the connecting link between wild and cultivated fields; as some states are civilized, and others half-civilized, and others savage or barbarous, so my field was, though not in a bad sense, a half-cultivated field. They were beans cheerfully returning to their wild and primitive state that I cultivated, and my hoe played the *Rans des Vaches*[14] for them.

Near at hand, upon the topmost spray of a birch, sings the brown-thrasher—or red mavis, as some love to call him—all the morning, glad of your society, that would find out another farmer's field if yours were not here. While you are planting the seed, he cries,—"Drop it, drop it,—cover it up, cover it up,—pull it up, pull it up, pull it up." But this was not corn, and so it was safe from such enemies as he. You may wonder what his rigmarole, his amateur Paganini[15] performances on one string or on twenty, have to do with your planting, and yet prefer it to leached ashes or plaster. It was a cheap sort of top dressing in which I had entire faith.

As I drew a still fresher soil about the rows with my hoe,

I disturbed the ashes of unchronicled nations who in primeval years lived under these heavens, and their small implements of war and hunting were brought to the light of this modern day. They lay mingled with other natural stones, some of which bore the marks of having been burned by Indian fires, and some by the sun, and also bits of pottery and glass brought hither by the recent cultivators of the soil. When my hoe tinkled against the stones, that music echoed to the woods and the sky, and was an accompaniment to my labor which yielded an instant and immeasurable crop. It was no longer beans that I hoed, nor I that hoed beans; and I remembered with as much pity as pride, if I remembered at all, my acquaintances who had gone to the city to attend the oratorios. The night-hawk circled overhead in the sunny afternoons—for I sometimes made a day of it—like a mote in the eye, or in heaven's eye, falling from time to time with a swoop and a sound as if the heavens were rent, torn at last to very rags and tatters, and yet a seamless cope remained; small imps that fill the air and lay their eggs on the ground on bare sand or rocks on the tops of hills, where few have found them; graceful and slender like ripples caught up from the pond, as leaves are raised by the wind to float in the heavens; such kindredship is in Nature. The hawk is aerial brother of the wave which he sails over and surveys, those his perfect air-inflated wings answering to the elemental unfledged pinions of the sea. Or sometimes I watched a pair of hen-hawks circling high in the sky, alternately, soaring and descending, approaching and leaving one another, as if they were the imbodiment of my own thoughts. Or I was attracted by the passage of wild pigeons from this wood to that, with a slight quivering winnowing sound and carrier haste; or from under a rotten stump my hoe turned up a sluggish portentous and outlandish spotted salamander, a trace of Egypt and the Nile, yet our contemporary. When I paused to lean on my hoe, these sounds and sights I heard and saw any where in the row, a part of the inexhaustible entertainment which the country offers.

On gala days the town fires its great guns, which echo like popguns to these woods, and some waifs of martial music occasionally penetrate thus far. To me, away there in my beanfield at the other end of the town, the big guns sounded as if a puff ball had burst; and when there was a military turnout of which I was ignorant, I have sometimes had a vague sense all the day of some sort of itching and disease in the horizon, as if some eruption would break out there soon, either scarlatina[16] or canker-rash, until at length some more favorable puff of wind, making haste over the fields and up the Wayland road, brought me information of the "trainers."[17] It seemed by the distant hum as if somebody's bees had swarmed, and that the neighbors, according to Virgil's advice, by a faint *tintinnabulum*[18] upon the most sonorous of their domestic utensils, were endeavoring to call them down into the hive again. And when the sound died quite away, and the hum had ceased, and the most favorable breezes told no tale, I knew that they had got the last drone of them all safely into the Middlesex hive, and that now their minds were bent on the honey with which it was smeared.

I felt proud to know that the liberties of Massachusetts and of our fatherland were in such safe keeping; and as I turned to my hoeing again I was filled with an inexpressible confidence, and pursued my labor cheerfully with a calm trust in the future.

When there were several bands of musicians, it sounded as if all the village was a vast bellows, and all the buildings expanded and collapsed alternately with a din. But sometimes it was a really noble and inspiring strain that reached these woods, and the trumpet that sings of fame,[19] and I felt as if I could spit a Mexican[20] with a good relish,—for why should we always stand for trifles?—and looked round for a woodchuck or a skunk to exercise my chivalry upon. These martial strains seemed as far away as Palestine, and reminded me of a march of crusaders in the horizon, with a slight tantivy and tremulous motion of the elm-tree tops which overhang the village. This was one of the *great* days; though the sky had from my clearing only the same everlastingly great look that it wears daily, and I saw no difference in it.

It was a singular experience that long acquaintance which I cultivated with beans, what with planting, and hoeing, and harvesting, and threshing, and picking over, and selling them, —the last was the hardest of all,—I might add eating, for I did taste. I was determined to know beans.[21] When they were growing, I used to hoe from five o'clock in the morning till noon, and commonly spent the rest of the day about other affairs. Consider the intimate and curious acquaintance one

makes with various kinds of weeds,—it will bear some iteration in the account, for there was no little iteration in the
labor,—disturbing their delicate organizations so ruthlessly,
and making such invidious distinctions with his hoe, levelling
whole ranks of one species, and sedulously cultivating another. That's Roman wormwood,—that's pigweed,—that's sorrel,—that's piper-grass,—have at him, chop him up, turn his
roots upward to the sun, don't let him have a fibre in the
shade, if you do he'll turn himself t'other side up and be as
green as a leek in two days. A long war not with cranes,[22]
but with weeds, those Trojans who had sun and rain and dews
on their side. Daily the beans saw me come to their rescue
armed with a hoe, and thin the ranks of their enemies, filling
up the trenches with weedy dead. Many a lusty crest-waving
Hector,[23] that towered a whole foot above his crowding comrades, fell before my weapon and rolled in the dust.

Those summer days which some of my contemporaries
devoted to the fine arts in Boston or Rome, and others to contemplation in India, and others to trade in London or New
York, I thus, with the other farmers of New England, devoted
to husbandry. Not that I wanted beans to eat, for I am by
nature a Pythagorean,[24] so far as beans are concerned, whether
they mean porridge or voting,[25] and exchanged them for rice;
but, perchance, as some must work in fields if only for the sake
of tropes and expression, to serve a parable-maker one day. It
was on the whole a rare amusement, which, continued too
long, might have become a dissipation. Though I gave them no
manure, and did not hoe them all once, I hoed them unusually
well as far as I went, and was paid for it in the end, "there
being in truth," as Evelyn says, "no compost or laetation what-
soever comparable to this continual motion, repastination, and
turning of the mould with the spade." "The earth," he adds
elsewhere, "especially if fresh, has a certain magnetism in it,
by which it attracts the salt, power, or virtue (call it either)
which gives it life, and is the logic of all the labor and
stir we keep about it, to sustain us; all dungings and other
sordid temperings being but the vicars succedaneous to this
improvement."[26] Moreover, this being one of those "worn-out
and exhausted lay fields which enjoy their sabbath," had perchance, as Sir Kenelm Digby thinks likely, attracted "vital
spirits"[27] from the air. I harvested twelve bushels of beans.

But to be more particular, for it is complained that Mr.

Coleman has reported chiefly the expensive experiments of gentlemen farmers, my outgoes were,—

For a hoe, ...	$0 54
Ploughing, harrowing, and furrowing, . .	7 50, Too much
Beans for seed, ...	3 12½
Potatoes "	1 33
Peas "	0 40
Turnip seed, ...	0 06
White line for crow fence,[28]	0 02
Horse cultivator and boy three hours, . .	1 00
Horse and cart to get crop, ...	0 75
In all, ...	$14 72½

My income was, (patrem familias vendacem, non emacem esse oportet,[29]) from

Nine bushels and twelve quarts of beans sold, . .	$16 94
Five " large potatoes, ...	2 50
Nine " small, ...	2 25
Grass, ...	1 00
Stalks, ...	0 75
In all, ...	$23 44

Leaving a pecuniary profit, as I have elsewhere said, of $8 71½.

This is the result of my experience in raising beans. Plant the common small white bush bean about the first of June, in rows three feet by eighteen inches apart, being careful to select fresh round and unmixed seed. First look out for worms, and supply vacancies by planting anew. Then look out for woodchucks, if it is an exposed place, for they will nibble off the earliest tender leaves almost clean as they go; and again, when the young tendrils make their appearance, they have notice of it, and will shear them off with both buds and young pods, sitting erect like a squirrel. But above all harvest as early as possible, if you would escape frosts and have a fair and salable crop; you may save much loss by this means.

This further experience also I gained. I said to myself, I will not plant beans and corn with so much industry another summer, but such seeds, if the seed is not lost, as sincerity, truth, simplicity, faith, innocence, and the like, and see if they will not grow in this soil, even with less toil and manurance, and sustain me, for surely it has not been exhausted for these crops. Alas! I said this to myself; but now another summer is gone, and another, and another, and I am obliged to say to you, Reader, that the seeds which I planted, if indeed they *were* the seeds of those virtues, were wormeaten or had lost their vitality, and so did not come up. Commonly men will only be brave as their fathers were brave, or timid. This generation is very sure to plant corn and beans each new year precisely as the Indians[30] did centuries ago and taught the first settlers to do, as if there were a fate in it. I saw an old man the other day, to my astonishment, making the holes with a hoe for the seventieth time at least, and not for himself to lie down in! But why should not the New Englander try new adventures, and not lay so much stress on his grain, his potato and grass crop, and his orchards,—raise other crops than these? Why concern ourselves so much about our beans for seed, and not be concerned at all about a new generation of men? We should really be fed and cheered if when we met a man we were sure to see that some of the qualities which I have named, which we all prize more than those other productions, but which are for the most part broadcast and floating in the air, had taken root and grown in him. Here comes such a subtile and ineffable quality, for instance, as truth or justice, though the slightest amount or new variety of it, along the road. Our ambassadors should be instructed to send home such seeds as these, and Congress[31] help to distribute them over all the land. We should never stand upon ceremony with sincerity. We should never cheat and insult and banish one another by our meanness, if there were present the kernel of worth and friendliness. We should not meet thus in haste. Most men I do not meet at all, for they seem not to have time; they are busy about their beans. We would not deal with a man thus plodding ever, leaning on a hoe or a spade as a staff between his work, not as a mushroom, but partially risen out of the earth, something more than erect, like swallows alighted and walking on the ground:—

> "And as he spake, his wings would now and then
>   Spread, as he meant to fly, then close again,"[32]

so that we should suspect that we might be conversing with an angel. Bread may not always nourish us; but it always does us good, it even takes stiffness out of our joints, and makes us supple and buoyant, when we knew not what ailed us, to recognize any generosity in man or Nature, to share any unmixed and heroic joy.

Ancient poetry and mythology suggest, at least, that husbandry was once a sacred art; but it is pursued with irreverent haste and heedlessness by us, our object being to have large farms and large crops merely. We have no festival, nor procession, nor ceremony, not excepting our Cattle-shows[33] and so called Thanksgivings, by which the farmer expresses a sense of the sacredness of his calling, or is reminded of its sacred origin. It is the premium and the feast which tempt him. He sacrifices not to Ceres[34] and the Terrestrial Jove,[35] but to the infernal Plutus[36] rather. By avarice and selfishness, and a grovelling habit, from which none of us is free, of regarding the soil as property, or the means of acquiring property chiefly, the landscape is deformed, husbandry is degraded with us, and the farmer leads the meanest of lives. He knows Nature but as a robber. Cato says that the profits of agriculture are particularly pious or just, *(maximeque pius quaestus,)*[37] and according to Varro the old Romans "called the same earth Mother and Ceres, and thought that they who cultivated it led a pious and useful life, and that they alone were left of the race of King Saturn."[38]

We are wont to forget that the sun looks on our cultivated fields and on the prairies and forests without distinction. They all reflect and absorb his rays alike,[39] and the former make but a small part of the glorious picture which he beholds in his daily course. In his view the earth is all equally cultivated like a garden. Therefore we should receive the benefit of his light and heat with a corresponding trust and magnanimity. What though I value the seed of these beans, and harvest that in the fall of the year? This broad field which I have looked at so long looks not to me as the principal cultivator, but away from me to influences more genial to it, which water and make it green. These beans have results which are not harvested by me. Do they not grow for woodchucks partly? The ear of wheat, (in Latin *spica,*[40] obsoletely *speca,* from *spe,* hope,) should not be the only hope of the husbandman; its kernel or grain (*granum,* from *gerendo,* bearing,) is not all that it bears. How, then, can our harvest fail? Shall I not rejoice also at the abundance of the weeds whose seeds are the granary of the birds? It matters little comparatively whether the fields fill the farmer's barns. The true husbandman will cease from anxiety, as the squirrels manifest no concern whether the woods will bear chestnuts this year or not, and finish his labor with every day, relinquishing all claim to the produce of his fields, and sacrificing in his mind not only his first but his last fruits also.

VIII

THE VILLAGE

AFTER hoeing, or perhaps reading and writing, in the forenoon, I usually bathed again in the pond, swimming across one of its coves for a stint,[1] and washed the dust of labor from my person, or smoothed out the last wrinkle which study had made, and for the afternoon was absolutely free. Every day or two I strolled to the village to hear some of the gossip which is incessantly going on there, circulating either from mouth to mouth, or from newspaper to newspaper, and which, taken in homoeopathic[2] doses, was really as refreshing in its way as the rustle of leaves and the peeping of frogs. As I walked in the woods to see the birds and squirrels, so I walked in the village to see the men and boys; instead of the wind among the pines I heard the carts rattle. In one direction from my house there was a colony of muskrats in the river meadows; under the grove of elms and buttonwoods in the other horizon was a village of busy men, as curious to me as if they had been prairie dogs, each sitting at the mouth of its burrow, or running over to a neighbor's to gossip. I went there frequently to observe their habits. The village appeared to me a great news room; and on one side, to support it, as once at Redding & Company's[3] on State Street, they kept nuts and raisins, or salt and meal and other groceries. Some have such a vast appetite for the former commodity, that is, the news, and such sound digestive organs, that they can sit forever in public avenues without stirring, and let it simmer and whisper through them like the Etesian winds,[4] or as if inhaling ether,[5] it only producing numbness and insensibility to pain,—otherwise it would often be painful to hear,—without affecting the consciousness. I hardly ever failed, when I rambled through the village, to see a row of such worthies, either sitting on a ladder sunning themselves, with their bodies inclined forward and their eyes glancing along the line this way and that, from time to time, with a voluptuous expression, or else leaning against a barn with their hands in their pockets, like caryatides, as if to prop it up.

They, being commonly out of doors, heard whatever was in the wind. These are the coarsest mills, in which all gossip is first rudely digested or cracked up before it is emptied into finer and more delicate hoppers within doors. I observed that the vitals of the village were the grocery, the bar-room, the post-office, and the bank; and, as necessary part of the machinery, they kept a bell, a big gun, and a fire-engine, at convenient places; and the houses were so arranged as to make the most of mankind, in lanes and fronting one another, so that every traveller had to run the gantlet,⁶ and every man, woman, and child might get a lick at him. Of course, those who were stationed nearest to the head of the line, where they could most see and be seen, and have the first blow at him, paid the highest prices for their places; and the few straggling inhabitants in the outskirts, where long gaps in the line began to occur, and the traveller could get over walls or turn aside into cow paths, and so escape, paid a very slight ground or window tax.⁷ Signs were hung out on all sides to allure him; some to catch him by the appetite, as the tavern and victualling cellar; some by the fancy, as the dry goods store and the jeweller's; and others by the hair or the feet or the skirts, as the barber, the shoemaker, or the tailor. Besides, there was a still more terrible standing invitation to call at every one of these houses, and company expected about these times. For the most part I escaped wonderfully from these dangers, either by proceeding at once boldly and without deliberation to the goal, as is recommended to those who run the gantlet, or by keeping my thoughts on high things, like Orpheus, who, "loudly singing the praises of the gods to his lyre, drowned the voices of the Sirens, and kept out of danger."⁸ Sometimes I bolted suddenly, and nobody could tell my whereabouts, for I did not stand much about gracefulness, and never hesitated at a gap in a fence. I was even accustomed to make an irruption into some houses, where I was well entertained, and after learning the kernels and very last sieve-ful of news, what had subsided, the prospects of war and peace, and whether the world was likely to hold together much longer, I was let out through the rear avenues,⁹ and so escaped to the woods again.

It was very pleasant, when I staid late in town, to launch myself into the night, especially if it was dark and tempestuous, and set sail from some bright village parlor or lecture room, with a bag of rye or Indian meal upon my shoulder, for my snug harbor in the woods, having made all tight without and withdrawn under hatches with a merry crew of thoughts, leaving only my outer man at the helm, or even tying up the helm when it was plain sailing. I had many a genial thought by the cabin fire "as I sailed."[10] I was never cast away nor distressed in any weather, though I encountered some severe storms. It is darker in the woods, even in common nights, than most suppose. I frequently had to look up at the opening between the trees above the path in order to learn my route, and, where there was no cart-path, to feel with my feet the faint track which I had worn, or steer by the known relation of particular trees which I felt with my hands, passing between two pines for instance, not more than eighteen inches apart, in the midst of the woods, invariably[11] in the darkest night. Sometimes, after coming home thus late in a dark and muggy night, when my feet felt the path which my eyes could not see, dreaming and absent-minded all the way, until I was aroused by having to raise my hand to lift the latch, I have not been able to recall a single step of my walk, and I have thought that perhaps my body would find its way home if its master should forsake it, as the hand finds its way to the mouth without assistance. Several times, when a visitor chanced to stay into evening, and it proved a dark night, I was obliged to conduct him to the cart-path in the rear of the house, and then point out to him the direction he was to pursue, and in keeping which he was to be guided rather by his feet than his eyes. One very dark night I directed thus on their way two young men who had been fishing in the pond. They lived about a mile off through the woods, and were quite used to the route. A day or two after one of them told me that they wandered about the greater part of the night, close by their own premises, and did not get home till toward morning, by which time, as there had been several heavy showers in the mean while, and the leaves were very wet, they were drenched to their skins. I have heard of many going astray even in the village streets, when the darkness was so thick that you could cut it with a knife, as the saying is. Some who live in the outskirts, having come to town a-shopping in their wagons, have been obliged to put up for the night; and gentlemen and ladies making a call have gone half a mile out of their way, feeling the sidewalk only with their feet, and not knowing when they turned. It is a surprising and memorable, as well as valuable experience, to be lost in the woods any time. Often in a storm, even by day, one will come out upon a well-known road and yet find it impossible to tell which way leads to the village. Though he knows that he has travelled it a thousand times, he cannot recognize a feature in it, but it is as strange to him as if it were a road in Siberia. By night, of course, the perplexity is infinitely greater. In our most trivial walks, we are constantly, though unconsciously, steering like pilots by certain well-known beacons and head-lands, and if we go beyond our usual course we still carry in our minds the bearing of some neighboring cape; and not till we are completely lost, or turned round,—for a man needs only to be turned round once with his eyes shut in this world to be lost,—do we appreciate the vastness and strangeness of Nature. Every man has to learn the points of compass again as often as he awakes, whether from sleep or any abstraction. Not till we are lost, in other words, not till we have lost the world, do we begin to find ourselves, and realize where we are and the infinite extent of our relations.

One afternoon, near the end of the first summer, when I went to the village to get a shoe from the cobbler's, I was seized and put into jail, because, as I have elsewhere related,[12] I did not pay a tax to, or recognize the authority of, the state which buys and sells men, women, and children, like cattle at the door of its senate-house. I had gone down to the woods for other purposes. But, wherever a man goes, men will pursue and paw him with their dirty institutions, and, if they can, constrain him to belong to their desperate odd-fellow[13] society. It is true, I might have resisted forcibly with more or less effect, might have run "amok" against society; but I preferred that society should run "amok" against me, it being the desperate party. However, I was released the next day, obtained my mended shoe, and returned to the woods in season to get my dinner of huckleberries on Fair Haven Hill.[14] I was never molested by any person but those who represented the state. I had no lock nor bolt but for the desk which held my papers, not even a nail to put over my latch or windows. I never fastened my door night or day, though I was to be absent several days; not even when the next fall I spent a fortnight in the woods of Maine.[15] And yet my house was more respected than if it had been surrounded by a file of soldiers. The tired rambler could rest and warm himself by my fire, the literary amuse himself with the few books on my table, or the curious, by opening my closet door, see what was left of my dinner, and what prospect I had of a supper. Yet, though many people of every class came this way to the pond, I suffered no serious inconvenience from these sources, and I never missed any thing but one small book, a volume of Homer,[16] which perhaps was improperly gilded, and this I trust a soldier of our camp[17] has found by this time. I am convinced, that if all men were to live as simply as I then did, thieving and robbery would be unknown. These take place only in communities where some have got more than is sufficient while others have not enough. The Pope's Homers would soon get properly distributed.—

> "Nec bella fuerunt,
> Faginus astabat dum scyphus ante dapes."

> "Nor wars did men molest,
> When only beechen bowls were in request."[18]

"You who govern public affairs, what need have you to employ punishments? Love virtue, and the people will be virtuous. The virtues of a superior man are like the wind; the virtues of a common man are like the grass; the grass, when the wind passes over it, bends."[19]

[IX]

THE PONDS

SOMETIMES, having had a surfeit of human society and gossip, and worn out all my village friends, I rambled still farther westward than I habitually dwell, into yet more unfrequented parts of the town, "to fresh woods and pastures new,"[1] or, while the sun was setting, made my supper of huckleberries and blueberries on Fair Haven Hill, and laid up a store for several days. The fruits do not yield their true flavor to the purchaser of them, nor to him who raises them for the market. There is but one way to obtain it, yet few take that way. If you would know the flavor of huckleberries, ask the cow-boy[2] or the partridge.[3] It is a vulgar error to suppose that you have tasted huckleberries who never plucked them. A huckleberry never reaches Boston; they have not been known there since they grew on her three hills.[4] The ambrosial and essential part of the fruit is lost with the bloom[5] which is rubbed off in the market cart, and they become mere provender. As long as Eternal Justice reigns, not one innocent huckleberry can be transported thither from the country's hills.

Occasionally, after my hoeing was done for the day, I joined some impatient companion who had been fishing on the pond since morning, as silent and motionless as a duck or a floating leaf, and, after practising various kinds of philosophy, had concluded commonly, by the time I arrived, that he belonged to the ancient sect of Coenobites.[6] There was one older man, an excellent fisher and skilled in all kinds of woodcraft, who was pleased to look upon my house as a building erected for the convenience of fishermen; and I was equally pleased when he sat in my doorway to arrange his lines. Once in a while we sat together on the pond, he at one end of the boat, and I at the other; but not many words passed between us, for he had grown deaf in his later years, but he occasionally hummed a psalm, which harmonized well enough with my philosophy. Our intercourse was thus altogether one of unbroken harmony, far more pleasing to remember than if it had been carried on

by speech. When, as was commonly the case, I had none to
commune with, I used to raise the echoes by striking with a
paddle on the side of my boat, filling the surrounding woods
with circling and dilating sound, stirring them up as the keeper
of a menagerie his wild beast, until I elicited a growl from
every wooded vale and hill-side.

In warm evenings I frequently sat in the boat playing the
flute, and saw the perch, which I seemed⁷ to have charmed,
hovering around me, and the moon travelling over the ribbed
bottom, which was strewed with the wrecks of the forest.
Formerly I had come to this pond adventurously, from time to
time, in dark summer nights, with a companion, and making a
fire close to the water's edge, which we thought attracted the
fishes, we caught pouts with a bunch of worms strung on a
thread; and when we had done, far in the night, threw the
burning brands high into the air like skyrockets, which, coming
down into the pond, were quenched with a loud hissing, and
we were suddenly groping in total darkness. Through this,
whistling a tune, we took our way to the haunts of men again.
But now I made my home by the shore.

Sometimes, after staying in a village parlor till the family
had all retired, I have returned to the woods, and, partly with
a view to the next day's dinner, spent the hours of midnight
fishing from a boat by moonlight, serenaded by owls and foxes,
and hearing, from time to time, the creaking note of some unknown bird close at hand. These experiences were very
memorable and valuable to me,—anchored in forty feet of
water, and twenty or thirty rods from the shore, surrounded
sometimes by thousands of small perch and shiners, dimpling
the surface with their tails in the moonlight, and communicat-
ing by a long flaxen line with mysterious nocturnal fishes
which had their dwelling forty feet below, or sometimes dragging sixty feet of line about the pond as I drifted in the gentle
night breeze, now and then feeling a slight vibration along it,
indicative of some life prowling about its extremity, of dull uncertain blundering purpose there, and slow to make up its
mind. At length you slowly raise, pulling hand over hand, some
horned pout squeaking and squirming to the upper air. It was
very queer, especially in dark nights, when your thoughts had
wandered to vast and cosmogonal themes in other spheres, to
feel this faint jerk, which came to interrupt your dreams and
link you to Nature again. It seemed as if I might next cast my

line upward into the air, as well as downward into this element which was scarcely more dense. Thus I caught two fishes, as it were, with one hook.

The scenery of Walden is on a humble scale, and, though very beautiful, does not approach to grandeur, nor can it much concern one who has not long frequented it or lived by its shore; yet this pond is so remarkable for its depth and purity as to merit a particular description. It is a clear and deep green well, half a mile long and a mile and three quarters in circumference, and contains about sixty-one and a half acres; a perennial spring in the midst of pine and oak woods, without any visible inlet or outlet except by the clouds and evaporation. The surrounding hills rise abruptly from the water to the height of forty to eighty feet, though on the south-east and east they attain to about one hundred and one hundred and fifty feet respectively, within a quarter and a third of a mile. They are exclusively woodland. All our Concord waters have two colors at least, one when viewed at a distance, and another, more proper, close at hand. The first depends more on the light, and follows the sky. In clear weather, in summer, they appear blue at a little distance, especially if agitated, and at a great distance all appear alike. In stormy weather they are sometimes of a dark slate color. The sea, however, is said to be blue one day and green another without any perceptible change in the atmosphere. I have seen our river, when, the landscape being covered with snow, both water and ice were almost as green as grass. Some consider blue "to be the color of pure water, whether liquid or solid."⁸ But, looking directly down into our waters from a boat, they are seen to be of very different colors. Walden is blue at one time and green at another, even from the same point of view. Lying between the earth and the heavens, it partakes of the color of both. Viewed from a hill-top it reflects the color of the sky, but near at hand it is of a yellowish tint next the shore where you can see the sand, then a light green, which gradually deepens to a uniform dark green in the body of the pond. In some lights, viewed even from a hill-top, it is of a vivid green next the shore. Some have referred this to the reflection of the verdure; but it is equally green there against the railroad sand-bank, and in the spring, before the leaves are expanded, and it may be simply the result of the prevailing blue mixed with the yellow of the sand. Such is the color of its iris. This is that portion, also, where in the spring, the ice being warmed by the heat of the sun reflected from the bottom, and also transmitted through the earth, melts first and forms a narrow canal about the still frozen middle. Like the rest of our waters, when much agitated, in clear weather, so that the surface of the waves may reflect the sky at the right angle, or because there is more light mixed with it, it appears at a little distance of a darker blue than the sky itself; and at such time, being on its surface, and looking with divided vision, so as to see the reflection, I have discerned a matchless and indescribable light blue, such as watered or changeable silks and sword blades suggest, more cerulean than the sky itself, alternating with the original dark green on the opposite sides of the waves, which last appeared but muddy in comparison. It is a vitreous greenish blue, as I remember it, like those patches of the winter sky seen through cloud vistas in the west before sundown. Yet a single glass of its water held up to the light is as colorless as an equal quantity of air. It is well known that a large plate of glass will have a green tint, owing, as the makers say, to its "body," but a small piece of the same will be colorless. How large a body of Walden water would be required to reflect a green tint I have never proved. The water of our river is black or a very dark brown to one looking directly down on it, and, like that of most ponds, imparts to the body of one bathing in it a yellowish tinge; but this water is of such crystalline purity that the body of the bather appears of an alabaster whiteness, still more unnatural, which, as the limbs are magnified and distorted withal, produces a monstrous effect, making fit studies for a Michael Angelo.°

The water is so transparent that the bottom can easily be discerned at the depth of twenty-five or thirty feet. Paddling over it, you may see many feet beneath the surface the schools of perch and shiners, perhaps only an inch long, yet the former easily distinguished by their transverse bars, and you think that they must be ascetic fish that find a subsistence there. Once, in the winter, many years ago, when I had been cutting holes through the ice in order to catch pickerel, as I stepped ashore I tossed my axe back on to the ice, but, as if some evil genius had directed it, it slid four or five rods directly into one of the holes, where the water was twenty-five feet deep. Out of curiosity, I lay down on the ice and looked through the hole, until

I saw the axe a little on one side, standing on its head, with its helve erect and gently swaying to and fro with the pulse of the pond; and there it might have stood erect and swaying till in the course of time the handle rotted off, if I had not disturbed it. Making another hole directly over it with an ice chisel which I had, and cutting down the longest birch which I could find in a neighborhood with my knife, I made a slip-noose, which I attached to its end, and, letting it down carefully, passed it over the knob of the handle, and drew it by a line along the birch, and so pulled the axe out again.

The shore is composed of a belt of smooth, rounded, white stones like paving stones, excepting one or two short sand beaches, and is so steep that in many places a single leap will carry you into water over your head; and were it not for its remarkable transparency, that would be the last to be seen of its bottom till it rose on the opposite side. Some think it is bottomless.[10] It is nowhere muddy, and a casual observer would say that there were no weeds at all in it; and of noticeable plants, except in the little meadows recently overflowed, which do not properly belong to it, a closer scrutiny does not detect a flag nor a bulrush, nor even a lily, yellow or white, but only a few small heart-leaves and potamogetons, and perhaps a water-target or two; all which however a bather might not perceive; and these plants are clean and bright like the element they grow in. The stones extend a rod or two into the water, and then the bottom is pure sand, except in the deepest parts, where there is usually a little sediment, probably from the decay of the leaves which have been wafted on to it so many successive falls, and a bright green weed is brought up on anchors even in midwinter.

We have one other pond just like this, White Pond in Nine Acre Corner,[11] about two and a half miles westerly; but, though I am acquainted with most of the ponds within a dozen miles of this centre, I do not know a third of this pure and well-like character. Successive nations perchance have drank at, admired, and fathomed it, and passed away, and still its water is green and pellucid as ever. Not an intermitting spring! Perhaps on that spring morning when Adam and Eve were driven out of Eden Walden Pond was already in existence, and even then breaking up in a gentle spring rain accompanied with mist and a southerly wind, and covered with myriads of ducks and geese, which had not heard of the fall, when still such pure lakes sufficed them. Even then it had commenced to rise and fall, and had clarified its waters and colored them of the hue they now wear, and obtained a patent of heaven to be the only Walden Pond in the world and distiller of celestial dews. Who knows in how many unremembered nations' literatures this has been the Castalian Fountain?[12] or what nymphs presided over it in the Golden Age? It is a gem of the first water which Concord wears in her coronet.

Yet perchance the first who came to this well have left some trace of their footsteps. I have been surprised to detect encircling the pond, even where a thick wood has just been cut down on the shore, a narrow shelf-like path[13] in the steep hillside, alternately rising and falling, approaching and receding from the water's edge, as old probably as the race of man here, worn by the feet of aboriginal hunters, and still from time to time unwittingly trodden by the present occupants of the land. This is particularly distinct to one standing on the middle of the pond in winter, just after a light snow has fallen, appearing as a clear undulating white line, unobscured by weeds and twigs, and very obvious a quarter of a mile off in many places where in summer it is hardly distinguishable close at hand. The snow reprints it, as it were, in clear white type alto-relievo. The ornamented grounds of villas[14] which will one day be built here may still preserve some trace of this.

The pond rises and falls, but whether regularly or not, and within what period, nobody knows, though, as usual, many pretend to know. It is commonly higher in the winter and lower in the summer, though not corresponding to the general wet and dryness. I can remember when it was a foot or two lower, and also when it was at least five feet higher, than when I lived by it. There is a narrow sand-bar running into it, with very deep water on one side, on which I helped boil a kettle of chowder, some six rods from the main shore, about the year 1824, which it has not been possible to do for twenty-five years; and on the other hand, my friends used to listen with incredulity when I told them, that a few years later I was accustomed to fish from a boat in a secluded cove in the woods, fifteen rods from the only shore they knew, which place was long since converted into a meadow. But the pond has risen steadily for two years, and now, in the summer of '52,[15] is just five feet higher than when I lived there, or as high as it was thirty years ago, and fishing goes on again in the meadow. This

makes a difference of level, at the outside, of six or seven feet;
and yet the water shed by the surrounding hills is insignificant
in amount, and this overflow must be referred to causes which
affect the deep springs. This same summer the pond has begun
to fall again. It is remarkable that the fluctuation, whether
periodical or not, appears thus to require many years for its
accomplishment. I have observed one rise and a part of two
falls, and I expect that a dozen or fifteen years hence the water
will again be as low as I have ever known it. Flints' Pond,[16] a
mile eastward, allowing for the disturbance occasioned by its
inlets and outlets, and the smaller intermediate ponds also,
sympathize with Walden, and recently attained their greatest
height at the same time with the latter. The same is true, as far
as my observation goes, of White Pond.

This rise and fall of Walden at long intervals serves this use
at least; the water standing at this great height for a year or
more, though it makes it difficult to walk round it, kills the
shrubs and trees which have sprung up about its edge since the
last rise, pitch-pines, birches, alders, aspens, and others, and,
falling again, leaves an unobstructed shore; for, unlike many
ponds and all waters which are subject to a daily tide, its shore
is cleanest when the water is lowest. On the side of the pond
next my house, a row of pitch-pines fifteen feet high has
been killed and tipped over as if by a lever, and thus a stop
put to their encroachments; and their size indicates how many
years have elapsed since the last rise to this height. By this
fluctuation the pond asserts its title to a shore, and thus the
shore is shorn, and the trees cannot hold it by right of possession. These are the lips of the lake on which no beard grows. It
licks its chaps from time to time. When the water is at its
height, the alders, willows, and maples send forth a mass of
fibrous red roots several feet long from all sides of their stems
in the water, and to the height of three or four feet from the
ground, in the effort to maintain themselves; and I have known
the high-blueberry bushes about the shore, which commonly
produce no fruit, bear an abundant crop under these circumstances.

Some have been puzzled to tell how the shore became so
regularly paved. My townsmen have all heard the tradition,[17]
the oldest people tell me that they heard it in their youth, that
anciently the Indians were holding a pow-wow upon a hill
here, which rose as high into the heavens as the pond now sinks

deep into the earth, and they used much profanity, as the story
goes, though this vice is one of which the Indians were never
guilty, and while they were thus engaged the hill shook and
suddenly sank, and only one old squaw, named Walden, escaped, and from her the pond was named. It has been conjec-
tured that when the hill shook these stones rolled down its side
and became the present shore. It is very certain, at any rate,
that once there was no pond here, and now there is one; and
this Indian fable does not in any respect conflict with the account of that ancient settler[18] whom I have mentioned, who remembers so well when he first came here with his divining
rod,[19] saw a thin vapor rising from the sward, and the hazel
pointed steadily downward, and he concluded to dig a well
here. As for the stones, many still think that they are hardly to
be accounted for by the action of the waves on these hills; but
I observe that the surrounding hills are remarkably full of the
same kind of stones, so that they have been obliged to pile
them up in walls on both sides of the railroad cut nearest the
pond; and, moreover, there are most stones where the shore is
most abrupt; so that, unfortunately, it is no longer a mystery
to me. I detect the paver.[20] If the name was not derived from
that of some English locality,—Saffron Walden,[21] for instance,
one might suppose that it was called, originally, *Walled-in*
Pond.[22]

The pond was my well ready dug. For four months in the
year its water is as cold as it is pure at all times; and I think
that it is then as good as any, if not the best, in the town.
In the winter, all water which is exposed to the air is colder
than springs and wells which are protected from it. The
temperature[23] of the pond water which had stood in the room
where I sat from five o'clock in the afternoon till noon the next
day, the sixth of March, 1846, the thermometer having been up
to 65° to 70° some of the time, owing partly to the sun on the
roof, was 42°, or one degree colder than the water of one of
the coldest wells in the village just drawn. The temperature
of the Boiling Spring[24] the same day was 45°, or the warmest
of any water tried, though it is the coldest that I know of in
summer, when, beside, shallow and stagnant surface water is
not mingled with it. Moreover, in summer, Walden never
becomes so warm as most water which is exposed to the sun,
on account of its depth. In the warmest weather I usually
placed a pailful in my cellar, where it became cool in the night,

and remained so during the day; though I also resorted to a spring in the neighborhood. It was as good when a week old as the day it was dipped, and had no taste to the pump. Whoever camps for a week in summer by the shore of a pond, needs only bury a pail of water a few feet deep in the shade of his camp to be independent on the luxury of ice.

There have been caught in Walden, pickerel, one weighing seven pounds, to say nothing of another which carried off a reel with great velocity, which the fisherman safely set down at eight pounds because he did not see him, perch and pouts, some of each weighing over two pounds, shiners, chivins or roach, (*Leuciscus pulchellus,*) a very few breams,[25] and a couple of eels, one weighing four pounds,—I am thus particular because the weight of a fish is commonly its only title to fame, and these are the only eels I have heard of here;—also, I have a faint recollection of a little fish some five inches long, with silvery sides and a greenish back, somewhat dace-like in its character, which I mention here chiefly to link my facts to fable. Nevertheless, this pond is not very fertile in fish. Its pickerel, though not abundant, are its chief boast. I have seen at one time lying on the ice pickerel of at least three different kinds; a long and shallow one, steel-colored, most like those caught in the river; a bright golden kind, with greenish reflections and remarkably deep, which is the most common here; and another, golden-colored, and shaped like the last, but peppered on the side with small dark brown or black spots, intermixed with a few faint blood-red ones, very much like a trout. The specific name *reticulatus* would not apply to this, it should be *guttatus* rather.[25a] These are all very firm fish, and weigh more than their size promises. The shiners, pouts, and perch also, and indeed all the fishes which inhabit this pond, are much cleaner, handsomer, and firmer fleshed than those in the river and most other ponds, as the water is purer, and they can easily be distinguished from them. Probably many ichthyologists would make new varieties of some of them. There are also a clean race of frogs and tortoises, and a few muscles in it; muskrats and minks leave their traces about it, and occasionally a travelling mud-turtle visits it. Sometimes, when I pushed off my boat in the morning, I disturbed a great mud-turtle which had secreted himself under the boat in the night. Ducks and geese frequent it in the spring and fall, the white-bellied swallows (*Hirundo bicolor*) skim over it,[26] and the

peetweets *(Totanus macularius)* "teter" along its stony shores
all summer. I have sometimes disturbed a fishhawk sitting on
a white-pine over the water; but I doubt if it is ever profaned
by the wing of a gull, like Fair Haven." At most, it tolerates
one annual loon. These are all the animals of consequence
which frequent it now.

You may see from a boat, in calm weather, near the sandy
eastern shore, where the water is eight or ten feet deep, and
also in some other parts of the pond, some circular heaps half
a dozen feet in diameter by a foot in height, consisting of small
stones less than a hen's egg in size, where all around is bare
sand. At first you wonder if the Indians could have formed
them on the ice for any purpose, and so, when the ice melted,
they sank to the bottom; but they are too regular and some of
them plainly too fresh for that. They are similar to those found
in rivers; but as there are no suckers nor lampreys here, I know
not by what fish they could be made. Perhaps they are the
nests of the chivin.²⁸ These lend a pleasing mystery to the
bottom.

The shore is irregular enough not to be monotonous. I have
in my mind's eye the western indented with deep bays, the
bolder northern, and the beautifully scolloped southern shore,
where successive capes overlap each other and suggest unexplored coves between. The forest has never so good a setting,
nor is so distinctly beautiful, as when seen from the middle of
a small lake amid hills which rise from the water's edge; for the
water in which it is reflected not only makes the best fore-
ground in such a case, but, with its winding shore, the most
natural and agreeable boundary to it. There is no rawness nor
imperfection in its edge there, as where the axe has cleared a
part, or a cultivated field abuts on it. The trees have ample
room to expand on the water side, and each sends forth its
most vigorous branch in that direction. There Nature has
woven a natural selvage, and the eye rises by just gradations
from the low shrubs of the shore to the highest trees. There
are few traces of man's hand to be seen. The water laves the
shore as it did a thousand years ago.

A lake is the landscape's most beautiful and expressive
feature. It is earth's eye; looking into which the beholder measures the depth of his own nature. The fluviatile trees next the
shore are the slender eyelashes which fringe it, and the
wooded hills and cliffs around are its overhanging brows.

Standing on the smooth sandy beach at the east end of the pond, in a calm September afternoon, when a slight haze makes the opposite shore line indistinct, I have seen whence came the expression, "the glassy surface of a lake." When you invert your head,[29] it looks like a thread of finest gossamer stretched across the valley, and gleaming against the distant pine woods, separating one stratum of the atmosphere from another. You would think that you could walk dry under it to the opposite hills, and that the swallows which skim over might perch on it. Indeed, they sometimes dive below the line, as it were by mistake, and are undeceived. As you look over the pond westward you are obliged to employ both your hands to defend your eyes against the reflected as well as the true sun, for they are equally bright; and if, between the two, you survey its surface critically, it is literally as smooth as glass, except where the skater insects,[30] at equal intervals scattered over its whole extent, by their motions in the sun produce the finest imaginable sparkle on it, or, perchance, a duck plumes itself, or, as I have said, a swallow skims so low as to touch it. It may be that in the distance a fish describes an arc of three or four feet in the air, and there is one bright flash where it emerges, and another where it strikes the water; sometimes the whole silvery arc is revealed; or here and there, perhaps, is a thistle-down floating on its surface, which the fishes dart at and so dimple it again. It is like molten glass cooled but not congealed, and the few motes in it are pure and beautiful like the imperfections in glass. You may often detect a yet smoother and darker water, separated from the rest as if by an invisible cobweb, boom of the water nymphs, resting on it. From a hill-top you can see a fish leap in almost any part; for not a pickerel or shiner picks an insect from this smooth surface but it manifestly disturbs the equilibrium of the whole lake. It is wonderful with what elaborateness this simple fact is advertised,—this piscine murder will out,[31]—and from my distant perch I distinguish the circling undulations when they are half a dozen rods in diameter. You can even detect a water-bug (*Gyrinus*) ceaselessly progressing over the smooth surface a quarter of a mile off; for they furrow the water slightly, making a conspicuous ripple bounded by two diverging lines, but the skaters glide over it without rippling it perceptibly. When the surface is considerably agitated there are no skaters nor water-bugs on it, but apparently, in calm days, they leave their havens and adventurously glide forth from the shore by short impulses till they completely cover it. It is a soothing employment, on one of those fine days in the fall when all the warmth of the sun is fully appreciated, to sit on a stump on such a height as this, overlooking the pond, and study the dimpling circles which are incessantly inscribed on its otherwise invisible surface amid the reflected skies and trees. Over this great expanse there is no disturbance but it is thus at once gently smoothed away and assuaged, as, when a vase of water is jarred, the trembling circles seek the shore and all is smooth again. Not a fish can leap or an insect fall on the pond but it is thus reported in circling dimples, in lines of beauty, as it were the constant welling up of its fountain, the gentle pulsing of its life, the heaving of its breast. The thrills of joy and thrills of pain are undistinguishable. How peaceful the phenomena of the lake! Again the works of man shine as in the spring. Ay, every leaf and twig and stone and cobweb sparkles now at mid-afternoon as when covered with dew in a spring morning. Every motion of an oar or an insect produces a flash of light; and if an oar falls, how sweet the echo!

In such a day, in September or October, Walden is a perfect forest mirror, set round with stones as precious to my eye as if fewer or rarer. Nothing so fair, so pure, and at the same time so large, as a lake, perchance, lies on the surface of the earth. Sky water. It needs no fence. Nations come and go without defiling it. It is a mirror which no stone can crack, whose quicksilver will never wear off, whose gilding Nature continually repairs; no storms, no dust, can dim its surface ever fresh;—a mirror in which all impurity presented to it sinks, swept and dusted by the sun's hazy brush,—this the light dust-cloth,—which retains no breath that is breathed on it, but sends its own to float as clouds high above its surface, and be reflected in its bosom still.

A field of water betrays the spirit that is in the air. It is continually receiving new life and motion from above. It is intermediate in its nature between land and sky. On land only the grass and trees wave, but the water itself is rippled by the wind. I see where the breeze dashes across it by the streaks or flakes of light. It is remarkable that we can look down on its surface. We shall, perhaps, look down thus on the surface of air at length, and mark where a still subtler spirit sweeps over it.

The skaters and water-bugs finally disappear in the latter part of October, when the severe frosts have come; and then and in November, usually, in a calm day, there is absolutely nothing to ripple the surface. One November afternoon, in the calm at the end of a rain storm of several days' duration, when the sky was still completely overcast and the air was full of mist, I observed that the pond was remarkably smooth, so that it was difficult to distinguish its surface; though it no longer reflected the bright tints of October, but the sombre November colors of the surrounding hills. Though I passed over it as gently as possible, the slight undulations produced by my boat extended almost as far as I could see, and gave a ribbed appearance to the reflections. But, as I was looking over the surface, I saw here and there at a distance a faint glimmer, as if some skater insects which had escaped the frosts might be collected there, or, perchance, the surface, being so smooth, betrayed where a spring welled up from the bottom. Paddling gently to one of these places, I was surprised to find myself surrounded by myriads of small perch, about five inches long, of a rich bronze color in the green water, sporting there and constantly rising to the surface and dimpling it, sometimes leaving bubbles on it. In such transparent and seemingly bottomless water, reflecting the clouds, I seemed to be floating through the air as in a balloon, and their swimming impressed me as a kind of flight or hovering, as if they were a compact flock of birds passing just beneath my level on the right or left, their fins, like sails, set all around them. There were many such schools in the pond, apparently improving the short season before winter would draw an icy shutter over their broad skylight, sometimes giving to the surface an appearance as if a slight breeze struck it, or a few rain-drops fell there. When I approached carelessly and alarmed them, they made a sudden plash and rippling with their tails, as if one had struck the water with a brushy bough, and instantly took refuge in the depths. At length the wind rose, the mist increased, and the waves began to run, and the perch leaped much higher than before, half out of water, a hundred black points, three inches long, at once above the surface. Even as late as the fifth of December, one year, I saw some dimples on the surface, and thinking it was going to rain hard immediately, the air being full of mist, I made haste to take my place at the oars and row homeward; already the rain seemed rapidly increasing, though I felt none on my cheek, and I anticipated a thorough soaking. But suddenly the dimples ceased, for they were produced by the perch, which the noise of my oars had scared into the depths, and I saw their schools dimly disappearing; so I spent a dry afternoon after all.

An old man who used to frequent this pond nearly sixty years ago, when it was dark with surrounding forests, tells me that in those days he sometimes saw it all alive with ducks and other water fowl, and that there were many eagles about it. He came here a-fishing, and used an old log canoe which he found on the shore. It was made of two white-pine logs dug out and pinned together, and was cut off square at the ends. It was very clumsy, but lasted a great many years before it became water-logged and perhaps sank to the bottom. He did not know whose it was; it belonged to the pond. He used to make a cable for his anchor of strips of hickory bark tied together. An old man, a potter, who lived by the pond before the Revolution, told him once that there was an iron chest at the bottom, and that he had seen it. Sometimes it would come floating up to the shore; but when you went toward it, it would go back into deep water and disappear. I was pleased to hear of the old log canoe, which took the place of an Indian one of the same material but more graceful construction, which perchance had first been a tree on the bank, and then, as it were, fell into the water, to float there for a generation, the most proper vessel for the lake. I remember that when I first looked into these depths there were many large trunks to be seen indistinctly lying on the bottom, which had either been blown over formerly, or left on the ice at the last cutting, when wood was cheaper; but now they have mostly disappeared.

When I first paddled a boat on Walden, it was completely surrounded by thick and lofty pine and oak woods, and in some of its coves grape vines had run over the trees next the water and formed bowers under which a boat could pass. The hills which form its shores are so steep, and the woods on them were then so high, that, as you looked down from the west end, it had the appearance of an amphitheatre for some kind of sylvan spectacle. I have spent many an hour, when I was younger, floating over its surface as the zephyr willed, having paddled my boat to the middle, and lying on my back across the seats, in a summer forenoon, dreaming awake, until I was aroused by the boat touching the sand, and I arose to see what shore my fates had impelled me to; days when idleness was the most attractive and productive industry. Many a forenoon have I stolen away, preferring to spend thus the most valued part of the day; for I was rich, if not in money, in sunny hours and summer days, and spent them lavishly; nor do I regret that I did not waste more of them in the workshop or the teacher's desk.[32] But since I left those shores the woodchoppers have still further laid them waste, and now for many a year there will be no more rambling through the aisles of the wood,[33] with occasional vistas through which you see the water. My Muse may be excused if she is silent henceforth. How can you expect the birds to sing when their groves are cut down?

Now the trunks of trees on the bottom, and the old log canoe, and the dark surrounding woods, are gone, and the villagers, who scarcely know where it lies, instead of going to the pond to bathe or drink, are thinking to bring its water, which should be as sacred as the Ganges at least, to the village[34] in a pipe, to wash their dishes with!—to earn their Walden by the turning of a cock or drawing of a plug! That devilish Iron Horse, whose ear-rending neigh is heard throughout the town, has muddied the Boiling Spring with his foot, and he it is that has browsed off all the woods on Walden shore; that Trojan horse,[35] with a thousand men in his belly, introduced by mercenary Greeks! Where is the country's champion, the Moore of Moore Hall,[36] to meet him at the Deep Cut[37] and thrust an avenging lance between the ribs of the bloated pest?

Nevertheless, of all the characters I have known, perhaps Walden wears best, and best preserves its purity. Many men have been likened to it, but few deserve that honor. Though the woodchoppers have laid bare first this shore and then that, and the Irish have built their sties by it, and the railroad has infringed on its border, and the ice-men have skimmed it once, it is itself unchanged, the same water which my youthful eyes fell on; all the change is in me. It has not acquired one permanent wrinkle after all its ripples. It is perennially young, and I may stand and see a swallow dip apparently to pick an insect from its surface as of yore. It struck me again to-night, as if I had not seen it almost daily

for more than twenty years,—Why, here is Walden, the same
woodland lake that I discovered so many years ago; where a
forest was cut down last winter another is springing up by
its shore as lustily as ever; the same thought is welling up to
its surface that was then; it is the same liquid joy and happi-
ness to itself and its Maker, ay, and it *may* be to me. It is the
work of a brave man surely, in whom there was no guile![38]
He rounded this water with his hand, deepened and clarified
it in his thought, and in his will bequeathed it to Concord.
I see by its face that it is visited by the same reflection; and
I can almost say, Walden, is it you?

> It is no dream of mine,
> To ornament a line;
> I cannot come nearer to God and Heaven
> Than I live to Walden even.
> I am its stony shore,
> And the breeze that passes o'er;
> In the hollow of my hand
> Are its water and its sand,
> And its deepest resort
> Lies high in my thought.[39]

The cars never pause to look at it; yet I fancy that the
engineers and firemen and brakemen, and those passengers
who have a season ticket and see it often, are better men for
the sight. The engineer does not forget at night, or his nature
does not, that he has beheld this vision of serenity and purity
once at least during the day. Though seen but once, it helps
to wash out State-street[40] and the engine's soot. One proposes
that it be called "God's Drop."[41]

I have said that Walden has no visible inlet nor outlet, but
it is on the one hand distantly and indirectly related to Flints'
Pond, which is more elevated, by a chain of small ponds coming from that quarter, and on the other directly and manifestly to Concord River, which is lower, by a similar chain of
ponds through which in some other geological period it may
have flowed, and by a little digging, which God forbid, it can
be made to flow thither again. If by living thus reserved and
austere, like a hermit in the woods, so long, it has acquired
such wonderful purity, who would not regret that the comparatively impure waters of Flints' Pond should be mingled

with it, or itself should ever go to waste its sweetness[42] in the ocean wave?

Flints', or Sandy Pond, in Lincoln, our greatest lake and inland sea, lies about a mile east of Walden. It is much larger, being said to contain one hundred and ninety-seven acres, and is more fertile in fish; but it is comparatively shallow, and not remarkably pure. A walk through the woods thither was often my recreation. It was worth the while, if only to feel the wind blow on your cheek freely, and see the waves run, and remember the life of mariners. I went a-chestnutting there in the fall, on windy days, when the nuts were dropping into the water and were washed to my feet; and one day, as I crept along its sedgy shore, the fresh spray blowing in my face, I came upon the mouldering wreck of a boat, the sides gone, and hardly more than the impression of its flat bottom left amid the rushes; yet its model was sharply defined, as if it were a large decayed pad, with its veins. It was as impressive a wreck as one could imagine on the sea-shore, and had as good a moral. It is by this time mere vegetable mould and undistinguishable pond shore, through which rushes and flags have pushed up. I used to admire the ripple marks on the sandy bottom, at the north end of this pond, made firm and hard to the feet of the wader by the pressure of the water, and the rushes which grew in Indian file, in waving lines, corresponding to these marks, rank behind rank, as if the waves had planted them. There also I have found, in considerable quantities, curious balls,[43] composed apparently of fine grass or roots, of pipewort perhaps, from half an inch to four inches in diameter, and perfectly spherical. These wash back and forth in shallow water on a sandy bottom, and are sometimes cast on the shore. They are either solid grass, or have a little sand in the middle. At first you would say that they were formed by the action of the waves, like a pebble; yet the smallest are made of equally coarse materials, half an inch long, and they are produced only at one season of the year. Moreover, the waves, I suspect, do not so much construct as wear down a material which has already acquired consistency. They preserve their form when dry for an indefinite period.

Flints' Pond! Such is the poverty of our nomenclature. What right had the unclean and stupid farmer,[44] whose farm abutted on this sky water, whose shores he has ruthlessly laid bare, to give his name to it? Some skin-flint, who loved better the reflecting surface of a dollar, or a bright cent, in which he could see his own brazen face; who regarded even the wild ducks which settled in it as trespassers; his fingers grown into crooked and horny talons from the long habit of grasping harpy-like;—so it is not named for me. I go not there to see him nor to hear of him; who never *saw* it, who never bathed in it, who never loved it, who never protected it, who never spoke a good word for it, nor thanked God that he had made it. Rather let it be named from the fishes that swim in it, the wild fowl or quadrupeds which frequent it, the wild flowers which grow by its shores, or some wild man or child the thread of whose history is interwoven with its own; not from him who could show no title to it but the deed which a like-minded neighbor or legislature gave him,—him who thought only of its money value; whose presence perchance cursed all the shore, who exhausted the land around it, and would fain have exhausted the waters within it; who regretted only that it was not English hay or cranberry meadow,— there was nothing to redeem it, forsooth, in his eyes,—and would have drained and sold it for the mud at its bottom. It did not turn his mill, and it was no *privilege*[45] to him to behold it. I respect not his labors, his farm where every thing has its price; who would carry the landscape, who would carry his God, to market, if he could get any thing for him; who goes to market *for* his god as it is; on whose farm nothing grows free, whose fields bear no crops, whose meadows no flowers, whose trees no fruits, but dollars; who loves not the beauty of his fruits, whose fruits are not ripe for him till they are turned to dollars. Give me the poverty that enjoys true wealth. Farmers are respectable and interesting to me in proportion as they are poor,—poor farmers. A model farm! where the house stands like a fungus in a muck-heap, chambers for men, horses, oxen, and swine, cleansed and uncleansed, all contiguous to one another! Stocked with men! A great grease-spot, redolent of manures and buttermilk! Under a high state of cultivation, being manured with the hearts and brains of men! As if you were to raise your potatoes in the church-yard! Such is a model farm.

No, no; if the fairest features of the landscape are to be named after men, let them be the noblest and worthiest men

alone. Let our lakes receive as true names at least as the
Icarian Sea,⁴⁶ where "still the shore" a "brave attempt resounds."⁴⁷

Goose Pond, of small extent, is on my way to Flints'; Fair-
Haven, an expansion of Concord River, said to contain some
seventy acres, is a mile south-west; and White Pond, of about
forty acres, is a mile and a half beyond Fair-Haven. This is
my lake country.⁴⁸ These, with Concord River, are my water
privileges; and night and day, year in year out, they grind
such grist as I carry to them.

Since the woodcutters, and the railroad, and I myself have
profaned Walden, perhaps the most attractive, if not the most
beautiful, of all our lakes, the gem of the woods, is White
Pond;—a poor name from its commonness, whether derived
from the remarkable purity of its waters or the color of its
sands. In these as in other respects, however, it is a lesser
twin of Walden. They are so much alike that you would say
they must be connected under ground. It has the same stony
shore, and its waters are of the same hue. As at Walden, in
sultry dog-day weather, looking down through the woods on
some of its bays which are not so deep but that the reflection
from the bottom tinges them, its waters are of a misty bluish-
green or glaucous color. Many years since I used to go there
to collect the sand by cart-loads, to make sand-paper⁴⁹ with,
and I have continued to visit it ever since. One who frequents
it proposes to call it Virid Lake.⁵⁰ Perhaps it might be called
Yellow-Pine Lake, from the following circumstance. About fifteen years ago you could see the top of a pitch-pine, of the
kind called yellow-pine hereabouts, though it is not a distinct
species, projecting above the surface in deep water, many
rods from the shore. It was even supposed by some that the
pond had sunk, and this was one of the primitive forest that
formerly stood there. I find that even so long ago as 1792,
in a "Topographical Description of the Town of Concord,"⁵¹
by one of its citizens, in the Collections of the Massachusetts
Historical Society, the author, after speaking of Walden and
White Ponds, adds: "In the middle of the latter may be seen,
when the water is very low, a tree which appears as if it grew
in the place where it now stands, although the roots are fifty
feet below the surface of the water; the top of this tree is
broken off, and at that place measures fourteen inches in

diameter." In the spring of '49 I talked with the man[52] who lives nearest the pond in Sudbury, who told me that it was he who got out this tree ten or fifteen years before. As near as he could remember, it stood twelve or fifteen rods from the shore, where the water was thirty or forty feet deep. It was in the winter, and he had been getting out ice in the forenoon, and had resolved that in the afternoon, with the aid of his neighbors, he would take out the old yellow-pine. He sawed a channel in the ice toward the shore, and hauled it over and along and out on to the ice with oxen; but, before he had gone far in his work, he was surprised to find that it was wrong end upward, with the stumps of the branches pointing down, and the small end firmly fastened in the sandy bottom. It was about a foot in diameter at the big end, and he had expected to get a good saw-log, but it was so rotten as to be fit only for fuel, if for that. He had some of it in his shed then. There were marks of an axe and of woodpeckers on the but. He thought that it might have been a dead tree on the shore, but was finally blown over into the pond, and after the top had become water-logged, while the but-end was still dry and light, had drifted out and sunk wrong end up. His father, eighty years old, could not remember when it was not there. Several pretty large logs may still be seen lying on the bottom, where, owing to the undulation of the surface, they look like huge water snakes in motion.

This pond has rarely been profaned by a boat, for there is little in it to tempt a fisherman. Instead of the white lily, which requires mud, or the common sweet flag, the blue flag *(Iris versicolor)* grows thinly in the pure water, rising from the stony bottom all around the shore, where it is visited by humming birds in June, and the color both of its bluish blades and its flowers, and especially their reflections, are in singular harmony with the glaucous water.

White Pond and Walden are great crystals on the surface of the earth, Lakes of Light. If they were permanently congealed, and small enough to be clutched, they would, perchance, be carried off by slaves, like precious stones, to adorn the heads of emperors; but being liquid, and ample, and secured to us and our successors forever, we disregard them, and run after the diamond of Kohinoor.[53] They are too pure to have a market value; they contain no muck. How much more beautiful than our lives, how much more transparent

than our characters, are they! We never learned meanness of
them. How much fairer than the pool before the farmer's door,
in which his ducks swim! Hither the clean wild ducks come.
Nature has no human inhabitant who appreciates her. The
birds with their plumage and their notes are in harmony with
the flowers, but what youth or maiden conspires with the wild
luxuriant beauty of Nature? She flourishes most alone, far
from the towns where they reside. Talk of heaven! ye disgrace
earth.

X

BAKER FARM

SOMETIMES I rambled to pine groves, standing like temples, or like fleets at sea, full-rigged, with wavy boughs, and rippling with light, so soft and green and shady that the Druids would have forsaken their oaks to worship in them; or to the cedar wood beyond Flints' Pond, where the trees, covered with hoary blue berries, spiring higher and higher, are fit to stand before Valhalla,[1] and the creeping juniper covers the ground with wreaths full of fruit; or to swamps where the usnea lichen hangs in festoons from the white-spruce[2] trees, and toad-stools, round tables of the swamp gods, cover the ground, and more beautiful fungi adorn the stumps, like butterflies or shells, vegetable winkles; where the swamp-pink and dogwood grow, the red alder-berry glows like eyes of imps, the waxwork[3] grooves and crushes the hardest woods in its folds, and the wild-holly berries make the beholder forget his home with their beauty, and he is dazzled and tempted by nameless other wild forbidden fruits, too fair for mortal taste. Instead of calling on some scholar, I paid many a visit to particular trees, of kinds which are rare in this neighborhood, standing far away in the middle of some pasture, or in the depths of a wood or swamp, or on a hill-top; such as the black-birch of which we have some handsome specimens two feet in diameter; its cousin the yellow-birch, with its loose golden vest, perfumed like the first; the beech, which has so neat a bole and beautifully lichen-painted, perfect in all its details, of which, excepting scattered specimens, I know but one small grove of sizable trees left in the township, supposed by some to have been planted by the pigeons[4] that were once baited with beech nuts near by; it is worth the while to see the silver grain sparkle when you split this wood; the bass; the hornbeam; the *celtis occidentalis*, or false elm, of which we have but one well-grown; some taller mast of a pine, a shingle tree, or a more perfect hemlock than usual, standing like a pagoda in the midst of the woods; and many others I could mention. These were the shrines I visited both summer and winter.

Once it chanced that I stood in the very abutment of a rainbow's⁵ arch, which filled the lower stratum of the atmosphere, tinging the grass and leaves around, and dazzling me as if I looked through colored crystal. It was a lake of rainbow light, in which, for a short while, I lived like a dolphin. If it had lasted longer it might have tinged my employments and life. As I walked on the railroad causeway, I used to wonder at the halo of light around my shadow, and would fain fancy myself one of the elect. One who visited me declared that the shadows of some Irishmen before him had no halo about them, that it was only natives that were so distinguished. Benvenuto Cellini⁶ tells us in his memoirs, that, after a certain terrible dream or vision which he had during his confinement in the castle of St. Angelo,⁷ a resplendent light appeared over the shadow of his head at morning and evening, whether he was in Italy or France, and it was particularly conspicuous when the grass was moist with dew. This was probably the same phenomenon to which I have referred, which is especially observed in the morning, but also at other times, and even by moonlight. Though a constant one, it is not commonly noticed, and, in the case of an excitable imagination like Cellini's, it would be basis enough for superstition. Beside, he tells us that he showed it to very few. But are they not indeed distinguished who are conscious that they are regarded at all?

I set out one afternoon to go a-fishing to Fair Haven, through the woods, to eke out my scanty fare of vegetables. My way led through Pleasant Meadow,⁸ an adjunct of the Baker Farm, that retreat of which a poet has since sung, beginning,—

> "Thy entry is a pleasant field,
> Which some mossy fruit trees yield
> Partly to a ruddy brook,
> By gliding musquash undertook,
> And mercurial trout,
> Darting about."⁹

I thought of living there before I went to Walden. I "hooked" the apples, leaped the brook, and scared the musquash¹⁰ and

the trout. It was one of those afternoons which seem indefinitely long before one, in which many events may happen, a
large portion of our natural life, though it was already half
spent when I started. By the way there came up a shower,
which compelled me to stand half an hour under a pine, piling
boughs over my head, and wearing my handkerchief for a
shed; and when at length I had made one cast over the
pickerel-weed, standing up to my middle in water, I found
myself suddenly in the shadow of a cloud, and the thunder
began to rumble with such emphasis that I could do no more
than listen to it. The gods must be proud, thought I, with
such forked flashes to rout a poor unarmed fisherman. So I
made haste for shelter to the nearest hut, which stood half a
mile from any road, but so much the nearer to the pond, and
had long been uninhabited:—

> "And here a poet builded,
> In the completed years,
> For behold a trivial cabin
> That to destruction steers."[11]

So the Muse fables. But therein, as I found, dwelt now John
Field,[12] an Irishman, and his wife, and several children, from
the broad-faced boy who assisted his father at his work, and
now came running by his side from the bog to escape the rain,
to the wrinkled, sibyl-like,[13] cone-headed infant that sat upon
its father's knee as in the palaces of nobles, and looked out
from its home in the midst of wet and hunger inquisitively
upon the stranger, with the privilege of infancy, not knowing
but it was the last of a noble line, and the hope and cynosure
of the world, instead of John Field's poor starveling brat.
There we sat together under that part of the roof which leaked
the least, while it showered and thundered without. I had sat
there many times of old before the ship was built that floated
this family to America. An honest, hard-working, but shiftless
man plainly was John Field; and his wife, she too was brave
to cook so many successive dinners in the recesses of that lofty
stove; with round greasy face and bare breast, still thinking
to improve her condition one day; with the never absent mop
in one hand, and yet no effect of it visible any where. The
chickens, which had also taken shelter here from the rain,
stalked about the room like members of the family, too hu-

manized methought to roast well. They stood and looked in
my eye or pecked at my shoe significantly. Meanwhile my
host told me his story, how hard he worked "bogging" for a
neighboring farmer, turning up a meadow with a spade or
bog hoe at the rate of ten dollars an acre and the use of the
land with manure for one year, and his little broad-faced son
worked cheerfully at his father's side the while, not knowing
how poor a bargain the latter had made. I tried to help him
with my experience, telling him that he was one of my nearest neighbors, and that I too, who came a-fishing here, and
looked like a loafer, was getting my living like himself; that
I lived in a tight, light, and clean house, which hardly cost
more than the annual rent of such a ruin as his commonly
amounts to; and how, if he chose, he might in a month or two
build himself a palace of his own; that I did not use tea, nor
coffee, nor butter, nor milk, nor fresh meat, and so did not
have to work to get them; again, as I did not work hard, I
did not have to eat hard, and it cost me but a trifle for my
food; but as he began with tea, and coffee, and butter, and
milk, and beef, he had to work hard to pay for them, and
when he had worked hard he had to eat hard again to repair
the waste of his system,—and so it was as broad as it was
long, indeed it was broader than it was long, for he was discontented and wasted his life into the bargain; and yet he had
rated it as a gain in coming to America, that here you could
get tea, and coffee, and meat every day. But the only true
America is that country where you are at liberty to pursue
such a mode of life as may enable you to do without these,
and where the state does not endeavor to compel you to sustain the slavery and war and other superfluous expenses which
directly or indirectly result from the use of such things. For
I purposely talked to him as if he were a philosopher, or desired to be one. I should be glad if all the meadows on the
earth were left in a wild state, if that were the consequence[14]
of men's beginning to redeem themselves. A man will not need
to study history to find out what is best for his own culture.
But alas! the culture of an Irishman is an enterprise to be
undertaken with a sort of moral bog hoe. I told him, that as
he worked so hard at bogging, he required thick boots and
stout clothing, which yet were soon soiled and worn out, but I
wore light shoes and thin clothing, which cost not half so
much, though he might think that I was dressed like a gentle-

man, (which, however, was not the case,) and in an hour or two, without labor, but as a recreation, I could, if I wished, catch as many fish as I should want for two days, or earn enough money to support me a week. If he and his family would live simply, they might all go a-huckleberrying in the summer for their amusement. John heaved a sigh at this, and his wife stared with arms a-kimbo, and both appeared to be wondering if they had capital enough to begin such a course with, or arithmetic enough to carry it through. It was sailing by dead reckoning to them, and they saw not clearly how to make their port so; therefore I suppose they still take life bravely, after their fashion, face to face, giving it tooth and nail, not having skill to split its massive columns with any fine entering wedge, and rout it in detail;—thinking to deal with it roughly, as one should handle a thistle. But they fight at an overwhelming disadvantage,—living, John Field, alas! without arithmetic, and failing so.

"Do you ever fish?" I asked. "O yes, I catch a mess now and then when I am lying by; good perch I catch." "What's your bait?" "I catch shiners with fish-worms, and bait the perch with them." "You'd better go now, John," said his wife with glistening and hopeful face; but John demurred.

The shower was now over, and a rainbow above the eastern woods promised a fair evening; so I took my departure. When I had got without I asked for a dish, hoping to get a sight of the well bottom, to complete my survey of the premises; but there, alas! are shallows and quicksands, and rope broken withal, and bucket irrecoverable. Meanwhile the right culinary vessel was selected, water was seemingly distilled, and after consultation and long delay passed out to the thirsty one,—not yet suffered to cool, not yet to settle. Such gruel sustains life here, I thought; so, shutting my eyes, and excluding the motes by a skilfully directed under-current, I drank to genuine hospitality the heartiest draught I could. I am not squeamish in such cases when manners are concerned.

As I was leaving the Irishman's roof after the rain, bending my steps again to the pond, my haste to catch pickerel, wading in retired meadows, in sloughs and bog-holes, in forlorn and savage places, appeared for an instant trivial to me who had been sent to school and college; but as I ran down the hill toward the reddening west, with the rainbow over my shoulder, and some faint tinkling sounds borne to my ear through the cleansed air, from I know not what quarter, my Good Genius seemed to say,—Go fish and hunt far and wide day by day,—farther and wider,—and rest thee by many brooks and hearthsides without misgiving. Remember thy Creator in the days of thy youth.¹⁵ Rise free from care before the dawn, and seek adventures. Let the noon find thee by other lakes, and the night overtake thee every where at home. There are no larger fields than these, no worthier games than may here be played. Grow wild according to thy nature, like these sedges and brakes, which will never become English hay. Let the thunder rumble; what if it threaten ruin to farmers' crops? that is not its errand to thee. Take shelter under the cloud, while they flee to carts and sheds. Let not to get a living be thy trade, but thy sport. Enjoy the land, but own it not. Through want of enterprise and faith men are where they are, buying and selling, and spending their lives like serfs.

O Baker Farm!

"Landscape where the richest element
    Is a little sunshine innocent." * *

"No one runs to revel
    On thy rail-fenced lea." * *

"Debate with no man hast thou,
        With questions art never perplexed,
As tame at the first sight as now,
        In thy plain russet gabardine dressed." * *

"Come ye who love,
        And ye who hate,
Children of the Holy Dove,
        And Guy Faux of the state,
And hang conspiracies
From the tough rafters of the trees!"¹⁶

Men come tamely home at night only from the next field or street, where their household echoes haunt, and their life pines because it breathes its own breath over again; their shadows morning and evening reach farther than their daily steps. We should come home from far, from adventures, and perils, and discoveries every day, with new experience and character.

Before I had reached the pond some fresh impulse had brought out John Field, with altered mind, letting go "bogging" ere this sunset. But he, poor man, disturbed only a couple of fins while I was catching a fair string, and he said it was his luck; but when we changed seats in the boat luck changed seats too. Poor John Field!—I trust he does not read this, unless he will improve by it,—thinking to live by some derivative old country mode in this primitive new country,— to catch perch with shiners. It is good bait sometimes, I allow. With his horizon all his own, yet he a poor man, born to be poor, with his inherited Irish poverty or poor life, his Adam's grandmother and boggy ways, not to rise in this world, he nor his posterity, till their wading webbed bog-trotting feet get *talaria* to their heels.

XI

HIGHER LAWS[1]

As I came home through the woods with my string of fish, trailing my pole, it being now quite dark, I caught a glimpse of a woodchuck[2] stealing across my path, and felt a strange thrill of savage delight, and was strongly tempted to seize and devour him raw; not that I was hungry then, except for that wildness which he represented. Once or twice, however, while I lived at the pond, I found myself ranging the woods, like a half-starved hound, with a strange abandonment, seeking some kind of venison which I might devour, and no morsel could have been too savage for me. The wildest scenes had become unaccountably familiar. I found in myself, and still find, an instinct toward a higher, or, as it is named, spiritual life, as do most men, and another toward a primitive rank and savage one, and I reverence them both. I love the wild[3] not less than the good. The wildness and adventure that are in fishing still recommended it to me. I like sometimes to take rank hold on life and spend my day more as the animals do. Perhaps I have owed to this employment and to hunting, when quite young, my closest acquaintance with Nature. They early introduce us to and detain us in scenery with which otherwise, at that age, we should have little acquaintance. Fishermen, hunters, woodchoppers, and others, spending their lives in the fields and woods, in a peculiar sense a part of Nature themselves, are often in a more favorable mood for observing her, in the intervals of their pursuits, than philosophers or poets even, who approach her with expectation. She is not afraid to exhibit herself to them. The traveller on the prairie is naturally a hunter, on the head waters of the Missouri and Columbia a trapper, and at the Falls of St. Mary[4] a fisherman. He who is only a traveller learns things at second-hand and by the halves, and is poor authority. We are most interested when science reports what those men already know practically or instinctively, for that alone is a true *humanity,* or account of human experience.

They mistake who assert that the Yankee has few amusements, because he has not so many public holidays, and men and boys do not play so many games as they do in England, for here the more primitive but solitary amusements of hunting, fishing and the like have not yet given place to the former. Almost every New England boy among my contemporaries shouldered a fowling piece between the ages of ten and fourteen; and his hunting and fishing grounds were not limited like the preserves of an English nobleman, but were more boundless even than those of a savage. No wonder, then, that he did not oftener stay to play on the common. But already a change is taking place, owing, not to an increased humanity, but to an increased scarcity of game, for perhaps the hunter is the greatest friend of the animals hunted, not excepting the Humane Society.

Moreover, when at the pond, I wished sometimes to add fish to my fare for variety. I have actually fished from the same kind of necessity that the first fishers did. Whatever humanity I might conjure up against it was all factitious and concerned my philosophy more than my feelings. I speak of fishing only now, for I had long felt differently about fowling, and sold my gun before I went to the woods. Not that I am less humane than others, but I did not perceive that my feelings were much affected. I did not pity the fishes nor the worms. This was habit. As for fowling, during the last years that I carried a gun my excuse was that I was studying ornithology, and sought only new or rare birds. But I confess that I am now inclined to think that there is a finer way of studying ornithology than this. It requires so much closer attention to the habits of the birds, that, if for that reason only, I have been willing to omit the gun. Yet notwithstanding the objection on the score of humanity, I am compelled to doubt if equally valuable sports are ever substituted for these; and when some of my friends have asked me anxiously about their boys, whether they should let them hunt, I have answered, yes,—remembering that it was one of the best parts of my education,—*make* them hunters, though sportsmen only at first, if possible, mighty hunters at last, so that they shall not find game large enough for them in this or any vegetable wilderness,—hunters as well as fishers of men.[5] Thus far I am of the opinion of Chaucer's nun, who

"yave not of the text a pulled hen
That saith that hunters ben not holy men."[6]

There is a period in the history of the individual, as of the race, when the hunters are the "best men," as the Algonquins[7] called them. We cannot but pity the boy who has never fired a gun; he is no more humane, while his education has been sadly neglected. This was my answer with respect to those youths who were bent on this pursuit, trusting that they would soon outgrow it. No humane being, past the thoughtless age of boyhood, will wantonly murder any creature, which holds its life by the same tenure that he does. The hare in its extremity cries like a child. I warn you, mothers, that my sympathies do not always make the usual *philanthropic*[8] distinctions.

Such is oftenest the young man's introduction to the forest, and the most original part of himself. He goes thither at first as a hunter and fisher, until at last, if he has the seeds of a better life in him, he distinguishes his proper objects, as a poet or naturalist it may be, and leaves the gun and fish-pole behind. The mass of men are still and always young in this respect. In some countries a hunting parson is no uncommon sight. Such a one might make a good shepherd's dog, but is far from being the Good Shepherd. I have been surprised to consider that the only obvious employment, except woodchopping, ice-cutting, or the like business, which ever to my knowledge detained at Walden Pond for a whole half day any of my fellow-citizens, whether fathers or children of the town, with just one exception, was fishing. Commonly they did not think that they were lucky, or well paid for their time, unless they got a long string of fish, though they had the opportunity of seeing the pond all the while. They might go there a thousand times before the sediment of fishing would sink to the bottom and leave their purpose pure; but no doubt such a clarifying process would be going on all the while. The governor and his council[9] faintly remember the pond, for they went a-fishing there when they were boys; but now they are too old and dignified to go a-fishing, and so they know it no more forever. Yet even they expect to go to heaven at last. If the legislature regards it, it is chiefly to regulate the number of hooks to be used there; but they know nothing about the hook of hooks with which to angle for the pond itself, impaling the legislature for a bait. Thus, even in civilized communities, the embryo man passes through the hunter stage of development.

I have found repeatedly, of late years, that I cannot fish without falling a little in self-respect. I have tried it again and again. I have skill at it, and, like many of my fellows, a certain instinct for it, which revives from time to time, but always when I have done I feel that it would have been better if I had not fished. I think that I do not mistake. It is a faint intimation, yet so are the first streaks of morning. There is unquestionably this instinct in me which belongs to the lower orders of creation; yet with every year I am less a fisherman, though without more humanity or even wisdom; at present I am no fisherman at all. But I see that if I were to live in a wilderness I should again be tempted to become a fisher and hunter in earnest. Beside, there is something essentially unclean about this diet and all flesh, and I began to see where housework commences, and whence the endeavor, which costs so much, to wear a tidy and respectable appearance each day, to keep the house sweet and free from all ill odors and sights. Having been my own butcher and scullion and cook, as well as the gentleman for whom the dishes were served up, I can speak from an unusually complete experience. The practical objection to animal food in my case was its uncleanness; and, besides, when I had caught and cleaned and cooked and eaten my fish, they seemed not to have fed me essentially. It was insignificant and unnecessary, and cost more than it came to. A little bread or a few potatoes would have done as well, with less trouble and filth. Like many of my contemporaries,[10] I had rarely for many years used animal food, or tea, or coffee, &c.; not so much because of any ill effects which I had traced to them, as because they were not agreeable to my imagination. The repugnance to animal food is not the effect of experience, but is an instinct. It appeared more beautiful to live low and fare hard in many respects; and though I never did so, I went far enough to please my imagination. I believe that every man who has been earnest to preserve his higher or poetic faculties in the best condition has been particularly inclined to abstain from animal food, and from much food of any kind. It is a significant fact, stated by entomologists, I find it in Kirby and Spence, that "some insects in their perfect state, though furnished with organs of feeding, make no use of them;" and they lay it down as "a general rule, that almost all insects in this state eat much less than in that of larvae. The voracious caterpillar when transformed into a butterfly," . . . "and the gluttonous maggot when become a fly,"[11] content themselves with a drop or two of honey or some other sweet liquid. The abdomen under the wings of the butterfly still represents the larva. This is the tid-bit which tempts his insectivorous fate. The gross feeder is a man in the larva state; and there are whole nations in that condition, nations without fancy or imagination, whose vast abdomens betray them.

It is hard to provide and cook so simple and clean a diet as will not offend the imagination; but this, I think, is to be fed when we feed the body; they should both sit down at the same table. Yet perhaps this may be done. The fruits eaten temperately need not make us ashamed of our appetites, nor interrupt the worthiest pursuits. But put an extra condiment into your dish, and it will poison you. It is not worth the while to live by rich cookery. Most men would feel shame if caught preparing with their own hands precisely such a dinner, whether of animal or vegetable food, as is every day prepared for them by others. Yet till this is otherwise we are not civilized, and, if gentlemen and ladies, are not true men and women. This certainly suggests what change is to be made. It may be vain to ask why the imagination will not be reconciled to flesh and fat. I am satisfied that it is not. Is it not a reproach that man is a carnivorous animal? True, he can and does live, in a great measure, by preying on other animals; but this is a miserable way,—as any one who will go to snaring rabbits, or slaughtering lambs, may learn,—and he will be regarded as a benefactor of his race who shall teach man to confine himself to a more innocent and wholesome diet. Whatever my own practice[12] may be, I have no doubt that it is a part of the destiny of the human race, in its gradual improvement, to leave off eating animals, as surely as the savage tribes have left off eating each other when they came in contact with the more civilized.

If one listens to the faintest but constant suggestions of his genius, which are certainly true, he sees not to what extremes, or even insanity, it may lead him; and yet that way, as he grows more resolute and faithful, his road lies. The faintest assured objection which one healthy man feels will at length prevail over the arguments and customs of mankind. No man ever followed his genius[13] till it misled him. Though the result were bodily weakness, yet perhaps no one can say that the consequences were to be regretted, for these were a life in conformity to higher principles. If the day and the night are such that you greet them with joy, and life emits a fragrance like flowers and sweet-scented herbs, is more elastic, more starry, more immortal,—that is your success. All nature is your congratulation, and you have cause momentarily to bless yourself. The greatest gains and values are farthest from being appreciated. We easily come to doubt if they exist. We soon forget them. They are the highest reality. Perhaps the facts most astounding and most real are never communicated by man to man. The true harvest of my daily life is somewhat as intangible and indescribable as the tints of morning or evening. It is a little star-dust caught, a segment of the rainbow which I have clutched.

Yet, for my part, I was never unusually squeamish; I could sometimes eat a fried rat with a good relish, if it were necessary. I am glad to have drunk water so long, for the same reason that I prefer the natural sky to an opium-eater's heaven.[14] I would fain keep sober always; and there are infinite degrees of drunkenness. I believe that water is the only drink for a wise man; wine is not so noble a liquor; and think of dashing the hopes of a morning with a cup of warm coffee, or of an evening with a dish of tea! Ah, how low I fall when I am tempted by them! Even music may be intoxicating. Such apparently slight causes destroyed Greece and Rome, and will destroy England and America. Of all ebriosity,[15] who does not prefer to be intoxicated by the air he breathes? I have found it to be the most serious objection to coarse labors long continued, that they compelled me to eat and drink coarsely also. But to tell the truth, I find myself at present somewhat less particular in these respects. I carry less religion to the table, ask no blessing; not because I am wiser than I was, but, I am obliged to confess, because, however much it is to be regretted, with years I have grown more coarse and indifferent. Perhaps these questions are entertained only in youth, as most believe of poetry. My practice is "nowhere," my opinion is here. Nevertheless I am far from regarding myself as one of those privileged ones to whom the Ved refers when it says, that "he who has true faith in the Omnipresent

Supreme Being may eat all that exists,"[16] that is, is not bound
to inquire what is his food, or who prepares it; and even in
their case it is to be observed, as a Hindoo commentator has
remarked, that the Vedant limits this privilege to "the time
of distress."

Who has not sometimes derived an inexpressible satisfaction
from his food in which appetite had no share? I have been
thrilled to think that I owed a mental perception to the commonly gross sense of taste, that I have been inspired through
the palate, that some berries which I had eaten on a hill-side
had fed my genius. "The soul not being mistress of herself,"
says Thseng-tseu, "one looks, and one does not see; one listens, and one does not hear; one eats, and one does not know
the savor of food."[17] He who distinguishes the true savor of
his food can never be a glutton; he who does not cannot be
otherwise. A puritan may go to his brown-bread crust with as
gross an appetite as ever an alderman to his turtle. Not that
food which entereth into the mouth defileth a man,[18] but the
appetite with which it is eaten. It is neither the quality nor
the quantity, but the devotion to sensual savors; when that
which is eaten is not a viand to sustain our animal, or inspire
our spiritual life, but food for the worms that possess us. If
the hunter has a taste for mud-turtles, muskrats, and other
such savage tid-bits, the fine lady indulges a taste for jelly
made of a calf's foot, or for sardines from over the sea, and
they are even. He goes to the mill-pond, she to her preserve-
pot. The wonder is how they, how you and I, can live this
slimy beastly life, eating and drinking.

Our whole life is startlingly moral. There is never an instant's truce between virtue and vice. Goodness is the only
investment that never fails. In the music of the harp which
trembles round the world it is the insisting on this which
thrills us. The harp is the travelling patterer for the Universe's
Insurance Company, recommending its laws, and our little
goodness is all the assessment that we pay. Though the youth
at last grows indifferent, the laws of the universe are not indifferent, but are forever on the side of the most sensitive.
Listen to every zephyr for some reproof, for it is surely there,
and he is unfortunate who does not hear it. We cannot touch
a string or move a stop but the charming moral transfixes us.
Many an irksome noise, go a long way off, is heard as music,
a proud sweet satire on the meanness of our lives.

We are conscious of an animal in us, which awakens in proportion as our higher nature slumbers. It is reptile[19] and sensual, and perhaps cannot be wholly expelled; like the worms which, even in life and health, occupy our bodies. Possibly we may withdraw from it, but never change its nature. I fear that it may enjoy a certain health of its own; that we may be well, yet not pure. The other day I picked up the lower jaw of a hog,[20] with white and sound teeth and tusks, which suggested that there was an animal health and vigor distinct from the spiritual. This creature succeeded by other means than temperance and purity. "That in which men differ from brute beasts," says Mencius, "is a thing very inconsiderable; the common herd lose it very soon; superior men preserve it carefully."[21] Who knows what sort of life would result if we had attained to purity? If I knew so wise a man as could teach me purity I would go to seek him forthwith. "A command over our passions, and over the external senses of the body, and good acts, are declared by the Ved to be indispensable in the mind's approximation to God."[22] Yet the spirit can for the time pervade and control every member and function of the body, and transmute what in form is the grossest sensuality into purity and devotion. The generative energy, which, when we are loose, dissipates and makes us unclean, when we are continent invigorates and inspires us. Chastity is the flowering of man; and what are called Genius, Heroism, Holiness, and the like, are but various fruits which succeed it. Man flows at once to God when the channel of purity is open. By turns our purity inspires and our impurity casts us down. He is blessed who is assured that the animal is dying out in him day by day, and the divine being established. Perhaps there is none but has cause for shame on account of the inferior and brutish nature to which he is allied. I fear that we are such gods or demigods only as fauns and satyrs,[23] the divine allied to beasts, the creatures of appetite, and that, to some extent, our very life is our disgrace.—

"How happy's he who hath due place assigned
To his beasts and disaforested his mind!

*   *   *   *   *

Can use his horse, goat, wolf, and ev'ry beast,
And is not ass himself to all the rest!

> Else man not only is the herd of swine,
> But he's those devils too which did incline
> Them to a headlong rage, and made them worse."[24]

All sensuality is one, though it takes many forms; all purity is one. It is the same whether a man eat, or drink, or cohabit, or sleep sensually. They are but one appetite, and we only need to see a person do any one of these things to know how great a sensualist he is. The impure can neither stand nor sit with purity. When the reptile is attacked at one mouth of his burrow, he shows himself at another. If you would be chaste, you must be temperate. What is chastity? How shall a man know if he is chaste? He shall not know it. We have heard of this virtue, but we know not what it is. We speak conformably to the rumor which we have heard. From exertion come wisdom and purity; from sloth ignorance and sensuality. In the student sensuality is a sluggish habit of mind. An unclean person is universally a slothful one, one who sits by a stove, whom the sun shines on prostrate, who reposes without being fatigued. If you would avoid uncleanness, and all the sins, work earnestly, though it be at cleaning a stable.[25] Nature is hard to be overcome, but she must be overcome. What avails it that you are Christian, if you are not purer than the heathen, if you deny yourself no more, if you are not more religious? I know of many systems of religion esteemed heathenish whose precepts fill the reader with shame, and provoke him to new endeavors, though it be to the performance of rites merely.

I hesitate to say these things, but it is not because of the subject,—I care not how obscene my *words* are,—but because I cannot speak of them without betraying my impurity. We discourse freely without shame of one form of sensuality, and are silent about another. We are so degraded that we cannot speak simply of the necessary functions of human nature. In earlier ages, in some countries, every function was reverently spoken of and regulated by law. Nothing was too trivial for the Hindoo lawgiver,[26] however offensive it may be to modern taste. He teaches how to eat, drink, cohabit, void excrement and urine, and the like, elevating what is mean, and does not falsely excuse himself by calling these things trifles.

Every man is the builder of a temple,[27] called his body, to the god he worships, after a style purely his own, nor can he get off by hammering marble instead. We are all sculptors and painters, and our material is our own flesh and blood and bones. Any nobleness begins at once to refine a man's features, any meanness or sensuality to imbrute them.

John Farmer[28] sat at his door one September evening, after a hard day's work, his mind still running on his labor more or less. Having bathed he sat down to recreate[29] his intellectual man. It was a rather cool evening, and some of his neighbors were apprehending a frost. He had not attended to the train of his thoughts long when he heard some one playing on a flute, and that sound harmonized with his mood. Still he thought of his work; but the burden of his thought was, that though this kept running in his head, and he found himself planning and contriving it against his will, yet it concerned him very little. It was no more than the scurf of his skin, which was constantly shuffled off. But the notes of the flute came home to his ears out of a different sphere from that he worked in, and suggested work for certain faculties which slumbered in him. They gently did away with the street, and the village, and the state in which he lived. A voice said to him,—Why do you stay here and live this mean moiling life, when a glorious existence is possible for you? Those same stars twinkle over other fields than these.—But how to come out of this condition and actually migrate thither? All that he could think of was to practise some new austerity, to let his mind descend into his body and redeem it, and treat himself with ever increasing respect.

XII

BRUTE NEIGHBORS

SOMETIMES I had a companion[1] in my fishing, who came through the village to my house from the other side of the town, and the catching of the dinner was as much a social exercise as the eating of it.

Hermit. I wonder what the world is doing now. I have not heard so much as a locust over the sweet-fern these three hours. The pigeons are all asleep upon their roosts,—no flutter from them. Was that a farmer's noon horn which sounded from beyond the woods just now? The hands are coming in to boiled salt beef and cider and Indian bread. Why will men worry themselves so? He that does not eat need not work. I wonder how much they have reaped. Who would live there where a body can never think for the barking of Bose?[2] And O, the housekeeping! to keep bright the devil's door-knobs, and scour his tubs this bright day! Better not keep a house. Say, some hollow tree; and then for morning calls and dinner-parties! Only a wood-pecker tapping. O, they swarm; the sun is too warm there, they are borne too far into life for me. I have water from the spring, and a loaf of brown bread on the shelf. —Hark! I hear a rustling of the leaves. Is it some ill-fed village hound yielding to the instinct of the chase? or the lost pig which is said to be in these woods, whose tracks I saw after the rain? It comes on apace; my sumachs and sweet-briers tremble.—Eh, Mr. Poet, is it you? How do you like the world to-day?

Poet. See those clouds; how they hang! That's the greatest thing I have seen to-day. There's nothing like it in old paintings, nothing like it in foreign lands,—unless when we were off the coast of Spain.[3] That's a true Mediterranean sky. I thought, as I have my living to get and have not eaten to-day, that I might go a-fishing. That's the true industry for poets. It is the only trade I have learned. Come, let's along.

Hermit. I cannot resist. My brown bread will soon be gone. I will go with you gladly soon, but I am just concluding a serious meditation. I think that I am near the end of it. Leave me alone, then, for a while. But that we may not be delayed, you shall be digging the bait meanwhile. Angle-worms are rarely to be met with in these parts, where the soil was never fattened with manure; the race is nearly extinct. The sport of digging the bait is nearly equal to that of catching the fish, when one's appetite is not too keen; and this you may have all to yourself to-day. I would advise you to set in the spade down yonder among the ground-nuts, where you see the johnswort waving. I think that I may warrant you one worm to every three sods you turn up, if you look well in among the roots of the grass, as if you were weeding. Or, if you choose to go farther, it will not be unwise, for I have found the increase of fair bait to be very nearly as the squares of the distances.

Hermit alone. Let me see; where was I? Methinks I was nearly in this frame of mind; the world lay about at this angle. Shall I go to heaven or a-fishing? If I should soon bring this meditation to an end, would another so sweet occasion be likely to offer? I was as near being resolved into the essence of things as ever I was in my life. I fear my thoughts will not come back to me. If it would do any good, I would whistle for them. When they make us an offer, is it wise to say, We will think of it? My thoughts have left no track, and I cannot find the path again. What was it that I was thinking of? It was a very hazy day. I will just try these three sentences of Con-fut-see;[4] they may fetch that state about again. I know not whether it was the dumps or a budding ecstasy. Mem.[5] There never is but one opportunity of a kind.

Poet. How now, Hermit, is it too soon? I have got just thirteen whole ones, beside several which are imperfect or undersized; but they will do for the smaller fry; they do not cover up the hook so much. Those village worms are quite too large; a shiner[6] may make a meal off one without finding the skewer.

Hermit. Well, then, let's be off. Shall we to the Concord? There's good sport there if the water be not too high.

Why do precisely these objects which we behold make a world? Why has man just these species of animals for his neighbors; as if nothing but a mouse could have filled this crevice? I suspect that Pilpay & Co.[7] have put animals to their best use, for they are all beasts of burden, in a sense, made to carry some portion of our thoughts.

The mice which haunted my house were not the common ones, which are said to have been introduced into the country, but a wild native kind[8] not found in the village. I sent one to a distinguished naturalist,[9] and it interested him much. When I was building, one of these had its nest underneath the house, and before I had laid the second floor, and swept out the shavings, would come out regularly at lunch time and pick up the crums at my feet. It probably had never seen a man before; and it soon became quite familiar, and would run over my shoes and up my clothes. It could readily ascend the sides of the room by short impulses, like a squirrel, which it resembled in its motions. At length, as I leaned with my elbow on the bench one day, it ran up my clothes, and along my sleeve, and round and round the paper which held my dinner, while I kept the latter close, and dodged and played at bo-peep with it; and when at last I held still a piece of cheese between my thumb and finger, it came and nibbled it, sitting in my hand, and afterward cleaned its face and paws, like a fly, and walked away.

A phoebe soon built in my shed, and a robin for protection in a pine which grew against the house. In June the partridge, (*Tetrao umbellus,*) which is so shy a bird, led her brood past my windows, from the woods in the rear to the front of my house, clucking and calling to them like a hen, and in all her behavior proving herself the hen of the woods. The young suddenly disperse on your approach, at a signal from the mother, as if a whirlwind had swept them away, and they so exactly resemble the dried leaves and twigs that many a traveller has placed his foot in the midst of a brood, and heard the whir of the old bird as she flew off, and her anxious calls and mewing, or seen her trail her wings to attract his attention, without suspecting their neighborhood. The parent will sometimes roll and spin round before you in such a dishabille, that you cannot, for a few moments, detect what kind of creature it is. The young squat still and flat, often running their heads under a leaf, and mind only their mother's directions given from a distance, nor will your approach make them run again and betray themselves. You may even tread on them, or have your eyes on them for a minute, without discovering them. I have held them in my open hand at such a time, and still their only care, obedient to their mother and their instinct, was to squat there without fear or trembling. So perfect is this instinct, that once, when I had laid them on the leaves again, and one accidentally fell on its side, it was found with the rest in exactly the same position ten minutes afterward. They are not callow like the young of most birds, but more perfectly developed and precocious even than chickens. The remarkably adult yet innocent expression of their open and serene eyes is very memorable. All intelligence seems reflected in them. They suggest not merely the purity of infancy, but a wisdom clarified by experience. Such an eye was not born when the bird was, but is coeval with the sky it reflects. The woods do not yield another such a gem. The traveller does not often look into such a limpid well. The ignorant or reckless sportsman often shoots the parent at such a time, and leaves these innocents to fall a prey to some prowling beast or bird, or gradually mingle with the decaying leaves which they so much resemble. It is said that when hatched by a hen they will directly disperse on some alarm, and so are lost, for they never hear the mother's call which gathers them again. These were my hens and chickens.

It is remarkable how many creatures live wild and free though secret in the woods, and still sustain themselves in the neighborhood of towns, suspected by hunters only. How retired the otter manages to live here! He grows to be four feet long, as big as a small boy, perhaps without any human being getting a glimpse of him. I formerly saw the raccoon in the woods behind where my house is built, and probably still heard their whinnering at night. Commonly I rested an hour or two in the shade at noon, after planting, and ate my lunch, and read a little by a spring which was the source of a swamp and of a brook, oozing from under Brister's Hill,[10] half a mile from my field. The approach to this was through a succession of descending grassy hollows, full of young pitch-pines, into a larger wood about the swamp. There, in a very secluded and shaded spot, under a spreading white-pine, there was yet a clean firm sward to sit on. I had dug out the spring and made a well of clear gray water, where I could dip up a pailful without roiling it, and thither I went for this purpose almost every day in midsummer, when the pond was warmest. Thither too the woodcock led her brood, to probe the mud for worms, flying but a foot above them down the bank, while they ran in a troop beneath; but at last, spying me, she would leave her young and circle round and round me, nearer and nearer till within four or five feet, pretending broken wings and legs, to attract my attention, and get off her young, who would already have taken up their march, with faint wiry peep, single file through the swamp, as she directed. Or I heard the peep of the young when I could not see the parent bird. There too the turtle-doves[11] sat over the spring, or fluttered from bough to bough of the soft white-pines over my head; or the red squirrel, coursing down the nearest bough, was particularly familiar and inquisitive. You only need sit still long enough in some attractive spot in the woods that all its inhabitants may exhibit themselves to you by turns.

I was witness to events of a less peaceful character. One day when I went out to my wood-pile, or rather my pile of stumps, I observed two large ants,[12] the one red, the other much larger, nearly half an inch long, and black, fiercely contending with one another. Having once got hold they never let go, but struggled and wrestled and rolled on the chips incessantly. Looking farther, I was surprised to find that the chips were covered with such combatants, that it was not a *duellum*, but a *bellum*, a war between two races of ants, the red always pitted against the black, and frequently two red ones to one black. The legions of these Myrmidons[13] covered all the hills and vales in my wood-yard, and the ground was already strewn with the dead and dying, both red and black. It was the only battle which I have ever witnessed, the only battle-field I ever trod while the battle was raging; internecine war; the red republicans on the one hand, and the black imperialists on the other. On every side they were engaged in deadly combat, yet without any noise that I could hear, and human soldiers never fought so resolutely. I watched a couple that were fast locked in each other's embraces, in a little sunny valley amid the chips, now at noon-day prepared to fight till the sun went down, or life went out. The smaller red champion had fastened himself like a vice to his adversary's front, and through all the tumblings on that field never for an instant ceased to gnaw at one of his feelers near the root, having already caused the other to go by the board;[14] while the stronger black one dashed him from side to side, and, as I saw on looking nearer, had already divested him of several of his members. They fought with more pertinacity than bull-dogs. Neither manifested the least disposition to retreat. It was evident that their battle-cry was Conquer or die.[15] In the mean while there came along a single red ant on the hill-side of his valley, evidently full of excitement, who either had despatched his foe, or had not yet taken part in the battle; probably the latter, for he had lost none of his limbs; whose mother had charged him to return with his shield[16] or upon it. Or perchance he was some Achilles,[17] who had nourished his wrath apart, and had now come to avenge or rescue his Patroclus. He saw this unequal combat from afar,—for the blacks were nearly twice the size of the red,—he drew near with rapid pace till he stood on his guard within half an inch of the combatants; then watching his opportunity, he sprang upon the black warrior, and commenced his operations near the root of his right fore-leg, leaving the foe to select among his own members; and so there were three united for life, as if a new kind of attraction had been invented which put all other locks and cements to shame. I should not have wondered by this time to find that they had their respective musical bands stationed on some eminent chip, and playing their national airs the while, to excite the slow and cheer the dying combatants. I was myself excited somewhat even as if they had been men. The more you think of it, the less the difference. And certainly there is not the fight recorded in Concord[18] history, at least, if in the history of America, that will bear a moment's comparison with this, whether for the numbers engaged in it, or for the patriotism and heroism displayed. For numbers and for carnage it was an Austerlitz or Dresden.[19] Concord Fight! Two killed on the patriots' side, and Luther Blanchard wounded! Why here every ant was a Buttrick,—"Fire! for God's sake fire!"—and thousands shared the fate of Davis and Hosmer. There was not one hireling there. I have no doubt that it was a principle they fought for, as much as our ancestors, and not to avoid a three-penny tax on their tea; and the results of this battle will be as important and memorable to those whom it concerns as those of the battle of Bunker Hill, at least.

I took up the chip on which the three I have particularly described were struggling, carried it into my house, and placed it under a tumbler on my window-sill, in order to see the issue. Holding a microscope to the first-mentioned red ant, I saw that, though he was assiduously gnawing at the near fore-leg of his enemy, having severed his remaining feeler, his own breast was all torn away, exposing what vitals he had there to the jaws of the black warrior, whose breast-plate was apparently too thick for him to pierce; and the dark carbuncles of the sufferer's eyes

shone with ferocity such as war only could excite. They struggled half an hour longer under the tumbler, and when I looked
again the black soldier had severed the heads of his foes from
their bodies, and the still living heads were hanging on either
side of him like ghastly trophies at his saddle-bow, still apparently as firmly fastened as ever, and he was endeavoring
with feeble struggles, being without feelers and with only the
remnant of a leg, and I know not how many other wounds,
to divest himself of them; which at length, after half an hour
more, he accomplished. I raised the glass, and he went off over
the window-sill in that crippled state. Whether he finally survived that combat, and spent the remainder of his days in some
Hotel des Invalides,²⁰ I do not know; but I thought that his
industry would not be worth much thereafter. I never learned
which party was victorious, nor the cause of the war; but I felt
for the rest of that day as if I had had my feelings excited
and harrowed by witnessing the struggle, the ferocity and carnage, of a human battle before my door.

Kirby and Spence tell us that the battles of ants have long
been celebrated and the date of them recorded, though they
say that Huber²¹ is the only modern author who appears to have
witnessed them. "Æneas Sylvius," say they, "after giving a
very circumstantial account of one contested with great
obstinacy by a great and small species on the trunk of a pear
tree," adds that " 'This action was fought in the pontificate of
Eugenius the Fourth, in the presence of Nicholas Pistoriensis,
an eminent lawyer, who related the whole history of the battle
with the greatest fidelity.' A similar engagement between great
and small ants is recorded by Olaus Magnus, in which the
small ones, being victorious, are said to have buried the bodies
of their own soldiers, but left those of their giant enemies a
prey to the birds. This event happened previous to the expul-
sion of the tyrant Christiern the Second from Sweden."²² The
battle which I witnessed took place in the Presidency of Polk,²³
five years before the passage of Webster's Fugitive-Slave Bill.²⁴

Many a village Bose, fit only to course a mud-turtle in a
victualling cellar, sported his heavy quarters in the woods,
without the knowledge of his master, and ineffectually smelled
at old fox burrows and woodchucks' holes; led perchance by
some slight cur which nimbly threaded the wood, and might
still inspire a natural terror in its denizens;—now far behind
his guide, barking like a canine bull toward some small squirrel

which had treed itself for scrutiny, then, cantering off, bending the bushes with his weight, imagining that he is on the track of some stray member of the jerbilla[25] family. Once I was surprised to see a cat walking along the stony shore of the pond, for they rarely wander so far from home. The surprise was mutual. Nevertheless the most domestic cat, which has lain on a rug all her days, appears quite at home in the woods, and, by her sly and stealthy behavior, proves herself more native there than the regular inhabitants. Once, when berrying, I met with a cat with young kittens in the woods, quite wild, and they all, like their mother, had their backs up and were fiercely spitting at me. A few years before I lived in the woods, there was what was called a "winged cat"[26] in one of the farm-houses in Lincoln nearest the pond, Mr. Gilian Baker's. When I called to see her in June, 1842, she was gone a-hunting in the woods, as was her wont, (I am not sure whether it was a male or female, and so use the more common pronoun,) but her mistress told me that she came into the neighborhood a little more than a year before, in April, and was finally taken into their house, that she was of a dark brownish-gray color, with a white spot on her throat, and white feet, and had a large bushy tail like a fox; that in the winter the fur grew thick and flatted out along her sides, forming strips ten or twelve inches long by two and a half wide, and under her chin like a muff, the upper side loose, the under matted like felt, and in the spring these appendages dropped off. They gave me a pair of her "wings," which I keep still. There is no appearance of a membrane about them. Some thought it was part fly-squirrel or some other wild animal, which is not impossible, for, according to naturalists, prolific hybrids have been produced by the union of the marten and domestic cat. This would have been the right kind of cat for me to keep, if I had kept any, for why should not a poet's cat be winged as well as his horse?[27]

In the fall the loon *(Colymbus glacialis)* came, as usual, to moult and bathe in the pond, making the woods ring with his wild laughter before I had risen. At rumor of his arrival all the Mill-dam[28] sportsmen are on the alert, in gigs and on foot, two by two and three by three, with patent rifles and conical balls and spy-glasses. They come rustling through the woods like autumn leaves, at least ten men to one loon. Some station themselves on this side of the pond, some on that, for the poor bird cannot be omnipresent; if he dive here he must come up there.

But now the kind October wind rises, rustling the leaves and rippling the surface of the water, so that no loon can be heard or seen, though his foes sweep the pond with spy-glasses, and make the woods resound with their discharges. The waves generously rise and dash angrily, taking sides with all waterfowl, and our sportsmen must beat a retreat to town and shop and unfinished jobs. But they were too often successful. When I went to get a pail of water in the morning I frequently saw this stately bird sailing out of my cove within a few rods. If I endeavored to overtake him in a boat, in order to see how he would manoeuvre, he would dive and be completely lost, so that I did not discover him again, sometimes, till the latter part of the day. But I was more than a match for him on the surface. He commonly went off in a rain.

As I was paddling along the north shore one very calm October afternoon,[29] for such days especially they settle on to the lakes, like the milkweed down, having looked in vain over the pond for a loon, suddenly one, sailing out from the shore toward the middle a few rods in front of me, set up his wild laugh and betrayed himself. I pursued with a paddle and he dived, but when he came up I was nearer than before. He dived again, but I miscalculated the direction he would take, and we were fifty rods apart when he came to the surface this time, for I had helped to widen the interval; and again he laughed long and loud, and with more reason than before. He manoeuvred so cunningly that I could not get within half a dozen rods of him. Each time, when he came to the surface, turning his head this way and that, he coolly surveyed the water and the land, and apparently chose his course so that he might come up where there was the widest expanse of water and at the greatest distance from the boat. It was surprising how quickly he made up his mind and put his resolve into execution. He led me at once to the widest part of the pond, and could not be driven from it. While he was thinking one thing in his brain, I was endeavoring to divine his thought in mine. It was a pretty game, played on the smooth surface of the pond, a man against a loon. Suddenly your adversary's checker disappears beneath the board, and the problem is to place yours nearest to where his will appear again. Sometimes he would come up unexpectedly on the opposite side of me, having apparently passed directly under the boat. So longwinded was he and so unweariable, that when he had swum farthest he would immediately plunge again, nevertheless; and then no wit could divine where in the deep pond, beneath the smooth surface, he might be speeding his way like a fish, for he had time and ability to visit the bottom of the pond in its deepest part. It is said that loons have been caught in New York lakes[30] eighty feet beneath the surface, with hooks set for trout,—though Walden is deeper than that. How surprised must the fishes be to see this ungainly visitor from another sphere speeding his way amid their schools! Yet he appeared to know his course as surely under water as on the surface, and swam much faster there. Once or twice I saw a ripple where he approached the surface, just put his head out to reconnoitre, and instantly dived again. I found that it was as well for me to rest on my oars and wait his reappearing as to endeavor to calculate where he would rise; for again and again, when I was straining my eyes over the surface one way, I would suddenly be startled by his unearthly laugh behind me. But why, after displaying so much cunning, did he invariably betray himself the moment he came up by that loud laugh? Did not his white breast enough betray him? He was indeed a silly loon, I thought. I could commonly hear the plash of the water when he came up, and so also detected him. But after an hour he seemed as fresh as ever, dived as willingly and swam yet farther than at first. It was surprising to see how serenely he sailed off with unruffled breast when he came to the surface, doing all the work with his webbed feet beneath. His usual note was this demoniac laughter, yet somewhat like that of a water-fowl; but occasionally, when he had balked me most successfully and come up a long way off, he uttered a long-drawn unearthly howl, probably more like that of a wolf than any bird; as when a beast puts his muzzle to the ground and deliberately howls. This was his looning,—perhaps the wildest sound that is ever heard here, making the woods ring far and wide. I concluded that he laughed in derision of my efforts, confident of his own resources. Though the sky was by this time overcast, the pond was so smooth that I could see where he broke the surface when I did not hear him. His white breast, the stillness of the air, and the smoothness of the water were all against him. At length, having come up fifty rods off, he uttered one of those prolonged howls, as if calling on the god of loons to aid him, and immediately there came a wind from the east and rippled the surface, and filled the whole air with misty rain, and I was impressed as if it were the prayer of the loon answered, and his god was angry with me; and so I left him disappearing far away on the tumultuous surface.

For hours, in fall days, I watched the ducks cunningly tack and veer and hold the middle of the pond, far from the sportsman; tricks which they will have less need to practise in Louisiana bayous. When compelled to rise they would sometimes circle round and round and over the pond at a considerable height, from which they could easily see to other ponds and the river, like black motes in the sky; and, when I thought they had gone off thither long since, they would settle down by a slanting flight of a quarter of a mile on to a distant part which was left free; but what beside safety they got by sailing in the middle of Walden I do not know, unless they love its water for the same reason that I do.

XIII

HOUSE-WARMING

In October I went a-graping to the river meadows, and loaded myself with clusters more precious for their beauty and fragrance than for food. There too I admired, though I did not gather, the cranberries, small waxen gems, pendants of the meadow grass, pearly and red, which the farmer plucks with an ugly rake, leaving the smooth meadow in a snarl, heedlessly measuring them by the bushel and the dollar only, and sells the spoils of the meads to Boston and New York; destined to be *jammed*, to satisfy the tastes of lovers of Nature there. So butchers rake the tongues of bison out of the prairie grass, regardless of the torn and drooping plant. The barberry's brilliant fruit was likewise food for my eyes merely; but I collected a small store of wild apples for coddling, which the proprietor and travellers had overlooked. When chestnuts¹ were ripe I laid up half a bushel for winter. It was very exciting at that season to roam the then boundless chestnut woods of Lincoln,—they now sleep their long sleep² under the railroad,—with a bag on my shoulder, and a stick to open burrs with in my hand, for I did not always wait for the frost, amid the rustling of leaves and the loud reproofs of the red-squirrels and the jays, whose half-consumed nuts I sometimes stole, for the burrs which they had selected were sure to contain sound ones. Occasionally I climbed and shook the trees. They grew also behind my house, and one large tree which almost overshadowed it, was, when in flower, a bouquet which scented the whole neighborhood, but the squirrels and the jays got most of its fruit; the last coming in flocks early in the morning and picking the nuts out of the burrs before they fell. I relinquished these trees to them and visited the more distant woods composed wholly of chestnut. These nuts, as far as they went, were a good substitute for bread. Many other substitutes might, perhaps, be found. Digging one day for fish-worms I discovered the ground-nut (*Apios tuberosa*) on its string, the potato of the aborigines, a sort of fabulous fruit, which I had begun to doubt if I had ever dug and eaten in childhood, as I had told, and had not dreamed it. I had often since seen its crimpled red velvety blossom supported by the stems of other plants without knowing it to be the same. Cultivation has well nigh exterminated it. It has a sweetish taste, much like that of a frostbitten potato, and I found it better boiled than roasted. This tuber seemed like a faint promise of Nature to rear her own children and feed them simply here at some future period. In these days of fatted cattle and waving grain-fields, this humble root, which was once the *totem*³ of an Indian tribe, is quite forgotten, or known only by its flowering vine; but let wild Nature reign here once more, and the tender and luxurious English grains will probably disappear before a myriad of foes, and without the care of man the crow may carry back even the last seed of corn to the great corn-field of the Indian's God in the south-west, whence he is said to have brought it; but the now al-most exterminated ground-nut will perhaps revive and flourish in spite of frosts and wildness, prove itself indigenous, and resume its ancient importance and dignity as the diet of the hunter tribe. Some Indian Ceres or Minerva⁴ must have been the inventor and bestower of it; and when the reign of poetry commences here, its leaves and string of nuts may be represented on our works of art.

Already, by the first of September, I had seen two or three small maples turned scarlet across the pond, beneath where the white stems of three aspens diverged, at the point of a prom-ontory, next the water. Ah, many a tale⁵ their color told! And gradually from week to week the character of each tree came out, and it admired itself reflected in the smooth mirror of the lake. Each morning the manager of this gallery substituted some new picture, distinguished by more brilliant or harmoni-ous coloring, for the old upon the walls.

The wasps came by thousands to my lodge in October, as to winter quarters, and settled on my windows within and on the walls over-head, sometimes deterring visitors from entering. Each morning, when they were numbed with cold, I swept some of them out, but I did not trouble myself much to get rid of them; I even felt complimented by their regarding my house as a desirable shelter. They never molested me seriously, though they bedded with me; and they gradually disappeared,

into what crevices I do not know, avoiding winter⁶ and unspeakable cold.

Like the wasps, before I finally went into winter quarters in
November, I used to resort to the north-east side of Walden,
which the sun, reflected from the pitch-pine woods and the
stone shore, made the fire-side of the pond; it is so much
pleasanter and wholesomer to be warmed by the sun while you
can be, than by an artificial fire. I thus warmed myself by the
still glowing embers which the summer, like a departed hunter,
had left.

When I came to build my chimney I studied masonry. My
bricks being second-hand ones required to be cleaned with a
trowel, so that I learned more than usual of the qualities of
bricks and trowels. The mortar on them was fifty years old, and
was said to be still growing harder; but this is one of those
sayings which men love to repeat whether they are true or not.
Such sayings themselves grow harder and adhere more firmly
with age, and it would take many blows with a trowel to clean
an old wiseacre of them. Many of the villages of Mesopotamia
are built of second-hand bricks of a very good quality, obtained from the ruins of Babylon, and the cement on them is
older and probably harder still. However that may be, I was
struck by the peculiar toughness of the steel which bore so
many violent blows without being worn out. As my bricks had
been in a chimney before, though I did not read the name of
Nebuchadnezzar⁷ on them, I picked out as many fireplace
bricks as I could find, to save work and waste, and I filled the
spaces between the bricks about the fireplace with stones from
the pond shore, and also made my mortar with the white sand
from the same place. I lingered most about the fireplace, as the
most vital part of the house. Indeed, I worked so deliberately,
that though I commenced at the ground in the morning, a
course of bricks raised a few inches above the floor served for
my pillow at night; yet I did not get a stiff neck for it that I
remember; my stiff neck is of older date. I took a poet⁸ to board
for a fortnight about those times, which caused me to be put
to it for room. He brought his own knife, though I had two,
and we used to scour them by thrusting them into the earth.
He shared with me the labors of cooking. I was pleased to see
my work rising so square and solid by degrees, and reflected,
that, if it proceeded slowly, it was calculated to endure a long

time. The chimney is to some extent an independent structure, standing on the ground and rising through the house to the heavens; even after the house is burned it still stands sometimes, and its importance and independence are apparent. This was toward the end of summer. It was now November.

The north wind had already begun to cool the pond, though it took many weeks of steady blowing to accomplish it, it is so deep. When I began to have a fire at evening, before I plastered my house, the chimney carried smoke particularly well, because of the numerous chinks between the boards. Yet I passed some cheerful evenings in that cool and airy apartment, surrounded by the rough brown boards full of knots, and rafters with the bark on high over-head. My house never pleased my eye so much after it was plastered, though I was obliged to confess that it was more comfortable. Should not every apartment in which man dwells be lofty enough to create some obscurity over-head, where flickering shadows may play at evening about the rafters? These forms are more agreeable to the fancy and imagination than fresco paintings or the other most expensive furniture. I now first began to inhabit my house, I may say, when I began to use it for warmth as well as shelter. I had got a couple of old fire-dogs to keep the wood from the hearth, and it did me good to see the soot form on the back of the chimney which I had built, and I poked the fire with more right and more satisfaction than usual. My dwelling was small, and I could hardly entertain an echo in it; but it seemed larger for being a single apartment and remote from neighbors. All the attractions of a house were concentrated in one room; it was kitchen, chamber, parlor, and keeping-room;[9] and whatever satisfaction parent or child, master or servant, derive from living in a house, I enjoyed it all. Cato says, the master of a family *(patremfamilias)* must have in his rustic villa "cellam oleariam, vinariam, dolia multa, uti lubeat caritatem expectare, et rei, et virtuti, et gloriae erit,"[10] that is, "an oil and wine cellar, many casks, so that it may be pleasant to expect hard times; it will be for his advantage, and virtue, and glory." I had in my cellar a firkin of potatoes, about two quarts of peas with the weevil in them, and on my shelf a little rice, a jug of molasses, and of rye and Indian meal a peck each.

I sometimes dream of a larger and more populous house, standing in a golden age, of enduring materials, and without ginger-bread[11] work, which shall still consist of only one room, a vast, rude, substantial, primitive hall, without ceiling or plastering, with bare rafters and purlins supporting a sort of lower heaven over one's head,—useful to keep off rain and snow; where the king and queen posts[12] stand out to receive your homage, when you have done reverence to the prostrate Saturn[13] of an older dynasty on stepping over the sill; a cavernous house, wherein you must reach up a torch upon a pole to see the roof; where some may live in the fire-place, some in the recess of a window, and some on settles, some at one end of the hall, some at another, and some aloft on rafters with the spiders, if they choose; a house which you have got into when you have opened the outside door, and the ceremony is over; where the weary traveller may wash, and eat, and converse, and sleep, without further journey; such a shelter as you would be glad to reach in a tempestuous night, containing all the essentials of a house, and nothing for housekeeping; where you can see all the treasures of the house at one view, and every thing hangs upon its peg that a man should use; at once kitchen, pantry, parlor, chamber, storehouse, and garret; where you can see so necessary a thing as a barrel or a ladder, so convenient a thing as a cupboard, and hear the pot boil, and pay your respects to the fire that cooks your dinner and the oven that bakes your bread, and the necessary furniture and utensils are the chief ornaments; where the washing is not put out, nor the fire, nor the mistress, and perhaps you are sometimes requested to move from off the trapdoor, when the cook would descend into the cellar, and so learn whether the ground is solid or hollow beneath you without stamping. A house whose inside is as open and manifest as a bird's nest, and you cannot go in at the front door[14] and out at the back without seeing some of its inhabitants; where to be a guest is to be presented with the freedom of the house, and not to be carefully excluded from seven eighths of it, shut up in a particular cell, and told to make yourself at home there,—in solitary confinement. Nowadays the host does not admit you to *his* hearth, but has got the mason to build one for yourself somewhere in his alley, and hospitality is the art of *keeping* you at the greatest distance. There is as much secrecy about the cooking as if he had a design to poison you. I am aware that I have been on many a man's premises, and might have been legally ordered off, but I am not aware that I have been

in many men's houses. I might visit in my old clothes a king
and queen who lived simply in such a house as I have
described, if I were going their way; but backing out[15] of a
modern palace will be all that I shall desire to learn, if ever I
am caught in one.

It would seem as if the very language of our parlors would
lose all its nerve and degenerate into *parlaver* wholly, our lives
pass at such remoteness from its symbols, and its metaphors
and tropes are necessarily so far fetched, through slides and
dumb-waiters, as it were; in other words, the parlor is so far
from the kitchen and workshop. The dinner even is only the
parable of a dinner, commonly. As if only the savage dwelt
near enough to Nature and Truth to borrow a trope from them.
How can the scholar, who dwells away in the North West
Territory or the Isle of Man, tell what is parliamentary in the
kitchen?

However, only one or two of my guests were ever bold
enough to stay and eat a hasty-pudding with me; but when
they saw that crisis approaching they beat a hasty retreat
rather, as if it would shake the house to its foundations. Nevertheless, it stood through a great many hasty-puddings.

I did not plaster[16] till it was freezing weather. I brought over
some whiter and cleaner sand for this purpose from the opposite shore of the pond in a boat, a sort of conveyance which
would have tempted me to go much farther if necessary. My
house had in the mean while been shingled down to the
ground on every side. In lathing I was pleased to be able to
send home each nail with a single blow of the hammer, and
it was my ambition to transfer the plaster from the board to
the wall neatly and rapidly. I remembered the story of a con-
ceited fellow, who, in fine clothes, was wont to lounge about
the village once, giving advice to workmen. Venturing one day
to substitute deeds for words, he turned up his cuffs, seized a
plasterer's board, and having loaded his trowel without mis-
hap, with a complacent look toward the lathing overhead,
made a bold gesture thitherward; and straightway, to his complete discomfiture, received the whole contents in his ruffled
bosom. I admired anew the economy and convenience of plastering, which so effectually shuts out the cold and takes a handsome finish, and I learned the various casualties to which the
plasterer is liable. I was surprised to see how thirsty the bricks
were which drank up all the moisture in my plaster before I

had smoothed it, and how many pailfuls of water it takes to christen a new hearth. I had the previous winter made a small quantity of lime by burning the shells of the *Unio fluviatilis*,¹¹ which our river affords, for the sake of the experiment; so that I knew where my materials came from. I might have got good limestone within a mile or two and burned it myself, if I had cared to do so.

The pond had in the mean while skimmed over in the shadiest and shallowest coves, some days or even weeks before the general freezing. The first ice is especially interesting and perfect, being hard, dark, and transparent, and affords the best opportunity that ever offers for examining the bottom where it is shallow; for you can lie at your length on ice only an inch thick, like a skater insect on the surface of the water, and study the bottom at your leisure, only two or three inches distant, like a picture behind a glass, and the water is necessarily always smooth then. There are many furrows in the sand where some creature has travelled about and doubled on its tracks; and, for wrecks, it is strewn with the cases of cadis worms made of minute grains of white quartz. Perhaps these have creased it, for you find some of their cases in the furrows, though they are deep and broad for them to make. But the ice itself is the object of most interest, though you must improve the earliest opportunity to study it. If you examine it closely the morning after it freezes, you find that the greater part of the bubbles, which at first appeared to be within it, are against its under surface, and that more are continually rising from the bottom; while the ice is as yet comparatively solid and dark, that is, you see the water through it. These bubbles are from an eightieth to an eighth of an inch in diameter, very clear and beautiful, and you see your face reflected in them through the ice. There may be thirty or forty of them to a square inch. There are also already within the ice narrow, oblong, perpendicular bubbles about half an inch long, sharp cones with the apex upward; or oftener, if the ice is quite fresh, minute spherical bubbles one directly above another, like a string of beads. But these within the ice are not so numerous nor obvious as those beneath. I sometimes used to cast on stones to try the strength of the ice, and those which broke through carried in air with them, which formed very large and conspicuous white bubbles beneath. One day when I came to the same place forty-eight hours afterward, I found that those large bubbles were still perfect, though an inch more of ice had formed, as I could see distinctly by the seam in the edge of a cake. But as the last two days had been very warm, like an Indian summer, the ice was not now transparent, showing the dark green color of the water, and the bottom, but opaque and whitish or gray, and though twice as thick was hardly stronger than before, for the air bubbles had greatly expanded under this heat and run together, and lost their regularity; they were no longer one directly over another, but often like silvery coins poured from a bag, one overlapping another, or in thin flakes, as if occupying slight cleavages. The beauty of the ice was gone, and it was too late to study the bottom. Being curious to know what position my great bubbles occupied with regard to the new ice, I broke out a cake containing a middling sized one, and turned it bottom upward. The new ice had formed around and under the bubble, so that it was included between the two ices. It was wholly in the lower ice, but close against the upper, and was flattish, or perhaps slightly lenticular, with a rounded edge, a quarter of an inch deep by four inches in diameter; and I was surprised to find that directly under the bubble the ice was melted with great regularity in the form of a saucer reversed, to the height of five eighths of an inch in the middle, leaving a thin partition there between the water and the bubble, hardly an eighth of an inch thick; and in many places the small bubbles in this partition had burst out downward, and probably there was no ice at all under the largest bubbles, which were a foot in diameter. I inferred that the infinite number of minute bubbles which I had first seen against the under surface of the ice were now frozen in likewise, and that each, in its degree, had operated like a burning glass on the ice beneath to melt and rot it. These are the little air-guns which contribute to make the ice crack and whoop.

At length the winter set in in good earnest, just as I had finished plastering, and the wind began to howl around the house as if it had not had permission to do so till then. Night after night the geese came lumbering in in the dark with a clangor and a whistling of wings, even after the ground was covered with snow, some to alight in Walden, and some flying low over the woods toward Fair Haven,[13] bound for Mexico. Several times, when returning from the village at ten or eleven o'clock at night, I heard the tread of a flock of geese, or else ducks, on the dry leaves in the woods by a pond-hole behind my dwelling, where they had come up to feed, and the faint honk or quack of their leader as they hurried off. In 1845 Walden froze entirely over for the first time on the night of the 22d of December, Flints' and other shallower ponds and the river having been frozen ten days or more; in '46, the 16th; in '49, about the 31st; and in '50, about the 27th of December; in '52, the 5th of January; in '53, the 31st of December. The snow had already covered the ground since the 25th of November, and surrounded me suddenly with the scenery of winter. I withdrew yet farther into my shell, and endeavored to keep a bright fire both within my house and within my breast. My employment out of doors now was to collect the dead wood in the forest, bringing it in my hands or on my shoulders, or sometimes trailing a dead pine tree under each arm to my shed. An old forest fence which had seen its best days was a great haul for me. I sacrificed it to Vulcan, for it was past serving the god Terminus.[19] How much more interesting an event is that man's supper who has just been forth in the snow to hunt, nay, you might say, steal, the fuel[20] to cook it with! His bread and meat are sweet.[21] There are enough fagots and waste wood of all kinds in the forests of most of our towns to support many fires, but which at present warm none, and, some think, hinder the growth of the young wood. There was also the drift-wood of the pond. In the course of the summer I had discovered a raft of pitch-pine logs with the bark on, pinned together by the Irish when the railroad was built. This I hauled up partly on the shore. After soaking two years and then lying high six months it was perfectly sound, though waterlogged past drying. I amused myself one winter day with sliding this piecemeal across the pond, nearly half a mile, skating behind with one end of a log fifteen feet long on my shoulder, and the other on the ice; or I tied several logs to-gether with a birch withe, and then, with a longer birch or alder which had a hook at the end, dragged them across. Though completely waterlogged and almost as heavy as lead, they not only burned long, but made a very hot fire; nay, I thought that they burned better for the soaking, as if the pitch, being confined by the water, burned longer as in a lamp.

Gilpin, in his account of the forest borderers of England,

says that "the encroachments of trespassers, and the houses and fences thus raised on the borders of the forest," were "considered as great nuisances by the old forest law, and were severely punished under the name of *purprestures*, as tending *ad terrorem ferarum—ad nocumentum forestae*, &c.,"[22] to the frightening of the game and the detriment of the forest. But I was interested in the preservation of the venison and the vert more than the hunters or wood-choppers, and as much as though I had been the Lord Warden[23] himself; and if any part was burned, though I burned it myself by accident, I grieved with a grief that lasted longer and was more inconsolable than that of the proprietors; nay, I grieved when it was cut down by the proprietors themselves. I would that our farmers when they cut down a forest felt some of that awe which the old Romans did when they came to thin, or let in the light to, a consecrated grove, *(lucum conlucare,)*[24] that is, would believe that it is sacred to some god. The Roman made an expiatory offering, and prayed, Whatever god or goddess thou art to whom this grove is sacred, be propitious to me, my family, and children, &c.

It is remarkable what a value is still put upon wood even in this age and in this new country, a value more permanent and universal than that of gold. After all our discoveries and inventions no man will go by a pile of wood. It is as precious to us as it was to our Saxon and Norman ancestors. If they made their bows of it, we make our gun-stocks of it. Michaux,[25] more than thirty years ago, says that the price of wood for fuel in New York and Philadelphia "nearly equals, and sometimes exceeds, that of the best wood in Paris, though this immense capital annually requires more than three hundred thousand cords, and is surrounded to the distance of three hundred miles by cultivated plains." In this town the price of wood rises almost steadily, and the only question is, how much higher it is to be this year than it was the last. Mechanics and tradesmen who come in person to the forest on no other errand, are sure to attend the wood auction, and even pay a high price for the privilege of gleaning after the wood-chopper. It is now many years that men have resorted to the forest for fuel and the materials of the arts; the New Englander and the New Hollander, the Parisian and the Celt, the farmer and Robinhood, Goody Blake and Harry Gill,[26] in most parts of the world the prince and the peasant, the scholar and the savage, equally require still a few sticks from the forest to warm them and cook their food. Neither could I do without them.

Every man looks at his wood-pile with a kind of affection. I loved to have mine before my window, and the more chips the better to remind me of my pleasing work. I had an old axe which nobody claimed, with which by spells in winter days, on the sunny side of the house, I played about the stumps which I had got out of my bean-field. As my driver prophesied when I was ploughing, they warmed me twice, once while I was splitting them, and again when they were on the fire, so that no fuel could give out more heat. As for the axe, I was advised to get the village blacksmith to "jump"[37] it; but I jumped him, and, putting a hickory helve from the woods into it, made it do. If it was dull, it was at least hung true.

A few pieces of fat pine were a great treasure. It is interesting to remember how much of this food for fire is still concealed in the bowels of the earth. In previous years I had often gone "prospecting" over some bare hill-side, where a pitch-pine wood had formerly stood, and got out the fat pine roots. They are almost indestructible. Stumps thirty or forty years old, at least, will still be sound at the core, though the sap-wood has all become vegetable mould, as appears by the scales of the thick bark forming a ring level with the earth four or five inches distant from the heart. With axe and shovel you explore this mine, and follow the marrowy store, yellow as beef tallow, or as if you had struck on a vein of gold, deep into the earth. But commonly I kindled my fire with the dry leaves of the forest, which I had stored up in my shed before the snow came. Green hickory finely split makes the wood-chopper's kindlings, when he has a camp in the woods. Once in a while I got a little of this. When the villagers were lighting their fires beyond the horizon, I too gave notice to the various wild inhabitants of Walden vale, by a smoky streamer from my chimney, that I was awake.—

> Light-winged Smoke, Icarian bird,
> Melting thy pinions in thy upward flight,
> Lark without song, and messenger of dawn,
> Circling above the hamlets as thy nest;
> Or else, departing dream, and shadowy form
> Of midnight vision, gathering up thy skirts;
> By night star-veiling, and by day

Darkening the light and blotting out the sun;
Go thou my incense upward from this hearth,
And ask the gods to pardon this clear flame.[28]

Hard green wood just cut, though I used but little of that,
answered my purpose better than any other. I sometimes left a
good fire when I went to take a walk in a winter afternoon;
and when I returned, three or four hours afterward, it would
be still alive and glowing. My house was not empty though I
was gone. It was as if I had left a cheerful housekeeper behind.
It was I and Fire that lived there; and commonly my housekeeper proved trustworthy. One day, however, as I was splitting wood, I thought that I would just look in at the window
and see if the house was not on fire; it was the only time I
remember to have been particularly anxious on this score; so I
looked and saw that a spark had caught my bed, and I went in
and extinguished it when it had burned a place as big as my
hand. But my house occupied so sunny and sheltered a position, and its roof was so low, that I could afford to let the fire
go out in the middle of almost any winter day.

The moles nested in my cellar, nibbling every third potato,
and making a snug bed even there of some hair left after
plastering and of brown paper; for even the wildest animals
love comfort and warmth as well as man, and they survive the
winter only because they are so careful to secure them. Some
of my friends spoke as if I was coming to the woods on purpose
to freeze myself. The animal merely makes a bed, which he
warms with his body in a sheltered place; but man, having
discovered fire, boxes up some air in a spacious apartment, and
warms that, instead of robbing himself, makes that his bed, in
which he can move about divested of more cumbrous clothing,
maintain a kind of summer in the midst of winter, and by
means of windows even admit the light, and with a lamp
lengthen out the day. Thus he goes a step or two beyond instinct, and saves a little time for the fine arts. Though, when
I had been exposed to the rudest blasts a long time, my whole
body began to grow torpid, when I reached the genial atmosphere of my house I soon recovered my faculties and prolonged my life. But the most luxuriously housed has little to
boast of in this respect, nor need we trouble ourselves to
speculate how the human race may be at last destroyed. It
would be easy to cut their threads[29] any time with a little

sharper blast from the north. We go on dating from Cold Fridays[30] and Great Snows; but a little colder Friday, or greater snow, would put a period to man's existence on the globe.

The next winter I used a small cooking-stove for economy, since I did not own the forest; but it did not keep fire so well as the open fire-place. Cooking was then, for the most part, no longer a poetic, but merely a chemic process. It will soon be forgotten, in these days of stoves, that we used to roast potatoes in the ashes, after the Indian fashion. The stove not only took up room and scented the house, but it concealed the fire, and I felt as if I had lost a companion. You can always see a face in the fire. The laborer, looking into it at evening, purifies his thoughts of the dross and earthiness which they have accumulated during the day. But I could no longer sit and look into the fire, and the pertinent words of a poet recurred to me with new force.—

"Never, bright flame, may be denied to me
 Thy dear, life imaging, close sympathy.
 What but my hopes shot upward e'er so bright?
 What but my fortunes sunk so low in night?

Why art thou banished from our hearth and hall,
 Thou who art welcomed and beloved by all?
 Was thy existence then too fanciful
 For our life's common light, who are so dull?
 Did thy bright gleam mysterious converse hold
 With our congenial souls? secrets too bold?

Well, we are safe and strong, for now we sit
 Beside a hearth where no dim shadows flit,
 Where nothing cheers nor saddens, but a fire
 Warms feet and hands—nor does to more aspire;
 By whose compact utilitarian heap
 The present may sit down and go to sleep,
 Nor fear the ghosts who from the dim past walked,
 And with us by the unequal light of the old wood fire
     talked."[31]

XIV

FORMER INHABITANTS;
AND WINTER VISITORS

I WEATHERED some merry snow storms, and spent some cheerful winter evenings by my fire-side, while the snow whirled wildly without, and even the hooting of the owl was hushed. For many weeks I met no one in my walks but those who came occasionally to cut wood and sled it to the village. The elements, however, abetted me in making a path through the deepest snow in the woods, for when I had once gone through the wind blew the oak leaves into my tracks, where they lodged, and by absorbing the rays of the sun melted the snow, and so not only made a dry bed for my feet, but in the night their dark line was my guide. For human society I was obliged to conjure up the former occupants of these woods. Within the memory of many of my townsmen the road near which my house stands resounded with the laugh and gossip of inhabitants, and the woods which border it were notched and dotted here and there with their little gardens and dwellings, though it was then much more shut in by the forest than now. In some places, within my own remembrance, the pines would scrape both sides of a chaise at once, and women and children who were compelled to go this way to Lincoln¹ alone and on foot did it with fear, and often ran a good part of the distance. Though mainly but a humble route to neighboring villages, or for the woodman's team, it once amused the traveller more than now by its variety, and lingered longer in his memory. Where now firm open fields stretch from the village to the woods, it then ran through a maple swamp on a foundation of logs, the remnants of which, doubtless, still underlie the present dusty highway, from the Stratten, now the Alms House² Farm, to Brister's Hill.

East of my bean-field, across the road, lived Cato Ingraham, slave of Duncan Ingraham,³ Esquire, gentleman of Concord village; who built his slave a house, and gave him permission to live in Walden Woods;—Cato,⁴ not Uticensis, but Concordiensis. Some say that he was a Guinea Negro. There are a few who remember his little patch among the walnuts, which he let grow up till he should be old and need them; but a younger and whiter speculator got them at last. He too, however, occupies an equally narrow house⁵ at present. Cato's half-obliterated cellar hole still remains, though known to few, being concealed from the traveller by a fringe of pines. It is now filled with the smooth sumach *(Rhus glabra)*, and one of the earliest species of golden-rod *(Solidago stricta)* grows there luxuriantly.

Here, by the very corner of my field, still nearer to town, Zilpha, a colored woman, had her little house, where she spun linen for the townsfolk, making the Walden Woods ring with her shrill singing, for she had a loud and notable voice. At length, in the war of 1812, her dwelling was set on fire by English soldiers,⁶ prisoners on parole, when she was away, and her cat and dog and hens were all burned up together. She led a hard life, and somewhat inhumane. One old frequenter of these woods remembers, that as he passed her house one noon he heard her muttering to herself over her gurgling pot,— "Ye are all bones, bones!" I have seen bricks amid the oak copse there.

Down the road, on the right hand, on Brister's Hill, lived Brister Freeman,⁷ "a handy Negro," slave of Squire Cummings⁸ once,—there where grow still the apple-trees which Brister planted and tended; large old trees now, but their fruit still wild and ciderish to my taste. Not long since I read his epitaph⁹ in the old Lincoln burying-ground, a little on one side, near the unmarked graves of some British grenadiers who fell in the retreat from Concord,—where he is styled "Sippio Brister,"—Scipio Africanus¹⁰ he had some title to be called,—"a man of color," as if he were discolored. It also told me, with staring emphasis, when he died; which was but an indirect way of informing me that he ever lived. With him dwelt Fenda, his hospitable wife, who told fortunes, yet pleasantly,—large, round, and black, blacker than any of the children of night, such a dusky orb never rose on Concord before or since.

Farther down the hill, on the left, on the old road in the woods are marks of some homestead of the Stratten¹¹ family; whose orchard once covered all the slope of Brister's Hill, but was long since killed out by pitch-pines, excepting a few stumps, whose old roots furnish still the wild stocks of many a thrifty village tree.[12]

Nearer yet to town, you come to Breed's location,[13] on the other side of the way, just on the edge of the wood; ground famous for the pranks of a demon not distinctly named in old mythology, who has acted a prominent and astounding part in our New England life, and deserves, as much as any mythological character, to have his biography written one day; who first comes in the guise of a friend or hired man, and then robs and murders the whole family,—New-England Rum. But history must not yet tell the tragedies enacted here; let time intervene in some measure to assuage and lend an azure tint to them. Here the most indistinct and dubious tradition says that once a tavern stood; the well the same, which tempered the traveller's beverage and refreshed his steed. Here then men saluted one another, and heard and told the news, and went their ways again.

Breed's hut was standing only a dozen years ago, though it had long been unoccupied. It was about the size of mine. It was set on fire by mischievous boys, one Election night,[14] if I do not mistake. I lived on the edge of the village then, and had just lost myself over Davenant's Gondibert,[15] that winter that I labored with a lethargy,—which, by the way, I never knew whether to regard as a family complaint, having an uncle[16] who goes to sleep shaving himself, and is obliged to sprout potatoes in a cellar Sundays, in order to keep awake and keep the Sabbath, or as the consequences of my attempt to read Chalmers' collection[17] of English poetry without skipping. It fairly overcame my Nervii.[18] I had just sunk my head on this when the bells rung fire, and in hot haste the engines rolled that way, led by a straggling troop of men and boys, and I among the foremost, for I had leaped the brook.[19] We thought it was far south over the woods,—we who had run to fires before,—barn, shop, or dwelling-house, or all together. "It's Baker's barn,"[20] cried one. "It is the Codman Place," affirmed another. And then fresh sparks went up above the wood, as if the roof fell in, and we all shouted "Concord to the rescue!" Wagons shot past with furious speed and crushing loads, bearing, perchance, among the rest, the agent of the Insurance Company,[21] who was bound to go however far; and ever and anon the engine bell tingled behind, more slow and sure, and rearmost of all, as it was afterward whispered, came they who set the fire and gave the alarm. Thus we kept on like true idealists, rejecting the evidence of our senses, until at a turn in the road we heard the crackling and actually felt the heat of the fire from over the wall, and realized, alas! that we were there. The very nearness of the fire but cooled our ardor. At first we thought to throw a frog-pond on to it; but concluded to let it burn, it was so far gone and so worthless. So we stood round our engine, jostled one another, expressed our sentiments through speaking trumpets, or in lower tone referred to the great conflagrations which the world has witnessed, including Bascom's shop,[22] and, between ourselves, we thought that, were we there in season with our "tub,"[23] and a full frog-pond by, we could turn that threatened last and universal one into another flood. We finally retreated without doing any mischief,—returned to sleep and Gondibert. But as for Gondibert, I would except that passage in the preface about wit being the soul's powder,—"but most of mankind are strangers to wit, as Indians are to powder."[24]

It chanced that I walked that way across the fields the following night, about the same hour, and hearing a low moaning at this spot, I drew near in the dark, and discovered the only survivor of the family that I know, the heir of both its virtues and its vices, who alone was interested in this burning, lying on his stomach and looking over the cellar wall at the still smouldering cinders beneath, muttering to himself, as is his wont. He had been working far off in the river meadows all day, and had improved the first moments that he could call his own to visit the home of his fathers and his youth. He gazed into the cellar from all sides and points of view by turns, always lying down to it, as if there was some treasure, which he remembered, concealed between the stones, where there was absolutely nothing but a heap of bricks and ashes. The house being gone, he looked at what there was left. He was soothed by the sympathy which my mere presence implied, and showed me, as well as the darkness permitted, where the well was covered up; which, thank Heaven, could never be burned; and he groped long about the wall to find the well-sweep which his father had cut and mounted, feeling for the iron hook or staple by which a burden had been fastened to the heavy end,—all that he could now cling to,— to convince me that it was no common "rider." I felt it, and still remark it almost daily in my walks, for by it hangs the history of a family.

Once more, on the left, where are seen the well and lilac bushes by the wall, in the now open field, lived Nutting and Le Grosse.[25] But to return toward Lincoln.

Farther in the woods than any of these, where the road approaches nearest to the pond, Wyman[26] the potter squatted, and furnished his townsmen with earthen ware, and left descendants to succeed him. Neither were they rich in worldly goods, holding the land by sufferance while they lived; and there often the sheriff came in vain to collect the taxes, and "attached a chip,"[27] for form's sake, as I have read in his accounts, there being nothing else that he could lay his hands on. One day in midsummer, when I was hoeing, a man who was carrying a load of pottery to market stopped his horse against my field and inquired concerning Wyman the younger. He had long ago bought a potter's wheel of him, and wished to know what had become of him. I had read of the potter's clay[28] and wheel in Scripture, but it had never occurred to me that the pots we use were not such as had come down unbroken from those days, or grown on trees like gourds somewhere, and I was pleased to hear that so fictile an art was ever practised in my neighborhood.

The last inhabitant of these woods before me was an Irishman, Hugh Quoil,[29] (if I have spelt his name with coil enough,) who occupied Wyman's tenement,—Col. Quoil, he was called. Rumor said that he had been a soldier at Waterloo. If he had lived I should have made him fight his battles over again. His trade here was that of a ditcher. Napoleon went to St. Helena; Quoil came to Walden Woods. All I know of him is tragic. He was a man of manners, like one who had seen the world, and was capable of more civil speech than you could well attend to. He wore a great coat in mid-summer, being affected with the trembling delirium, and his face was the color of carmine. He died in the road at the foot of Brister's Hill shortly after I came to the woods, so that I have not remembered him as a neighbor. Before his house was pulled down, when his comrades avoided it as "an unlucky castle," I visited it. There lay his old clothes curled up by use, as if they were himself, upon his raised plank bed. His pipe lay broken on the hearth, instead of a bowl[30] broken at the fountain. The last could never have been the symbol of

his death, for he confessed to me that, though he had heard
of Brister's Spring, he had never seen it; and soiled cards,
kings of diamonds, spades and hearts, were scattered over the
floor. One black chicken which the administrator could not
catch, black as night and as silent, not even croaking, awaiting Reynard,[31] still went to roost in the next apartment. In
the rear there was the dim outline of a garden, which had
been planted but had never received its first hoeing, owing
to those terrible shaking fits, though it was now harvest time.
It was over-run with Roman wormwood and beggar-ticks,
which last stuck to my clothes for all fruit. The skin of a
woodchuck was freshly stretched upon the back of the house,
a trophy of his last Waterloo; but no warm cap or mittens
would he want more.

Now only a dent in the earth marks the site of these dwellings, with buried cellar stones, and strawberries, raspberries,
thimbleberries, hazel-bushes, and sumachs growing in the
sunny sward there; some pitch-pine or gnarled oak occupies
what was the chimney nook, and a sweet-scented black-birch,
perhaps, waves where the door-stone was. Sometimes the well
dent is visible, where once a spring oozed; now dry and tear-
less grass; or it was covered deep,—not to be discovered till
some late day,—with a flat stone under the sod, when the
last of the race departed. What a sorrowful act must that be,
—the covering up of wells! coincident with the opening of
wells of tears. These cellar dents, like deserted fox burrows,
old holes, are all that is left where once were the stir and
bustle of human life, and "fate, free-will, foreknowledge absolute,"[32] in some form and dialect or other were by turns
discussed. But all I can learn of their conclusions amounts
to just this, that "Cato and Brister pulled wool;" which is
about as edifying as the history of more famous schools of
philosophy.

Still grows the vivacious lilac a generation after the door
and lintel and the sill are gone, unfolding its sweet-scented
flowers each spring, to be plucked by the musing traveller;
planted and tended once by children's hands, in front-yard
plots,—now standing by wall-sides in retired pastures, and
giving place to new-rising forests;—the last of that stirp, sole
survivor of that family. Little did the dusky children think
that the puny slip with its two eyes only, which they stuck
in the ground in the shadow of the house and daily watered,

would root itself so, and outlive them, and house itself in the rear that shaded it, and grown man's garden and orchard, and tell their story faintly to the lone wanderer a half century after they had grown up and died,—blossoming as fair, and smelling as sweet, as in that first spring. I mark its still tender, civil, cheerful, lilac colors.

But this small village, germ of something more, why did it fail while Concord keeps its ground? Were there no natural advantages,—no water privileges, forsooth? Ay, the deep Walden Pond and cool Brister's Spring,—privilege to drink long and healthy draughts at these, all unimproved by these men but to dilute their glass. They were universally a thirsty race. Might not the basket, stable-broom, mat-making, corn-parching, linen-spinning, and pottery business have thrived here, making the wilderness[33] to blossom like the rose, and a numerous posterity have inherited the land of their fathers? The sterile soil would at least have been proof against a low-land degeneracy. Alas! how little does the memory of these human inhabitants enhance the beauty of the landscape! Again, perhaps, Nature will try, with me for a first settler, and my house raised last spring to be the oldest in the hamlet.

I am not aware that any man has ever built on the spot which I occupy. Deliver me from a city built on the site of a more ancient city,[34] whose materials are ruins, whose gardens cemeteries. The soil is blanched and accursed there, and before that becomes necessary the earth itself will be destroyed. With such reminiscences I repeopled the woods and lulled myself asleep.

At this season I seldom had a visitor. When the snow lay deepest no wanderer ventured near my house for a week or fortnight at a time, but there I lived as snug as a meadow mouse, or as cattle and poultry[35] which are said to have survived for a long time buried in drifts, even without food; or like that early settler's family in the town of Sutton, in this state, whose cottage was completely covered by the great snow of 1717 when he was absent, and an Indian found it only by the hole which the chimney's breath made in the drift, and so relieved the family. But no friendly Indian concerned himself about me; nor needed he, for the master of the house was at home. The Great Snow! How cheerful it is to hear of! When the farmers could not get to the woods and swamps with their teams, and were obliged to cut down the shade trees before their houses, and when the crust was harder cut off the trees in the swamps ten feet from the ground, as it appeared the next spring.

In the deepest snows, the path which I used from the highway to my house, about half a mile long, might have been represented by a meandering dotted line, with wide intervals between the dots. For a week of even weather I took exactly the same number of steps, and of the same length, coming and going, stepping deliberately and with the precision of a pair of dividers in my own deep tracks,—to such routine the winter reduces us,—yet often they were filled with heaven's own blue. But no weather interfered fatally with my walks, or rather my going abroad, for I frequently tramped eight or ten miles through the deepest snow to keep an appointment with a beech-tree, or a yellow-birch, or an old acquaintance among the pines; when the ice and snow causing their limbs to droop, and so sharpening their tops, had changed the pines into fir-trees; wading to the tops of the highest hills when the snow was nearly two feet deep on a level, and shaking down another snow-storm on my head at every step; or sometimes creeping and floundering thither on my hands and knees, when the hunters had gone into winter quarters. One afternoon I amused myself by watching a barred owl *(Strix nebulosa)* sitting on one of the lower dead limbs of a white-pine, close to the trunk, in broad daylight, I standing within a rod of him. He could hear me when I moved and cronched the snow with my feet, but could not plainly see me. When I made most noise he would stretch out his neck, and erect his neck feathers, and open his eyes wide; but their lids soon fell again, and he began to nod. I too felt a slumberous influence after watching him half an hour, as he sat thus with his eyes half open, like a cat, winged brother of the cat. There was only a narrow slit left between their lids, by which he preserved a peninsular relation to me; thus, with half-shut eyes, looking out from the land of dreams, and endeavoring to realize me, vague object or mote that interrupted his visions. At length, on some louder noise or my nearer approach, he would grow uneasy and sluggishly turn about on his perch, as if impatient at having his dreams disturbed; and when he launched himself off and flapped through the pines, spread-

ing his wings to unexpected breadth, I could not hear the
slightest sound from them. Thus, guided amid the pine
boughs rather by a delicate sense of their neighborhood than
by sight, feeling his twilight way, as it were, with his sensitive
pinions, he found a new perch, where he might in peace
await the dawning of his day.

As I walked over the long causeway made for the railroad
through the meadows, I encountered many a blustering and
nipping wind, for nowhere has it freer play; and when the
frost had smitten me on one cheek,[36] heathen as I was, I
turned to it the other also. Nor was it much better by the
carriage road from Brister's Hill. For I came to town still,
like a friendly Indian, when the contents of the broad open
fields were all piled up between the walls of the Walden road,
and half an hour sufficed to obliterate the tracks of the last
traveller. And when I returned new drifts would have formed,
through which I floundered, where the busy north-west wind
had been depositing the powdery snow round a sharp angle in
the road, and not a rabbit's track, nor even the fine print, the
small type, of a meadow[37] mouse was to be seen. Yet I rarely
failed to find, even in mid-winter, some warm and springy
swamp where the grass and the skunk-cabbage still put forth
with perennial verdure, and some hardier bird occasionally
awaited the return of spring.

Sometimes, notwithstanding the snow, when I returned
from my walk at evening I crossed the deep tracks of a wood-
chopper[38] leading from my door, and found his pile of whit-
tlings on the hearth, and my house filled with the odor of his
pipe. Or on a Sunday afternoon, if I chanced to be at home,
I heard the cronching of the snow made by the step of a
long-headed farmer[39] who from far through the woods sought
my house, to have a social "crack;" one of the few of his vocation who are "men on their farms;" who donned a frock instead of a professor's gown, and is as ready to extract the
moral out of church or state as to haul a load of manure from
his barn-yard. We talked of rude and simple times, when men
sat about large fires in cold bracing weather, with clear heads;
and when other dessert failed, we tried our teeth on many a
nut which wise squirrels have long since abandoned, for those
which have the thickest shells are commonly empty.

The one who came from farthest to my lodge, through
deepest snows and most dismal tempests, was a poet.[40] A

farmer, a hunter, a soldier, a reporter, even a philosopher, may be daunted; but nothing can deter a poet, for he is actuated by pure love. Who can predict his comings and goings? His business calls him out at all hours, even when doctors sleep. We made that small house ring with boisterous mirth and resound with the murmur of much sober talk, making amends then to Walden vale for the long silences. Broadway was still and deserted in comparison. At suitable intervals there were regular salutes of laughter, which might have been referred indifferently to the last uttered or the forth-coming jest. We made many a "bran new" theory of life over a thin dish of gruel, which combined the advantages of conviviality with the clear-headedness which philosophy requires.

I should not forget that during my last winter at the pond there was another welcome visitor,[41] who at one time came through the village, through snow and rain and darkness, till he saw my lamp through the trees, and shared with me some long winter evenings. One of the last of the philosophers,— Connecticut gave him to the world,—he peddled first her wares, afterwards, as he declares, his brains. These he peddles still, prompting God and disgracing man, bearing for fruit his brain only, like the nut its kernel. I think that he must be the man of the most faith of any alive. His words and attitude always suppose a better state of things than other men are acquainted with, and he will be the last man to be disappointed as the ages revolve. He has no venture in the present. But though comparatively disregarded now, when his day comes, laws unsuspected by most will take effect, and masters of families and rulers will come to him for advice.—

"How blind that cannot see serenity!"[42]

A true friend of man; almost the only friend of human progress. An Old Mortality,[43] say rather an Immortality, with unwearied patience and faith making plain the image engraven in men's bodies, the God of whom they are but defaced and leaning monuments. With his hospitable intellect he embraces children, beggars, insane, and scholars, and entertains the thought of all, adding to it commonly some breadth and elegance. I think that he should keep a caravansary on the world's highway, where philosophers of all nations might put up, and on his sign should be printed, "Entertainment for man, but not for his beast."⁴⁴ Enter ye that have leisure and a quiet mind, who earnestly seek the right road." He is perhaps the sanest man and has the fewest crotchets of any I chance to know; the same yesterday and to-morrow. Of yore we had sauntered and talked, and effectually put the world behind us; for he was pledged to no institution in it, freeborn, *ingenuus*. Whichever way we turned, it seemed that the heavens and the earth had met together, since he enhanced the beauty of the landscape. A blue-robed man, whose fittest roof is the overarching sky which reflects his serenity. I do not see how he can ever die; Nature cannot spare him.

Having each some shingles of thought well dried, we sat and whittled them, trying our knives, and admiring the clear yellowish grain of the pumpkin pine.⁴⁵ We waded so gently and reverently, or we pulled together so smoothly, that the fishes of thought were not scared from the stream, nor feared any angler on the bank, but came and went grandly, like the clouds which float through the western sky, and the mother-o'-pearl flocks which sometimes form and dissolve there. There we worked, revising mythology, rounding a fable here and there, and building castles in the air for which earth offered no worthy foundation. Great Looker! Great Expecter! to converse with whom was a New England Night's Entertainment.⁴⁶ Ah! such discourse we had, hermit and philosopher, and the old settler⁴⁷ I have spoken of,—we three,⁴⁸—it expanded and racked my little house; I should not dare to say how many pounds' weight there was above the atmospheric pressure on every circular inch; it opened its seams so that they had to be calked with much dulness thereafter to stop the consequent leak;—but I had enough of that kind of oakum already picked.

There was one other⁴⁹ with whom I had "solid seasons," long to be remembered, at his house in the village, and who looked in upon me from time to time; but I had no more for society there.

There too, as every where, I sometimes expected the Visitor who never comes. The Vishnu Purana says, "The house-holder is to remain at eventide in his courtyard as long as it takes to milk a cow, or longer if he pleases, to await the arrival of a guest."⁵⁰ I often performed this duty of hospitality, waited long enough to milk a whole herd of cows, but did not see the man approaching from the town.⁵¹

XV

WINTER ANIMALS

WHEN the ponds were firmly frozen, they afforded not only new and shorter routes to many points, but new views from their surfaces of the familiar landscape around them. When I crossed Flints' Pond, after it was covered with snow, though I had often paddled about and skated over it, it was so unexpectedly wide and so strange that I could think of nothing but Baffin's Bay.[1] The Lincoln hills rose up around me at the extremity of a snowy plain, in which I did not remember to have stood before; and the fishermen, at an indeterminable distance over the ice, moving slowly about with their wolfish dogs, passed for sealers or Esquimaux, or in misty weather loomed like fabulous creatures, and I did not know whether they were giants or pygmies. I took this course when I went to lecture[2] in Lincoln in the evening, travelling in no road and passing no house between my own hut[3] and the lecture room. In Goose Pond,[4] which lay in my way, a colony of muskrats dwelt, and raised their cabins high above the ice, though none could be seen abroad when I crossed it. Walden, being like the rest usually bare of snow, or with only shallow and interrupted drifts on it, was my yard, where I could walk freely when the snow was nearly two feet deep on a level elsewhere and the villagers were confined to their streets. There, far from the village street, and except at very long intervals, from the jingle of sleigh-bells, I slid and skated, as in a vast moose-yard well trodden, overhung by oak woods and solemn pines bent down with snow or bristling with icicles.

For sounds in winter nights, and often in winter days, I heard the forlorn but melodious note of a hooting owl indefinitely far; such a sound as the frozen earth would yield if struck with a suitable plectrum, the very *lingua vernacula* of Walden Wood, and quite familiar to me at last, though I never saw the bird while it was making it. I seldom opened my door in a winter evening without hearing it; *Hoo hoo hoo, hoorer hoo,* sounded sonorously, and the first three syllables accented somewhat like *how der do;* or sometimes *hoo hoo* only. One night in the beginning of winter, before the pond froze over, about nine o'clock, I was startled by the loud honking of a goose, and, stepping to the door, heard the sound of their wings like a tempest in the woods as they flew low over my house. They passed over the pond toward Fair Haven, seemingly deterred from settling by my light, their commodore honking all the while with a regular beat. Suddenly an unmistakable cat-owl from very near me, with the most harsh and tremendous voice I ever heard from any inhabitant of the woods, responded at regular intervals to the goose, as if determined to expose and disgrace this intruder from Hudson's Bay by exhibiting a greater compass and volume of voice in a native, and *boo-hoo* him out of Concord horizon. What do you mean by alarming the citadel[5] at this time of night consecrated to me? Do you think I am ever caught napping at such an hour, and that I have not got lungs and a larynx as well as yourself? *Boo-hoo, boo-hoo, boo-hoo!* It was one of the most thrilling discords I ever heard. And yet, if you had a discriminating ear, there were in it the elements of a concord such as these plains never saw nor heard.

I also heard the whooping[6] of the ice in the pond, my great bed-fellow in that part of Concord, as if it were restless in its bed and would fain turn over, were troubled with flatulency and bad dreams; or I was waked by the cracking of the ground by the frost, as if some one had driven a team against my door, and in the morning would find a crack in the earth a quarter of a mile long and a third of an inch wide.

Sometimes I heard the foxes as they ranged over the snow crust, in moonlight nights, in search of a partridge or other game, barking raggedly and demoniacally like forest dogs, as if laboring with some anxiety, or seeking expression, struggling for light and to be dogs outright and run freely in the streets; for if we take the ages into our account, may there not be a civilization going on among brutes as well as men? They seemed to me to be rudimental, burrowing men, still standing on their defence, awaiting their transformation. Sometimes one came near to my window, attracted by my light, barked a vulpine curse at me, and then retreated.

Usually the red squirrel (*Sciurus Hudsonius*) waked me in the dawn, coursing over the roof and up and down the sides

of the house, as if sent out of the woods for this purpose. In
the course of the winter I threw out half a bushel of ears of
sweet-corn, which had not got ripe, on to the snow crust by
my door, and was amused by watching the motions of the
various animals which were baited by it. In the twilight and
the night the rabbits came regularly and made a hearty meal.
All day long the red squirrels came and went, and afforded
me much entertainment by their manoeuvres. One would approach at first warily through the shrub-oaks, running over
the snow crust by fits and starts like a leaf blown by the wind,
now a few paces this way, with wonderful speed and waste of
energy, making inconceivable haste with his "trotters," as if
it were for a wager, and now as many paces that way, but
never getting on more than half a rod at a time; and then
suddenly pausing with a ludicrous expression and a gratuitous
somerset, as if all the eyes in the universe were fixed on him,
—for all the motions of a squirrel, even in the most solitary
recesses of the forest, imply spectators as much as those of a
dancing girl,—wasting more time in delay and circumspection
than would have sufficed to walk the whole distance,—I
never saw one walk,—and then suddenly, before you could
say Jack Robinson, he would be in the top of a young pitch-
pine, winding up his clock[7] and chiding all imaginary spectators, soliloquizing and talking to all the universe at the
same time,—for no reason that I could ever detect, or he
himself was aware of, I suspect. At length he would reach
the corn, and selecting a suitable ear, brisk[8] about in the
same uncertain trigonometrical way to the top-most stick of
my wood-pile, before my window, where he looked me in
the face, and there sit for hours, supplying himself with a
new ear from time to time, nibbling at first voraciously and
throwing the half-naked cobs about; till at length he grew
more dainty still and played with his food, tasting only the
inside of the kernel, and the ear, which was held balanced
over the stick by one paw, slipped from his careless grasp and
fell to the ground, when he would look over at it with a
ludicrous expression of uncertainty, as if suspecting that it had
life, with a mind not made up whether to get it again, or a
new one, or be off; now thinking of corn, then listening to
hear what was in the wind. So the little impudent fellow
would waste many an ear in a forenoon; till at last, seizing
some longer and plumper one, considerably bigger than him-

self, and skilfully balancing it, he would set out with it to the woods, like a tiger with a buffalo, by the same zig-zag course and frequent pauses, scratching along with it as if it were too heavy for him and falling all the while, making its fall a diagonal between a perpendicular and horizontal, being determined to put it through at any rate;—a singularly frivolous and whimsical fellow;—and so he would get off with it to where he lived, perhaps carry it to the top of a pine tree forty or fifty rods distant, and I would afterwards find the cobs strewn about the woods in various directions.

At length the jays arrive, whose discordant screams were heard long before, as they were warily making their approach an eighth of a mile off, and in a stealthy and sneaking manner they flit from tree to tree, nearer and nearer, and pick up the kernels which the squirrels have dropped. Then, sitting on a pitch-pine bough, they attempt to swallow in their haste a kernel which is too big for their throats and chokes them; and after great labor they disgorge it, and spend an hour in the endeavor to crack it by repeated blows with their bills. They were manifestly thieves, and I had not much respect for them; but the squirrels, though at first shy, went to work as if they were taking what was their own.

Meanwhile also came the chicadees in flocks, which, picking up the crums the squirrels had dropped, flew to the nearest twig, and, placing them under their claws, hammered away at them with their little bills, as if it were an insect in the bark, till they were sufficiently reduced for their slender throats. A little flock of these tit-mice came daily to pick a dinner out of my wood-pile, or the crums at my door, with faint flitting lisping notes, like the tinkling of icicles in the grass, or else with sprightly *day day day*, or more rarely, in spring-like days, a wiry summery *phe-be* from the wood-side. They were so familiar that at length one alighted on an armful of wood which I was carrying in, and pecked at the sticks without fear. I once had a sparrow alight upon my shoulder for a moment while I was hoeing in a village garden, and I felt that I was more distinguished by that circumstance than I should have been by any epaulet I could have worn. The squirrels also grew at last to be quite familiar, and occasionally stepped upon my shoe, when that was the nearest way.

When the ground was not yet quite covered, and again near the end of winter, when the snow was melted on my south

hill-side and about my wood-pile, the partridges came out of
the woods morning and evening to feed there. Whichever side
you walk in the woods the partridge bursts away on whirring
wings, jarring the snow from the dry leaves and twigs on high,
which comes sifting down in the sun-beams like golden dust,
for this brave bird is not to be scared by winter. It is frequently
covered up by drifts, and, it is said, "sometimes plunges from
on wing into the soft snow, where it remains concealed for a
day or two."⁹ I used to start them in the open land also, where
they had come out of the woods at sunset to "bud" the wild
apple-trees. They will come regularly every evening to particular trees, where the cunning sportsman lies in wait for them,
and the distant orchards next the woods suffer thus not a little.
I am glad that the partridge gets fed, at any rate. It is Nature's
own bird which lives on buds and diet-drink.

In dark winter mornings, or in short winter afternoons, I
sometimes heard a pack of hounds threading all the woods with
hounding cry and yelp, unable to resist the instinct of the
chase, and the note of the hunting horn at intervals, proving
that man was in the rear. The woods ring again, and yet no fox
bursts forth on to the open level of the pond, nor following
pack pursuing their Actaeon.¹⁰ And perhaps at evening I see
the hunters returning with a single brush trailing from their
sleigh for a trophy, seeking their inn. They tell me that if the
fox would remain in the bosom of the frozen earth he would be
safe, or if he would run in a straight line away no fox-hound
could overtake him; but, having left his pursuers far behind,
he stops to rest and listen till they come up, and when he
runs he circles round to his old haunts, where the hunters
await him. Sometimes, however, he will run upon a wall many
rods, and then leap off far to one side, and he appears to
know that water will not retain his scent. A hunter told me
that he once saw a fox pursued by hounds burst out on to
Walden when the ice was covered with shallow puddles, run
part way across, and then return to the same shore. Ere long
the hounds arrived, but here they lost the scent. Sometimes
a pack hunting by themselves would pass my door, and circle
round my house, and yelp and hound without regarding me, as
if afflicted by a species of madness, so that nothing could divert
them from the pursuit. Thus they circle until they fall upon
the recent trail of a fox, for a wise hound will forsake every
thing else for this. One day a man¹¹ came to my hut from

Lexington to inquire after his hound that made a large track, and had been hunting for a week by himself. But I fear that he was not the wiser for all I told him, for every time I attempted to answer his questions he interrupted me by asking, "What do you do here?" He had lost a dog, but found a man.

One old hunter who has a dry tongue, who used to come to bathe[12] in Walden once every year when the water was warmest, and at such times looked in upon me, told me, that many years ago he took his gun one afternoon and went out for a cruise in Walden Wood; and as he walked the Wayland[13] road he heard the cry of hounds approaching, and ere long a fox leaped the wall into the road, and as quick as thought leaped the other wall out of the road, and his swift bullet had not touched him. Some way behind came an old hound and her three pups in full pursuit, hunting on their own account, and disappeared again in the woods. Late in the afternoon, as he was resting in the thick woods south of Walden, he heard the voices of the hounds far over toward Fair Haven still pursuing the fox; and on they came, their hounding cry which made all the woods ring sounding nearer and nearer, now from Well-Meadow,[14] now from the Baker Farm. For a long time he stood still and listened to their music, so sweet to a hunter's ear, when suddenly the fox appeared, threading the solemn aisles with an easy coursing pace, whose sound was concealed by a sympathetic rustle of the leaves, swift and still, keeping the ground, leaving his pursuers far behind; and, leaping upon a rock amid the woods, he sat erect and listening, with his back to the hunter. For a moment compassion restrained the latter's arm; but that was a short-lived mood, and as quick as thought can follow thought his piece was levelled, and *whang!*—the fox rolling over the rock lay dead on the ground. The hunter still kept his place and listened to the hounds. Still on they came, and now the near woods resounded through all their aisles with their demoniac cry. At length the old hound burst into view with muzzle to the ground, and snapping the air as if possessed, and ran directly to the rock; but spying the dead fox she suddenly ceased her hounding, as if struck dumb with amazement, and walked round and round him in silence; and one by one her pups arrived, and, like their mother, were sobered into silence by the mystery. Then the hunter came forward and stood in their midst, and the mystery was solved. They waited in silence while he skinned the fox, then followed the brush a while, and at length turned off into the woods again. That evening a Weston[15] Squire came to the Concord hunter's cottage to inquire for his hounds, and told how for a week they had been hunting on their own account from Weston woods. The Concord hunter told him what he knew and offered him the skin; but the other declined it and departed. He did not find his hounds that night, but the next day learned that they had crossed the river and put up at a farm-house for the night, whence, having been well fed, they took their departure early in the morning.

The hunter who told me this could remember one Sam Nutting,[16] who used to hunt bears on Fair Haven Ledges, and exchange their skins for rum in Concord village; who told him, even, that he had seen a moose there. Nutting had a famous fox-hound named Burgoyne,—he pronounced it Bugine,— which my informant used to borrow. In the "Wast Book"[17] of an old trader of this town, who was also a captain, town-clerk, and representative, I find the following entry. Jan. 18th, 1742-3, "John Melven Cr. by 1 Grey Fox 0—2—3;" they are not now found here; and in his leger, Feb. 7th, 1743, Hezekiah Stratton has credit "by ½ a Catt[18] skin 0—1—4½;" of course, a wild-cat, for Stratton was a sergeant in the old French war, and would not have got credit for hunting less noble game. Credit is given for deer skins also, and they were daily sold. One man still preserves the horns of the last deer[19] that was killed in this vicinity, and another has told me the particulars of the hunt in which his uncle was engaged. The hunters were formerly a numerous and merry crew here. I remember well one gaunt Nimrod[20] who would catch up a leaf by the roadside and play a strain on it wilder and more melodious, if my memory serves me, than any hunting horn.

At midnight, when there was a moon, I sometimes met with hounds in my path prowling about the woods, which would skulk out of my way, as if afraid, and stand silent amid the bushes till I had passed.

Squirrels and wild mice disputed for my store of nuts. There were scores of pitch-pines around my house, from one to four inches in diameter, which had been gnawed by mice the previous winter,—a Norwegian winter for them, for the snow lay long and deep, and they were obliged to mix a large proportion of pine bark with their other diet. These trees were alive and apparently flourishing at mid-summer, and many of them had grown a foot, though completely girdled; but after another winter such were without exception dead. It is remarkable that a single mouse should thus be allowed a whole pine tree for its dinner, gnawing round instead of up and down it; but perhaps it is necessary in order to thin these trees, which are wont to grow up densely.

The hares (*Lepus Americanus*) were very familiar. One had her form under my house all winter, separated from me only by the flooring, and she startled me each morning by her hasty departure when I began to stir,—thump, thump, thump, striking her head against the floor timbers in her hurry. They used to come round my door at dusk to nibble the potato parings which I had thrown out, and were so nearly the color of the ground that they could hardly be distinguished when still. Sometimes in the twilight I alternately lost and recovered sight of one sitting motionless under my window. When I opened my door in the evening, off they would go with a squeak and a bounce. Near at hand they only excited my pity. One evening one sat by my door two paces from me, at first trembling with fear, yet unwilling to move; a poor wee thing, lean and bony, with ragged ears and sharp nose, scant tail and slender paws. It looked as if Nature no longer contained the breed of nobler bloods,²¹ but stood on her last toes. Its large eyes appeared young and unhealthy, almost dropsical. I took a step, and lo, away it scud with an elastic spring over the snow crust, straightening its body and its limbs into graceful length, and soon put the forest between me and itself,—the wild free venison, asserting its vigor and the dignity of Nature. Not without reason was its slenderness. Such then was its nature. (*Lepus, levipes,* light-foot, some think.)²²

What is a country without rabbits and partridges? They are among the most simple and indigenous animal products; ancient and venerable families known to antiquity as to modern times; of the very hue and substance of Nature, nearest allied to leaves and to the ground,—and to one another; it is either winged or it is legged. It is hardly as if you had seen a wild creature when a rabbit or a partridge bursts away, only a natural one, as much to be expected as rustling leaves. The partridge and the rabbit are still sure to thrive, like true natives of the soil, whatever revolutions occur. If the forest is cut off, the sprouts and bushes which spring up afford them concealment, and they become more numerous than ever. That must be a poor country indeed that does not support a hare. Our woods teem with them both, and around every swamp may be seen the partridge or rabbit walk, beset with twiggy fences[23] and horse-hair snares, which some cow-boy[24] tends.

XVI

THE POND IN WINTER

AFTER a still winter night I awoke with the impression that some question had been put to me, which I had been endeavoring in vain to answer in my sleep, as what—how—when—where? But there was dawning Nature, in whom all creatures live, looking in at my broad windows with serene and satisfied face, and no question on *her* lips. I awoke to an answered question, to Nature and daylight. The snow lying deep on the earth dotted with young pines, and the very slope of the hill on which my house is placed, seemed to say, Forward! Nature puts on question and answers none which we mortals ask. She has long ago taken her resolution. "O Prince, our eyes contemplate with admiration and transmit to the soul the wonderful and varied spectacle of this universe. The night veils without doubt a part of this glorious creation; but day comes to reveal to us this great work, which extends from earth even into the plains of the ether."[1]

Then to my morning work. First I take an axe and pail and go in search of water, if that be not a dream. After a cold and snowy night it needed a divining rod[2] to find it. Every winter the liquid and trembling surface of the pond, which was so sensitive to every breath, and reflected every light and shadow, becomes solid to the depth of a foot or a foot and a half, so that it will support the heaviest teams, and perchance the snow covers it to an equal depth, and it is not to be distinguished from any level field. Like the marmots[3] in the surrounding hills, it closes its eye-lids and becomes dormant for three months or more. Standing on the snow-covered plain, as if in a pasture amid the hills, I cut my way first through a foot of snow, and then a foot of ice, and open a window under my feet, where, kneeling to drink, I look down into the quiet parlor of the fishes, pervaded by a softened light as through a window of ground glass, with its bright sanded floor the same as in summer; there a perennial waveless serenity reigns as in the amber twilight sky, corresponding to the cool and even temperament

of the inhabitants. Heaven is under our feet as well as over
our heads.

Early in the morning, while all things are crisp with frost,
men come with fishing reels and slender lunch, and let down
their fine lines through the snowy field to take pickerel and
perch; wild men, who instinctively follow other fashions and
trust other authorities than their townsmen, and by their goings
and comings stitch towns together in parts where else they
would be ripped. They sit and eat their luncheon in stout fear-
naughts⁴ on the dry oak leaves on the shore, as wise in natural
lore as the citizen is in artificial. They never consulted with
books, and know and can tell much less than they have done.
The things which they practise are said not yet to be known.
Here is one fishing for pickerel with grown perch for bait. You
look into his pail with wonder as into a summer pond, as if he
kept summer locked up at home, or knew where she had retreated. How, pray, did he get these in mid-winter? O, he got
worms out of rotten logs since the ground froze, and so he
caught them. His life itself passes deeper in Nature than the
studies of the naturalist penetrate; himself a subject for the
naturalist. The latter raises the moss and bark gently with his
knife in search of insects; the former lays open logs to their
core with his axe, and moss and bark fly far and wide. He gets
his living by barking trees. Such a man has some right to fish,
and I love to see Nature carried out in him. The perch swallows
the grub-worm, the pickerel swallows the perch, and the
fisherman swallows the pickerel; and so all the chinks in the
scale of being⁵ are filled.

When I strolled around the pond in misty weather I was
sometimes amused by the primitive mode which some ruder
fisherman had adopted. He would perhaps have placed alder
branches over the narrow holes in the ice, which were four or
five rods apart and an equal distance from the shore, and
having fastened the end of the line to a stick to prevent its
being pulled through, have passed the slack line over a twig of
the alder, a foot or more above the ice, and tied a dry oak leaf
to it, which, being pulled down, would show when he had a
bite. These alders loomed through the mist at regular intervals
as you walked half way round the pond.

Ah, the pickerel of Walden! when I see them lying on the
ice, or in the well which the fisherman cuts in the ice, making a
little hole to admit the water, I am always surprised by their

rare beauty, as if they were fabulous fishes, they are so foreign to the streets, even to the woods, foreign as Arabia to our Concord life. They possess a quite dazzling and transcendent beauty which separates them by a wide interval from the cadaverous cod and haddock whose fame is trumpeted[e] in our streets. They are not green like the pines, nor gray like the stones, nor blue like the sky; but they have, to my eyes, if possible, yet rarer colors, like flowers and precious stones, as if they were the pearls, the animalized *nuclei* or crystals of the Walden water. They, of course, are Walden all over and all through; are themselves small Waldens in the animal kingdom, Waldenses.[7] It is surprising that they are caught here,—that in this deep and capacious spring, far beneath the rattling teams and chaises and tinkling sleighs that travel the Walden road, this great gold and emerald fish swims. I never chanced to see its kind in any market; it would be the cynosure of all eyes there. Easily, with a few convulsive quirks, they give up their watery ghosts, like a mortal translated before his time to the thin air of heaven.

As I was desirous to recover the long lost bottom of Walden Pond, I surveyed it[8] carefully, before the ice broke up, early in '46, with compass and chain and sounding line. There have been many stories told about the bottom, or rather no bottom, of this pond, which certainly had no foundation for themselves. It is remarkable how long men will believe in the bottomlessness of a pond without taking the trouble to sound it. I have visited two such Bottomless Ponds[9] in one walk in this neighborhood. Many have believed that Walden reached quite through to the other side of the globe. Some who have lain flat on the ice for a long time, looking down through the illusive medium, perchance with watery eyes into the bargain, and driven to hasty conclusions by the fear of catching cold in their breasts, have seen vast holes "into which a load of hay might be driven," if there were any body to drive it, the undoubted source of the Styx[10] and entrance to the Infernal Regions from these parts. Others have gone down from the village with a "fifty-six"[11] and a wagon load of inch rope, but yet have failed to find any bottom; for while the "fifty-six" was resting by the way, they were paying out the rope in the vain attempt to fathom their truly immeasurable capacity for marvellousness. But I can assure my readers that Walden has a reasonably tight

bottom at a not unreasonable, though at an unusual, depth. I
fathomed it easily with a cod-line and a stone weighing about
a pound and a half, and could tell accurately when the stone
left the bottom, by having to pull so much harder before the
water got underneath to help me. The greatest depth was
exactly one hundred and two feet; to which may be added the
five feet which it has risen since, making one hundred and
seven. This is a remarkable depth for so small an area; yet not
an inch of it can be spared by the imagination. What if all
ponds were shallow? Would it not react on the minds of men?
I am thankful that this pond was made deep and pure for a
symbol. While men believe in the infinite some ponds will be
thought to be bottomless.

A factory owner, hearing what depth I had found, thought
that it could not be true, for, judging from his acquaintance
with dams, sand would not lie at so steep an angle. But the
deepest ponds are not so deep in proportion to their area as
most suppose, and, if drained, would not leave very remarkable
valleys. They are not like cups between the hills; for this one,
which is so unusually deep for its area, appears in a vertical
section through its centre not deeper than a shallow plate. Most
ponds, emptied, would leave a meadow no more hollow than
we frequently see. William Gilpin, who is so admirable in all
that relates to landscapes, and usually so correct, standing at
the head of Loch Fyne, in Scotland, which he describes as "a
bay of salt water, sixty or seventy fathoms deep, four miles
in breadth," and about fifty miles long, surrounded by mountains, observes, "If we could have seen it immediately after
the diluvian crash, or whatever convulsion of Nature occasioned it, before the waters gushed in, what a horrid chasm it
must have appeared!"[12]

> So high as heaved the tumid hills, so low
> Down sunk a hollow bottom, broad, and deep,
> Capacious bed of waters——."[13]

But if, using the shortest diameter of Loch Fyne, we apply
these proportions to Walden, which, as we have seen, appears
already in a vertical section only like a shallow plate, it will
appear four times as shallow. So much for the *increased*
horrors of the chasm of Loch Fyne when emptied. No doubt
many a smiling valley with its stretching cornfields occupies

exactly such a "horrid chasm," from which the waters have
receded, though it requires the insight and the far sight of
the geologist to convince the unsuspecting inhabitants of this
fact. Often an inquisitive eye may detect the shores of a primitive lake in the low horizon hills, and no subsequent elevation[13a] of the plain have been necessary to conceal their history.
But it is easiest, as they who work on the highways know, to
find the hollows by the puddles after a shower. The amount of
it is, the imagination, give it the least license, dives deeper and
soars higher than Nature goes. So, probably, the depth of the
ocean will be found to be very inconsiderable compared with
its breadth.

As I sounded through the ice I could determine the shape of
the bottom with greater accuracy than is possible in surveying
harbors which do not freeze over, and I was surprised at its
general regularity. In the deepest part there are several acres
more level than almost any field which is exposed to the sun,
wind and plough. In one instance, on a line arbitrarily chosen,
the depth did not vary more than one foot in thirty rods; and
generally, near the middle, I could calculate the variation for
each one hundred feet in any direction beforehand within three
or four inches. Some are accustomed to speak of deep and
dangerous holes even in quiet sandy ponds like this, but the
effect of water under these circumstances is to level all in-
equalities. The regularity of the bottom and its conformity to
the shores and the range of the neighboring hills were so perfect that a distant promontory betrayed itself in the soundings
quite across the pond, and its direction could be determined by
observing the opposite shore. Cape becomes bar, and plain
shoal, and valley and gorge deep water and channel.

When I had mapped the pond[14] by the scale of ten rods to
an inch, and put down the soundings, more than a hundred in
all, I observed this remarkable coincidence. Having noticed
that the number indicating the greatest depth was apparently
in the centre of the map, I laid a rule on the map lengthwise,
and then breadthwise, and found, to my surprise, that the line
of greatest length intersected the line of greatest breadth
exactly at the point of greatest depth, notwithstanding that the
middle is so nearly level, the outline of the pond far from
regular, and the extreme length and breadth were got by
measuring into the coves; and I said to myself, Who knows
but this hint would conduct to the deepest part of the ocean

as well as of a pond or puddle? Is not this the rule also for the height of mountains, regarded as the opposite of valleys? We know that a hill is not highest at its narrowest part.

Of five coves, three, or all which had been sounded, were observed to have a bar quite across their mouths and deeper water within, so that the bay tended to be an expansion of water within the land not only horizontally but vertically, and to form a basin or independent pond, the direction of the two capes showing the course of the bar. Every harbor on the sea-coast, also, has its bar at its entrance. In proportion as the mouth of the cove was wider compared with its length, the water over the bar was deeper compared with that in the basin. Given, then, the length and breadth of the cove, and the char-acter of the surrounding shore, and you have almost elements enough to make out a formula for all cases.

In order to see how nearly I could guess, with this experi-ence, at the deepest point in a pond, by observing the outlines of its surface and the character of its shores alone, I made a plan of White Pond, which contains about forty-one acres, and, like this, has no island in it, nor any visible inlet or outlet; and as the line of greatest breadth fell very near the line of least breadth, where two opposite capes approached each other and two opposite bays receded, I ventured to mark a point a short distance from the latter line, but still on the line of greatest length, as the deepest. The deepest part was found to be within one hundred feet of this, still farther in the direction to which I had inclined, and was only one foot deeper, namely, sixty feet. Of course, a stream running through, or an island in the pond, would make the problem much more complicated.

If we knew all the laws of Nature, we should need only one fact, or the description of one actual phenomenon, to infer all the particular results at that point. Now we know only a few laws, and our result is vitiated, not, of course, by any confusion or irregularity in Nature, but by our ignorance of essential ele-ments in the calculation. Our notions of law and harmony are commonly confined to those instances which we detect; but the harmony which results from a far greater number of seemingly conflicting, but really concurring, laws, which we have not detected, is still more wonderful. The particular laws are as our points of view, as, to the traveller, a mountain outline varies with every step, and it has an infinite number of profiles, though absolutely but one form. Even when cleft or bored through it is not comprehended in its entirety.

What I have observed of the pond is no less true in ethics. It is the law of average. Such a rule of the two diameters not only guides us toward the sun in the system and the heart in man, but draw lines through the length and breadth of the aggregate of a man's particular daily behaviors and waves of life into his coves and inlets, and where they intersect will be the height or depth of his character. Perhaps we need only to know how his shores trend and his adjacent country or circumstances, to infer his depth and concealed bottom. If he is surrounded by mountainous circumstances, an Achillean shore,[15] whose peaks overshadow and are reflected in his bosom, they suggest a corresponding depth in him. But a low and smooth shore proves him shallow on that side. In our bodies, a bold projecting brow falls off to and indicates a corresponding depth of thought. Also there is a bar across the entrance of our every cove, or particular inclination; each is our harbor for a season, in which we are detained and partially land-locked. These inclinations are not whimsical usually, but their form, size, and direction are determined by the promontories of the shore, the ancient axes of elevation. When this bar is gradually increased by storms, tides, or currents, or there is a subsidence of the waters, so that it reaches to the surface, that which was at first but an inclination in the shore in which a thought was harbored becomes an individual lake, cut off from the ocean, wherein the thought secures its own conditions, changes, perhaps, from salt to fresh, becomes a sweet sea, dead sea, or a marsh. At the advent of each individual into this life, may we not suppose that such a bar has risen to the surface somewhere? It is true, we are such poor navigators that our thoughts, for the most part, stand off and on upon a harborless coast, are conversant only with the bights of the bays of poesy, or steer for the public ports of entry, and go into the dry docks of science, where[16] they merely refit for this world, and no natural currents concur to individualize them.

As for the inlet or outlet of Walden, I have not discovered any but rain and snow and evaporation, though perhaps, with a thermometer and a line, such places may be found, for where the water flows into the pond it will probably be coldest in summer and warmest in winter. When the ice-men[17] were at work here in '46-7, the cakes sent to the shore were one day rejected by those who were stacking them up there, not being thick enough to lie side by side with the rest; and the cutters thus discovered that the ice over a small space was two or three inches thinner than elsewhere, which made them think that there was an inlet there. They also showed me in another place what they thought was a "leach hole," through which the pond leaked out under a hill into a neighboring meadow, pushing me out on a cake of ice to see it. It was a small cavity under ten feet of water; but I think that I can warrant the pond not to need soldering till they find a worse leak than that. One has suggested, that if such a "leach hole" should be found, its connection with the meadow, if any existed, might be proved by conveying some colored powder or sawdust to the mouth of the hole, and then putting a strainer over the spring in the meadow, which would catch some of the particles carried through by the current.

While I was surveying, the ice, which was sixteen inches thick, undulated under a slight wind like water. It is well known that a level cannot be used on ice. At one rod from the shore its greatest fluctuation, when observed by means of a level on land directed toward a graduated staff on the ice, was three quarters of an inch, though the ice appeared firmly attached to the shore. It was probably greater in the middle. Who knows but if our instruments were delicate enough we might detect an undulation in the crust of the earth? When two legs of my level were on the shore and the third on the ice, and the sights were directed over the latter, a rise or fall of the ice of an almost infinitesimal amount made a difference of several feet on a tree across the pond. When I began to cut holes for sounding, there were three or four inches of water on the ice under a deep snow which had sunk it thus far; but the water began immediately to run into these holes, and continued to run for two days in deep streams, which wore away the ice on every side, and contributed essentially, if not mainly, to dry the surface of the pond; for, as the water ran in, it raised and floated the ice. This was somewhat like cutting a hole in the bottom of a ship to let the water out. When such holes freeze, and a rain succeeds, and finally a new freezing forms a fresh smooth ice over all, it is beautifully mottled internally by dark figures, shaped somewhat like a spider's web, what you may call ice rosettes, produced by the channels worn by the water

flowing from all sides to a centre. Sometimes, also, when the
ice was covered with shallow puddles, I saw a double shadow
of myself, one standing on the head of the other, one on the
ice, the other on the trees or hill-side.

While yet it is cold January, and snow and ice are thick and
solid, the prudent landlord comes from the village to get ice
to cool his summer drink; impressively, even pathetically wise,
to foresee the heat and thirst of July now in January,—wearing
a thick coat and mittens! when so many things are not provided
for. It may be that he lays up no treasures[18] in this world which
will cool his summer drink in the next. He cuts and saws the
solid pond, unroofs the house of fishes, and carts off their very
element and air, held fast by chains and stakes like corded
wood, through the favoring winter air, to wintry cellars, to
underlie the summer there. It looks like solidified azure, as, far
off, it is drawn through the streets. These ice-cutters are a
merry race, full of jest and sport, and when I went among them
they were wont to invite me to saw pit-fashion with them, I
standing underneath.

In the winter of '46-7 there came a hundred men of Hyper-
borean[19] extraction swoop down on to our pond one morning,
with many car-loads of ungainly-looking farming tools, sleds,
ploughs, drill-barrows, turf-knives, spades, saws, rakes, and
each man was armed with a double-pointed pike-staff, such as
is not described in the New-England Farmer[20] or the Cultivator. I did not know whether they had come to sow a crop of
winter rye, or some other kind of grain recently introduced
from Iceland. As I saw no manure, I judged that they meant to
skim the land, as I had done, thinking the soil was deep and
had lain fallow long enough. They said that a gentleman
farmer,[21] who was behind the scenes, wanted to double his
money, which, as I understood, amounted to half a million already; but in order to cover each one of his dollars with another, he took off the only coat, ay, the skin itself, of Walden
Pond in the midst of a hard winter. They went to work at
once, ploughing, harrowing, rolling, furrowing, in admirable
order, as if they were bent on making this a model farm; but
when I was looking sharp to see what kind of seed they
dropped into the furrow, a gang of fellows by my side suddenly
began to hook up the virgin mould itself, with a peculiar jerk,
clean down to the sand, or rather water,—for it was a very
springy soil,—indeed all the *terra firma* there was,—and haul

it away on sleds, and then I guessed that they must be cutting peat in a bog. So they came and went every day, with a peculiar shriek from the locomotive, from and to some point of the polar regions, as it seemed to me, like a flock of arctic snow-birds. But sometimes Squaw Walden had her revenge, and a hired man, walking behind his team, slipped through a crack in the ground down toward Tartarus,[22] and he who was so brave before suddenly became but the ninth part[23] of a man, almost gave up his animal heat, and was glad to take refuge in my house, and acknowledged that there was some virtue in a stove; or sometimes the frozen soil took a piece of steel out of a ploughshare, or a plough got set in the furrow and had to be cut out.

To speak literally, a hundred Irishmen, with Yankee over-seers, came from Cambridge every day to get out the ice. They divided it into cakes by methods too well known to require description, and these, being sledded to the shore, were rapidly hauled off on to an ice platform, and raised by grappling irons and block and tackle, worked by horses, on to a stack, as surely as so many barrels of flour, and there placed evenly side by side, and row upon row, as if they formed the solid base of an obelisk designed to pierce the clouds. They told me that in a good day they could get out a thousand tons, which was the yield of about one acre. Deep ruts and "cradle holes" were worn in the ice, as on *terra firma*, by the passage of the sleds over the same track, and the horses invariably ate their oats out of cakes of ice hollowed out like buckets. They stacked up the cakes thus in the open air in a pile thirty-five feet high on one side and six or seven rods square, putting hay between the out-side layers to exclude the air; for when the wind, though never so cold, finds a passage through, it will wear large cavities, leaving slight supports or studs only here and there, and finally topple it down. At first it looked like a vast blue fort or Valhalla;[24] but when they began to tuck the coarse meadow hay into the crevices, and this became covered with rime and icicles, it looked like a venerable moss-grown and hoary ruin, built of azure-tinted marble, the abode of Winter, that old man we see in the almanac,[25]—his shanty, as if he had a design to estivate with us. They calculated that not twenty-five per cent. of this would reach its destination, and that two or three per cent. would be wasted in the cars. However, a still greater part of this heap had a different destiny from what was intended; for, either because the ice was found not to keep so well as was expected, containing more air than usual, or for some other reason, it never got to market. This heap, made in the winter of '46-7 and estimated to contain ten thousand tons, was finally covered with hay and boards; and though it was unroofed the following July, and a part of it carried off, the rest remaining exposed to the sun, it stood over that summer and the next winter, and was not quite melted till September 1848. Thus the pond recovered the greater part.

Like the water, the Walden ice, seen near at hand, has a green tint, but at a distance is beautifully blue, and you can easily tell it from the white ice of the river or the merely greenish ice of some ponds, a quarter of a mile off. Sometimes one of those great cakes slips from the ice-man's sled into the village street, and lies there for a week like a great emerald, an object of interest to all passers. I have noticed that a portion of Walden which in the state of water was green will often, when frozen, appear from the same point of view blue. So the hollows about this pond will, sometimes, in the winter, be filled with a greenish water somewhat like its own, but the next day will have frozen blue. Perhaps the blue color of water and ice is due to the light and air they contain, and the most transparent is the bluest. Ice is an interesting subject for contemplation. They told me that they had some in the ice-house at Fresh Pond[26] five years old which was as good as ever. Why is it that a bucket of water soon becomes putrid, but frozen remains sweet forever? It is commonly said that this is the difference between the affections and the intellect.

Thus for sixteen days I saw from my window a hundred men at work like busy husbandmen, with teams and horses and apparently all the implements of farming, such a picture as we see on the first page of the almanac;[27] and as often as I looked out I was reminded of the fable[28] of the lark and the reapers, or the parable[29] of the sower, and the like; and now they are all gone, and in thirty days more, probably, I shall look for the same window on the pure sea-green Walden water there, reflecting the clouds and the trees, and sending up its evaporations in solitude, and no traces will appear that a man has ever stood there. Perhaps I shall hear a solitary loon laugh as he dives and plumes himself, or shall see a lonely fisher in his boat, like a floating leaf, beholding his form reflected in the waves, where lately a hundred men securely labored.

Thus[30] it appears that the sweltering inhabitants of Charleston and New Orleans, of Madras and Bombay and Calcutta,[31] drink at my well. In the morning I bathe my intellect in the stupendous and cosmogonal philosophy of the Bhagvat Geeta,[32] since whose composition years of the gods have elapsed, and in comparison with which our modern world and its literature seem puny and trivial; and I doubt if that philosophy is not to be referred to a previous state of existence, so remote is its sublimity from our conceptions. I lay down the book and go to my well for water, and lo! there I meet the servant of the Bramin, priest of Brahma and Vishnu and Indra, who still sits in his temple on the Ganges reading the Vedas,[33] or dwells at the root of a tree with his crust and water jug. I meet his servant come to draw water for his master, and our buckets as it were grate together in the same well. The pure Walden water is mingled with the sacred water of the Ganges. With favoring winds it is wafted past the site of the fabulous islands of Atlantis and the Hesperides,[34] makes the periplus[35] of Hanno, and, floating by Ternate and Tidore[36] and the mouth of the Persian Gulf, melts in the tropic gales of the Indian seas, and is landed in ports of which Alexander[37] only heard the names.

[XVII]

SPRING

THE opening[1] of large tracts by the ice-cutters commonly causes a pond to break up earlier; for the water, agitated by the wind, even in cold weather wears away the surrounding ice. But such was not the effect on Walden that year, for she had soon got a thick new garment to take the place of the old. This pond never breaks up so soon as the others in this neighborhood, on account both of its greater depth and its having no stream passing through it to melt or wear away the ice. I never knew it to open in the course of a winter, not excepting that of '52-3, which gave the ponds so severe a trial. It commonly opens about the first of April, a week or ten days later than Flints' Pond and Fair Haven, beginning to melt on the north side and in the shallower parts where it began to freeze. It indicates better than any water hereabouts the absolute progress of the season, being least affected by transient changes of temperature. A severe cold of a few days' duration in March may very much retard the opening of the former ponds, while the temperature of Walden increases almost uninterruptedly. A thermometer[2] thrust into the middle of Walden on the 6th of March, 1847, stood at 32°, or freezing point; near the shore at 33°; in the middle of Flints' Pond, the same day, at 32½°; at a dozen rods from the shore, in shallow water, under ice a foot thick, at 36°. This difference of three and a half degrees between the temperature of the deep water and the shallow in the latter pond, and the fact that a great proportion of it is comparatively shallow, show why it should break up so much sooner than Walden. The ice in the shallowest part was at this time several inches thinner than in the middle. In mid-winter the middle had been the warmest and the ice thinnest there. So, also, every one who has waded about the shores of a pond in summer must have perceived how much warmer the water is close to the shore, where only three or four inches deep, than a little distance out, and on the surface where it is deep, than near the bottom. In spring the sun not only exerts an influence through the increased temperature of the air and earth, but its heat passes through ice a foot or more thick, and is reflected from the bottom in shallow water, and so also warms the water and melts the under side of the ice, at the same time that it is melting it more directly above, making it uneven, and causing the air bubbles which it contains to extend themselves upward and downward until it is completely honey-combed, and at last disappears suddenly in a single spring rain. Ice has its grain as well as wood, and when a cake begins to rot or "comb," that is, assume the appearance of honey-comb, whatever may be its position, the air cells are at right angles with what was the water surface. Where there is a rock or a log rising near to the surface the ice over it is much thinner, and is frequently quite dissolved by this reflected heat; and I have been told that in the experiment[3] at Cambridge to freeze water in a shallow wooden pond, though the cold air circulated underneath, and so had access to both sides, the reflection of the sun from the bottom more than counterbalanced this advantage. When a warm rain in the middle of the winter melts off the snow-ice from Walden, and leaves a hard dark or transparent ice on the middle, there will be a strip of rotten though thicker white ice, a rod or more wide, about the shores, created by this reflected heat. Also, as I have said, the bubbles themselves within the ice operate as burning glasses to melt the ice beneath.

The phenomena of the year take place every day in a pond on a small scale. Every morning, generally speaking, the shallow water is being warmed more rapidly than the deep, though it may not be made so warm after all, and every evening it is being cooled more rapidly until the morning. The day is an epitome[4] of the year. The night is the winter, the morning and evening are the spring and fall, and the noon is the summer. The cracking and booming of the ice indicate a change of temperature. One pleasant morning after a cold night, February 24th, 1850, having gone to Flints' Pond to spend the day, I noticed with surprise, that when I struck the ice with the head of my axe, it resounded like a gong for many rods around, or as if I had struck on a tight drum-head. The pond began to boom about an hour after sunrise, when it felt the influence of the sun's rays slanted upon it from over the hills; it stretched itself and yawned like a waking man with a gradually increasing tumult, which was kept up three or four hours. It took a short siesta at noon, and boomed once more toward night, as the sun was withdrawing his influence. In the right stage of the weather a pond fires its evening gun with great regularity. But in the middle of the day, being full of cracks, and the air also being less elastic, it had completely lost its resonance, and probably fishes and muskrats could not then have been stunned by a blow on it. The fishermen say that the "thundering of the pond" scares the fishes and prevents their biting. The pond does not thunder every evening, and I cannot tell surely when to expect its thundering; but though I may perceive no difference in the weather, it does. Who would have suspected so large and cold and thick-skinned a thing to be so sensitive? Yet it has its law to which it thunders obedience when it should as surely as the buds expand in the spring. The earth is all alive and covered with papillae. The largest pond is as sensitive to atmospheric changes as the globule of mercury in its tube.

One attraction in coming to the woods to live was that I should have leisure and opportunity to see the spring come in. The ice in the pond at length begins to be honey-combed, and I can set my heel in it as I walk. Fogs and rains and warmer suns are gradually melting the snow; the days have grown sensibly longer; and I see how I shall get through the winter without adding to my wood-pile, for large fires are no longer necessary. I am on the alert for the first signs of spring, to hear the chance note of some arriving bird, or the striped squirrel's chirp, for his stores must be now nearly exhausted, or see the woodchuck venture out of his winter quarters. On the 13th of March, after I had heard the bluebird, song-sparrow, and red-wing, the ice was still nearly a foot thick. As the weather grew warmer it was not sensibly worn away by the water, nor broken up and floated off as in rivers, but, though it was completely melted for half a rod in width about the shore, the middle was merely honey-combed and saturated with water, so that you could put your foot through it when six inches thick; but by the next day, evening, perhaps, after a warm rain followed by fog, it would have wholly disappeared, all gone off with the fog, spirited away. One year I went across the middle only five days before it disappeared entirely. In 1845 Walden was first completely open on the

1st of April; in '46, the 25th of March; in '47, the 8th of April; in '51, the 28th of March; in '52, the 18th of April; in '53, the 23d of March; in '54,⁵ about the 7th of April.

Every incident connected with the breaking up of the rivers and ponds and the settling of the weather is particularly interesting to us who live in a climate of so great extremes. When the warmer days come, they who dwell near the river hear the ice crack at night with a startling whoop as loud as artillery, as if its icy fetters were rent from end to end, and within a few days see it rapidly going out. So the alligator comes out of the mud with quakings of the earth. One old man, who has been a close observer of Nature, and seems as thoroughly wise in regard to all her operations as if she had been put upon the stocks when he was a boy, and he had helped to lay her keel,—who has come to his growth, and can hardly acquire more of natural lore if he should live to the age of Methuselah,⁶—told me, and I was surprised to hear him express wonder at any of Nature's operations, for I thought that there were no secrets between them, that one spring day he took his gun and boat, and thought that he would have a little sport with the ducks. There was ice still on the meadows, but it was all gone out of the river, and he dropped down without obstruction from Sudbury,⁷ where he lived, to Fair Haven Pond, which he found, unexpectedly, covered for the most part with a firm field of ice. It was a warm day, and he was surprised to see so great a body of ice remaining. Not seeing any ducks, he hid his boat on the north or back side of an island in the pond, and then concealed himself in the bushes on the south side, to await them. The ice was melted for three or four rods from the shore, and there was a smooth and warm sheet of water, with a muddy bottom, such as the ducks love, within, and he thought it likely that some would be along pretty soon. After he had lain still there about an hour he heard a low and seemingly very distant sound, but singularly grand and impressive, unlike any thing he had ever heard, gradually swelling and increasing as if it would have a universal and memorable ending, a sullen rush and roar, which seemed to him all at once like the sound of a vast body of fowl coming in to settle there, and, seizing his gun, he started up in haste and excited; but he found, to his surprise, that the whole body of the ice had started while he lay there, and drifted in to the shore, and the sound he had heard was made by its edge grating on the shore,—at first gently nibbled and crumbled off, but at length heaving up and scattering its wrecks along the island to a considerable height before it came to a stand still.

At length the sun's rays have attained the right angle, and warm winds blow up mist and rain and melt the snow banks, and the sun dispersing the mist smiles on a checkered landscape of russet and white smoking with incense, through which the traveller picks his way from islet to islet, cheered by the music of a thousand tinkling rills and rivulets whose veins are filled with the blood of winter which they are bearing off.

Few phenomena gave me more delight than to observe the forms which thawing sand and clay assume in flowing down the sides of a deep cut on the railroad through which I passed on my way to the village, a phenomenon not very common on so large a scale, though the number of freshly exposed banks of the right material must have been greatly multiplied since railroads were invented. The material was sand of every degree of fineness and of various rich colors, commonly mixed with a little clay. When the frost comes out in the spring, and even in a thawing day in the winter, the sand begins to flow down the slopes like lava, sometimes bursting out through the snow and overflowing it where no sand was to be seen before. Innumerable little streams overlap and interlace one with another, exhibiting a sort of hybrid product, which obeys half way the law of currents, and half way that of vegetation. As it flows it takes the forms of sappy leaves or vines, making heaps of pulpy sprays a foot or more in depth, and resembling, as you look down on them, the laciniated, lobed and imbricated thalluses of some lichens; or you are reminded of coral, of leopards' paws or birds' feet, of brains or lungs or bowels, and excrements of all kinds. It is a truly *grotesque* vegetation, whose forms and color we see imitated in bronze, a sort of architectural foliage more ancient and typical than acanthus, chiccory, ivy, vine,⁸ or any vegetable leaves; destined perhaps, under some circumstances, to become a puzzle to future geologists. The whole cut impressed me as if it were a cave with its stalactites laid open to the light. The various shades of the sand are singularly rich and agreeable, embracing the different iron colors, brown, gray, yellowish, and reddish. When the flowing mass reaches the drain at the

foot of the bank it spreads out flatter into *strands*, the separate streams losing their semi-cylindrical form and gradually
becoming more flat and broad, running together as they are
more moist, till they form an almost flat *sand*, still variously
and beautifully shaded, but in which you can trace the original forms of vegetation; till at length, in the water itself, they
are converted into *banks*, like those formed off the mouths
of rivers, and the forms of vegetation are lost in the ripple
marks on the bottom.

The whole bank, which is from twenty to forty feet high,
is sometimes overlaid with a mass of this kind of foliage, or
sandy rupture, for a quarter of a mile on one or both sides,
the produce of one spring day. What makes this sand foliage
remarkable is its springing into existence thus suddenly. When
I see on the one side the inert bank,—for the sun acts on one
side first,—and on the other this luxuriant foliage, the creation
of an hour, I am affected as if in a peculiar sense I stood in
the laboratory of the Artist who made the world and me,—
had come to where he was still at work, sporting on this bank,
and with excess of energy strewing his fresh designs about. I
feel as if I were nearer to the vitals of the globe, for this sandy
overflow is something such a foliaceous mass as the vitals of
the animal body. You find thus in the very sands an anticipa-
tion of the vegetable leaf. No wonder that the earth expresses
itself outwardly in leaves, it so labors with the idea inwardly.
The atoms have already learned this law, and are pregnant by
it. The overhanging leaf sees here its prototype. *Internally*,
whether in the globe or animal body, it is a moist thick *lobe*,
a word especially applicable to the liver and lungs and the
leaves of fat, (λείβω, *labor, lapsus*, to flow or slip downward,
a lapsing; λοβός, *globus*, lobe, globe; also lap, flap, and
many other words,) *externally* a dry thin *leaf*, even as the *f*
and *v* are a pressed and dried *b*. The radicals of lobe are *lb*,
the soft mass of the *b* (single lobed, or B, double lobed,)
with a liquid *l* behind it pressing it forward. In globe, *glb*,
the guttural *g* adds to the meaning the capacity of the throat.
The feathers and wings of birds are still drier and thinner
leaves. Thus, also, you pass from the lumpish grub in the
earth to the airy and fluttering butterfly. The very globe continually transcends and translates itself, and becomes winged
in its orbit. Even ice begins with delicate crystal leaves, as
if it had flowed into moulds which the fronds of water plants

have impressed on the watery mirror. The whole tree itself
is but one leaf, and rivers are still vaster leaves whose pulp is
intervening earth, and towns and cities are the ova of insects
in their axils.

When the sun withdraws the sand ceases to flow, but in the
morning the streams will start once more and branch and
branch again into a myriad of others. You here see perchance
how blood vessels are formed. If you look closely you observe
that first there pushes forward from the thawing mass a
stream of softened sand with a drop-like point, like the ball
of the finger, feeling its way slowly and blindly downward,
until at last with more heat and moisture, as the sun gets
higher, the most fluid portion, in its effort to obey the law to
which the most inert also yields, separates from the latter and
forms for itself a meandering channel or artery within that,
in which is seen a little silvery stream glancing like lightning
from one stage of pulpy leaves or branches to another, and
ever and anon swallowed up in the sand. It is wonderful how
rapidly yet perfectly the sand organizes itself as it flows, using
the best material its mass affords to form the sharp edges of
its channel. Such are the sources of rivers. In the silicious
matter which the water deposits is perhaps the bony system,
and in the still finer soil and organic matter the fleshy fibre
or cellular tissue. What is man but a mass of thawing clay?[10]
The ball of the human finger is but a drop congealed. The
fingers and toes flow to their extent from the thawing mass of
the body. Who knows what the human body would expand
and flow out to under a more genial heaven? Is not the hand
a spreading *palm* leaf with its lobes and veins? The ear may
be regarded, fancifully, as a lichen, *umbilicaria*, on the side
of the head, with its lobe or drop. The lip—*labium*, from
labor (?)—laps or lapses from the sides of the cavernous
mouth. The nose is a manifest congealed drop or stalactite.
The chin is a still larger drop, the confluent dripping of the
face. The cheeks are a slide from the brows into the valley
of the face, opposed and diffused by the cheek bones. Each
rounded lobe of the vegetable leaf, too, is a thick and now
loitering drop, larger or smaller; the lobes are the fingers of
the leaf; and as many lobes as it has, in so many directions it
tends to flow, and more heat or other genial influences would
have caused it to flow yet farther.

Thus it seemed that this one hillside illustrated the prin-

ciple of all the operations of Nature. The Maker of this earth
but patented a leaf. What Champollion[11] will decipher this
hieroglyphic for us, that we may turn over a new leaf at last?
This phenomenon is more exhilarating to me than the luxuriance and fertility of vineyards. True, it is somewhat ex-
crementitious in its character, and there is no end to the heaps
of liver, lights and bowels, as if the globe were turned wrong
side outward; but this suggests at least that Nature has some
bowels,[12] and there again is mother of humanity. This is the
frost coming out of the ground; this is Spring. It precedes the
green and flowery spring, as mythology precedes regular
poetry. I know of nothing more purgative of winter fumes and
indigestions. It convinces me that Earth is still in her swad-
dling clothes, and stretches forth baby fingers on every side.
Fresh curls spring from the baldest brow. There is nothing
inorganic. These foliaceous heaps lie along the bank like the
slag of a furnace, showing that Nature is "in full blast" within.
The earth is not a mere fragment of dead history, stratum[13]
upon stratum like the leaves of a book, to be studied by geologists and antiquaries chiefly, but living poetry like the leaves
of a tree, which precede flowers and fruit,—not a fossil earth,
but a living earth; compared with whose great central life all
animal and vegetable life is merely parasitic. Its throes will
heave our exuviae from their graves. You may melt your
metals and cast them into the most beautiful moulds you can;
they will never excite me like the forms which this molten
earth flows out into. And not only it, but the institutions upon
it, are plastic like clay[14] in the hands of the potter.

Ere long, not only on these banks, but on every hill and
plain and in every hollow, the frost comes out of the ground
like a dormant quadruped from its burrow, and seeks the
sea with music, or migrates to other climes in clouds. Thaw
with his gentle persuasion is more powerful than Thor[15] with
his hammer. The one melts, the other but breaks in pieces.

When the ground was partially bare of snow, and a few
warm days had dried its surface somewhat, it was pleasant to
compare the first tender signs of the infant year just peeping
forth with the stately beauty of the withered vegetation which
had withstood the winter,—life-everlasting, golden-rods, pin-
weeds, and graceful wild grasses, more obvious and interesting frequently than in summer even, as if their beauty was

not ripe till then; even cotton-grass, cat-tails, mulleins, johnswort, hard-hack, meadow-sweet, and other strong stemmed
plants, those unexhausted granaries which entertain the earliest birds,—decent weeds, at least, which widowed Nature
wears. I am particularly attracted by the arching and sheaf-
like top of the wool-grass; it brings back the summer to our
winter memories, and is among the forms which art loves to
copy, and which, in the vegetable kingdom, have the same
relation to types already in the mind of man that astronomy
has. It is an antique style older than Greek or Egyptian. Many
of the phenomena of Winter are suggestive of an inexpressible
tenderness and fragile delicacy. We are accustomed to hear
this king described as a rude and boisterous tyrant; but with
the gentleness of a lover he adorns the tresses of Summer.

At the approach of spring the red-squirrels got under my
house, two at a time, directly under my feet as I sat reading
or writing, and kept up the queerest chuckling and chirrup-
ing and vocal pirouetting and gurgling sounds that ever were
heard; and when I stamped they only chirruped the louder,
as if past all fear and respect in their mad pranks, defying
humanity to stop them. No you don't—chickaree—chickaree.
They were wholly deaf to my arguments, or failed to perceive
their force, and fell into a strain of invective that was irresistible.

The first sparrow of spring! The year beginning with younger hope than ever! The faint silvery warblings heard over the
partially bare and moist fields from the blue-bird, the song-
sparrow, and the red-wing, as if the last flakes of winter
tinkled as they fell! What at such a time are histories, chro-
nologies, traditions, and all written revelations? The brooks
sing carols and glees to the spring. The marsh-hawk sailing
low over the meadow is already seeking the first slimy life
that awakes. The sinking sound of melting snow is heard in
all dells, and the ice dissolves apace in the ponds. The grass
flames up on the hillsides like a spring fire,—"et primitus
oritur herba imbribus primoribus evocata,"[16]—as if the earth
sent forth an inward heat to greet the returning sun; not yellow but green is the color of its flame;—the symbol of perpetual youth, the grass-blade, like a long green ribbon, streams
from the sod into the summer, checked indeed by the frost,
but anon pushing on again, lifting its spear of last year's hay
with the fresh life below. It grows as steadily as the rill oozes

out of the ground. It is almost identical with that, for in the growing days of June, when the rills are dry, the grass blades are their channels, and from year to year the herds drink at this perennial green stream, and the mower draws from it betimes their winter supply. So our human life but dies down to its root, and still puts forth its green blade to eternity.

Walden is melting apace. There is a canal two rods wide along the northerly and westerly sides, and wider still at the east end. A great field of ice has cracked off from the main body. I hear a song-sparrow singing from the bushes on the shore,—*olit, olit, olit,*—*chip, chip, chip, che char,*—*che wiss, wiss, wiss.* He too is helping to crack it. How handsome the great sweeping curves in the edge of the ice, answering somewhat to those of the shore, but more regular! It is unusually hard, owing to the recent severe but transient cold, and all watered or waved like a palace floor. But the wind slides eastward over its opaque surface in vain, till it reaches the living surface beyond. It is glorious to behold this ribbon of water sparkling in the sun, the bare face of the pond full of glee and youth, as if it spoke the joy of the fishes within it, and of the sands on its shore,—a silvery sheen as from the scales of a *leuciscus,*[17] as it were all one active fish. Such is the contrast between winter and spring. Walden was dead and is alive again.[18] But this spring it broke up more steadily, as I have said.

The change from storm and winter to serene and mild weather, from dark and sluggish hours to bright and elastic ones, is a memorable crisis which all things proclaim. It is seemingly instantaneous at last. Suddenly an influx of light filled my house, though the evening was at hand, and the clouds of winter still overhung it, and the eaves were dripping with sleety rain. I looked out the window, and lo! where yesterday was cold gray ice there lay the transparent pond already calm and full of hope as in a summer evening, reflecting a summer evening sky in its bosom, though none was visible overhead, as if it had intelligence with some remote horizon. I heard a robin in the distance, the first I had heard for many a thousand years, methought, whose note I shall not forget for many a thousand more,—the same sweet and powerful song as of yore. O the evening robin, at the end of a New England summer day! If I could ever find the twig he sits upon! I mean *he;* I mean *the twig.* This at least is not the *Turdus migratorius*.[19] The pitch-pines and shrub-oaks about my house, which had so long drooped, suddenly resumed their several characters, looked brighter, greener, and more erect and alive, as if effectually cleaned and restored by the rain. I knew that it would not rain any more. You may tell by looking at any twig of the forest, ay, at your very wood-pile, whether its winter is past or not. As it grew darker, I was startled by the *honking* of geese flying low over the woods, like weary travellers getting in late from southern lakes, and indulging at last in unrestrained complaint and mutual consolation. Standing at my door, I could hear the rush of their wings; when, driving toward my house, they suddenly spied my light, and with hushed clamor wheeled and settled in the pond. So I came in, and shut the door, and passed my first spring night in the woods.

In the morning I watched the geese from the door through the mist, sailing in the middle of the pond, fifty rods off, so large and tumultuous that Walden appeared like an artificial pond for their amusement. But when I stood on the shore they at once rose up with a great flapping of wings at the signal of their commander, and when they had got into rank circled about over my head, twenty-nine of them, and then steered straight to Canada, with a regular *honk* from the leader at intervals, trusting to break their fast in muddier pools. A "plump" of ducks rose at the same time and took the route to the north in the wake of their noisier cousins.

For a week I heard the circling groping clangor of some solitary goose in the foggy mornings, seeking its companion, and still peopling the woods with the sound of a larger life than they could sustain. In April the pigeons were seen again flying express in small flocks, and in due time I heard the martins twittering over my clearing, though it had not seemed that the township contained so many that it could afford me any, and I fancied that they were peculiarly of the ancient race that dwelt in hollow trees ere white men came. In almost all climes the tortoise and the frog are among the precursors and heralds of this season, and birds fly with song and glancing plumage, and plants spring and bloom, and winds blow, to correct this slight oscillation of the poles and preserve the equilibrium of Nature.

As every season seems best to us in its turn, so the coming

in of spring is like the creation of Cosmos out of Chaos and the
realization of the Golden Age.—

> "Eurus ad Auroram, Nabathacaque regna recessit,
> Persidaque, et radiis juga subdita matutinis."

"The East-Wind withdrew to Aurora and the Nabathæan
  kingdom,[20]
And the Persian, and the ridges placed under the morning
  rays.

* * * *

Man was born. Whether that Artificer of things,
The origin of a better world, made him from the divine seed;
Or the earth being recent and lately sundered from the high
Ether, retained some seeds of cognate heaven."[21]

A single gentle rain makes the grass many shades greener.
So our prospects brighten on the influx of better thoughts. We
should be blessed if we lived in the present always and took
advantage of every accident that befell us, like the grass
which confesses the influence of the slightest dew that falls on
it; and did not spend our time in atoning for the neglect of
past opportunities, which we call doing our duty. We loiter
in winter while it is already spring. In a pleasant spring morning all man's sins are forgiven. Such a day is a truce to vice.
While such a sun holds out to burn,[22] the vilest sinner may
return. Through our own recovered innocence we discern
the innocence of our neighbors. You may have known your
neighbor yesterday for a thief, a drunkard, or a sensualist,
and merely pitied or despised him, and despaired of the world;
but the sun shines bright and warm this first spring morning,
recreating the world, and you meet him at some serene work,
and see how his exhausted and debauched veins expand with
still joy and bless the new day, feel the spring influence with
the innocence of infancy,[23] and all his faults are forgotten.
There is not only an atmosphere of good will about him, but
even a savor of holiness groping for expression, blindly and
ineffectually perhaps, like a new-born instinct, and for a short
hour the south hill-side echoes to no vulgar jest. You see some
innocent fair shoots preparing to burst from his gnarled rind
and try another year's life, tender and fresh as the youngest
plant. Even he has entered into the joy[24] of his Lord. Why the

jailer does not leave open his prison doors,—why the judge
does not dismiss his case,—why the preacher does not dismiss
his congregation! It is because they do not obey the hint
which God gives them, nor accept the pardon which he
freely offers to all.

"A return to goodness produced each day in the tranquil
and beneficent breath of the morning, causes that in respect
to the love of virtue and the hatred of vice, one approaches a
little the primitive nature of man, as the sprouts of the forest
which has been felled. In like manner the evil which one
does in the interval of a day prevents the germs of virtues
which began to spring up again from developing themselves
and destroys them.

"After the germs of virtue have thus been prevented many
times from developing themselves, then the beneficent breath
of evening does not suffice to preserve them. As soon as the
breath of evening does not suffice longer to preserve them,
then the nature of man does not differ much from that of the
brute. Men seeing the nature of this man like that of the
brute, think that he has never possessed the innate faculty of
reason. Are those the true and natural sentiments of man?"[25]

"The Golden Age was first created, which without any avenger
Spontaneously without law cherished fidelity and rectitude.
Punishment and fear were not; nor were threatening words
    read
On suspended brass; nor did the suppliant crowd fear
The words of their judge; but were safe without an avenger.
Not yet the pine felled on its mountains had descended
To the liquid waves that it might see a foreign world,
And mortals knew no shores but their own.

   *   *   *   *

There was eternal spring, and placid zephyrs with warm
Blasts soothed the flowers born without seed."[26]

On the 29th of April, as I was fishing from the bank of the
river near the Nine-Acre-Corner bridge,[27] standing on the
quaking grass and willow roots, where the muskrats lurk, I
heard a singular rattling sound, somewhat like that of the
sticks[28] which boys play with their fingers, when, looking up,
I observed a very slight and graceful hawk,[29] like a night-
hawk, alternately soaring like a ripple and tumbling a rod

or two over and over, showing the underside of its wings, which gleamed like a satin ribbon in the sun, or like the pearly inside of a shell. This sight reminded me of falconry and what nobleness and poetry are associated with that sport. The Merlin it seemed to me it might be called: but I care not for its name. It was the most ethereal flight I had ever witnessed. It did not simply flutter like a butterfly, nor soar like the larger hawks, but it sported with proud reliance in the fields of air; mounting again and again with its strange chuckle, it repeated its free and beautiful fall, turning over and over like a kite, and then recovering from its lofty tumbling, as if it had never set its foot on *terra firma*. It appeared to have no companion in the universe,—sporting there alone,—and to need none but the morning and the ether with which it played. It was not lonely, but made all the earth lonely beneath it. Where was the parent which hatched it, its kindred, and its father in the heavens? The tenant of the air, it seemed related to the earth but by an egg hatched some time in the crevice of a crag;—or was its native nest made in the angle of a cloud, woven of the rainbow's trimmings and the sunset sky, and lined with some soft midsummer haze caught up from earth? Its eyry now some cliffy cloud.

Beside this I got a rare mess of golden and silver and bright cupreous fishes, which looked like a string of jewels. Ah! I have penetrated to those meadows on the morning of many a first spring day, jumping from hummock to hummock, from willow root to willow root, when the wild river valley and the woods were bathed in so pure and bright a light as would have waked the dead, if they had been slumbering in their graves, as some suppose. There needs no stronger proof of immortality. All things must live in such a light. O Death,[30] where was thy sting? O Grave, where was thy victory, then?

Our village life would stagnate if it were not for the un-explored forests and meadows which surround it. We need the tonic of wildness,—to wade sometimes in marshes where the bittern and the meadow-hen[31] lurk, and hear the booming of the snipe; to smell the whispering sedge where only some wilder and more solitary fowl builds her nest, and the mink crawls with its belly close to the ground. At the same time that we are earnest to explore and learn all things, we require that all things be mysterious and unexplorable, that land and sea be infinitely wild, unsurveyed and unfathomed by us be-

cause unfathomable. We can never have enough of Nature.
We must be refreshed by the sight of inexhaustible vigor,
vast and Titanic features, the sea-coast with its wrecks, the
wilderness with its living and its decaying trees, the thunder
cloud, and the rain which lasts three weeks and produces
freshets. We need to witness our own limits transgressed, and
some life pasturing freely where we never wander. We are
cheered when we observe the vulture feeding on the carrion
which disgusts and disheartens us and deriving health and
strength from the repast. There was a dead horse in the hollow by the path to my house, which compelled me sometimes to go out of my way, especially in the night when the
air was heavy, but the assurance it gave me of the strong appetite and inviolable health of Nature was my compensation
for this. I love to see that Nature is so rife with life that
myriads can be afforded to be sacrificed and suffered to prey
on one another; that tender organizations can be so serenely
squashed out of existence like pulp,—tadpoles which herons
gobble up, and tortoises and toads run over in the road; and
that sometimes it has rained flesh and blood! With the liability
to accident, we must see how little account is to be made
of it. The impression made on a wise man is that of universal
innocence. Poison is not poisonous after all, nor are any
wounds fatal. Compassion is a very untenable ground. It must
be expeditious. Its pleadings will not bear to be stereotyped.

Early in May, the oaks, hickories, maples, and other trees,
just putting out amidst the pine woods around the pond, imparted a brightness like sunshine to the landscape, especially
in cloudy days, as if the sun were breaking through mists and
shining faintly on the hill-sides here and there. On the third
or fourth of May I saw a loon in the pond, and during the
first week of the month I heard the whippoorwill, the brown-
thrasher, the veery, the wood-pewee, the chewink, and other
birds. I had heard the wood-thrush[a] long before. The phoebe
had already come once more and looked in at my door and
window, to see if my house was cavern-like enough for her,
sustaining herself on humming wings with clinched talons,
as if she held by the air, while she surveyed the premises.
The sulphur-like pollen of the pitch-pine soon covered the
pond and the stones and rotten wood along the shore, so that
you could have collected a barrel-ful. This is the "sulphur
showers" we hear of. Even in Calidas' drama of Sacontala,

we read of "rills dyed yellow with the golden dust of the lotus."[33] And so the seasons went rolling on into summer, as one rambles into higher and higher grass.

Thus was my first year's life[34] in the woods completed; and the second year was similar to it. I finally left Walden September 6th, 1847.

CONCLUSION

To the sick the doctors wisely recommend a change of air and scenery. Thank Heaven, here is not all the world. The buckeye does not grow in New England, and the mockingbird is rarely heard here. The wild-goose is more of a cosmopolite than we; he breaks his fast in Canada, takes a luncheon in the Ohio, and plumes himself for the night in a southern bayou. Even the bison, to some extent, keeps pace with the seasons, cropping the pastures of the Colorado only till a greener and sweeter grass awaits him by the Yellowstone. Yet we think that if rail-fences are pulled down, and stone-walls piled up on our farms, bounds are henceforth set to our lives and our fates decided. If you are chosen town-clerk, forsooth, you cannot go to Tierra del Fuego[1] this summer: but you may go to the land of infernal fire nevertheless. The universe is wider than our views of it.

Yet we should oftener look over the tafferel of our craft, like curious passengers, and not make the voyage like stupid sailors picking oakum.[2] The other side of the globe is but the home of our correspondent. Our voyaging is only great-circle[3] sailing, and the doctors prescribe for diseases of the skin merely. One hastens to Southern Africa to chase the giraffe; but surely that is not the game he would be after. How long, pray, would a man hunt giraffes if he could? Snipes and wood-cocks also may afford rare sport; but I trust it would be nobler game to shoot one's self.—

> "Direct your eye right inward, and you'll find
> A thousand regions in your mind
> Yet undiscovered. Travel them, and be
> Expert in home-cosmography."[4]

What does Africa,—what does the West stand for? Is not our own interior[5] white on the chart[6] black though it may prove, like the coast, when discovered. Is it the source of the Nile,

or the Niger, or the Mississippi, or a North-West Passage
around this continent, that we would find? Are these the problems which most concern mankind? Is Franklin⁷ the only
man who is lost, that his wife should be so earnest to find
him? Does Mr. Grinnell⁸ know where he himself is? Be rather
the Mungo Park, the Lewis and Clarke and Frobisher,⁹ of
your own streams and oceans; explore your own higher latitudes,—with shiploads of preserved meats to support you, if
they be necessary; and pile the empty cans¹⁰ sky-high for a
sign. Were preserved meats invented to preserve meat merely?
Nay, be a Columbus to whole new continents and worlds
within you, opening new channels, not of trade, but of
thought. Every man is the lord of a realm beside which the
earthly empire of the Czar¹¹ is but a petty state, a hummock
left by the ice. Yet some can be patriotic who have no *self*-
respect, and sacrifice the greater to the less. They love the
soil which makes their graves, but have no sympathy with
the spirit which may still animate their clay. Patriotism is a
maggot in their heads. What was the meaning of that South-
Sea Exploring Expedition,¹² with all its parade and expense,
but an indirect recognition of the fact, that there are continents and seas in the moral world, to which every man is an
isthmus or an inlet, yet unexplored by him, but that it is
easier to sail many thousand miles through cold and storm
and cannibals, in a government ship, with five hundred men
and boys to assist one, than it is to explore the private sea,
the Atlantic and Pacific Ocean of one's being alone.—

> "Erret, et extremos alter scrutetur Iberos.
>   Plus habet hic vitæ, plus habet ille viæ."

Let them wander and scrutinize the outlandish Australians.
I have more of God, they more of the road.¹³

It is not worth the while to go round the world to count the
cats in Zanzibar.¹⁴ Yet do this even till you can do better, and
you may perhaps find some "Symmes' Hole"¹⁵ by which to get
at the inside at last. England and France, Spain and Portugal,
Gold Coast and Slave Coast, all front on this private sea; but
no bark from them has ventured out of sight of land, though
it is without doubt the direct way to India. If you would learn
to speak all tongues and conform to the customs of all nations,

if you would travel farther than all travellers, be naturalized in all climes, and cause the Sphinx[16] to dash her head against a stone, even obey the precept of the old philosopher, and Explore thyself.[17] Herein are demanded the eye and the nerve. Only the defeated and deserters go to the wars, cowards that run away and enlist. Start now on that farthest western way,[18] which does not pause at the Mississippi or the Pacific, nor conduct toward a worn-out China or Japan, but leads on direct a tangent to this sphere, summer and winter, day and night, sun down, moon down, and at last earth down too.

It is said that Mirabeau[19] took to highway robbery "to ascertain what degree of resolution was necessary in order to place one's self in formal opposition to the most sacred laws of society." He declared that "a soldier who fights in the ranks does not require half so much courage as a foot-pad,"—"that honor and religion have never stood in the way of a well-considered and firm resolve." This was manly, as the world goes; and yet it was idle, if not desperate. A saner man would have found himself often enough "in formal opposition" to what are deemed "the most sacred laws of society," through obedience to yet more sacred laws, and so have tested his resolution without going out of his way. It is not for a man to put himself in such an attitude to society, but to maintain himself in whatever attitude he find himself through obedience to the laws of his being, which will never be one of opposition to a just government, if he should chance to meet with such.

I left the woods[20] for as good a reason as I went there. Perhaps it seemed to me that I had several more lives to live, and could not spare any more time for that one. It is remarkable how easily and insensibly we fall into a particular route, and make a beaten track for ourselves. I had not lived there a week before my feet wore a path[21] from my door to the pondside; and though it is five or six years since I trod it, it is still quite distinct. It is true, I fear that others may have fallen into it, and so helped to keep it open. The surface of the earth is soft and impressible by the feet of men; and so with the paths which the mind travels. How worn and dusty, then, must be the highways of the world, how deep the ruts of tradition and conformity! I did not wish to take a cabin passage, but rather to go before the mast[22] and on the deck of the world, for there I could best see the moonlight[23] amid the mountains. I do not wish to go below now.

I learned this, at least, by my experiment; that if one advances confidently in the direction of his dreams, and endeavors to live the life he has imagined, he will meet with a success unexpected in common hours. He will put some things behind, will pass an invisible boundary; new, universal, and more liberal laws will begin to establish themselves around and within him; or the old laws be expanded, and interpreted in his favor in a more liberal sense, and he will live with the license of a higher order of beings. In proportion as he simplifies his life, the laws of the universe will appear less complex, and solitude will not be solitude, nor poverty poverty, nor weakness weakness. If you have built castles in the air, your work need not be lost; that is where they should be. Now put the foundations under them.

It is a ridiculous demand which England and America make, that you shall speak so that they can understand you. Neither men nor toad-stools grow so. As if that were important, and there were not enough to understand you without them. As if Nature could support but one order of understandings, could not sustain birds as well as quadrupeds, flying as well as creeping things, and *hush* and *who*,²⁴ which Bright can understand, were the best English. As if there were safety in stupidity alone. I fear chiefly lest my expression may not be *extra-vagant* enough, may not wander far enough beyond the narrow limits of my daily experience, so as to be adequate to the truth of which I have been convinced. *Extra vagance!* it depends on how you are yarded. The migrating buffalo, which seeks new pastures in another latitude, is not extravagant like the cow which kicks over the pail, leaps the cow-yard fence, and runs after her calf, in milking time. I desire to speak somewhere *without* bounds; like a man in a waking moment, to men in their waking moments; for I am convinced that I cannot exaggerate enough even to lay the foundation of a true expression. Who that has heard a strain of music feared then lest he should speak extravagantly any more forever? In view of the future or possible, we should live quite laxly and undefined in front, our outlines dim and misty on that side; as our shadows reveal an insensible perspiration toward the sun. The volatile truth of our words should continually betray the inadequacy of the residual statement. Their truth is instantly *translated;* its literal monument alone remains. The words which express our faith and piety are not definite; yet they are significant and fragrant like frankincense to superior natures.

Why level downward to our dullest perception always, and praise that as common sense? The commonest sense is the sense of men asleep, which they express by snoring. Sometimes we are inclined to class those who are once-and-a-half witted with the half-witted, because we appreciate only a third part of their wit. Some would find fault with the morning-red, if they ever got up early enough. "They pretend," as I hear, "that the verses of Kabir have four different senses; illusion, spirit, intellect, and the exoteric doctrine of the Vedas;"[25] but in this part of the world it is considered a ground for complaint if a man's writings admit of more than one interpretation. While England endeavors to cure the potato-rot,[26] will not any endeavor to cure the brain-rot, which prevails so much more widely and fatally?

I do not suppose that I have attained to obscurity, but I should be proud if no more fatal fault were found with my pages on this score than was found with the Walden ice. Southern customers objected to its blue color, which is the evidence of its purity, as if it were muddy, and preferred the Cambridge ice, which is white, but tastes of weeds. The purity men love is like the mists which envelop the earth, and not like the azure ether beyond.

Some are dinning in our ears that we Americans, and moderns generally, are intellectual dwarfs compared with the ancients, or even the Elizabethan men. But what is that to the purpose? A living dog[27] is better than a dead lion. Shall a man go and hang himself because he belongs to the race of pygmies, and not be the biggest pygmy that he can? Let every one mind his own business, and endeavor to be what he was made.

Why should we be in such desperate haste to succeed, and in such desperate enterprises? If a man does not keep pace with his companions, perhaps it is because he hears a different drummer.[28] Let him step to the music which he hears, however measured or far away. It is not important that he should mature as soon as an apple-tree or an oak. Shall he turn his spring into summer? If the condition of things which we were made for is not yet, what were any reality which we can substitute? We will not be shipwrecked on a vain reality. Shall we with pains erect a heaven of blue glass over ourselves, though when it is done we shall be sure to gaze still at the true ethereal heaven far above, as if the former were not?

There was an artist[29] in the city of Kouroo who was disposed to strive after perfection. One day it came into his mind to make a staff. Having considered that in an imperfect work time is an ingredient, but into a perfect work time does not enter, he said to himself, It shall be perfect in all respects, though I should do nothing else in my life. He proceeded instantly to the forest for wood, being resolved that it should not be made of unsuitable material; and as he searched for and rejected stick after stick, his friends gradually deserted him, for they grew old in their works and died, but he grew not older by a moment. His singleness of purpose and resolution, and his elevated piety, endowed him, without his knowledge, with perennial youth. As he made no compromise with Time, Time kept out of his way, and only sighed at a distance because he could not overcome him. Before he had found a stock[29a] in all respects suitable the city of Kouroo was a hoary ruin, and he sat on one of its mounds to peel the stick. Before he had given it the proper shape the dynasty of the Candahars was at an end, and with the point of the stick he wrote the name of the last of that race in the sand, and then resumed his work. By the time he had smoothed and polished the staff Kalpa[30] was no longer the pole-star; and ere he had put on the ferule and the head adorned with precious stones, Brahma[31] had awoke and slumbered many times. But why do I stay to mention these things? When the finishing stroke was put to his work, it suddenly expanded before the eyes of the astonished artist into the fairest of all the creations of Brahma. He had made a new system in making a staff, a world with full and fair proportions; in which, though the old cities and dynasties had passed away, fairer and more glorious ones had taken their places. And now he saw by the heap of shavings still fresh at his feet, that, for him and his work, the former lapse of time had been an illusion, and that no more time had elapsed than is required for a single scintillation from the brain of Brahma to fall on and inflame the tinder of a mortal brain. The material was pure, and his art was pure; how could the result be other than wonderful?

No face which we can give to a matter will stead us so well at last as the truth. This alone wears well. For the most part, we are not where we are, but in a false position. Through an infirmity of our natures, we suppose a case, and put ourselves into it, and hence are in two cases at the same time, and it is doubly difficult to get out. In sane moments we regard only the facts, the case that is. Say what you have to say, not what you ought. Any truth is better than make-believe. Tom Hyde,[32] the tinker, standing on the gallows, was asked if he had any thing to say. "Tell the tailors," said he, "to remember to make a knot in their thread before they take the first stitch." His companion's prayer is forgotten.

However mean your life is, meet it and live it; do not shun it and call it hard names. It is not so bad as you are. It looks poorest when you are richest. The fault-finder will find faults even in paradise. Love your life, poor as it is. You may perhaps have some pleasant, thrilling, glorious hours, even in a poorhouse. The setting sun is reflected from the windows of the alms-house as brightly as from the rich man's abode; the snow melts before its door as early in the spring. I do not see but a quiet mind may live as contentedly there, and have as cheering thoughts, as in a palace. The town's poor seem to me often to live the most independent lives of any. May be they are simply great enough to receive without misgiving. Most think that they are above being supported by the town; but it oftener happens that they are not above supporting themselves by dishonest means, which should be more disreputable. Cultivate poverty like a garden herb, like sage. Do not trouble yourself much to get new things, whether clothes or friends. Turn the old; return to them. Things do not change; we change. Sell your clothes and keep your thoughts. God will see that you do not want society. If I were confined to a corner of a garret all my days, like a spider, the world would be just as large to me while I had my thoughts about me. The philosopher said: "From an army of three divisions one can take away its general, and put it in disorder; from the man the most abject and vulgar one cannot take away his thought."[33] Do not seek so anxiously to be developed, to subject yourself to many influences to be played on; it is all dissipation. Humility like darkness reveals the heavenly lights. The shadows of poverty and meanness gather around us, "and lo! creation widens to our view."[34] We are often reminded that if there were bestowed on us the wealth of Croesus,[35] our aims must still be the same, and our means essentially the same. Moreover, if you are restricted in your range of poverty, if you cannot buy books and newspapers, for instance, you are but confined to the most significant and vital experiences; you are compelled to deal with the material which yields the most sugar and the most starch. It is life near the bone[36] where it is sweetest. You are defended from being a trifler. No man loses ever on a lower level by magnanimity on a higher. Superfluous wealth can buy superfluities only. Money is not required to buy one necessary of the soul.

I live in the angle of a leaden wall, into whose composition was poured a little alloy of bell metal. Often, in the repose of my mid-day, there reaches my ears a confused *tintinnabulum*[37] from without. It is the noise of my contemporaries. My neighbors tell me of their adventures with famous gentlemen and ladies, what notabilities they met at the dinner-table; but I am no more interested in such things than in the contents of the Daily Times. The interest and the conversation are about costume and manners chiefly; but a goose is a goose still, dress it as you will. They tell me of California and Texas, of England and the Indies, of the Hon. Mr. ————[38] of Georgia or of Massachusetts, all transient and fleeting phenomena, till I am ready to leap from their court-yard like the Mameluke bey.[39] I delight to come to my bearings,—not walk in procession with pomp and parade, in a conspicuous place, but to walk even with the Builder of the universe, if I may,—not to live in this restless, nervous, bustling, trivial Nineteenth Century, but stand or sit thoughtfully while it goes by. What are men celebrating? They are all on a committee of arrangements, and hourly expect a speech from somebody. God is only the president of the day, and Webster[40] is his orator. I love to weigh, to settle, to gravitate toward that which most strongly and rightfully attracts me;—not hang by the beam of the scale and try to weigh less,—not suppose a case, but take the case that is; to travel the only path I can, and that on which no power can resist me. It affords me no satisfaction to commence to spring an arch before I have got a solid foundation. Let us not play at kittlybenders.[41] There is a solid bottom every where. We read that the traveller asked the boy if the swamp before him had a hard bottom. The boy replied that it had. But presently the traveller's horse sank in up to the girths, and he observed to the boy, "I thought you said that this bog had a hard bottom." "So it has," answered the latter, "but you have not got half way to it yet." So it is with the bogs and quicksands of society;

but he is an old boy that knows it. Only what is thought said
or done at a certain rare coincidence is good. I would not be
one of those who will foolishly drive a nail into mere lath and
plastering; such a deed would keep me awake nights. Give me
a hammer, and let me feel for the furrowing. Do not depend
on the putty. Drive a nail home and clinch it so faithfully that
you can wake up in the night and think of your work with
satisfaction,—a work at which you would not be ashamed to
invoke the Muse.[42] So will help you God, and so only. Every
nail driven should be as another rivet in the machine of the
universe, you carrying on the work.

Rather than love, than money, than fame, give me truth.
I sat at a table where were rich food and wine in abundance,
and obsequious attendance, but sincerity and truth were not;
and I went away hungry from the inhospitable board. The
hospitality was as cold as the ices. I thought that there was no
need of ice to freeze them. They talked to me of the age of the
wine and the fame of the vintage; but I thought of an older, a
newer, and purer wine, of a more glorious vintage, which they
had not got, and could not buy. The style, the house and
grounds and "entertainment" pass for nothing with me. I called
on the king, but he made me wait in his hall, and conducted
like a man incapacitated for hospitality. There was a man in
my neighborhood who lived in a hollow tree.[43] His manners
were truly regal. I should have done better had I called on
him.

How long shall we sit in our porticoes practising idle and
musty virtues, which any work would make impertinent? As if
one were to begin the day with long-suffering, and hire a man
to hoe his potatoes; and in the afternoon go forth to practise
Christian meekness and charity with goodness aforethought!
Consider the China pride and stagnant self-complacency of
mankind. This generation reclines a little to congratulate itself
on being the last of an illustrious line; and in Boston and London and Paris and Rome, thinking of its long descent, it speaks
of its progress in art and science and literature with satisfaction. There are the Records of the Philosophical Societies, and
the public Eulogies of *Great Men!* It is the good Adam contemplating his own virtue. "Yes, we have done great deeds,
and sung divine songs, which shall never die,"[44]—that is, as
long as *we* can remember them. The learned societies and
great men of Assyria,—where are they? What youthful philoso-

phers and experimentalists we are! There is not one of my readers who has yet lived a whole human life. These may be but the spring months in the life of the race. If we have had the seven-years' itch,[45] we have not seen the seventeen-year locust[46] yet in Concord. We are acquainted with a mere pellicle of the globe on which we live. Most have not delved six feet beneath the surface, nor leaped as many above it. We know not where we are. Beside, we are sound asleep nearly half our time. Yet we esteem ourselves wise, and have an established order on the surface. Truly, we are deep thinkers, we are ambitious spirits! As I stand over the insect crawling amid the pine needles on the forest floor, and endeavoring to conceal itself from my sight, and ask myself why it will cherish those humble thoughts, and hide its head from me who might, perhaps, be its benefactor, and impart to its race some cheering information, I am reminded of the greater Benefactor and Intelligence that stands over me the human insect.

There is an incessant influx of novelty into the world, and yet we tolerate incredible dulness. I need only suggest what kind of sermons are still listened to in the most enlightened countries. There are such words as joy and sorrow, but they are only the burden of a psalm, sung with a nasal twang, while we believe in the ordinary and mean. We think that we can change our clothes only. It is said that the British Empire is very large and respectable, and that the United States are a first-rate power. We do not believe that a tide rises and falls behind every man which can float the British Empire like a chip, if he should ever harbor it in his mind. Who knows what sort of seventeen-year locust will next come out of the ground? The government of the world I live in was not framed, like that of Britain, in after-dinner conversations over the wine.

The life in us is like the water in the river. It may rise this year higher than man has ever known it, and flood the parched uplands; even this may be the eventful year, which will drown out all our muskrats.[47] It was not always dry land where we dwell. I see far inland the banks which the stream anciently washed, before science began to record its freshets. Every one has heard the story[48] which has gone the rounds of New England, of a strong and beautiful bug which came out of the dry leaf of an old table of apple-tree wood, which had stood in a farmer's kitchen for sixty years, first in Connecticut, and afterward in Massachusetts,—from an egg deposited in the living tree many years earlier still, as appeared by counting the annual layers beyond it; which was heard gnawing out for several weeks, hatched perchance by the heat of an urn. Who does not feel his faith in a resurrection and immortality strengthened by hearing of this? Who knows what beautiful and winged life, whose egg has been buried for ages under many concentric layers of woodenness in the dead dry life of society, deposited at first in the alburnum of the green and living tree, which has been gradually converted into the semblance of its well-seasoned tomb,—heard perchance gnawing out now for years by the astonished family of man, as they sat round the festive board,—may unexpectedly come forth from amidst society's most trivial and handselled furniture, to enjoy its perfect summer life at last!

I do not say that John or Jonathan[49] will realize all this; but such is the character of that morrow which mere lapse of time can never make to dawn. The light which puts out our eyes is darkness to us. Only that day dawns to which we are awake. There is more day to dawn. The sun[50] is but a morning star.

NOTES

ECONOMY

1. Although the first edition gives the title *Walden: or, Life in the Woods,* on March 4, 1862, two months before he died, Thoreau wrote to his publishers, Ticknor & Fields, asking them to omit "Or Life in the Woods" from the title of a new edition. They complied with this request, although it has rarely been followed since. Sherman Paul (*The Shores of America,* Urbana, 1958, p. 75) suggests that Thoreau may have dropped the subtitle because he feared his audience was taking it too literally and thus missing the more important philosophy permeating the book.

Although a book by J. T. Headley entitled *The Adirondack: or Life in the Woods* (New York, 1849) preceded *Walden* by five years, it seems unlikely that it was the source of Thoreau's subtitle, for its preface is dated March 31, 1849, and Thoreau's *A Week* was published in May, 1849, with the appended announcement that *Walden: or, Life in the Woods* would soon be published. *A Week* had been set up in type for at least five months before publication since its page proofs are copyrighted 1848.

A possible source of this subtitle of *Walden* is the essay by Charles Lane in the *Dial,* IV (1844), 415, entitled "Life in the Woods."

The drawing of Thoreau's cabin was made by his sister Sophia. It was described by Ellery Channing as "a feeble caricature" of the building. Another drawing by an eyewitness, that published in the "Thoreau Annex" of the *Concord Freeman* in the 1880's (reprinted in *TSB* 23 [1948] shows the cabin in the middle of an open field.

The quotation is from the second chapter of *Walden.* It is omitted from the title page of many modern editions, and unfortunately so, for it sets the mood for the entire book. John C. Broderick, in "Imagery in Walden," (*UTSE* XXXIII [1954], 80-89), points out how this awakening and morning theme is a basic image carried throughout the book.

A possible source for Thoreau's idea is Orestes Brownson's statement in his *Boston Quarterly Review* in 1838 that he "aimed to startle, and made it a point to be as paradoxical and extravagant as he could."

The Bibliophile Edition of *Walden* includes a facsimile of a manuscript title page by Thoreau which includes a drawing of Chanticleer and the following quotation from Saadi: "The clouds, wind, moon, sun and sky, act in cooperation, that thou mayest get thy daily bread, and not eat it with indifference; all render for thy sake, and are obedient to command; it must be an equitable condition, that thou shall be obedient also."

2. Although Thoreau is undoubtedly referring to many direct inquiries, some of which he describes later in the book, he is also probably referring to the fact that he was asked to deliver at least three lectures on his Walden experiences before the Concord Lyceum. The texts of these lectures were later incorporated into the book itself. Much of the material on this page, for example, was taken from his lecture of February 10, 1847.

3. Note the particular audience to whom Thoreau is addressing the book. Later he suggests his book is primarily for those who are dissatisfied with their present life.

4. The common nineteenth-century name for Hawaiians.

5. Upper-caste Hindus, who frequently subjected themselves to various penances as acts of devotion. I have not been able to trace down the specific source of the following quotation.

6. For an exposition of the theory that the sun image is the key symbol of *Walden*, see Stanley Edgar Hyman "Henry Thoreau in Our Time," *Atlantic Monthly*, CLXXVIII (1946), 137-46. I am not at all convinced that the theory presented has any validity.

7. Hercules, the most celebrated of all heroes of antiquity, was commanded to perform twelve feats before he could obtain his release from servitude to Eurystheus. They included such tasks as fetching the golden apples of the Hesperides and cleansing the stables of Augeas.

8. One of the labors of Hercules was to fight the Lernaean Hydra, a lion with nine heads. As fast as Hercules cut off a head, two grew in its place. But finally with the aid of his servant Iolaus he burned away the heads and buried the ninth immortal one beneath a rock.

9. Romulus, the founder of Rome, and his brother Remus, are fabled to have been stranded as babes at the foot of the Palatine hill and adopted and suckled by a she-wolf.

10. "We must eat a peck of dirt before we die" is an old proverb that can be traced at least as far back as Oswald Dykes' *English Proverbs* of 1709.

11. One of the twelve labors of Hercules. Augeas had 3,000 oxen, and his stables had not been cleansed for thirty years.

12. "Lay not up for yourselves treasures upon earth, where moth and rust doth corrupt, and where thieves break through and steal" (Matthew 6:19.) Thoreau's referring to the Holy Bible as "an old book" did not win him any friends among his conservative contemporaries.

13. Deucalion, the son of Prometheus, and his wife Pyrrha, were the only mortals saved when Zeus determined to annihilate the degenerate race of men. Upon the advice of Themis, they covered their heads and cast stones over their shoulders which turned into men and thus repeopled the earth.

14. Ovid's *Metamorphoses*, Book 1, lines 414-15.

15. Sir Walter Raleigh's *History of the World*, Book 1, Part 1, Chap. 2, Sec. 5.

16. The amount up to which a particular customer of a bank is not permitted to overdraw *(NED)*.

17. *Cf.* "I could be bounded in a nutshell" (Hamlet, II, ii, 260).

18. Thoreau was one of the first Americans to protest against the factory system. He favored beginning one's reforms at home, not in a distant land.

19. Although the Puritans concerned themselves with man as a sinner, the Unitarians of Thoreau's day talked more of the divinity of man. *Cf.* Emerson's "Divinity School Address," *passim.*

20. "Tis the Divinity that stirs within us" (Joseph Addison, *Cato*, V, i).

21. Although this name does not occur in *The Pilgrim's Progress*, it is certainly in that tradition.

22. William Wilberforce (1759-1833), English antislavery crusader who led the parliamentary battle for the abolition of slavery in the British West Indies.

23. Embroidered cushions used in ladies' dressing rooms *(DAE)*.

24. "What is the chief end of man? Man's chief end is to glorify God and to enjoy him forever" (The Shorter Catechism from the *New England Primer*).

25. A reference to the railroad, which, in the 1840's, was just beginning to spread its network about the country.

26. Although Thoreau was eight days short of twenty-eight

years when he went to Walden, he wrote a large portion of the book in later years, not completing it until 1854, when he was thirty-six.

27. Although Thoreau was not an absolute vegetarian as were some of his transcendentalist friends, he did follow a modified vegetarian diet through a large part of his mature life.

28. John Evelyn, *Silva: or, a Discourse of Forest-Trees* (London, 1729, p. 246).

29. I have searched numerous editions of the works of Hippocrates, but have been unable to find any such reference. Is it possible that Thoreau is confusing him with some other ancient author?

30. "Be not afflicted, my child, for who shall efface what thou hast formerly done, or shall assign to thee what thou hast left undone?" (H. H. Wilson, trans., *The Vishńu Puráńa* [London, 1840, p. 87]).

31. "The days of our years are three-score and ten" (Psalms 90:10).

32. *Confucian Analects,* Book II, Chap. XVII. For a detailed analysis of this and other quotations from Confucius, see Lyman C. Cady, "Thoreau's Quotations from the Confucian Books in *Walden,*" *AL,* XXXIII (1961), 20-32.

33. In several places in his *Journals* (I, 474; VI, 69) Thoreau records his delight in going over the old account books of Concord merchants. See also, "Winter Animals," below.

34. Except for the fact that so many have called Thoreau "without humor," it would seem almost pointless to note that Thoreau particularly delighted in a pun. For a catalog of the puns in *Walden,* see David Skwire, "A Check List of Wordplays in *Walden,*" *AL,* XXXI (1959), 282-89.

35. "We were well clothed, and though sitting close to the fire, were far from too warm; yet these naked savages, though further off, were observed, to our great surprise, to be streaming with perspiration at undergoing such a roasting" (Charles Darwin, *Journal of Research . . . During the Voyage of H.M.S. Beagle* [New York, 1846, I, 284]).

36. Thoreau was probably recalling his reading of *The Voyages of Captain James Cook Round the World,* particularly Vol. III, p. vi.

37. Justus Liebig (1803-1873), professor of Chemistry in the University of Giessen, wrote many volumes using this metaphor. Among them is *Animal Chemistry* (Philadelphia, 1842?, *passim*).

38. The supposed home of the virtuous in the after-life in Greek mythology.

39. When Thoreau wrote his book, the clipper trade with the Orient was at its height.

40. It was the pet theory of Thoreau's friend and neighbor Amos Bronson Alcott that man's diet should not be confined to vegetables merely, but to those species of plant life which showed their higher nature by growing up towards the sun and not downward into the earth. Thus he would eat corn, but not carrots. See C. E. Sears, *Bronson Alcott's Fruitlands* (Boston, 1915, p. 39).

41. Thoreau once again calls the reader's attention to the fact that he is addressing his book not to the general public, but to a special audience—those who are dissatisfied with their present life.

42. Thoreau was probably thinking of Robinson Crusoe's method of keeping his calendar.

43. "One Life; a little gleam of Time between two Eternities" (Thomas Carlyle, *On Heroes and Hero-Worship,* Lecture V).

44. This cryptic passage is one of the most discussed in *Walden.* At least three different people attempted to learn Thoreau's own interpretation directly from him:

(1) Miss Ellen Watson, in "Thoreau Visits Plymouth" (*TSB* 21, 1947), reports that when Thoreau visited Plymouth, Mass., a year or two after the publication of *Walden,* he met there "Uncle Ed" Watson who asked him what he meant when he said he lost "a hound, a horse, and a dove." Thoreau replied, "Well, Sir, I suppose we all have our losses." "That's a pretty way to answer a fellow," replied Uncle Ed.

(2) When Thoreau's friend B. B. Wiley wrote from Chicago inquiring as to the meaning of the symbols, Thoreau replied in a letter of April 26, 1857 (VI, 301-2): "How shall we account for our pursuits, if they are original? We get the language with which to describe our various lives out of a common mint. If others have their losses which they are busy repairing, so have I mine, and their hound and horse may *perhaps* be the symbols of some of them. But also I have lost, or am in danger of losing, a far finer and more ethereal treasure which commonly no loss, of which they are conscious, will symbolize. This I answer hastily and with some hesitation, according as I now understand my words."

(3) T. M. Raysor, speaking of Thoreau's love for Ellen Sewall, says, "When Thoreau discovered Miss Ward's knowledge of the affair, he told her that the references in the first chapter of Walden to 'a hound, a bay horse, and a turtle-dove' which he had lost long ago were allusions to the boy Edmund Sewall, to John Thoreau, and to Ellen Sewall" ("The Love Story of Thoreau," *SP,* XXIII [1926], 460, which also contains further information on Thoreau's relationships with the Sewall family). For further details of this interpretation, see Raymond Adams, "Thoreau's Growth at Walden," *Christian Register,* CCXXIV (1945), 268-70. It is only fair to state

however, that virtually none of the major biographers of Thoreau has accepted this story as fact.

Among the many interpretations offered by various critics are these:

Ralph Waldo Emerson, in his biographical sketch of Thoreau (Centenary Edition, X, 476), says, "He had many reserves, an unwillingness to exhibit to profane eyes what was still sacred in his own, and knew well how to throw a poetic veil over his experience. All readers of *Walden* will remember his mythical record of his disappointments:—

[He then quotes the passage.]

"His riddles are worth the reading, and I confide that if at any time I do not understand the expression, it is yet just. Such was the wealth of his truth that it was not worth his while to use words in vain."

Vivian Hopkins, in *Spires of Form* (Cambridge, 1951, p. 243n), tells us that, "In a late manuscript fragment, Notes on Thoreau, Emerson records Thoreau's own statement from his Journal, 1840, on 'the hound': 'A good book will not be dropped by its author but thrown up. It will be so long a promise that he will not overtake it soon. He will have slipped leash of a fleet hound.' Emerson adds: 'The bay horse might be such command of property as he desired, and the turtle dove might be the wife of his dream.'"

John Burroughs, in "Henry D. Thoreau" (*Century Magazine*, II [1882], 377), says that Thoreau states in his Journal, "'The ultimate expression of fruit of any created thing is a fine effluence, which only the most ingenuous worshipper perceives at a reverent distance from its surface even.' This 'fine effluence' he was always reaching after, and often grasping or inhaling. This is the mythical hound and horse and turtle-dove which he says in 'Walden' he long ago lost, and has been on their trail ever since. He never abandons the search, and in every woodchuck-hole or muskrat-den, in retreat of bird, or squirrel, or mouse, or fox that he pries into, in every walk and expedition to the fields or swamps, or to distant woods, in every spring note and call that he listens to so patiently, he hopes to get some clew to his lost treasures, to the effluence that so provokingly eludes him."

Samuel Arthur Jones says, "To this man Thoreau every created thing was a divine message from its Maker and his. Oh, if he could but catch the meaning of the message or of the messenger. . . Alas for us all! they had lost them, even as we have: for what is the hound but the divine scent that finds the trail; what the bay horse but sagacity and strength to carry us in pursuit; what the turtle-dove but innocence to secure us the Divine protection? And we have lost them all." (*Thoreau: a Glimpse* [Concord, 1903], pp. 19-20).

Mark Van Doren says, "The parable of the hound, the bay horse, and the turtle-dove is plainly a 'mythical record of disappointments.' . . . It is clear enough that Thoreau's quest was not for any metaphysical entity, because he wore his metaphysics as comfortably as any one. It is clear enough that this single disappointment of his life was not an intellectual but an emotional one, and that it arose in the domain of the human relations. His ideal was perfect in human intercourse, and his quest was for an absolutely satisfactory condition of friendship" (*Henry David Thoreau: A Critical Study* [Boston, 1916], pp. 16-17).

Mr. John Girdler presents a 118-page analysis of this allusion in his unpublished master's thesis. But he sheds little light on the problem. Most of his space is devoted to a refutation of Mark Van Doren's interpretation. In conclusion he states: Thoreau "is an idealist. He is searching for the thing which he thinks will most benefit man, and he is using the methods that he believes best suit his genius. Consequently, his fables must, in his own words, be given the 'most generous interpretation.' It is not enough to seek a narrow and personal interpretation of the hound and bay horse allegory for, to quote him again, those thoughts which are 'contemporaneous with social and personal connections, though they may be humane and tender, are not the wisest and most universal' " (John Girdler, *A Study of the Hound, Bay Horse, and Turtle-dove Allusion in Thoreau's Walden* [University of Southern California, 1935; Unpublished master's thesis], p. 110).

Miss Edith Peairs, in "The Hound, the Bay Horse, and the Turtle-dove: A Study of Thoreau and Voltaire" (*PMLA* LII [1937], 863-69), attempts to prove that Thoreau's source for these symbols was Voltaire's *Zadig*. I am unconvinced.

Henry Seidel Canby states, "In the symbolic language of the Persian poets which he so often read, he is clearly describing a search for no lost maid or boy, but for that sense of the spiritual reality behind nature, which again and again in his Journal he deplores as something felt in youth, but never quite regained" (*Thoreau* [Boston, 1939], p. 294).

Frank Davidson suggests that "The hound, the bay horse, and the turtle-dove seem to be respectively for Thoreau symbols of a wildness that keeps man in touch with nature, intellectual stimulus, and purification of spirit" ("Thoreau's Hound, Bay Horse, and Turtle-Dove," *NEQ*, XXVII [1954], 521-24).

Among other possible sources for Thoreau's symbols are these: In 1843, Thoreau edited passages from the "Chinese Four Books" for the *Dial* (IV, 206), and one passage there, which Thoreau later included in *A Week* (I, 208) resembles Thoreau's parable remarkably: "Benevolence is man's heart, and justice is man's path. If a man lose his fowl or his dogs, he knows how to seek them. There are those who lose their hearts and know not how to seek them. The duty of the student is no other than to seek his lost heart."

It might also be noted that many of the old ballads such as "The Twa Corbies" associate together a hound, a horse, and a bird—although the bird is usually a falcon rather than a turtle-dove.

William Bysshe Stein, in "Thoreau's Hound, Bay Horse, and Turtle-Dove" (*TSB* 67 [1959], 1) suggests "The Story of Conn-eda; or the Golden Apples of Lough Erne," an old Irish folk tale, as a specific source for the images.

Emerson's poem "Forerunners" (Centennial Edition, IX, 85-86) also hints of the combination of hound, horse, and dove.

In conclusion, however, it should be pointed out that there is no unanimity on interpretation of these symbols and the individual critic is left free to interpret as he wishes.

45. *Gazette* was, and still is a popular name for small town newspapers and Thoreau was probably thinking in particular of Concord's own *Yeoman's Gazette*.

46. The food wherewith God fed the children of Israel in the deserts of Arabia, which rained from the heavens, and which melted with the heat of the sun (Numbers 11:8).

47. Thoreau may be referring facetiously either to his own *Journal,* which was not published until forty-four years after his death, or to the *Dial,* whose editors, Emerson and Margaret Fuller, rejected a number of his contributions, and whose circulation never exceeded several hundred.

48. Thoreau felt any day wasted in which he did not spend at least four or five hours walking in the woods and fields of Concord taking note of the world of nature. In his later years he became more and more concerned with keeping a precise record of the progress of the seasons and hoped to publish an "Atlas of Concord" with a complete record of its natural phenomena.

49. For the last ten or fifteen years of his life, Thoreau earned a large portion of his income by surveying.

50. All of these species were rarities in Concord and thus especially cherished by Thoreau.

51. In his *Journal* (II, 84) Thoreau identifies the "well-known lawyer" as Mr. Samuel Hoar, who lived but a stone's throw from Thoreau's Main Street house, and whose daughter Elizabeth was an intimate friend of both Emerson and Thoreau.

52. Sherman Paul (*The Shores of America*, Urbana, 1958, p. 322) suggests that Thoreau is here giving a thinly veiled account of the publishing failure of *A Week*.

53. At least one piece of "private business" which Thoreau wished to transact at Walden Pond was the writing of *A Week*, his memorial tribute to his brother John, who had died in 1842. For three years he had been kept from the task by worldly affairs. By retiring to the pond he was able to find time to complete the book.

54. Thoreau wrote his book at the height of the clipper ship trade with the Orient, particularly with China, the Celestial Empire. Salem, Mass., was the center of this trade. The products listed were all prominent in the trade. See S. E. Morison, *The Maritime History of Massachusetts* (Boston, 1921, *passim*).

55. The coast of New Jersey was long noted as the site of many shipwrecks.

56. Jean François de Gallup La Pérouse (1741-88), French explorer whose ship was wrecked in the New Hebrides in 1788.

57. Carthaginian navigator of the 6th and 5th centuries B.C.

58. The two ordinary deductions in calculating the net weight of goods to be sold by retail *(NED)*.

59. In Thoreau's own copy of *Walden*, he corrected "post" to "port" and it is said to be clearly "port" in the manuscript.

60. St. Petersburg, now Leningrad, is built in the lowlands of the Neva River.

61. The relationship of the following material on clothing to the "clothes philosophy" of Carlyle's *Sartor Resartus* will quickly be seen by any student familiar with that work.

62. Thoreau did not have the usual mid-Victorian objections to nudity, but delighted in swimming and wading along the rivers' edges naked. The modern nudists claim him as one of their precursors. See Lawrence MacDonald, "Henry Thoreau-Liberal, Unconventional, Nudist" (*Sunshine & Health*, January, 1943).

63. Ida Pfeiffer, *A Lady's Voyage Round the World* (New York, 1852), p. 265.

64. "Neither do men put new wine into old bottles else the bottles break" (Matthew 9:17).

65. "When we have shuffled off this mortal coil" (*Hamlet*, III, i).

66. Thoreau was thinking of Bias (circa 6th century B.C.), as he indicates in his *Journal* (I, 169-70).

67. Sanborn, in the Bibliophile *Walden*, identifies this as Miss Mary Minot (I, 79).

68. The Roman goddesses of charm and beauty.

69. The Fates in Roman mythology.

70. Although stories of seeds germinating after thousands of years have generally been discredited, in recent years several attempts have succeeded. See, for example, the *New York Times,* March 7, 1951, for the sprouting of lotus seeds estimated to be 50,000 years old.

In Thoreau's own copy of *Walden,* he revised the "was" of this sentence to "is said to have been."

Alexander Japp, in his biography of Thoreau (p. 237) suggests that Thoreau derived this idea from his reading of Coleman's report on the trees and shrubs of Massachusetts, but the idea was so frequently expressed in Thoreau's day that it seems unlikely we can be so precise as to its particular source.

71. Thoreau originally made these statements on costume about a group of Tyrolese singers who visited Concord in 1841 (cf. *Journal,* I, 196), but now applies it more generally.

72. A droll character in comedy and pantomime usually dressed in parti-colored clothes.

73. An interesting grammatical error. Since he is comparing only two patterns, he should say "more," just as immediately above he correctly said "latter" rather than "last."

74. Here again it is significant that Thoreau was one of the earliest Americans to protest against the evils of the factory system that were already producing slums and paupers in the New England cities.

75. Samuel Laing, *Journal of a Residence in Norway* (London, 1837), p. 295.

76. Terming the Bible a "fable" alienated some of Thoreau's more devout contemporaries. But he was not one to mince words to sooth his neighbor's feelings.

77. Any complicated structure, but specifically a building in Crete built by Daedalus where the Minotaur was housed. Theseus was able to penetrate the structure, slay the Minotaur, and then escape with the aid of Ariadne, who gave him the clue—a thread to follow.

78. The Penobscot Indians from Northern Maine frequently visited Concord and encamped outside the town.

79. "If I have freedom in my love, / And in my soul am free" (Richard Lovelace, "To Althea from Prison").

80. Daniel Gookin, *Historical Collections of the Indians in New England* (Boston, 1792), Chap. III, p. 9.

81. "The foxes have holes, and the birds of the air have nests; but the Son of man hath not where to lay his head" (Matthew 8:20).

82. A non-smoking stove invented by Benjamin Thompson, Count Rumford (1753-1814).

83. Formerly builders plastered between the studding; now thick paper takes the place of this "back plaster."

84. "For ye have the poor always with you" (Matthew 26:11).

85. "The fathers have eaten sour grapes, and the children's teeth are set on edge" (Ezekiel 18:2).

86. Ezekiel 18:3-4.

87. The Middlesex County cattle show was held in Concord each September and Thoreau usually joined the throng visiting it. In 1860 he was its principal speaker, delivering his paper on "The Succession of Forest Trees."

88. A dialect word meaning "proceeding regularly," and usually spelled "suant" *(NED)*. Thoreau's usage is so unique that it is cited in most dictionaries. Thoreau comments in some detail on this word in his *Journal*, III, 272.

89. An Elizabethan word meaning "trap." Thus a trap so delicate that a hair would spring it.

90. George Chapman, *The Tragedy of Caesar and Pompey*, V, ii.

91. A god of pleasantry among the ancients, son of Nox, according to Hesiod. The quotation is from the entry under Momus in Lempriere's *Bibliotheca Classica* (New York, 1842, p. 744).

92. This refers to a fund established in Concord in the eighteenth century, and still used for the care of the "silent poor," that is, those who hide their poverty to avoid going to the poorhouse.

93. "There are writings on the pyramid in Egyptian characters showing how much was spent on purges and onions and garlic for the workmen" *(Herodotus* 2. 125).

94. It was still the custom to leave all unexplored areas white on maps.

95. The slaves. Although Thoreau never formally joined the Abolitionist movement, he was deeply interested in the welfare of the slaves and at least once used his Walden cabin as a station on the underground railroad aiding Negroes to freedom in Canada.

96. In his own copy of *Walden*, Thoreau questioned the italicizing of this word.

97. Galoshes, or overshoes for wet weather. The *DAE* lists several variants of this word.

98. The Roman goddess of the dawn.

99. A king of Egypt. His subjects erected a statue of him which uttered a melodious sound every morning when the first rays of the sun fell upon it.

100. The last king of Assyria, whose effeminacy irritated his

officers and led them to revolt. See Byron's tragedy of this name. Thoreau may have read of him in Diodorus 2. 23.

101. There was a vogue for Oriental decoration in the mid-nineteenth century, inspired by the clipper ship trade with the Far East.

102. The type-name for Americans as "John Bull" is for the British.

103. A reference to his friend Nathaniel Hawthorne's delightful satire on the liberal religions, "The Celestial Railroad." "Malaria" means literally "bad air."

104. The division calls attention to the derivation of the word from the Latin *agri cultura*, the culture, or tilling of a field.

105. Gaudy trifles (*NED*).

106. "Wonder-Working Providence of Sions Saviour," *A History of New England* (London, 1654), Chap. 36, p. 83. Thoreau has modernized the English slightly.

107. E. B. O'Callaghan, *The Documentary History of the State of New York* (Albany, 1851), IV, 31-32. A set of this work was in Thoreau's personal library.

108. Thoreau was probably thinking of his friend Alcott's book *The Doctrine and Discipline of Human Culture* (Boston, 1836).

109. According to tradition, Thoreau borrowed the axe from his friend and neighbor Amos Bronson Alcott, and Alcott in "Mr. Alcott on Thoreau" (*Concord Freeman*, August 19, 1880) states, "When he [Thoreau] projected the Walden cabin he came to me and said, 'Mr. Alcott, lend me an ax,' and with this he built the temple of a grand primeval man." But George Willis Cooke, in his introduction to *Early Letters of George Wm. Curtis to John S. Dwight* (New York, 1898, p. 81) says Emerson was the lender; and Ellery Channing, in his own copy of *Walden*, has a note claiming the axe as his.

110. Thoreau refers to the meadowlark and the phoebe. Both begin singing in the Concord area in late March. He is not referring to the wood pewee, which does not arrive in Concord until late May.

111. "Now is the winter of our discontent, / Made glorious summer by this sun of York" (*Richard III*, I, i).

112. This is Thoreau's own poem. Although he quotes other authors frequently, he is always careful to put all but his own poetry within quotation marks.

113. There is no James Collins listed in the *Concord Vital Records*. But there is a family, now residents of Lowell, Mass., who claim to be descendants of this Collins. He was one of the many Irish who left their native country because of the potato famine,

and came to this country to work on the railroads as day laborers.

114. Concord Town Records list a William Seley, but no Seeleys.

115. Discussed in Book II of Virgil's *Aeneid*, particularly circa line 351.

116. Ellery Channing has written in his copy of *Walden* at this point, "There is nothing like a hill here and never was. . . . H. means the small rise in the ground, but it is no hill, no 20 foot rise" (F. B. Sanborn, *Recollections* [Boston], pp. 391-92).

117. There is still a noticeable dent in the earth a century after Thoreau's hut was taken away!

118. George Willis Cooke, in his introduction to *Early Letters of George Wm. Curtis to John S. Dwight* (New York, 1898, p. 81) says these acquaintances were Emerson, Alcott, W. E. Channing, Burrill and George Curtis, Edmund Hosmer and his sons John, Edmund and Andrew. The Curtis brothers were former residents of Brook Farm, but now residents of Concord. George later became a well-known critic and editor. Hosmer was Thoreau's favorite Concord farmer.

119. The American cowbird and the English cuckoo lay their eggs in other birds' nests and thus avoid the task of providing for their offspring.

120. "Nine tailors make but one man" is an old proverb that can be traced at least as far back as John Ray's *English Proverbs* of 1678.

121. As Thoreau points out in his *Journal* for January 11, 1852 (III, 182-83), this was Horatio Greenough, the sculptor. F. O. Matthiessen (in *American Renaissance* [New York, 1941], pp. 153-57) and Charles R. Metzger (in *Emerson and Greenough* [Berkeley, 1954], p. 79) both point out that this paragraph seems to reflect a gross misunderstanding of Greenough's ideas. But William J. Griffin ("Thoreau's Reactions to Horatio Greenough," *NEQ*, XXX [1957], pp. 508-12) demonstrates that Thoreau's opinions were based on a letter Greenough had written Emerson and not upon his published theories.

122. This is the fundamental theory of modern functional architecture. Significantly enough, Frank Lloyd Wright, our greatest modern architect, has said in a letter to this editor, "The history of American Architecture would be incomplete without Thoreau's wise observations on the subject."

123. The famous old Trinity Church in downtown New York, on Broadway opposite Wall Street.

124. The vogue of the "picturesque" in the early nineteenth century was considerable, and Thoreau read avidly all the works of Rev. William Gilpin on the picturesque. Cf. William D. Temple-

man, "Thoreau, Moralist of the Picturesque," *PMLA*, XLVII (1932), pp. 846-89.

125. That is, who do not have rare and expensive foods in their houses.

126. That is, in Thoreau's time one would order a coffin to be made by the local carpenter.

127. The grave.

128. Thoreau is apparently referring to the old Greek tradition of paying Charon a small piece of money to be ferried across the River Styx at death.

129. The details of building his chimney will be found below in the chapter on "House-Warming."

130. He did not plaster the house till late fall (cf. chapter on "House-Warming" below). A detailed discussion of the construction of the cabin will be found in Roland Wells Robbins, *Discovery at Walden* (Stoneham, Mass., 1947, *passim*). Mr. Robbins rediscovered and excavated the site of the cabin in 1945 and 1946.

131. Roland Robbins has pointed out to me that at 1845 price levels this should have provided enough nails to build an entire house. When Robbins excavated the site of the cabin in 1945, he discovered an unusually large number of bent nails, indicating that Thoreau's aim with a hammer was not all it might have been.

132. Although Thoreau liked to pretend that he was no more than a squatter on Emerson's land at Walden Pond, Henry Seidel Canby (*Thoreau* [Boston, 1939], p. 215) asserts that Thoreau had made an arrangement with Emerson to clear the land in return for its use.

133. Main Street in Concord still displays a notable line of grand and luxurious dwellings, one of the loveliest in any New England town.

134. The many Biblical allusions (as Jeremiah 23:28) to the difficulty of separating chaff from wheat.

135. In the Roman Catholic Church it is the custom to appoint a cardinal devil's advocate to bring up every conceivable argument against the raising of a candidate to sainthood.

136. Harvard College in Cambridge, Mass., from which Thoreau graduated in 1837.

137. According to Crawford (p. 362), Thoreau once occupied a fourth-floor room in Hollis Hall, the dormitory at Harvard.

138. Another reference to the fact that the then-recent Irish immigrants were hired chiefly to do menial labor.

139. In 1846 William Lassell discovered a satellite to Neptune only a few months after the planet itself was located.

140. "And why beholdest thou the mote that is in thy brother's

eye, but perceivest not the beam that is in thine own?" (Luke 6:41).

141. Manufactured by Joseph Rodgers [*sic*] & Sons, Sheffield, England, long one of the most noted cutlers.

142. The Harvard College catalogs of the 1830's list "nautical astronomy" as one part of sophomore mathematics.

143. Adam Smith (1723-90), Scottish economist, author of *The Wealth of Nations;* David Ricardo (1772-1823), English economist; and a family of French economists including Jean Baptiste Say (1767-1832).

144. In the Bibliophile *Walden,* Sanborn identifies this as Harriet Martineau, who made a famous tour of America in 1834 and 1835.

145. Possibly the Princess Adelaide (1792-1849) who in 1818 married the Duke of Clarence, who became William IV in 1830.

146. John the Baptist lived on locusts and wild honey in the wilderness (Matthew 3:4).

147. A famous race horse in eighteenth-century England, owned by a Mr. Childers of Carr House, and reputed to have been able to run a mile in one minute.

148. The terminus of the Boston and Fitchburg Railroad which passed by Walden Pond.

149. It is an interesting indication of Thoreau's preciseness that in the manuscript this reads one dollar, then is corrected to seventy cents, only to be changed in the page proof to ninety cents with the marginal comment to the printer, "They have changed the fare within the last week" (J. Lyndon Shanley, *The Making of Walden* [Chicago, 1957], p. 36).

150. A typical newspaper headline of Thoreau's time.

151. Thoreau may be thinking of Robert Clive (Baron Clive of Passey) who served the British government in India and also wrote some poetry.

152. Emerson records the purchase of the Walden wood-lot in his letter to his brother William on October 4, 1844 (Ralph L. Rusk, *The Letters of Ralph Waldo Emerson* [New York, 1939], III, 262).

153. Arthur Young was the author of many volumes on agriculture, including *Rural Oeconomy, or Essays on the Practical Parts of Husbandry* (London, 1773).

154. "I understand you well, said my master, it is now very plain, from all you have spoken, that whatever share of reason the *Yahoos* pretend to, the *Houyhnhnms* are your masters" (Jonathan Swift, *Gulliver's Travels*, IV, iv).

155. Thoreau may have been thinking of his friend Bronson

Alcott, whose transcendental community at nearby Harvard, Mass., was conducted without the use of animal labor.

156. "Gain cannot be made without some other person's loss" (Publilius Syrus).

157. Thoreau was speaking from bitter experience. In 1844 when Emerson wished to address a gathering of Abolitionists on the anniversary of the liberation of the West Indian slaves, no Concord church would open its doors to the convention, and Thoreau finally obtained the use of the courthouse and rang the bell (James Elliot Cabot, *A Memoir of Ralph Waldo Emerson* [Boston, 1887], p. 430).

158. Thoreau's favorite Oriental work. A classic of Hindu religious literature.

159. A pastoral region in ancient Greece now used figuratively as the name of an ideal land.

160. Not the famous Greek city, but an ancient city in Egypt, called also Hecatompylos for its hundred gates. Thoreau may have read about it in Diodorus 1. 15.

161. Emerson, in his Journals for August 18, 1852 (VIII, 320), attributes a very similar opinion of the worth of the pyramids to Horatio Greenough. But Greenough apparently made his statement that month, whereas Thoreau's is recorded in his own *Journal* for April 21, 1852 (III, 454).

162. While there is a Balcom family listed in the Concord records of Thoreau's time, I can find none of that name listed in the Massachusetts directories of architects in that period.

163. A celebrated architect in the age of Augustus. He wrote the only book on architecture among the ancients that is still extant.

164. I can find no trace of any Dobsons in either Concord records or in the directories of Massachusetts stonecutters of Thoreau's time.

165. Thoreau probably meant to say "forty centuries." Napoleon, in a short address to his soldiers in Egypt, said of the pyramids, "From the summit of those monuments forty centuries look down upon you."

166. I have been unable to discover the particular person (if any) to whom Thoreau was referring, although Concord, like any town of its day, had its share of eccentrics.

167. The bracket covering "experiments which failed," in the first edition did not include salt, but through a printer's error it was extended in later editions. Careful editors since then have made the correction. Thus this offers a simple check as to whether any particular edition has been edited with care or not.

168. There is a pleasant little anecdote that Thoreau caught alive in a boxtrap one of the woodchucks that had been ravaging his beans. But not having the heart to kill it, he carted it off two miles and freed it, letting it be someone else's worry, not his own. See Henry S. Canby, *Thoreau* (Boston, 1939), p. 219.

169. A resident of central Asia. Most of the Oriental religions include the doctrine of transmigration of the souls after death, even for animals.

170. His mother and sisters did most of such work for him as a friendly service.

171. Barthalow Crawford, *Thoreau: Representative Selections* (New York, 1934), states that the fractions did not occur in the original manuscripts and that they were "whimsical additions" by Thoreau, but Prof. Shanley informs me the fractions are in the manuscript.

172. It is one of the favorite statements of those who belittle Thoreau's experiment that he lived within sound of the Emerson dinner bell, which is without question true. But he has effectively answered their charge in the following sentence. George Willis Cooke, in *Early Letters of George Wm. Curtis to John S. Dwight* (New York, 1898; p. 81) states, "It was Thoreau's custom while at Walden to dine on Sundays with Emerson, and to stop at [Edmund] Hosmer's on his way back to the pond, often remaining to supper."

173. He is using the word in the biological sense of specific, as distinguished from generic name. Thoreau is exceedingly careful in his choice of words, and one will often find his use of them enlightening.

174. "For they the Egyptians do not use the birds for hatching the eggs, in effecting this themselves artificially by their own wit and skill in an astounding manner, they are not surpassed by the operations of nature" (Diodorus 1. 74. 4).

175. Apparently Thoreau's own coinage, but quite obvious in its meaning and a pun on "cerulean."

176. Marcus Porcius Cato *De agri cultura*, Chap. 74. Ethel Seybold (*Thoreau: The Quest and the Classics* [New Haven, 1951], p. 55) points out that Thoreau apparently did not have access to this volume until 1851 and so it was a late addition to *Walden*. Note that Thoreau almost invariably follows any Latin or Greek quotation with an English translation (often his own) for the convenience of the reader. John Paul Pritchard in "Cato in Concord" (*Classical Weekly*, XXXVI [1942], 3-5), makes a special study of Thoreau's interest in Cato.

177. Thoreau undoubtedly used John Warner Barber, *His-*

torical Collections . . . of . . . Massachusetts (Worcester, 1839),
p. 195, where the whole, an untitled poem, is quoted.

178. Ellery Channing in his copy of *Walden* suggests that Thoreau was thinking of his friend Isaac Hecker here.

179. A widow's share, according to the laws of inheritance, is a
third.

180. Most of the furniture which Thoreau used at Walden is
now on display in a special Thoreau Room in the Concord Antiquarian Society. In his *Journal* (III, 200), Thoreau says he carted
all his furniture out to Walden in a hay-rigging.

181. Mr. Laurence E. Richardson informs me that the name
Spaulding was a common one in the neighboring towns of Carlisle
and Chelmsford in Thoreau's time, though there is no record of a
Concord Spaulding. Byron Rees (*Walden* [New York, 1910]),
states, without citing his source, that Thoreau was referring to a
Carlisle family.

182. Latin for castoff.

183. A reference to Aesop's fable "The Fox without a Tail."

184. A collegiate term meaning a complete failure in recitation
(*DAE*).

185. Neat, trim-looking.

186. "Arise, take up thy bed, and go unto thine house" (Matthew 9:6).

187. A common old superstition.

188. Economical New England housewives once kept the curtains drawn in their parlors to keep the sun from fading their
carpets.

189. Channing comments in his copy of *Walden*, "Deacon
Brown, a penurious old curmudgeon, who lived next house to me in
the middle of the town,—a human rat." Thoreau gives further details of this auction in his *Journal* (VI, 80).

190. "The evil, that men do, lives after them; / The good is oft
interred with their bones" (*Julius Caesar*, III, ii).

191. The word was formerly applied to fires for the burning of
heretics, proscribed books, etc.

192. The emphasis is on the derivation of the word from the
Latin *auctio*, meaning an increasing, that is, of the price by bidding.

193. Thoreau is probably thinking of the *Iliad* 22. 330, wherein
the death of Hector is usually described as his "kicking the dust."

194. Frank Davidson, in "Thoreau's Contribution to Hawthorne's
Mosses" (*NEQ*, XX [1947], 539), points out the similarity between
this description of the busk and Hawthorne's short story "Earth's

Holocaust" and suggests that Thoreau may have inspired Hawthorne to write the story.

195. William Bartram, *Travels through North and South Carolina* . . . (Philadelphia, 1791, p. 507; Part IV, Chap. 3).

196. William H. Prescott, *History of the Conquest of Mexico* (New York, 1843, Book I, Chap. IV).

197. Noah Webster, *An American Dictionary of the English Language* (New York, 1828).

198. In his Commencement Speech at his graduation from Harvard, Thoreau suggested we should reverse the biblical order, working one day and resting six. He thus was practicing roughly what he had preached.

199. Thoreau had three experiences as a school teacher. In order to earn more money, he left Harvard for a few months and taught in Canton, Mass. After graduation, he taught for a few weeks in the public schools in Concord. But when the authorities insisted that he use the rod, he whipped six children at random and handed in his resignation. Shortly thereafter he started a private school with his brother John. This was a pioneer in many of the principles of modern education and was so successful that there was a waiting list of students. But it was later abandoned when John became too ill to teach. Thoreau also spent a number of months as a private tutor for Emerson's nephews on Staten Island.

200. Apollo, when banished from heaven, was forced to tend the flocks of Admetus, son of the king of Pherae, for nine years. This is a favorite allusion of Thoreau's and it will be found over and over again in his writings. Ethel Seybold (*Thoreau: The Quest and the Classics* [New Haven, 1951], p. 59) thinks that Thoreau derived this legend from his reading of *Alcestis* while a student at Harvard. But the legend occurs so frequently that this hardly seems a safe guess.

201. The Greek revival in American architecture was nearing its end by the time Thoreau went to Walden, and it was being replaced by the rococo pseudo-Gothic style.

202. Referring to the custom in colonial America of emigrants indenturing themselves to pay for their passage across the Atlantic.

203. This paragraph is taken almost word for word from a letter Thoreau wrote Horace Greeley on May 19, 1848, thus giving an interesting insight into his methods of composition.

204. An interesting parallel to the story of the rich young man, told in Luke 18.

205. It is important to call attention to this line, for so many ask, "What if everyone lived like Thoreau?" An anonymous reviewer of *Walden* in the *National Anti-Slavery Standard* for Dec.

16, 1854, aptly commented, "No man could pursue his course who was a mere superficial imitator, any more than it would be a real imitation of Christ if all men were to make it their main business to go about preaching the gospel to each other."

206. Fugitive slaves trying to make their way to Canada, used the North Star as their guide.

207. Thoreau is probably thinking in particular of J. A. Etzler's proposals in his *The Paradise within the Reach of All Men* that the construction of huge apartment houses would save much time, money, and energy. Thoreau wrote a devastating review of the book for the *Democratic Review* (XIII [1843], 427ff).

208. Despite Thoreau's protests here to the contrary, he did perhaps more than any other Concordian to better the conditions of the Irish laborers of the town. Cf. Frank Buckley, "Thoreau and the Irish" (*NEQ*, XIII [1940], 389-400).

209. "The devil finds work for idle hands" is an old proverb that can be traced at least as far back as John Ray's *Compleat Collection of English Proverbs* of 1670.

210. Probably a reference to Cotton Mather's *Essays to Do Good* (1710) or Benjamin Franklin's *Dogood Papers* (1722).

211. A merry domestic fairy known also as Puck. See *Midsummer Night's Dream*, II, i.

212. The son of the sun in Greek mythology. The tale is told in the *Aeneid* and many other classical sources.

213. John Howard (1726?-90), English philanthropist and prison reformer.

214. There are many such incidents recorded in *The Jesuit Relations and Allied Documents*. See, for example, Vol. XVII, p. 109 (Cleveland, 1898).

215. "And as ye would that men should do to you, do ye also to them likewise" (Luke 6:31).

216. "Love your enemies" (Matthew 5:44).

217. "Then said Jesus, Father, forgive them; for they know not what they do" (Luke 23:34).

218. Latin for *outside* and *inside*.

219. The biblical custom of tithing one's income for the Lord.

220. William Penn (1644-1718), Quaker reformer and founder of Pennsylvania; John Howard (1726?-90), English prison reformer; and Elizabeth Fry (1780-1845), Quaker prison reformer.

221. "Charity shall cover the multitude of sins" (I Peter 4:8).

222. An ancient belief, as, for example, in Song of Solomon 5:4: "And my bowels were moved for him."

223. "But when thou doest alms, let not thy left hand know what thy right hand doeth" (Matthew 6:3).

224. "Evil communications corrupt good manners" (I Corinthians 15:33).

225. The opening lines of the "Shorter Catechism" in the *New England Primer* are "Man's chief End is to Glorify God, and to Enjoy Him for ever."

226. One of the popular healing fads of Thoreau's day was mesmerism or animal magnetism.

227. Another name for the Tigris River. Also spelled Dijla or Dojail.

228. Musee-Huddeen Sheik Saadi, *The Gulistan or Rose Garden.* Saadi was a famous Persian poet of the thirteenth century who was particularly popular among the transcendentalists. Emerson wrote a preface to an English translation. Thoreau's quotation occurs in Chapter VIII ("Rules for Conduct in Life"), No. 105.

229. " 'Complemental' to round out a one-sided view of things; Thoreau in printing Carew's poem, permits his opposition a rebuttal to the arguments of 'Economy' " (Joseph Jones, *Index to Walden* [Austin, 1955], p. 11). J. H. Birss, in *Notes & Queries*, CLXIV (1933), 63, states that this poem was taken from the Cavalier poet Thomas Carew's masque *Coelum Britannicum.* They are the words of Mercury after "the fifth anti-masque of Gipsies." Thoreau has modernized the text somewhat and added his own title.

[II]

WHERE I LIVED, AND WHAT I LIVED FOR

1. The first, second, third, and fifth paragraphs of this chapter were first published as "A Poet Buying a Farm" in *Sartain's Union Magazine*, (XI [1852], 127), with slight variations in punctuation and wording, for example, "rotten" for "blasted" in the first paragraph, and "proprietorship" for "possession" and "a poorman" for "not rich man" in the second paragraph.

For earlier publication of another segment in the same magazine, see the chapter on "Sounds." Since the August, 1852, is the final issue of the magazine, it raises the interesting question, did Thoreau originally intend to serialize more of *Walden* only to have the magazine fail on him?

2. An old farm on the Sudbury River just below Hubbard's Bridge, in Concord.

3. From "Verses supposed to be written by Alexander Selkirk"

by William Cowper. "Survey" is italicized to call attention to the pun on Thoreau's own means of earning a living.

4. According to Greek mythology, Atlas carried the world on his shoulders.

5. A *"Boston Cultivator"* was published in Thoreau's lifetime at 22 North Market Street, Boston; and a *"New England Cultivator"* at 26 Washington Street, Boston.

6. From Cato's *De agri cultura* 1. 1. Thoreau could have little complaint about the current Ash-Hooper translation, for it says, "When you are thinking of acquiring a farm, keep in mind these points: that you be not overeager in buying nor spare your pains in examining, and that you consider it not sufficient to go over it once. However often you go, a good piece of land will please you more at each visit."

7. Note the structure of the book. To give it unity, he combined the experience of two years (and, indeed, some of the experiences of the period from 1847 to 1854, when the book was finally published) into one. This was a favorite device of Thoreau's. Thus he used the unit of a week for his first book, and in *Cape Cod* combined several excursions into one.

8. He said this before on the title page where these lines were set forth as the theme of the book. The ode to dejection refers to Coleridge's poem of that name.

9. A house he had seen in the Catskill Mountains in 1844, as he tells us in his *Journal* (I, 361).

10. The supposed residence of the gods in Greek mythology.

11. Thoreau built the boat himself and used it on his excursion on the Concord and Merrimack rivers. He sold it to Nathaniel Hawthorne, who was then residing in the Old Manse, who in turn passed it on to Thoreau's friend Ellery Channing. Hawthorne tells at some length the story of his acquiring the boat in his *American Notebooks* in the entries for September 1 and 2, 1842.

12. *"Et un sejour sans oiseaux est comme un mets sans assaisonnement"* (M. A. Langlois, trans. *Harivansa ou Histoire de la Famille de Hari* [Paris, 1834], I, 282). The translation into English is undoubtedly Thoreau's.

13. Note that Thoreau did not retire from civilization. He was within easy walking distance of Concord village and only twenty miles from Boston.

14. Site of the battle of April 19, 1775, the opening skirmish of the American Revolution.

15. Channing identifies this as Heywood's Peak, which is directly south of Walden Pond.

16. The Peterborough range in southern New Hampshire.

17. It was a frequent custom in the days before modern re-frigeration to lower the butter into the well on summer days to keep it from melting and spoiling.

18. The rivers of Concord (including the Sudbury) overflow their banks each spring.

19. The grasslands of Asiatic Russia.

20. *"Il n'y a d'heureux dans le monde que les êtres qui jouissent librement d'un vaste horizon"* (M. A. Langlois, *Harivansa ou Histoire de la Famille de Hari* [Paris, 1834], I, 283). The translation into English is undoubtedly Thoreau's. Damodara is another name for Krishna.

21. The names of various stars and constellations.

22. The author of these lines is unknown, but they were set to music in 1611 by Robert Jones as the ninth song in *The Muses Gardin for Delights, or the Fift Booke of Ayres.* According to Joseph Leach (*American Notes & Queries*, II [1943], 171) Thoreau may have found it in Thomas Evans' *Old Ballads* I ([London, 1810], 248). Further discussion of Thoreau's use of the poem will be found in Howard Schultz, "A Fragment of Jacobean Song in Thoreau's *Walden*" (*MLN*, LXIII [1948], 271-72).

23. The Roman goddess of the dawn.

24. Confucius, *The Great Learning*, "Commentary of the Philosopher Tsang," Chap. I, p. i.

25. "And the trumpet that sings of fame" (Felecia Hemans, "The Landing of the Pilgrims," pp. 177-223).

26. The opening lines of the *Iliad* and the *Odyssey* speak of the wrath and wanderings of the Greeks.

27. This phrase, abbreviated "t f" is the printer's sign for a standing advertisement.

28. I have been unable to locate this quotation more precisely.

29. The statue erected in ancient times to Memnon, king of Ethiopia, uttered a melodious sound every morning when the first rays of the sun fell on it.

30. The ancient Spartans were noted for their idealization of bravery and hardship.

31. Thoreau usually referred to his travel essays as "excursions."

32. The opening lines of the "Shorter Catechism" in the *New England Primer* are "Man's chief End is to Glorify God, and to Enjoy Him for ever."

33. Aeacus, son of Jupiter in Greek mythology, was king of Oenopia. When a pestilence destroyed his subjects, he entreated Jupiter to repeople his kingdom by changing all the ants in an old oak tree into men.

34. The opening lines of *Iliad,* III, compare the Trojans to cranes fighting with pygmies.

35. "If we can get a garment to cover without / Our other garments are clout upon clout" ("New England Annoyances" which Thoreau was familiar with, in John Warner Barber, *Historical Collections . . . of . . . Massachusetts* [Worcester, 1841], p. 195).

36. Until it was unified in 1871, the German Confederacy was constantly changing its borders.

37. Ties upon which the railroad tracks are laid. Note the pun on the word.

38. Another reference to Hawthorne's short story "The Celestial Railroad."

39. Note the punning allusion to running a person out of town.

40. An old proverb which can be traced at least as far back as Thomas Fuller's *Gnomologia* (1732).

41. A nervous disease marked by involuntary motions of the limbs.

42. The parish bell was rung in one way (known as "setting the bell") to call the people to church, and in another to call the people to a fire.

43. In May, 1844, Thoreau and his friend Edward Hoar went on a fishing expedition on Fairhaven Bay, a short distance from Walden Pond. The fire they built to cook the fish got away from them and burned down a large area of woods. Thoreau ran to fetch the fire company, then returned to put out the flames. But soon seeing his solitary efforts were futile, he climbed a nearby hill to enjoy the spectacle. He thus enraged his fellow-townsmen, who, it is thought, had not his companion been the son of the town's leading citizen, would have jailed him. Echoes of that fire still reverberate against Thoreau in Concord today. A contemporary account of the fire from the *Concord Freeman* of May 3, 1844, is reproduced in *TSB* 32 (1950). Thoreau's own account of the fire will be found in his *Journal* (II, 21-25).

44. The Washita or Ouachita River, as it is now called, flows from Arkansas into the Red River in Louisiana. The residents of that area were prone to gouge out their opponents' eyes with a turn of the thumb (Francis Allen, *Walden* [Boston, 1910], p. 382).

45. Referring to the famous blind fish in the Mammoth Cave in Kentucky.

46. A railroad formerly connecting Worcester, Massachusetts, and Albany, New York. Now a part of the Boston and Albany Railroad.

47. Bartholow Crawford (*Henry David Thoreau: Representa-*

tive Selections [New York, 1934], p. 367) states: "The persons here named appear prominently in the annals of Spain during the 'thirties and early 'forties. During the first part of the period, King Ferdinand and his brother Don Carlos were struggling for power. With the death of the king in 1839, Maria Christina succeeded to the throne as regent. In 1841 she was temporarily replaced by General Espartero, also as regent; but in 1843 the thirteen-year-old Infanta was crowned Queen Isabella."

48. When the Commonwealth under Cromwell abolished the British monarchy.

49. In Thoreau's personal copy of *Walden* he changed "come . . . them" to "accomplish it."

50. *Confucian Analects,* Book XIV, xxvi, 2. The "h" in Kieou-he-yu is apparently a typographical error for "p."

51. According to Genesis, Sabbath is the last day of the week, rather than the first as in the modern calendar. The Seventh-Day Adventists were active in calling attention to this in Thoreau's time.

52. Possibly an allusion to Father Taylor of the Boston Seaman's Bethel, who was famous for the nautical allusions in his sermons. He was the original for the character of Father Mapple in Melville's *Moby Dick.*

53. The idea, so common to the English Romanticists and the American transcendentalists and most notably expressed in Wordsworth's "Intimations of Immortality," that the child has a superior understanding of the universe which he loses as he matures.

54. I have been unable to locate this quotation more precisely.

55. The shopping center of Concord.

56. The new railroad trains then just spreading their networks over New England were easily derailed. Note the large number of figures relating to the railroad in this and the preceding paragraph.

57. So that he might hear the Sirens yet not succumb to the fatal desire to go to them, Ulysses had himself tied to the mast of the ship and had his sailors' ears filled with wax.

58. A point of support.

59. "And because of the anxiety occasioned by the rise of the river the kings have constructed a Nilometer at Memphis, where those who are charged with the administration of it accurately measure the rise and despatch messages to the cities" (Diodorus of Sicily 1. 36. 10).

60. Once again the romantic idea of the superior wisdom of the child.

[III]

READING

1. *"Etant assis, parcourir la région du monde spirituel: j'ai eu cet avantage dans les livres. Être enivré par une seule coupe de vin: j'ai éprouvé ce plaisir lorsque j'ai bu la liqueur des doctrines ésotériques"* (M. Garcin de Tassy, *Histoire de la Littérature Hindoui* [Paris, 1839], I, 331). The translation from the French is undoubtedly Thoreau's own. Mast was a Hindu poet of the eighteenth century.

2. For the influence of Homer upon Thoreau, particularly in the writing of *Walden,* see Ethel Seybold, *Thoreau: The Quest and the Classics* (New Haven, 1951), *passim.*

3. Thoreau had, perhaps, a better knowledge of Greek and Latin than any other transcendentalist, and translated a number of the classics into modern English.

4. The two most famous oracles of ancient Greece.

5. "Except a man be born again, he cannot see the kingdom of God" (John 3:3).

6. Refers to the fact that some of the ancient classics have survived only because churchmen of the Middle Ages, not appreciating their value, used the manuscripts as scrap paper for their own notes.

7. It is important to remember that Thoreau was not always a successful lecturer, and after a failure was wont to deride the value of the lecture platform.

8. This fact is recorded in Plutarch's life of Alexander.

9. It need hardly be said that he did not intend us to take this statement literally. He means simply that no translation has ever succeeded in fully carrying over the spirit of the original into a new language.

10. The Vatican houses one of the greatest libraries of ancient classics in the world.

11. The Vedas are the entire sacred scriptures of the Hindus; the Zendavesta, the scripture of Zoroastrianism. Thoreau was always ready to point out that the Bibles of other religions meant as much to him as the Christian.

12. An allusion to the building of the Tower of Babel.

13. This is the first part of the mnemonic device once used in country schools to teach the children the alphabet.

14. In one-room country schools, the youngest children sat on the lowest benches in the front row.

15. The *Catalogue of Concord Social Library* for 1836 (Concord, 1836, p. 20) includes a book entitled *Much Instruction from Little Reading*.

16. An old bit of folklore that Thoreau may have become familiar with through Sir Thomas Browne's discussion of "That the Ostrich Digesteth Iron" in the *Pseudodoxia Epidemica*, Book III, Chapter 22.

17. Apparently an allusion to typical characters in the sentimental novels of Thoreau's day.

18. "The course of true love never did run smooth" (*Midsummer Night's Dream*, I, i).

19. Perhaps a reference to one of the most famous of the Baron Munchausen tales, where in a great snowstorm he ties his horse to a post, only to discover when the snow melts that he has tied it to the top of a church steeple.

20. O. T. M., in *American Notes & Queries* (1942), II, 141, suggests that this may be a jibe at Cooper's *The Wept of the Wish-ton-Wish*. E. E. Leisy, in *American Notes & Queries* (1942), II, 121, suggests that it might be taken from the *Arabian Nights*.

21. In his essay on "Walking" (V, 236), Thoreau speaks of "the child's rigmarole, Iery wiery ichery van, tittle-tol-tan."

22. It was a common practice in the mid-nineteenth century to issue long novels first in monthly parts. Dickens is the outstanding example.

23. Again a reference to the fact that in the country schools the small children sat on little benches without desks in the front of the schoolroom.

24. Just at the time that Thoreau was at Walden, Dr. Sylvester Graham was leading his campaign for a reform of the diet, substituting whole grain flours for the more highly milled products. There was a wide interest in these reforms among the transcendentalists and at least several of Thoreau's friends followed the Graham diets.

25. Francis Allen (*Walden* [Boston, 1910], p. 383) identifies this as Alek Therien, who is described at greater length in the chapter on "Visitors." But this man is described as "middle-aged" and Therien as "twenty-eight years old." Prof. Shanley suggests to me that with the life expectancy of the 1850's, twenty-eight might be middle-aged, but I doubt if Thoreau, then in his thirties, would so use the term.

26. Thoreau may have been thinking of *Easy Reading for Little Folks* (Boston, n.d.).

27. "Tit" means "little," as in the bird name "titlark."

28. "Except a man be born again, he cannot see the kingdom of God" (John 3:3). The religious conversion of a person is thus often spoken of as his second birth.

29. A Persian religious teacher of about the year 1000 B.C., and one of Thoreau's favorite religious philosophers.

30. Literally, "to fall overboard," that is, to permit to be lost.

31. For a suggestion that Thoreau derived the ideas expressed here from Elizabeth Peabody's "The Dorian Measure, with a Modern Application" (*Aesthetic Papers*, I [1849], 109-10), see Joseph Jones, "Villages as Universities: *Aesthetic Papers* and a Passage in *Walden*" (*ESQ*, VII [1957], 40-42).

32. A famous French scholastic philosopher, teacher, and theologian who lived from 1079 to 1142.

33. The Lyceum was a common educational institution in the small towns of New England of the mid-nineteenth century. Its main purpose was to sponsor a series of lectures each winter. Thoreau was a frequent lecturer at such Lyceums and was one of the officials of the Concord Lyceum. As F. B. Sanborn tells in his *Recollections of Seventy Years* (Boston, 1909, pp. 569-70) Thoreau was curator for the year 1842-43, and with a budget of $109.20, paid for the renting, lighting, and heating of a lecture hall and provided for twenty-three speakers—including such famous men as Emerson, Horace Greeley, Theodore Parker, and Wendell Phillips—and yet was able to turn $9.20 unexpended back to the treasury at the end of the year. For Thoreau's own experiences as a lecturer, see Hubert H. Hoeltze, "Thoreau as Lecturer," *NEQ*, XIX (1946), 485-94, and Walter Harding, "Thoreau on the Lecture Platform," *NEQ*, XXIV (1951), 365-74.

34. Apparently an allusion to those periodicals which did not take sides on political issues, but were to provide matter for every member of the family.

35. The *Olive Branch* was published weekly under the editorship of Rev. Thomas F. Norris at 5 Washington St., Boston, Mass.

36. Harper & Brothers is a New York publishing concern, (now Harper & Row), still one of the leading publishers today. Redding & Co. was a firm of booksellers and publishers at 8 State Street, Boston, Mass.

[IV]

SOUNDS

1. Notice how the opening paragraph carries over the idea from the preceding chapter. This was one of the many devices Thoreau used to unify the seemingly unrelated essays of the book. Note also that the sounds described in the chapter are listed in chronological order, starting with the morning, going on through the afternoon, evening, night, and ending up with morning once again. Thus, just as the whole book epitomizes the year, so this chapter epitomizes the day, and both end on the theme of renewal—the book on the renewal of spring; the chapter, the renewal of dawn.

2. The long passage following is one of the most famous in *Walden* and is considered by many to be one of the outstanding expressions of the mystical experience in literature. For a detailed analysis of Thoreau's use of sound and silence in achieving the mystical experience, see Sherman Paul, "The Wise Silence: Sound as the Agency of Correspondence in Thoreau" (*NEQ*, XXII [1949], 511-27).

3. Thoreau took his daily bath in the cove of Walden Pond nearest his cabin.

4. Corn is one of the most rapid-growing of the common garden vegetables.

5. The days of our week are, of course, named after heathen gods—Thor, Woden, etc.

6. Ida Pfeiffer, *A Lady's Voyage Round the World* (New York, 1852), p. 36. The Puri Indians are natives of eastern Brazil.

7. Roland Robbins, in *Discovery at Walden* (Stoneham, 1947; p. 10), points out that the actual distance is more than a dozen rods.

8. Compare this passage with Thoreau's description of the occasion when he heard a tree fall in the dead of the night in the Maine wilderness (*Maine Woods*, p. 115), which he thought one of the most impressive sounds he had ever heard. Note throughout this chapter, and particularly from this point on, the emphasis upon sounds and onomatopoeia.

9. The following nine paragraphs were first published as "The Iron Horse" in *Sartain's Union Magazine* (XI [1852], 66-68), with numerous revisions of spelling, punctuation, and word choice. A

few new words are interpolated and a few others dropped, few if any of which are of great import.

10. A rush.

11. Probably the passenger pigeons which were once so prevalent, but which by Thoreau's time were beginning to become scarce and now have been extinct for nearly forty years.

12. As Roland Robbins discovered when he began his research on the location of Thoreau's cabin, the passage about the mink was not in Thoreau's original journal entry for August 6, 1845, but was added later when he had left Walden and had forgotten that he could not see the marsh from his cabin door (Roland Robbins, *Discovery at Walden* [Stoneham, Mass., 1947], p. 17).

13. Thoreau was probably referring to the bobolinks or to almost any small bird that inhabits marshlands.

14. The ruffed grouse or partridge produces a loud noise by beating its wings.

15. The lines quoted are from Ellery Channing's "Walden Spring" from *The Woodman, and Other Poems*. Channing was one of Thoreau's closest friends and his biographer.

16. The railroad from Boston to Fitchburg was constructed through Concord in the early 1840's. It is now the Boston and Maine line to Albany. An interesting analysis of Thoreau's attitude toward the railroad may be found in G. Ferris Cronkhite, "The Transcendental Railroad" (*NEQ,* XXIV [1951], 306-28).

17. Thoreau was probably thinking of "Come unto me, all ye that labour and are heavy laden, and I will give you rest" (Matthew 11:28).

18. Zeus, the Greek god of weather, was sometimes referred to as "cloud-compeller."

19. The passage parallels in many respects Job 39:19-25.

20. Notice the antithesis here to point up the triviality of the passengers' errands.

21. Still another reference to Hawthorne's satire "The Celestial Railroad."

22. A machine for sowing seeds (*DAE*).

23. An extensive swamp in southeastern Virginia and northeastern North Carolina.

24. In his own copy of *Walden*, Thoreau changed "are" to "were" and "rings" to "rang."

25. According to Greek mythology, one of the three Fates who presided over the birth and the life of mankind. She cut the thread of human life with a pair of scissors.

Nathalia Wright, in "Emily Dickinson's Boanerges and Thoreau's Atropos" (*MLN,* LXXII [1957], 101-03) points out certain parallels between this passage in *Walden* and Emily Dickinson's later poem "I like to see it lap the miles."

26. A battlefield in northern Mexico where the American forces withstood a severe attack in the Mexican War in 1847. Thoreau opposed the Mexican War as a war to extend the dominions of slavery. See his essay on "Civil Disobedience."

27. In the *Mémorial de Ste-Hélène* (Dec. 4-5, 1815) Las Cases explains Napoleon's meaning, though the reference is to "two o'clock in the morning courage": "As to moral courage, he had, he said, very rarely met with the two o'clock in the morning courage, unprepared courage" (*John O'London's Weekly*, June 9, 1950, p. 344).

28. Thoreau was probably thinking of the "Great Snow" of February, 1717, which Cotton Mather described at length and which Thoreau quoted in his *Journal* for February 3, 1856, although he was unquestionably familiar with it earlier.

29. He is thinking, of course, of two poems by Robert Burns: "To a Mouse" and "To a Mountain Daisy."

30. Long Wharf is one of the major wharves of Boston harbor and would be the source of much of the freight carried on the Fitchburg Railroad, some of which might be destined for Lake Champlain, on the New York-Vermont border.

31. In the *Sartain's Union Magazine* version of these paragraphs, the word "parts" reads "ports," which makes more sense and would seem to indicate that "parts" is an uncorrected typographical error, although Prof. Shanley informs me that it is "parts" in the manuscript.

32. Summer hats popular at the time were made from palm leaves.

33. Cocoanut husks were used in making matting, particularly doormats.

34. Gunny is a coarse material made from jute and used for bagging.

35. Old cloth is frequently pulverized and used in the making of paper for books.

36. Thoreau frequently visited the Maine woods and so saw the results of spring freshets which strewed the lumber being floated down to the mills high along the banks or washed it out to sea.

37. Thomaston, Maine, was one of the major sources of lime in Thoreau's day.

38. The Grand Banks, an extensive shoal southeast of Newfoundland, is the major fishing ground of the New England fishermen.

39. Emerson in his *Journal* (V, 36-37) says that Thoreau told him this storekeeper was Deacon Parkman.

40. Thoreau was probably thinking of the parlor guessing-game known as "Twenty Questions" in which all substances are divided into the three classifications of animal, vegetable, or mineral.

41. Codfish cured by drying.

42. Charles Wilkins, trans., *Fables and Proverbs from the Sanskrit being the Hitopadesa,* "The Lion and the Rabbit," Chap. II, Fable IX.

43. Another of Thoreau's many puns.

44. Cuttingsville is a post office in Shrewsbury, Rutland County, Vermont.

45. Milton's *Paradise Lost,* I, 293-94.

46. "The cattle upon a thousand hills" (Psalms, 50:10).

47. "The mountains skipped like rams, and the little hills like lambs" (Psalms 114:4). Note Thoreau's misspelling of bellwether.

48. A range of hills in southwestern New Hampshire, visible from the heights of Concord.

49. Thoreau's own poem.

50. All towns in the vicinity of Concord.

51. The word seems to have been adapted by Thoreau from the Latin *ululo,* to howl, to utter a mournful cry. *Ulula* was the Latin name for a species of owl. The word is translated "screech owl," but the bird was not nearly related to our American screech owl. Poe used the same Latin word as a basis for his poem "Ulalume."

52. Was Thoreau thinking of "We give thee a shout: Hoo!" (Ben Jonson, *Masque of Queens,* ll. 317-18)?

53. "Then nightly sings the staring owl, 'Tu-whit, tu-who!'" Song from *Love's Labour's Lost.*

54. "Allas! that I was born!" (Chaucer, *The Book of the Duchess,* l. 686).

55. "Abandon hope, all ye who enter here" (Dante, *Inferno,* 3. 1. 9).

56. In his own copy of *Walden,* Thoreau corrected this to "double spruce," which is an old name for the black spruce, the common spruce of the New England *swamps,* and the only species found in the neighborhood of Concord. The "single," or white spruce is more northerly in its range, and is found on the Maine coast and in the forests of northern New England. Adding to the irony of Thoreau's confusion of these species is his statement in his *Journal* for December 22, 1853 (VI, 22), before *Walden* was published, "It is remarkable how few inhabitants of Concord can tell

a spruce from a fir, and probably not two a white from a black spruce, unless they are together."

57. According to Greek mythology, the river Styx encircled Hades. Therefore Stygian means "of the lower world."

58. In drinking bouts it was customary to pass around a large cup with marks on the inside to indicate how much each man was expected to drink.

59. That is, "under the table."

60. "Early to bed and early to rise, / Makes a man healthy, wealthy, and wise" (Benjamin Franklin, Maxims prefixed to *Poor Richard's Almanack*, 1757).

61. Referring to the custom of Cape Cod ship captains taking a coop of hens along on their whaling ships.

62. The meadowlark, a common resident of New England fields.

63. See note 28, above.

[V]

SOLITUDE

1. "And leaves the world to darkness and to me" (Thomas Gray, "Elegy in a Country Churchyard").

2. In the ancient physiological theory of the humors, the predominance of black bile caused melancholy.

3. Aeolus was the Greek god of the winds. One of Thoreau's favorite musical instruments was the Aeolian harp, a stringed instrument placed in an open window and vibrated by the winds. Thoreau's own instrument is now in the Concord Antiquarian Society.

4. From Patrick MacGregor's blank verse translation of Ossian, *The Genuine Remains of Ossian*, "Croma" (London, 1841, p. 193).

5. Beacon Hill is the eminence on which the State House stands in Boston, Massachusetts. Five Points was a section of downtown New York notorious for its squalor and crime.

6. Brighton, a suburb of Boston, was then the site of numerous slaughterhouses.

7. "Bright" was a common farm name for a favored ox.

8. Confucius, *The Doctrine of the Mean*, XVI, 1-3.

9. *Confucian Analects*, Book IV, xxv.

10. In Hindu mythology, the Vedic god who presides over the deities of the middle realm (the air).

11. Thoreau was constantly aware of the fact that he was never able to lose himself completely in any emotion. It offers an interesting psychological problem.

12. Once again, Harvard College in Cambridge, Massachusetts.

13. In the first edition, the comma appears after "remunerate" rather than before. Thoreau struck out the comma in his copy of *Walden*, but it is often moved back to after "thinks," where it quite logically belongs, by some modern editors.

14. A famous sociological experiment of the time was conducted in nearby Lowell, Mass., where girls were hired to work in the textile mills and lived in factory dormitories. Reformers loudly praised the artistic products of their leisure, but Thoreau questioned the effect on their individual spirits.

15. I have been unable to discover the source of this story.

16. Hypochondriac melancholy *(NED)*.

17. A common natural phenomenon, known as a parhelion or sun-dog.

18. When Jesus cast the evil spirit out of an unclean man: "He asked him, 'What is thy name?' and he answered, saying, 'My name is Legion: for we are many'" (Mark 5:9).

19. The Mill Brook still flows through the center of Concord.

20. Since Thoreau a few lines later refers to him as one thought to be dead, it is likely that he was referring to Pan, the Greek god of all the inhabitants of the country. "The great God Pan is dead" is from Plutarch's "Why the Oracles cease to give Answers."

21. Two of the regicides under indictment for killing King Charles I. They remained in hiding at various places in the Connecticut River Valley.

22. Mother Nature.

23. He is perhaps thinking of "Morrison's Pill" which Carlyle describes in the chapter of that name in *Past and Present*.

24. Thomas Parr, reputedly born in 1483, who died in Salop, England, in 1635, aged 152 years.

25. Patent medicines of the day hawked from village to village in covered wagons.

26. The modern Souli River, which according to Greek mythology was in communication with the realms of Pluto.

27. A Roman goddess, the forerunner of the sun.

28. The Greek goddess of health.

29. The "blameless physician" of the *Iliad*.

30. According to some ancient authorities, Juno conceived Hebe after eating lettuce.

[VI]

VISITORS

1. Three well-known hotels in Thoreau's time in Boston, New York, and Concord, respectively.

2. Thoreau is probably thinking of *"Parturient montes, nascetur ridiculus mus"* (Mountains will labor, to bring forth a ridiculous mouse; Horace, *De Arte Poetica*, l. 139).

3. Thoreau returns to the original meaning of the word drawing room—a room to which the ladies withdrew after dinner.

4. The old New England custom of keeping the shades drawn in the parlor to keep the sun from fading the rug.

5. Indian-meal mush.

6. Pluto's three-headed dog who stood watch at the entrance to hell.

7. Edmund Spenser's *Faerie Queene*, Book 1, Canto i, Stanza 35.

8. *A Relation or Journall of the Beginning and Proceedings of the English Plantation at Plimouth in New England* (London, 1622), Part II: "A Journey to Packanokik."

9. A country of Asia Minor in ancient times. The man was Alex Therien, one of Thoreau's favorite fellow townsmen. (See J. Lyndon Shanley, *The Making of Walden* [Chicago, 1957], p. 170). Calvin Greene, in his copy of *Walden* in Princeton University Library, adds: "He afterward took to drinking, said Miss Thoreau. He was always very friendly to her brother, felt quite pleased over the above notice, and in Thoreau's last sickness, often visited him. At one time, (when somewhat intoxicated), Thoreau said to him, 'Why don't you take a gun and shoot yourself?' O! he answered, he wouldn't do *that* for the world! 'Well' added Thoreau, 'you might better do that and done with it, than keep on as you have been doing.'" See Thoreau's *Journal* (I, 365) for further identification of Therien as the Homeric man.

10. The *Iliad*, beginning of Book XVI.

11. White oak bark is a powerful astringent frequently used in medicine.

12. The passenger pigeons which in Thoreau's day were common, but which are now extinct.

13. The ruffed grouse.

14. "The days of our years are three-score years and ten" (Psalms 90:10).

15. Homespun, manufactured in Vermont.

16. The Latin word for money, *pecunia,* is derived from *pecus,* cattle.

17. "Plato defined man thus: 'Man is a two-footed, featherless animal,' and was much praised for the definition; so Diogenes plucked a cock and brought it into his school, and said, "This is Plato's Man.'" (From an essay on Diogenes in Diogenes Laertes, *The Lives and Opinions of Eminent Philosophers.*)

18. In his *Journal* (III, 198) Thoreau tells an anecdote of two young women who borrowed this dipper and failed to return it.

19. The Concord almshouse (poor house) was comparatively near Walden Pond, situated just across the fields from Emerson's house.

20. In many small New England towns the offices of selectman and overseer of the poor are combined.

21. Channing suggests this might have been one David Flint. A David Flint is listed in the Concord Register as born March 28, 1791.

22. "Whosoever shall exalt himself shall be abased; and he that shall humble himself shall be exalted" (Matthew 23:12).

23. The Walden cabin was a station on the famous Underground Railroad aiding escaped slaves on their way to Canada. Moncure Conway, in his *Autobiography, Memories and Experiences* (Boston, 1904, I, 141), gives a detailed account of Thoreau's caring for a fugitive slave.

24. A reference to Aesop's fable "The Cock and the Fox."

25. I have been unable to discover the source of this quotation.

26. "Ay, there's the rub" (Hamlet, III, i).

27. Dr. Josiah Bartlett was a Concord physician for over half a century.

28. Emerson's home in Concord was a Mecca for reformers and geniuses from all over the world. Thoreau met many of these. There is a memorable account of one such meeting with three "ultra-reformers" in his Journals (V, 263-65).

29. A parody of the familiar nursery rhyme "This is the house that Jack built."

30. Most of the larger hawks were called "hen-hawks" or "hen-harriers" by the farmers.

31. Samoset's greeting to the Pilgrim Fathers. Calvin Greene, in his copy of *Walden* in Princeton University Library, tells us that it can be found in Willson's *American History,* p. 181. C. B. Cooper (*Walden,* Chicago, 1938) suggests that Thoreau was thinking of his

English friend Thomas Cholmondeley here, but that is impossible since he did not meet Cholmondeley until the fall of 1854—after *Walden* was published.

[VII]

THE BEAN-FIELD

1. This may seem an exaggerated figure, but a mathematician assures me that it is quite probable for a bean-patch the size of Thoreau's.

2. Hercules was forced by Zeus to perform twelve labors for Eurystheus, among them the cleaning of the Augean stables and destruction of the Lernaean Hydra.

3. A giant of Libya, son of the Earth. Because he regained his strength whenever he touched his mother, Hercules finally defeated him by lifting him up in the air and squeezing him to death in his arms.

4. According to legend, Thoreau could not bear to kill this offending woodchuck, so he caught it in a boxtrap, releasing it several miles away to feed on someone else's garden. See Henry S. Canby, *Thoreau* (Boston, 1939), p. 219.

5. In his *Journal* for August, 1845 (I, 380) Thoreau says he was five at the time of this visit.

6. Although Thoreau was born in Concord, Mass., in 1818 his family moved to nearby Chelmsford, and then in 1821 to Boston, returning to Concord to settle permanently in 1823.

7. Thoreau's favorite instrument was the flute, and his own flute may still be seen among the relics in the Concord Antiquarian Society.

8. Thoreau had a lifelong interest in the Indians and assembled a large collection of Indian artifacts that is now in the Peabody Museum at Harvard University. His friend William Ellery Channing tells a story: "In a walk, his companion, a citizen, said, 'I do not see where you find your Indian arrowheads.' Stooping to the ground, Henry picked one up, and presented it to him, crying, 'Here is one'" (*Thoreau the Poet-Naturalist* [Boston, 1902], p. 271). Thoreau tells a somewhat similar anecdote in his *Journal* for October 29, 1837 (I, 7).

9. "And sprinkled dust upon their heads towards heaven" (Job 2:12).

10. The road past Walden Pond leads from Concord to the neighboring town of Lincoln, and thence to Wayland. *Agricola laboriosus* means "hard-working farmer."

11. The ministerial husbandman was the Rev. Henry Colman, mentioned immediately below.

12. Rev. Henry Colman (1785-1849) published for the state a series of four surveys of the agriculture of Massachusetts from 1838 to 1841.

13. The various grass crops grown for fodder in New England are not native but imported, and are thus known as English hay to distinguish them from meadow hay harvested for bedding.

14. A song sung or played by Swiss herdsmen to call their cattle.

15. Nicolò Paganini (1784-1840), perhaps the most noted violinist of all times, was particularly noted for his ability to play on a single string.

16. Scarlatina is now more usually called "scarlet fever"; canker-rash is a form of malignant sore throat.

17. Concord was the home of the Concord Artillery, a unit of the state militia. The participants were known as "trainers."

18. According to the Virgil concordance, he does not use the word *tintinnabulum*.

19. "And the trumpet that sings of fame" (Felicia Hemans, "The Landing of the Pilgrims").

20. The war with Mexico was carried on during Thoreau's stay at Walden. Need it be said that this is irony?

21. A common expression in New England is "He doesn't know beans," meaning the person is ignorant.

22. A reference to the simile in the opening lines of *Iliad*, III.

23. The son of King Priam and Hecuba, he was the most valiant of the Trojan warriors against the Greeks. The falling and rolling in the dust is described in *Iliad*, Book XXII, l. 330.

24. Pythagoras was an ancient Greek philosopher who forbade his disciples to eat beans because he supposed them to have been produced from the same putrefied matter from which, at the creation of the world, man was formed.

25. It was a common custom in the ancient world to use beans as voting tallies.

26. John Evelyn, *Terra: a Philosophical Discourse of Earth* (London, 1729), pp. 14 and 16.

27. I have been unable to locate this quotation more precisely.

28. That is, a scarecrow device.

29. "The master should have the selling habit, not the buying habit" (Cato *De agri cultura* 2. 7).

30. An account of Squanto teaching the Pilgrims how to plant corn may be found in Alexander Young, *Chronicles of the Pilgrim Fathers* (Boston, 1841), p. 231.

31. It was a popular custom in Thoreau's day for Congressmen to distribute free seeds to their constituents.

32. Francis Quarles, "The Shepheard's Oracles," Ec. V.

33. The county of Middlesex held a cattle-show or county fair in Concord each year.

34. The Roman goddess of corn and harvests.

35. Jupiter, the Roman god of the earth.

36. The god of riches, not to be confused with Pluto, the god of hell.

37. Cato's *De agri cultura*, Introduction, Section 4.

38. *"Nec sine causa terram eandem appellabant matrem et Cererem"* (M. Terenti Varronis *Rerum Rusticarum* 3. 1. 5).

"It was also not without reason that they called the same earth 'mother' and 'Ceres'" (Varro *On Agriculture*). When Saturn was banished from his throne by Jupiter, he fled to Italy and taught the natives the art of agriculture.

39. "For he maketh his sun to rise on the evil and on the good, and sendeth rain on the just and unjust" (Matthew 5:45).

40. "The grain is so called from *gerere;* for the seed is planted that the ear may 'bear' *(gerat)* the grain. . . . The ear, however, which the peasants, in their old-fashioned way, call *speca,* seems to have got its name from *spes;* for it is because they hope *(sperant)* to have this grow that they plant" (Varro *Rerum Rusticarum* 1. 48. 2-3).

[VIII]

THE VILLAGE

1. In *TSB* 38 (1952), F. H. Allen tells an amusing tale of the difficulties the French translator of *Walden* had with this word. "The word 'stint' had been unfamiliar to M. Fabulet, but he had evidently found in a dictionary that it was used, especially in England, for a small sandpiper, and had translated "for a 'stint' by 'en chasse d'une bécassine,' that is, 'in pursuit of a snipe.'"

2. Homeopathic doctors are noted for giving medicine in minute doses.

3. Redding & Co. were booksellers at 8 State Street, Boston, in Thoreau's time.

4. A local Mediterranean summer wind from the north frequently mentioned by the classical authors.

5. Early experimentation on anaesthetics was going on in Boston during the 1840's under the leadership of Emerson's brother-in-law, Dr. Charles Jackson, and Oliver Wendell Holmes, Sr.

6. A punishment formerly common among sailors: the crew, provided with rope ends, were drawn up into two rows, and the delinquent had to run between them as they delivered as severe a chastisement as they could.

7. In the early years of the Republic the federal government imposed a tax on windows, which incidentally led to Fries Rebellion of 1799. Ground tax is the still prevalent real estate tax.

8. This is apparently a translation (possibly Thoreau's own) of the *Argonautica* of Apollonius Rhodius 4. 903.

9. Thoreau was probably thinking of Emerson in particular here, for it was but a short walk from Emerson's back door, through the fields and woods to the Walden cabin.

10. The refrain of the old American "Ballad of Captain Robert Kidd."

11. In his copy of *Walden*, Thoreau inserted a comma after "invariably."

12. Thoreau has told in further detail the story of his personal rebellion against slavery in "Resistance to Civil Government" which was published in *Aesthetic Papers* in 1849. It has been widely reprinted as "Civil Disobedience" and had a strong influence on Gandhi.

13. A pun on the Independent Order of Odd Fellows, a popular fraternal lodge.

14. A short distance southwest of Walden on the shore of the Sudbury River.

15. Thoreau left Walden for Maine on August 31, 1846. The account of this excursion is the first ("Ktaadn") chapter of his *Maine Woods.*

16. In the catalog of his library (Walter Harding, *Thoreau's Library* [Charlottesville, 1957], p. 59), Thoreau notes that it was the first volume of his Pope translation of the *Iliad* (Baltimore, 1812) that was stolen.

17. In the "Sayings of Confucius" which Thoreau edited for the *Dial*, III, 494, he quotes, "A soldier of the kingdom of Ci lost his buckler; and having sought after it a long time in vain; he comforted himself with this reflection; 'A soldier has lost his buckler, but a soldier in our camp will find it; he will use it.'" He had apparently found it in *The Phenix: A Collection of Old and Rare Fragments*

(New York, 1836, p. 83), where it is printed as one of the "Morals of Confucius."

18. *"Nev bella fuerant, Faginus abstabat quum [sic] scyphus ante dapes"* (*Elegies of Tibullus* 3. 11. 7-8). It is interesting to note that John Evelyn quotes these two lines and gives almost exactly the same translation in *Silva; or a Discourse of Forest-Trees* (London, 1729, p. 46), so it is quite possible that Thoreau derived this quotation from this secondary source.

19. *Confucian Analects*, Book XII, xix.

[IX]

THE PONDS

1. Line 193 of Milton's "Lycidas."

2. "Would you know the ripest cherries? Ask the boys and the blackbirds" (Goethe), "Sprichwortlich."

3. The ruffed grouse, in New England.

4. Copp's, Fort, and Beacon Hills, where the city was first founded.

5. Although there is a common confusion of huckleberries and blueberries, it is what is most commonly called the blueberry that has a bloom, not the huckleberry.

6. One of a religious order living in a convent or community. Here used as one of Thoreau's best puns, that is, "See, no bites."

7. In many later editions this has been corrupted to "seem."

8. I have been unable to discover the source of this definition.

9. One pronounced characteristic of the male figures in Michelangelo's paintings is the overdevelopment of muscles.

10. Seemingly every community in New England has its so-called "bottomless ponds." I am familiar with a number of them and Thoreau mentions some in his Journals. See, for example, *Journal*, II, 68.

11. Nine Acre Corner is a little over a mile southwest of Walden Pond, near the Sudbury town line.

12. A spring sacred to the Muses, flowing from the slope of Parnassus.

13. The path is still visible and has, in fact, been worn much deeper by visitors to the Pond.

14. Presumably Walden Pond has been preserved from such a fate, for it is now a state reservation.

15. One of the many indications that a large part of *Walden*

was written in the seven years intervening between his leaving the Pond and the publication of the book in 1854.

16. Also known as Sandy Pond, in the town of Lincoln, about a mile southeast of Walden. Thoreau's college classmate Charles Stearns Wheeler built a hut there in 1836 and spent a part of his vacations there for the next six years. It is almost certain that Thoreau spent some time there with him, and thus it was possibly one of the sources of his idea of building at Walden.

17. In Thoreau's own copy of *Walden* he has noted that this tale is told of Alexander's Lake, Killingly, Conn., in Barber's *Connecticut Historical Collections* (New Haven, 1838, p. 431). But Kenneth Cameron, in "Thoreau and the Folklore of Walden Pond" (*ESQ*, III [1956], 11) cites an article in the Concord newspaper, the *Middlesex Gazette* for August 11, 1821, which attributes this legend to Walden Pond itself. Mr. Cameron also reprints an article by Wayne Hanley in the *Boston Herald* for January 15, 1956, which cites a theory expounded by Dr. Joseph H. Hartshorn, a geologist of Boxboro, Mass.:

> Walden Pond could have been a high hill, covered with an earth crust and supporting growing trees. And it could have collapsed into a pond, because the heart of the hill would have been a huge ice pocket left by the glacier. When the ice pocket melted, the thin earth crust would have sunk to become the bottom of Walden Pond.

18. Pan, see Chapter V.

19. A forked hazel stick, which, according to tradition, if held properly, will bend down when placed over water. It is still used in rural regions to locate appropriate sites for wells.

20. Glacial action.

21. According to a note in his own copy of *Walden*, Thoreau got this name from Evelyn's Diary. But the Concord Minot family, which was related to Thoreau by marriage, originally came from Saffron Walden, a suburb of London, and it seems likely Thoreau heard the name in family tradition. Thoreau himself speaks of this tradition in his *Journal* for December 2, 1857 (X, 219). Yet in an unpublished manuscript in the Huntington Library (HM924). Thoreau points out that the Minot family did not come to Concord until after Walden was named.

Hannah Hudson, in "Concord Books" (*Harper's Monthly*, LI [1875], 29), suggests that the pond may have been named for Richard Walden, speaker of the General Court of Massachusetts from 1666 to 1679, and an associate of Major Simon Willard, one of pioneers of Concord.

22. Kenneth Cameron, in "Thoreau and the Folklore of Walden

Pond" (*ESQ*, III [1956], 10) cites a reference in the Concord newspaper, the *Yeoman's Gazette* for August 21, 1830, to Walden as "Wall'd in." So Thoreau obviously did not invent this version of the source of its name.

23. Although these seemingly unimportant facts so carefully recorded by Thoreau occasionally irritate the modern reader, like the measurements of the whales in *Moby Dick,* they indicate the growing interest in scientific research in this country in the mid-nineteenth century. In later years Thoreau sometimes bewailed the fact that the recording of such minutia was gradually usurping his time and leaving him little for philosophical speculation. See, for example, his *Journal,* II, 406.

24. Slightly west of Walden Pond. A boiling spring is not a hot spring, but merely one in which the water can be seen bubbling up from the bottom.

25. In his own copy of *Walden,* after the word "breams," Thoreau inserts "Pomotis obesus [Nov. 26-58] one trout weighing a little over 5 lbs—(Nov. 14-57)." In his *Journal* for the latter date, he records the catching of a trout by Gardiner Heywood (X, 180), and for the former date, discusses various types of fresh-water fish (XI, 344-47).

25a. *Reticulatus* means "net-like," *guttatus,* "speckled."

26. In his own copy of *Walden,* Thoreau inserted the words "kingfisher dart away from its cover" after the word "it."

27. A widening of the Sudbury River southwest of Walden Pond.

28. Thoreau's guess was correct. An account of this fish and its nestbuilding habits will be found in *The Fishes of the Connecticut Lakes and Neighboring Waters,* by W. C. Kendall and E. L. Goldsborough, published as Document No. 633 of the United States Bureau of Fisheries.

29. It was a favorite habit of Thoreau's to bend over and peer at the landscape through his legs, thus providing a novel (and framed) view.

30. In his own copy, Thoreau inserted the word "(Hydrometer)" after the word "insects."

31. "Mordre wol out" (Chaucer, "The Prioress' Tale," l. 1766).

32. Thoreau had been previously employed as a school teacher and as a worker in his father's pencil shop.

33. Now, thanks to the fact that it is a state reservation, the woods have returned to Walden's shores, though the great hurricane of 1938 and the county commissioners of 1957 destroyed many large trees.

34. At one time the citizens of Concord considered piping

Walden water into town, but later decided upon Sandy Pond since it was higher and would provide more pressure.

35. The Greeks finally entered Troy by hiding in a wooden horse and persuading the Trojans to drag it into the city as a god.

36. "But More of More-Hall, with nothing at all, / He slew the dragon of Wantley" (From "The Dragon of Wantley" in Bishop Percy's *Reliques of Ancient English Poetry*).

37. Just west of Walden Pond, the earth was cut away to permit the railroad to proceed on a level track.

38. "Behold an Israelite indeed, in whom is no guile!" (John 1:47).

39. Thoreau's own poem. As always he is careful to put others' poems in quotation marks.

40. The financial district in Boston.

41. Emerson thus refers to Walden Pond in his *Journal* for April 9, 1840 (V, 381).

42. "And waste its sweetness on the desert air" (Gray's "Elegy in a Country Churchyard").

43. An article explaining these balls, which are not peculiar to Flint's Pond, may be found in W. F. Ganong, "On Balls of Vegetable Matter from Sandy Shores," *Rhodora*, VII (March, 1905), 41-47. Mr. Ganong makes particular reference to Thoreau's comment.

44. As John Olin Eidson points out in his *Charles Stearns Wheeler* (Athens, Georgia, 1951, p. 53), Thoreau had first hoped to build his cabin on the shore of Flint's Pond but had been thwarted by the owner, Mr. Flint—thus his anger.

45. Landowners in New England were required to obtain a written "privilege" from the community before they could dam up a stream for water power.

46. The part of the Aegean Sea where Icarus was drowned.

47. "For still the shore my brave attempt resounds" (William Drummond of Hawthornden, "Icarus").

48. England's lake country was made famous by Wordsworth.

49. Part of the Thoreau family business was the manufacture of sandpaper, no piece of which, so far as I know, now exists.

50. Sanborn (*Recollections of Seventy Years* [Boston, 1909], II, 323) suggests that it was Ellery Channing who gave White Pond this name.

51. William Jones, "A Topographical Description of Concord," *Mass. Hist. Soc. Col.*, I (1792), 238.

52. The man was a Mr. Haynes. His grandson, Adrian Hayward, gives an amusing account of the pulling out of the tree in *Nature Outlook* (IV, [1945], 29-36) in an article entitled "The White

Pond Tree." Haynes later commented to his son, "Thoreau was as anxious for all the particulars as if apples of gold had grown on it."

53. One of the world's largest diamonds—109 carats—first discovered in India and now part of the British crown jewels.

[X]

BAKER FARM

1. In Scandinavian mythology, the hall of immortality into which the souls of heroes slain in battle are received.

2. In Thoreau's personal copy this is changed to "black." See note in "Sounds" on his confusion of these species.

3. Now more commonly known as bittersweet.

4. The passenger pigeons which once were so numerous as to be trapped and slaughtered by the thousands but which since Thoreau's day have become extinct.

5. This is, of course, a physical impossibility, since rainbows are an optical illusion and always appear directly ahead of the observer. Charles D. Stewart, in "A Word for Thoreau" (*Atlantic Monthly*, CLVI [1935], 110-16) attempts to convince us that Thoreau could have experienced this phenomenon.

6. A noted Italian sculptor, artist, and autobiographer (1500-71). Thoreau quotes frequently from the *Autobiography* in his *Journal*. For comment on the shadow over his head, see Chapter 26.

7. A castle in Rome which was originally the tomb of the Emperor Hadrian.

8. On the shore of Fair Haven Bay, a short distance southwest of Walden. Baker Farm has since been incorporated into a large estate.

9. William Ellery Channing, "Baker Farm," in *Thoreau the Poet-Naturalist* (Boston, 1902; p. 225), which gives slight variations in the lines.

10. The Indian name for the muskrat.

11. William Ellery Channing, "Baker Farm," p. 371 (again, slight variations).

12. I am grateful to Mr. Laurence Richardson for pointing out to me that a walk from Walden to Fair Haven Bay would be taken through Lincoln and that in the Vital Records of Lincoln one finds recorded the birth of one Mary Field, daughter of "John, Irish laborer, and Mary" in May, 1844.

13. In Greek mythology, a Sibyl was granted as many years of

life as she had grains of sand in her hand. The older she grew, the more decrepit and haggard she looked.

14. It is important to note this "if-clause" before one condemns Thoreau as one who would lead us back to the life of the savage.

15. Remember now thy Creator in the days of thy youth" (Ecclesiastes 12:1).

16. William Ellery Channing, "Baker Farm," pp. 370, 372 (again slight variations).

[XI]

HIGHER LAWS

1. The phrase "Higher Laws" was one commonly used by the various transcendentalists—and the Abolitionists, too, in their fight against the proslavery laws passed by Congress. Theodore Parker, for example, once said, "To say that there is no law higher than what the State can make is practical atheism" (quoted in Henry Steele Commager, *Theodore Parker* [Boston, 1936], p. 208). "Higher Laws," then, are the god-given laws of one's conscience that, according to the transcendentalists, must be obeyed even at the cost of disobeying the laws of one's government. Thoreau expounds further on this idea in his essay on "Civil Disobedience."

2. "Cynics may be inclined to suspect that an almost exclusive diet of rice, Indian meal, and molasses might reasonably be expected to make even woodchuck look strangely attractive to any man" (Joseph Wood Krutch, *Henry David Thoreau* [New York, 1948], p. 83).

3. John Burroughs has written an essay on "Thoreau's Wildness" in *Literary Values* (Boston, 1902; pp. 197-202).

4. Thoreau is probably referring to the Falls of the St. Mary River in southeastern British Columbia.

5. "And Jesus said unto them, Come after me, and I will make you to become fishers of men" (Mark 1:17).

6. "He yaf nat of that text a pulled hen, / That seith that hunters beth nat hooly men" (Chaucer, Prologue to *Canterbury Tales*, ll. 177-78). But it was said of the monk rather than the nun.

7. The Indians of northeastern North America.

8. It means literally "love of man." Thoreau is merely pointing out that his love is wider than that.

9. In Massachusetts, a special body of men known as "the council" is elected to advise the governor in affairs of state.

10. The 1840's and 1850's were a period of food reform, with Dr. Sylvester Graham of "Graham cracker" fame at the helm. See Grace Adams and Edward Hutter's *The Mad Forties* (New York, 1942) for an amusing account of some of the food reforms suggested.

Ethel Seybold (*Thoreau: The Quest and the Classics* [New Haven, 1951], p. 42) suggests that some of Thoreau's ideas on food reform expressed in this chapter were derived from his reading of Porphyry's "On Abstinence from Animal Food."

11. William Kirby and William Spence, *An Introduction to Entomology* (Philadelphia, 1846), p. 258.

12. Although Thoreau frequently practiced vegetarianism, he did not confine himself wholly to that diet. For a discussion of Thoreau's vegetarian principles in relation to those of his contemporaries, see Joseph Jones, "Transcendental Grocery Bills: Thoreau's *Walden* and Some Aspects of American Vegetarianism" (*UTSE*, XXXVI [1957], 141-54).

13. Before one condemns this statement as gross exaggeration, he should read Emerson's essay on "Self-reliance," which is a further exposition of this theme.

14. Opium-taking was comparatively prevalent in Thoreau's day. Witness De Quincey's *Confessions*, etc.

15. Compare Emily Dickinson's: "Inebriate of air am I, / And debauchee of dew" ("I Taste a Liquor Never Brewed").

16. Rajah Rammohun Roy, trans., *Translation of Several . . . of the Veds* (London, 1832), p. 21.

17. Confucius, *The Great Learning*, "Commentary of the Philosopher Tsang," Chap. VII, 2.

18. "But those things which proceed out of the mouth come forth from the heart; and they defile the man" (Matthew 15:18).

19. Frank Davidson, in "Thoreau's Contributions to Hawthorne's *Mosses*" (*NEQ*, XX [1947], 538), points out that Thoreau was quite possibly thinking here of Hawthorne's short story "Egotism, or the Bosom Serpent."

20. This incident is described in his Journal entry for June 9, 1850 (II, 36). A later discovery by Thoreau of a hog's jawbones is discussed at length in F. B. Sanborn's *Recollections of Seventy Years* (Boston, 1909; p. 320).

21. *Works of Mencius*, Book IV ("Le Low") Part II, Chap. XIX, p. 1.

22. Rajah Rammohun Roy, *Translation of Several . . . of the Veds* (London, 1832), p. 19.

23. Fauns and satyrs were demigods, half man and half goat.

24. John Donne, "To Sr Edward Herbert at Iulyers."

25. That Thoreau practiced what he preached is evidenced by his Journal entry for April 20, 1841: "To-day I earned seventy-five cents heaving manure out of a pen" (I, 250-51).

26. Thoreau was unquestionably thinking of the Hindu *Laws of Menu* or the *Vishńu Puráńa*, which he had read in the H. H. Wilson translation (London, 1840).

27. "Ye are the temple of God" (I Corinthians 3:16).

28. Although Farmer was a common family name in Concord in Thoreau's time, it is more likely that Thoreau is using it here as a type-name rather than as a reference to a specific person.

29. In the first edition, this word came at the end of a line of type and was broken into "rec reate." In Thoreau's own copy, he corrected the syllabification, and thus apparently the hyphen crept into the word in some editions.

[XII]

BRUTE NEIGHBORS

1. William Ellery Channing the younger. In the dialogue that follows, Thoreau is the hermit and Channing the poet. J. Lyndon Shanley (*The Making of Walden* [Chicago, 1957], p. 80) suggests that Thoreau introduced this dialogue as a comic interlude because he felt the need of a descent from the level of "Higher Laws" to Brute Neighbors.

2. A name for dogs popular in the mid-nineteenth century.

3. Channing had sailed along the coast of Spain on his way to Italy in 1846.

4. A variant spelling of Confucius.

5. Abbreviation for "memorandum."

6. A New England term for any small fresh-water fish.

7. Pilpay, known also as Bidpai, was the reputed author of a collection of fables of East Indian origin. Thoreau was familiar with them in the Charles Wilkins translation, and Emerson had used some of them in the *Dial* (III [1842], 82-85).

8. In his own copy, Thoreau inserted "(mus leucopus)" after the word "kind."

9. Louis Agassiz. In the late 1840's, Thoreau collected various species of fish, reptiles, and mammals for Agassiz, who was working on the classification of species at Harvard. See the letters to and from Agassiz and his assistant J. Elliott Cabot in Thoreau's published correspondence.

10. A small elevation about half a mile north of Walden Pond.

11. Now more commonly called mourning doves.

12. The battle of the ants which follows is one of the most famous passages in *Walden*. Thoreau here uses the technique of the mock-heroic, describing the battle in terms of a major encounter of nations.

13. The warlike people of ancient Thessaly who accompanied Achilles, their king, to the Trojan War.

14. Literally, to fall overboard (*NED*).

15. The motto of the Duke of Kent.

16. "Another [Spartan woman], as she handed her son his shield, exhorted him, saying, 'Either this or upon this.'" (Plutarch, *Sayings of Spartan Women*, 16).

17. Achilles, filled with resentment against Agamemnon, refused to participate in the Trojan War until his friend Patroclus was killed, when he went forth to battle.

18. The battle of Concord of April 19, 1775, was of course one of the most famous in American history. The names and quotations given are familiar to any student of that battle.

19. The sites of two of Napoleon's bloodiest battles.

20. A hospital for invalid veterans in Paris; now the site of Napoleon's tomb.

21. François Huber (1750-1831) was a great Swiss entomologist. Aeneas Sylvius (1405-64) was Pope Pius II. Eugenius IV was pope from 1431-47. Olaus Magnus (1490-1558) was archbishop of Uppsala. Christiern II was ruler of Denmark and Norway in the sixteenth century.

22. William Kirby and William Spence, *An Introduction to Entomology* (Philadelphia, 1846), pp. 361-62.

23. James Knox Polk was president from 1845 to 1849.

24. Daniel Webster was not the author of the Fugitive Slave Bill, but he was roundly condemned by northern Abolitionists for his part in its passage. See, for example, Whittier's famous poem "Ichabod."

25. This is apparently a variant spelling of *Gerbillus,* a member of the mouse family.

26. *TSB* 68 (1959), p. 1, describes a similar "winged cat" discovered in West Virginia in 1959.

27. Pegasus, the winged horse of Greek mythology, was a favorite of the Muses, and thus is now considered the steed of poets.

28. The shopping center of Concord.

29. Thoreau notes in his *Journal* (IV, 380) that this occurred on October 8, 1852.

30. "Not long since we saw one of those birds loons of un-

usual size . . . it had been caught in Seneca Lake on the hook of what fishermen call a set-line, dropped to the depth of ninety-five feet, the bird having dived that distance to reach the bait. Several others have been caught in the same manner in Seneca Lake upon lines sunk from eighty to one hundred feet" [Susan Fenimore Cooper], *Rural Hours* [New York, 1850], p. 10). Thoreau in his *Journal* (IV, 380) said he also found this information in a newspaper.

[XIII]

HOUSE-WARMING

1. Some thirty years ago, a blight killed off the chestnut trees throughout New England and they have never succeeded in re-establishing themselves.

2. Thoreau is punning on the word "sleeper," another name for railroad ties.

3. Thoreau found this in E. B. O'Callaghan, *The Documentary History of the State of New York* (Albany, 1849) I, 10. A copy of this was in Thoreau's personal library.

4. Roman goddesses: Ceres, of harvests and corn; and Minerva, goddess of wisdom, who gave man the olive tree.

5. "Those evening bells! those evening bells! / How many a tale their music tells" (Thomas Moore, "Those Evening Bells").

6. *Iliad*, Book III, l. 4, is often translated as "avoiding winter and unspeakable cold."

7. Thoreau is apparently referring to the handwriting on the wall (cf. Daniel 5).

8. William Ellery Channing.

9. A New England term for sitting room (*DAE*).

10. Cato *De agri cultura* 3. 2.

11. The rococo scrollwork so popular in the decoration of houses of the mid-nineteenth century.

12. Two different types of support for a peaked roof. A king post is a vertical member connecting the apex of a triangular truss with its base. Queen posts, also vertical, connect the mid-points of the sides with the base.

13. A Roman god who was worshiped by uncovering the head. Note the length of Thoreau's sentence.

14. There is an apochryphal legend that once Thoreau and Channing set their compass in a direct line with a distant mountain

peak, determining to walk to it in a straight line. Midway on their journey they found a country farmhouse to be directly in their path, but since the front and back doors (connected as is usual by a long hall) were open and no one was in evidence, the two proceeded directly through the house.

15. According to court etiquette, one should never turn his back on royalty.

16. According to his *Journal* (I, 387), Thoreau "Left house on account of plastering, Wednesday, November 12th, at night; returned Saturday, December 6th."

17. The common fresh-water clam.

18. An expansion of the Sudbury River, about a mile southwest of Walden.

19. The Roman gods of fires and boundaries, respectively (that is, the wood was too rotten to use as fence posts).

20. In his *Journal* (III, 308), Thoreau tells us that this comment was inspired by seeing the Irishman Patrick Riordan carrying home an armful of faggots.

21. "Stolen waters are sweet, and bread eaten in secret is pleasant" (Proverbs 9:17).

22. William Gilpin, *Remarks on Forest Scenery* (Edinburgh, 1834), II, 122. For a study of Gilpin's influence on Thoreau, see William D. Templeman, "Thoreau, Moralist of the Picturesque," *PMLA*, XLVII (1932), 864-89.

23. William Gilpin, *Remarks on Forest Scenery* (Edinburgh, 1834), II, 101ff. Thoreau comments at length on these passages in his *Journal*, III, 407-8.

24. "The following is the Roman formula to be observed in thinning a grove: A pig is to be sacrificed, and [a] . . . prayer uttered." (Cato *De agri cultura* 139).

25. This is undoubtedly in F. Andrew Michaux's great *North American Sylva*, first published in Philadelphia in 1818, but I have been unable to find the specific reference in any of the editions I have checked. In his *Journal* for May, 1851 (II, 201), Thoreau cites frequently from Michaux and says he is using the edition of 1819.

26. See the poem of this name by William Wordsworth.

27. If an axe is becoming blunt and some cutting steel remains, it can be improved by heating and hammering it to thin the head and lengthen it.

28. Thoreau's own poem, and one of his most famous. For extensive analyses of this poem, see F. O. Matthiessen, *American Renaissance* (New York, 1941), pp. 165-66 and Delmer Rodabaugh, "Thoreau's SMOKE," *Explicator*, XVII (1959), 47.

29. A reference to the three Parcae (Fates) of Greek mythology; the first held the distaff of life, the second spun out the thread, and the third cut it.

30. The Cold Friday was January 19, 1810. Thoreau collects some reminiscences of it in his *Journal* for January 22, 1857 (IX, 230). The Great Snow was probably that of December 10, 1717, a famous description of which, by Cotton Mather, Thoreau quotes in his *Journal* for February 3, 1856 (VIII, 163-65).

31. These lines are from a poem by Ellen Hooper, published in the transcendentalist periodical the *Dial* (I [1840], 193). Thoreau omits the first portion of the poem and changes the stanza breaks of the portion he prints. In his own copy of *Walden*, Thoreau adds the identification "(Mrs. Hooper)" after the poem.

[XIV]

FORMER INHABITANTS; AND WINTER VISITORS

1. The road nearest Thoreau's cabin led from Concord to Lincoln.

2. The Concord almshouse is still on Walden Road, just to the rear of Emerson's house. Brister's Hill is now cut by Walden Street.

3. According to Townsend Scudder's *Concord: American Town* (Boston, 1947; pp. 135, 139), Duncan Ingraham was Concord's wealthiest citizen in the late eighteenth century, and one of the founders of its famous Social Circle.

4. Cato Uticensis, a grandson of M. Porcius Cato, whom Thoreau so frequently quotes in this book, was so named from his death at Utica.

5. The grave.

6. Concord, an inland town, was chosen for the residence of paroled prisoners awaiting their exchange in the War of 1812.

7. For a further account of Brister Freeman, see F. B. Sanborn, *Henry D. Thoreau* (Boston, 1882), pp. 206-7.

8. F. B. Sanborn (*Walden*, Boston, 1909; II, 154) identifies Cummings as a Concord physician of Scotch parentage who died in 1788.

9. The epitaph on the gravestone, which still stands, reads, "In memory of Sippio Brister, a man of Colour who died Nov. 1, 1820. Et. 61."

10. Scipio Africanus led the Romans against Carthage in 202 B.C.

11. In his own copy of *Walden,* Thoreau corrected the spelling from "Stratten" to "Stratton."

12. In his own copy of *Walden,* Thoreau adds at the end of this paragraph: "Surveying for Cyrus Jarvis Dec. 23 '56—he shows me a deed of this lot containing 6 A. 52 rods all on the W. of the Wayland Road—& 'consisting of plowland, orcharding & woodland' —sold by Joseph Stratton to Samuel Swan of Concord In holder Aug. 11th 1777."

13. According to Thoreau's *Journal* for 1850 (II, 20), John C. Breed was a Concord barber. Byron Rees (*Walden,* New York, 1910; p. 372) quotes a manuscript in the Concord Free Public Library, "John C. Breed, barber and drunkard; found dead in the road at last, in 1824 . . . an extreme instance of the power of appetite for rum . . . was its complete slave. He was all absorbed in it; he had no other want, no other affection. If he had opportunity to earn six cents by shaving, he would spend one cent for a cracker and five cents for his rum."

14. Election nights were often the occasion for mischief-making on the part of the young men of the town.

15. William Davenant, *Gondibert: An Heroick Poem,* (London, 1672).

16. Thoreau's maternal uncle Charles Dunbar. Thoreau tells many tales of this eccentric uncle in his *Journal.* (See, for example, VIII, 229-46). I have summarized these in "Uncle Charlie Comes to Concord," *Nature Outlook* (VII [1948], 7-9).

17. Alexander Chalmers, *The Works of the English Poets from Chaucer to Cowper* (21 vols.; London, 1810). Thoreau is said to have read the entire set through in his "spare" time while a student at Harvard.

18. A mixed Celto-Germanic tribe, occupying Flanders, and defeated by Caesar in 57 B.C.

19. Mrs. Caleb Wheeler has pointed out to me that if Thoreau "leaped the brook," the fire probably occurred when he was living at Emerson's house. (Note that earlier in the paragraph he says, "I lived on the edge of the village then—" a description that would aptly fit Emerson's house), and the brook he jumped was probably the Mill Brook which still courses along between Emerson's house and Walden Street.

20. James Baker lived in Lincoln about a mile south of Walden Pond. It was his farm that Thoreau speaks of as Baker Farm. The Codman place was that of Lincoln's wealthiest family, a magnifi-

cent three-story house still standing west of the Lincoln railroad station, between the railroad and the Waltham Road.

21. The Middlesex Mutual Fire Insurance Company was established in Concord in 1826.

22. Bascom's fire occurred in the spring of 1828, when Thoreau was still a schoolboy, and is described in the Concord newspaper *Yeoman's Gazette* for May 3, 1828.

23. In Thoreau's day, fires were fought with little hand-drawn vehicles, usually referred to as "tubs."

24. This is a quotation from William Davenant's "The Author's Preface" to his *Gondibert*.

25. Mrs. Caleb Wheeler has suggested to me that Nutting was probably the Sam Nutting mentioned below in "Winter Animals," and that he was a bachelor brother to Nathaniel Nutting, who was for many years sexton of the First Parish Church. John Le Grosse she identifies as a farmer who lived on Westford Road.

26. According to *Concord Births, Marriages, and Death* (Concord, n.d., p. 356), Thomas Wyman died on September 28, 1843, at the age of sixty-nine. I find no record of his son.

27. Old custom of sheriff attaching a chip if there were no other possessions to place a lien on.

28. In his own copy of *Walden*, Thoreau apparently deleted the words "clay and" and inserted a "(?)" after the word "use" in the next line.

29. A brief account of the death of Hugh Coyle [*sic*] from the *Concord Freeman* of October 3, 1845, is reprinted in *TSB* 33 (1950, p. 3). Thoreau writes at great length on Quoil in his *Journal* (I, 414ff). There is further description of Hugh Quoil's hut in Thoreau's "A Winter Walk" (V, 172-73).

30. "The golden bowl be broken, or the pitcher be broken at the fountain" (Ecclesiastes 12:6).

31. The traditional literary name for fox.

32. "Fix'd fate, free-will, forknowledge absolute" (Milton, *Paradise Lost*, II, 560).

33. "The wilderness and the solitary place shall be glad for them; and the desert shall rejoice, and blossom as the rose" (Isaiah 35:1).

34. Some of the major archeological discoveries occurred during Thoreau's lifetime, including the exploration of Babylon, the exhumation of Assyrian artifacts, and the rediscovery of Petra.

In the fall of 1853, Thoreau read Austen Henry Layard, *Nineveh and Its Remains* (New York, 1849) and was much interested in the account of the discovery of the various layers of archeological remains indicating the successive cities. See his *Journal*, VI, 11, 15.

35. Here Thoreau is quoting extensively from Cotton Mather's description of the Great Snow referred to in the previous chapter.

36. "Whosoever shall smite thee on thy right cheek, turn to him the other also" (Matthew 5:39).

37. In his own copy, Thoreau inserted the word "deer" between "meadow" and "mouse."

38. Aleck Therien, who was described at length in the chapter on "Visitors" above.

39. In the Bibliophile edition of *Walden*, Sanborn (Boston 1909; II, 167), identifies him as Edmund Hosmer. A detailed account of Thoreau's friendship with Hosmer may be found in Mary Hosmer Brown, *Memories of Concord* (Boston, 1926), pp. 88-111.

40. William Ellery Channing the younger, who lived on Ponkawtasset Hill on the opposite side of Concord.

41. Amos Bronson Alcott, father of Louisa May Alcott of *Little Women* fame. (Thoreau makes the identification in his *Journal* for May 9, 1853). In his youth Alcott had been a peddler through the South. Thoreau was one of the earliest to recognize Alcott's strange genius.

42. "How blind that cannot see serenitie?" ("Wolseius Triumphans," in Thomas Storer, *The Life and Death of Thomas Wolsey Cardinall* [London, 1599]).

43. The title character of a novel by Sir Walter Scott.

44. Inns were accustomed to advertise "Entertainment for man and beast."

45. First growth white pine—so called from the yellowish color of its wood.

46. A play on the *Arabian Nights' Entertainment.*

47. See the chapter on "Solitude" above.

48. Thoreau, in his own copy, placed a "(?)" in the margin by this line.

49. Ralph Waldo Emerson.

50. "The householder is then to remain at eventide in his courtyard as long as it takes to milk a cow, or longer if he pleases, to await the arrival of a guest" (H. H. Wilson, trans., *The Vishńu Puráńa* [London, 1840], p. 305).

51. "But never more could see the man Approaching from the town" (From the Old English ballad, "The Children in the Wood").

[XV]

WINTER ANIMALS

1. Now more commonly Baffin Bay, a part of the Arctic Ocean between Greenland and the Canadian arctic islands.

2. In his *Journal* for January 7, 1852 (III, 177), Thoreau describes walking to Lincoln in a snowstorm to lecture.

3. Although most people refer to the building at Walden Pond as a "hut," it is interesting to note that Thoreau uses that term only twice in his whole book; once here and again once eight paragraphs below. Roland Robbins, in *Discovery at Walden* (Stoneham, 1947, p. 10), points out that Thoreau refers to it as a "house" eighty-odd times, a "lodge" three times, a "dwelling" twice, and a "homestead" once.

4. Strangely enough Goose Pond is about a quarter of a mile northeast of Walden, while Lincoln is southeast.

5. Thoreau is undoubtedly referring to the incident of the geese alarming the citadel when the Gauls took Rome in 390 B.C. See Livy, *History of Rome*, 5. 47.

6. Caused by expansion and contraction of ice. See below, the chapter on "The Pond in Winter" for more on this phenomenon.

7. The squirrel, when angry, makes a chattering noise much like a noisy clock.

8. In his own copy, Thoreau corrected "brisk" to "frisk."

9. I have been unable to find the source of this quotation. Prof. Shanley informs me that in the *Walden* manuscript, the quotation is attributed to Audubon, but I have been unable to trace it further.

10. A famous Greek hunter who, when he saw Artemis bathing, was changed into a stag and devoured by his own dogs.

11. Thoreau gives the detailed conversation with this man in his *Journal* (I, 398-99).

12. As Thoreau knew only too well, the hunter with his one bath a year was probably outdoing many of his neighbors. In his *Journal* for July 8, 1852 (IV, 202), Thoreau says, "One farmer, who came to bathe in Walden one Sunday while I lived there, told me it was the first bath he had had for fifteen years."

13. A small town south of Concord.

14. On the shore of Fair Haven Bay, about a mile southwest of Walden.

15. A town nearby Concord.

16. In his *Journal* for March 10, 1853 (V, 16), Thoreau calls him "Old Fox" Nutting and records that he had killed moose as well as bear. Thoreau also records that he lived in Jacob Baker's house in Lincoln.

17. This old record book was found in Deacon R. Brown's attic, and Thoreau quotes from it at length in his *Journal* for January 27, 1854 (VI, 77–79). Channing says it was Ephraim Jones's book.

18. In his own copy, Thoreau queried whether this should be "calf" and adds "v. Mott ledger near beginning." But various types of wildcat have been caught in Concord, and on October 13, 1860, he wrote a letter to the Boston Society of Natural History presenting it with the skin of a Canada lynx killed in nearby Carlisle.

19. Thanks to the efforts of conservationists, deer are once more common in the Concord woods.

20. "Nimrod, the mighty hunter before the Lord" (Genesis 10:9).

21. "Rome, thou hast lost the breed of noble bloods" (*Julius Caesar*, I, ii).

22. "Lucius Aelius thought that the hare received its name *lepus* because of its swiftness, being *levipes*, nimblefoot" (Varro *Rerum Rusticarum* 3. 12).

23. Small fence built of twigs and placed across a rabbit's run to divert it into a snare.

24. Not in the modern sense of the word, of course, but "a boy who attends cows."

[XVI]

THE POND IN WINTER

1. Prof. Charles Anderson has identified this quotation as coming from *Harivanea*.

2. A forked hazel stick used by the superstitious to locate water.

3. Woodchucks.

4. Stout woolen coats of great thickness.

5. The idea of the "great chain of being" popular particularly in eighteenth-century England. See Arthur O. Lovejoy, *The Great Chain of Being* (Cambridge, 1933).

6. In Thoreau's day, fish peddlers blew horns to announce their presence as they walked through the streets.

7. A Protestant Christian sect which arose after 1170 in southern France.

8. In 1939, Edward S. Deevey, Jr., of the Osborn Zoological Laboratory of Yale University, rechecked Thoreau's survey and analysis of Walden Pond with the latest scientific instruments. His conclusions, published as "A Re-examination of Thoreau's 'Walden'" (*Quarterly Review of Biology*, XVII [1942], 1-11), are that Thoreau was phenomenally accurate in his observations when one considers he was using the crudest of instruments, and that his contribution to the science of limnology was "original and genuine."

9. In his *Journal* for September 15, 1850 (II, 68), Thoreau records visiting "Bottomless Ponds" in Sudbury and beyond.

10. The river which flows around Hades.

11. A fifty-six-pound weight.

12. William Gilpin, *Observations on . . . the High-lands of Scotland* (London, 1808), II, 4.

13. Milton, *Paradise Lost*, VII, 288-90.

13a. Gordon S. Haight (*Walden*, New York, Classics Club, 1942, p. 312) states, "The text here is obviously corrupt. . . . Probably the first printer of Thoreau's manuscript dropped out a whole line after the word elevation." It is true that the verb does not agree in number with the subject, but the error must have been caused by a misprinting of the verb itself, for we can trace the sentence back to the *Journal* (IV, 339) where the subject and the verb agree.

14. In the first edition of *Walden*, Thoreau inserted his own map of Walden Pond, but it has been omitted in most recent editions. See p. XII.

15. Achilles was born in Thessaly, according to tradition. Thoreau is probably referring to a rugged, mountainous shore.

16. In his own copy of *Walden*, Thoreau placed a "(?)" in the margin by these lines.

17. Frederic Tudor, the "ice king" of the nineteenth-century New England ice industry, and his former partner, Nathaniel Jarvis Wyeth, engaged in a trade war in the mid-1840's. Rather than be forced to buy ice from Wyeth, who had a monopoly of the sources, Tudor, who shipped ice all over the world, did his own harvesting at Walden Pond. When Tudor won the war, he had no need for the Walden ice, so it was left to melt on the shores of the pond. See Richard O. Cummings, *The American Ice Harvests* (Berkeley, 1949), *passim*.

18. "But lay up for yourselves treasures in heaven" (Matthew 6:20).

19. According to Greek legend, a people supposed to live in a

land of plenty and perpetual sunshine beyond the north wind. Thoreau may have read of them in Diodorus 2.47.

20. The *New England Farmer* was an agricultural journal published at Quincy Hall in Boston. There were both a *New England Cultivator* and a *Boston Cultivator* published in Boston.

21. In the Bibliophile Society Edition of *Walden* (Boston, 1909; II, 205) Thoreau identifies this as Mr. Tudor.

22. A region of the Greek Hell.

23. An old proverb which can be traced back at least as far as John Ray's *English Proverbs* of 1678 is "Nine tailors make but one man."

24. In Scandinavian mythology, the hall of immortality.

25. The issues of the *Old Farmer's Almanac* of the 1850's depict winter as an old man on the January page.

26. In Cambridge, Massachusetts.

27. Thoreau was probably again thinking of the *Old Farmer's Almanac* which featured these illustrations on the front cover.

28. He is probably referring to La Fontaine's fable (IV, 22) on "The Lark and Her Young Ones with the Owner of the Field," which Emerson speaks of at some length under the title of "The Lark and the Reaper" in *Dial*, III, 414. In his manuscript commonplace book now in the Library of Congress, Thoreau mentions reading this fable in J. Payne Collier, *Old Ballads* (London, 1843).

29. The parable as told by Jesus in Matthew 13.

30. Mark Van Doren (*Henry David Thoreau*, Boston, 1916; p. 81) feels that this final paragraph of the chapter shows the direct influence of Sir Thomas Browne in its style.

31. Ice-harvesting was a major industry in nineteenth-century New England, and ice was shipped to all these and many other ports.

32. One of the major Hindu sacred writings. Below are listed the three major gods of Hindu mythology.

33. The sacred scriptures of the Hindus. Thoreau would be pleased to know that the Hindus received not only ice from Walden Pond, but his own writings as well. His works had a profound influence on the late Gandhi and his followers.

34. Atlantis was a fabled land now supposedly at the bottom of the Atlantic Ocean. The Hesperides were legendary Greek islands supposedly at the western extremity of the world.

35. Hanno, a Carthaginian explorer, went to West Africa in 480 B.C. His report, "The Periplus of Hanno," is supposedly the earliest extant eye-witness report of an explorer. Thoreau was probably familiar with it in *The Phenix: a Collection of Old and Rare*

Fragments (New York, 1835), the entire text of which is translated into English.

36. "Of Ternate and Tidor, whence merchants bring / Their spicy drugs" (*Paradise Lost*, II, 639). They are two of the Spice Islands in the Dutch East Indies.

37. Alexander the Great became the most widely traveled man of his time.

[XVII]

SPRING

1. For a discussion of the spring and rebirth imagery throughout the book and particularly in this chapter, see Richard P. Adams, "Romanticism and the American Renaissance" (*AL*, XXIII [1952], 424-28).

2. Thoreau here reflects the mid-nineteenth-century interest in scientific phenomena almost for its own sake alone—an interest which Melville parodied so ably in portions of *Moby Dick*. Thoreau found to his dismay that as he grew older he became more and more interested in merely recording statistics and less in interpreting the statistics for a better understanding of life.

3. The *Concord Freeman* for September 30, 1842 announces that "they are building a reservoir on a very large scale at Fresh Pond, for the purpose of *manufacturing ice*, the coming winter. It is intended to pump up the water into the basin and allow it to freeze, which it will more readily do, than in the pond, as the depth will be but little, and it can be but slightly disturbed."

4. It was a favorite fancy of Thoreau's to see the world in microcosm, the Atlantic Ocean in Walden Pond, etc. Emerson reflects much the same sentiment in almost the same words in his *Journal* entry for 1836 (IV, 26): "A Day is a miniature Eternity."

5. Since in his *Journal* for March 28, 1854 (VI, 176) Thoreau notes that he has received the first proofs of *Walden*, this last entry must have been inserted into the final text. It is thus revealed that Thoreau kept revising his text up to the last possible moment. In his *Journal* for April 9, 1854 (XII, 191), he records his discovery that Walden had opened several days before. It is possible however that the first proofs did not cover this material.

6. "All the days of Methuselah were 969 years" (Genesis 5:27).

7. The next town southwest of Concord.

8. All of these leaves have been used as decorative motifs in various schools of architecture. Interestingly enough, I am told by one who is attempting a psychoanalysis of Thoreau from his writings, that Thoreau's interpretations of the shapes of thawing sand indicates "the character-orientation Freud called 'Anal.'"

9. These lines reflect Thoreau's constant interest in word divisions. An accomplished linguist, he had ample background for such speculation.

10. "Your bodies are like to bodies of clay" (Job 13:12).

11. Jean François Champollion (1790-1832), French Egyptologist who deciphered the Rosetta stone.

12. In old physiology, the bowels were thought to be the source of compassion.

13. See note on the excavation of Ninevah in Chapter Fourteen.

14. "As clay is in the potter's hand" (Jeremiah 18:6).

15. The Scandinavian god of thunder.

16. M. Terenti Varronis [Varro] *Rerum Rusticarum* ["On Agriculture"] 2. 2. 14. "And the grass which is called forth by the early rains is just growing."

17. A genus of fresh-water fish. Allen states that in Thoreau's time it was considered to include such fish as the dace, roach, minnow, and shiner, but that at the present time no fish included in that genus are known to exist in Massachusetts.

18. "For this my son was dead, and is alive again" (Luke 15:24).

19. Although in Thoreau's day the robin was listed by ornithologists under this name, it has now been changed to *Planesticus migratorius*.

20. An ancient Arab country east of present-day Israel.

21. Ovid's *Metamorphoses*, Book 1, ll. 61-62, 78-81.

22. "And while the lamp holds out to burn / The vilest sinner may return" (Isaac Watts, *Hymns and Spiritual Songs*, 1. 88).

23. Once again the romantic theme of the innocence of childhood exemplified in Wordsworth's "Ode on the Intimations of Immortality."

24. "Enter thou into the joy of thy Lord" (Matthew 25:23).

25. *Works of Mencius*, Book VI, "Kaou Tsze," Part I, Chapter VIII, p. 2.

26. Ovid's *Metamorphoses*, Book 1, ll. 89-96, 107-8.

27. In the southwest portion of Concord.

28. "Bones" or "clappers" which children use as a rhythmical instrument.

29. Edwin Way Teale (*Walden*, New York, 1946; p. 262) identifies this as "undoubtedly a male marsh hawk."

30. "O death, where is thy sting? O grave, where is thy victory?" (I Corinthians 15:55).

31. Edwin Way Teale (*Walden*, New York, 1946; p. 263) suggests that this was probably the coot, although possibly either a Virginia rail or a sora rail.

32. As Francis H. Allen has pointed out in his *Thoreau's Bird-Lore* (Boston, 1910; p. 377ff.), Thoreau almost invariably confuses the wood thrush and the hermit thrush. And since the wood thrush is a late spring arrival in Massachusetts, it is probable that Thoreau is actually referring to the hermit thrush here.

33. Cálidás, *Sacontalá; or, the Fatal Ring* (Sir William Jones translation), Speech of Dushmanta in Act V.

34. Once again Thoreau reminds us that he has condensed the experiences of two years into one for the sake of unity.

[XVIII]

CONCLUSION

1. A group of islands at the southern tip of South America. Translated from the Spanish it means "land of fire."

2. On the old sailing vessels, sailors were often kept busy untwisting old pieces of rope to use in calking the seams of the ship.

3. The shortest distance between two points on a sphere is the arc of a circular plane passed through the center of the sphere; thus ships (and now airplanes) navigate between any two points on the great circle.

4. "Direct your eye-sight inward, and you'l find / A thousand regions in your mind / Yet undiscover'd. Travell them, and be / Expert in home cosmographie" (William Habington, "To My Honoured Friend Sir Ed. P. Knight," which Thoreau probably found in Chalmers' *Works of the English Poets*, VI, 468. Notice Thoreau's modernization of the poem and his misreading of the first line).

5. As J. W. Krutch points out in the *TSB* 29 (1949), Thoreau is apparently echoing "We carry with us the wonders we seek without us, there is all Africa and her prodigies in us," from Book One of Sir Thomas Browne's *Religio Medici*.

6. Unknown and unexplored regions are left blank, thus white, on charts and maps.

7. Sir John Franklin (1786-1847), a British explorer who was lost in the Arctic and the object of many expeditions sent out to search for him.

8. Henry Grinnell of New York was "the author, advocate, and patron of the United States expedition in search of Sir John Franklin."

9. Mungo Park (1771-1806?) was a Scottish explorer in Africa; Lewis and Clark led our famous exploration trip through the Louisiana Purchase; and Sir Martin Frobisher (1535?-94) was a famous British navigator and explorer.

10. Elisha Kent Kane, in his *The United States Grinnell Expedition in Search of Sir John Franklin* (Philadelphia, 1856; p. 164) describes the finding of six hundred preserved meat cans left by Franklin.

11. The realms of the Czar of Russia were the largest body of land under one dominion in Thoreau's time.

12. Charles Wilkes (1798-1877) led an exploring expedition to the antarctic islands of the Pacific from 1839 to 1842. An indication of the interest of the transcendentalists in the expedition may be found in the report on it in the *Dial*, III, 132.

13. In his *Journal* for May 10, 1841 (I, 259-60), Thoreau tells us that these are the last verses of Claudian's "Old Man of Verona." Thoreau has changed "Iberos" (Spaniards) to "Australians" to make its application more appropriate to his time.

14. Thoreau was undoubtedly thinking of Charles Pickering's *The Races of Man* (London, 1851), which, according to his *Journal* (V, 392), he read in 1853. Pickering's book is a report of a world tour and, amazingly enough, gives a report (p. 349) on the domestic cats in Zanzibar!

15. Capt. John Cleves Symmes in 1818 advanced a theory that the earth was hollow and open at both poles. A detailed description of his theory may be found in *Blackwood's Magazine*, CCXXVI (1829), 856-57. Poe also made literary use of the theory in several of his tales, as for example "MS Found in a Bottle."

16. A mythical monster inhabiting Thebes and propounding a riddle to all who encountered her. When Oedipus solved the riddle, she dashed her head against a rock, killing herself.

17. The expression "Know thyself" has been attributed at various times to nearly all of the great Greek philosophers.

18. Thoreau wrote *Walden* at the height of the migration to the West.

19. The Count de Mirabeau (1749-91) was a statesman of the French Revolution. In his *Journal* for July 21, 1851 (II, 332-33)

he quotes the following passage at greater length from *Harper's New Monthly*, I, 648.

20. The immediate reason for Thoreau's leaving Walden was that Emerson planned to go abroad on a lecture tour and wished Thoreau to take over the care of his house and family.

21. The path from Thoreau's cabin site to the pond is still visible, kept open nowadays by visitors to his cabin from all over the world.

22. Thoreau's Harvard classmate Richard Henry Dana, Jr. was the author of the then celebrated *Two Years Before the Mast* (1840) based on his own experiences on a voyage around Cape Horn. Common sailors sailed "before the mast," passengers, "below."

23. Channing says Thoreau refers to a trip they took up the Hudson together by boat, when they spent the night in the bow of the ship because it was bright moonlight.

24. In the first edition of *Walden*, Thoreau wrote "*hush* and *who*." When Francis H. Allen edited Thoreau's *Writings* for Houghton Mifflin in 1906, thinking that Thoreau had slipped, he changed it to "*hish* and *whoa*," which has been followed in most modern editions. However, Mr. Allen has written me that he now believes Thoreau was correct and would suggest reverting to the original form. A long discussion of the terms used in calling oxen ("Bright" was a common mid-nineteenth-century pet name for an ox) was submitted to Mr. Allen anonymously shortly after his edition appeared and is now in the Francis H. Allen Papers in the Thoreau Society Archives in the Concord Free Public Library.

25. "*On prétend que les vers de Kabir ont quatre sens différents: L'illusion (mâyâ), l'esprit (âtmâ), l'intellect (man), et la doctrine exotérique des Védas*" (M. Garcin de Tassy, *Histoire de la Littérature Hindoui* [Paris, 1839], p. 279). The translation is apparently Thoreau's.

26. The potato blight or rot struck the United States in 1845 and the British Isles in 1846. Many attempts were made to develop protection against it.

27. "A living dog is better than a dead lion" (Ecclesiastes 9:4).

28. Compare: "For years I marched as to music in comparison with which the military music of the streets is noise and discord" (Thoreau, *Journal*, II, 307).

29. I have as yet been unable to find any source for this legend, and all earlier annotators have assumed that it was original with Thoreau. Sherman Paul (*The Shores of America* [Urbana, 1958], p. 353) suggests that "Kouros was clearly Kuru, Kooroo, or Curu,

the nation that fought the Pandoos in the *Mahabharata,* the sacred land that Arjuna was assigned to protect in the *Bhagavad-Gita.* Thoreau may have come across it in the *Laws of Menu,* where it is referred to as the country of Brahmanical sages (see the Dial, III [1843], 332). These Brahmins also carried staves."

"I have long thought of it as an allegory of Thoreau's own life, of his love for the Beautiful, the True, and the Good, and of his search for Perfection. I find in it a veiled suggestion of the reason he went to Walden, of his indifference to criticism and the social standards of his time" (Arthur Christy, *The Orient in American Transcendentalism* [New York, 1932], p. 193).

29a. Although this reads *stock* in the first edition, it obviously is a misprint for *stick*.

30. In Hindu literature, Kalpa is not a star but a long period of time, cited specifically by some authors as 4,354,560,000 years. The Hindus also knew that over a great period of time the pole star changed. Thoreau may have remembered both of these facts from his reading of H. T. Colebrooke, *Miscellaneous Essays* (London, 1837), II, 288, 364.

31. A day of Brahma supposedly lasted two billion, one hundred and sixty million years, at the end of which time he slept.

32. I have been unable to find any further clue to the identity of Tom Hyde except for the fact that in a manuscript in the Huntington Library, Thoreau adds here, "You Boston folks & Roxbury people will want Tom Hyde to mend your kettle,"—which might imply that he was a character in eastern Massachusetts folklore or fact.

33. *Confucian Analects,* 9, 25.

34. "And lo! Creation widened in man's view" (Joseph Blanco White, Sonnet: "To Night").

35. A ruler of Lydia in ancient times who was known as the richest member of mankind.

36. "The nearer the bone the sweeter the flesh" (Old English proverb).

37. A small tinkling bell (*NED*).

38. C. B. Cooper (*Walden,* Chicago, 1938; p. 206) suggests that this was probably Senator Robert Toombs but does not explain why.

39. In 1811, Pasha of Egypt ordered the massacre of all the Mamelukes. They were trapped in a citadel, but one escaped by leaping on his horse from the ramparts and fleeing to Syria.

40. Daniel Webster (1782-1852), senator from Massachusetts and the most famous orator of his day.

41. A child's game of running out onto thin ice without break-ing through. Thoreau's source for the following anecdote is the Concord newspaper *Yeoman's Gazette* for November 22, 1828.

42. In ancient times it was the custom to invoke the aid of the Muses whenever one embarked upon a major literary effort.

43. Emerson in his journals (as quoted in his son's *Emerson in Concord* [Boston, 1888], p. 210) also mentions "a divine man dwelt near me in a hollow tree," but I have been unable to trace the allusion further.

44. I have been unable to trace the source of this quotation.

45. A long-lasting itch (*DAE.*) Interestingly enough, the *DAE's* earliest entry for this term is 1899. (See Walter Harding, "Thoreau and the Seven Years' Itch," *American Speech*, XXIX [1954], 237).

46. When Thoreau visited Staten Island in 1843, he was much impressed with the seventeen-year locust (cicada), which he had not known in Concord.

47. Muskrats build their houses with the upper chamber above the water level and the entrance below. Thus if the water rises high enough, they run the risk of being drowned. Thoreau was ap-parently inspired by the high waters of 1850 to make this com-ment. See his *Journal* (II, 18, 33).

48. Although this story reached print in a number of places in Thoreau's lifetime (see Douglas Sackman, "The Original of Mel-ville's Apple-Tree Table," *AL*, XI [1940], 448-51, for a list), it is probable he derived it from Timothy Dwight, *Travels in New Eng-land and New York* (New Haven, 1821; II, 398), or from J. W. Barber, *Massachusetts Historical Collections* (Worcester, 1839; pp. 108-9), since he was familiar with both of these books. Herman Melville later used the story as the basis for his "The Apple-Tree Table" in *Putnam's Monthly Magazine* (VII [1856], 465-75). Al-though Mr. Sackman does not list *Walden* as one of Melville's pos-sible sources, certain verbal similarities make it seem likely. I have recounted the history of the apple-tree table legend from its be-ginning in an obscure Vermont periodical, on through Thoreau to Melville, in "The Apple-Tree Table Tale" (*BPLQ*, VIII [1956], 213-15).

Mr. Edwin Way Teale, the distinguished entomologist, has pointed out to me that it is quite possible for this incident to have occurred, and cites W. J. Showalter's *Our Insect Friends and Foes* (Washington, 1935; p. 84), which points out a case of the grub of the long-horned beetle remaining in a bookcase for fifty years.

49. Colloquial names for a typical British and a typical Ameri-can citizen, respectively.

50. An interesting parallel to this can be found in Emerson's "Politics": "We think our civilization near its meridian, but we are yet only at the cock-crowing and the morning star."

The Variorum

CIVIL DISOBEDIENCE

INTRODUCTION

ONE evening late in July of 1846, probably the 23rd or 24th, Thoreau walked in to Concord village from Walden Pond to pick up a shoe he had left at the cobbler's shop to be repaired. He was stopped on the street by Sam Staples, the local constable, tax collector, and jailer, and asked to pay his poll tax for the last several years. "I'll pay your tax, Henry, if you're hard up," Staples said. He also offered to try to persuade the selectmen to reduce the tax if Thoreau thought it too high, but Thoreau replied that he had not paid it as a matter of principle and didn't intend to pay it now. When Staples asked what he should do about it, Thoreau suggested that if he didn't like it, he could resign his office. But Staples, not taking kindly to that suggestion, replied, "Henry, if you don't pay, I shall have to lock you up pretty soon." "As well now as any time, Sam," was the answer. "Well, come along then," said Staples, and took him to jail.

Thoreau was not the first to be arrested in Concord for non-payment of his poll taxes. More than three years before, on January 17, 1843, Staples had arrested Thoreau's friend, Bronson Alcott, on the same charge. The Massachusetts poll tax (not a voting tax, but a head tax imposed on every male between the ages of twenty and seventy) had long been unpopular, and the Abolitionists seized upon protesting against paying it as a dramatic way of demonstrating their abhorrence of a government that supported slavery. Although Alcott was arrested, he was never jailed, for Squire Hoar, the town's leading citizen, paid Alcott's taxes himself rather than permit such a blot on the town escutcheon. And in the succeeding years, despite his pleas for "the privilege of non-payment of taxes," Alcott's wife's family paid his taxes in advance to avoid the embarrassment of having a relative in jail. In December 1843 Alcott's English friend, Charles Lane, also refused to pay his poll tax in Concord and was arrested. Again Squire Hoar paid the tax, and Lane was quickly released.

The examples of Alcott and Lane set Thoreau to thinking. The agitation against slavery had grown in recent years from the work of a few rare individuals to that of the beginnings of a mass movement. William Lloyd Garrison was beginning to become a household name. Ex-President John Quincy Adams, through his constant barrage of petitions and speeches in the national House of Representatives, was slowly making more and more people aware of the vast gap between the democratic principles the country vocally avowed and the slavery legally practiced in the South. The antislavery movement had by no means attained respectability (ironically it was not to attain that until after the Civil War when the need for its activities no longer existed), and Garrison could still be dragged through the streets of Boston with a noose around his neck. But at least it was causing twinges in the American conscience.

Thoreau himself was made particularly aware of the issues involved by the antislavery activities of the members of his own household—his mother and sisters—by the antislavery periodicals they regularly subscribed to, and by the fact that the antislavery agitators who visited Concord invariably put up for the night in his mother's boarding house. It is safe to say that there was probably hardly a single prominent New England Abolitionist of those times that Thoreau did not meet at least once across his mother's dining table.

The Abolitionists had, in recent years, split, philosophically at least, into two groups. Those led by William Lloyd Garrison were activists. They denounced loudly and vehemently those institutions such as the church, the state, and the press which they felt were the most ardent defenders of the status quo on the slavery question. Feeling their only weapon against these institutions to be mass action, they stressed the development of larger and more aggressive antislavery societies. The other group, which until his recent death had been led by Nathaniel P. Rogers, believed the only possible solution was the reformation of mankind. They feared that Garrison's plans would lead to the institutionalizing of the antislavery societies themselves and argued that a utopian society could be achieved only through self-reformation of each individual in a society. This kind of a philosophy was inevitably attractive to a Transcendentalist such as Thoreau. He had already endorsed Rogers' principles in the pages of *The Dial.* Now that he felt called to action himself, he quite naturally took the individualistic rather than the organizational approach, and adopting the ideas and actions of Lane and Alcott, he refused to pay his own poll tax.

Unfortunately for Thoreau's principles, Staples for several years simply ignored Thoreau's tax resistance. Although Staples, like many of the "more practical" townspeople, was pretty skeptical of the "Transcendentalist crowd" (he used to say of Emerson, "I suppose there's a great many things that Mr. Emerson knows that I couldn't understand; but I *know* that there's a damn sight of things that I know that he don't know anything about"), he always had a high opinion of Thoreau. Therefore, if Thoreau chose to ignore paying his taxes, Staples chose to ignore his non-payment.

Why Staples suddenly decided to take action in the summer of 1846 is not known for certain. He was about to give up his position as tax collector and so might have been faced with the prospect of paying Thoreau's taxes himself to clear the books. Or it might have been that the recent declaration of war against Mexico had inflamed a patriotism that demanded the collection of all taxes. At any rate, he gave Thoreau several warnings before finally arresting him and said afterwards that he was not worried about Thoreau's running off; he knew he could get him when he wanted to.

The Concord jail, now long since torn down, was no small-town lockup. Concord was the shire town of Middlesex County and this was the county jail. It stood just off the Mill Dam, behind the stores, near the present site of the Roman Catholic rectory, and was built of granite, three stories high, sixty-five feet long, thirty-two feet wide, and surrounded with a brick wall about ten feet high, mounted with iron pickets. It had eighteen cells, each twenty-six feet long and eight and a half feet high. Each cell had two double-grated windows. A formidable jail indeed.

The prisoners were enjoying a chat and the evening air in the prison yard when Thoreau and Staples entered. Staples told the men it was time to return to their cells and introduced Thoreau to his cellmate. When the door was locked, he showed Thoreau where to hang his hat and how to manage matters there. After inquiring about Thoreau's arrest, he explained that he had been accused of burning down a barn and had been waiting three months for his trial—although since he was given free board and room and was permitted to go out and work in the hayfields by the day, he thought he was being well treated and was contented.

Thoreau made the most of what he thought to be a rare opportunity and pumped his cellmate for all he was worth about the history of the jail and its occupants and its gossip, which he realized never circulated outside, but eventually his informant tired of the inquisition and went to bed, leaving Thoreau to blow out the lamp. Thoreau, however, was much too excited to sleep and stood at the window for some time, looking out through the grating and listening to the activities in the nearby hotel. Later in the night a prisoner in a nearby cell began calling out with painful monotony, "What is life? So this is life!" Finally tiring of the repetition, Thoreau put his head to the window bars and called out in a loud voice, "Well, what *is* life, then?" His only answer was silence and his reward a quiet night's sleep.

Meanwhile, word of Thoreau's arrest had rapidly spread through the village. When his mother heard of it, she rushed to the jail to ascertain the truth of the rumor and then back home to tell the family the news. Sam Staples had gone out for a while that evening, and on his return his daughter Ellen informed him that someone had knocked at the door in his absence and, passing in a package, had said, "Here is the money to pay Mr. Thoreau's tax." Staples had taken off his boots and was sitting by the fire when his daughter told him, and he declared that he wasn't going to take the trouble to put them back on. Thoreau could just as well spend the night in jail and be released in the morning.

Just who the person was who knocked on Staples' door and handed in the package has never been absolutely ascertained. Some have claimed that it was Emerson; others, Aunt Jane Thoreau, Elizabeth Hoar, Rockwood Hoar, or Samuel Hoar. Staples, himself, told so many stories in later years—that it was a man, a young woman, an old woman, two women— that his word, as he readily admitted to one of his inquisitors, was not to be depended on. As a matter of fact, neither he nor his daughter probably ever knew, for tradition has it that the person was heavily veiled. But the preponderance of evidence points to Aunt Maria Thoreau. And Eben J. Loomis, who was an old friend of the Thoreau family, was almost certain in his old age that Aunt Maria had once admitted to him that she was the one.

Probably what happened is that when Thoreau's mother returned home with the news, Aunt Maria was understandably upset to learn that her nephew was in jail. It seems likely that Thoreau had extracted a promise from his mother not to interfere with his plans. But Aunt Maria was bound by no such promise and so stepped in and paid the tax. And regularly thereafter, possibly even until the time of Thoreau's death, she or others paid his tax in advance so that the incident could not occur again.

When morning came, the prisoners were fed their breakfast of bread and a pint of chocolate, and Thoreau's cellmate, leaving for his day's stint in the hayfields, bade him goodbye, saying that he doubted if he would see Thoreau again. (Later Thoreau was to find out that when his cellmate came to trial, he was found innocent of the charges and released. Apparently he had fallen asleep in the barn while smoking and so had inadvertently burned it down.)

When Staples came to release Thoreau, he was astounded to discover that Thoreau was not willing to leave the jail, the only prisoner he ever had who did not want to leave as soon as he could. In fact, said Staples, Thoreau was "as mad as the devil" at being released. It had been the whole purpose of his refusal to pay taxes to get arrested and so to call dramatically to the attention of his fellow citizens the cause of abolitionism that he had espoused. When Aunt Maria paid his taxes, she had destroyed the whole point of his campaign, and, to put it mildly, he was not pleased. Since he himself had not paid those taxes, he felt he had the right to stay in jail and said so. But Staples said, "Henry, if you will not go of your own accord I shall put you out, for you cannot stay here any longer." Capitulating, Thoreau finally went on his way, picked up his shoe at the cobbler's, and within half an hour was picking huckleberries on a hill two miles off where, as he said rejoicingly, "the State was nowhere to be seen."

Word of his arrest and release had, of course, spread rapidly throughout the town. Many stared at him, he noticed, as though he had been on a long journey. And little Georgie Bartlett said that he thought from the excitement he was seeing a Siberian exile or John Bunyan himself. Many of his townsmen of course did not agree with or approve of Thoreau's action.

James Garty, who readily admitted that Thoreau "was a good sort of man" and "would pay every cent he owed to any man," complained at the time that "it wouldn't do to have everybody like him, or his way of thinking." Emerson complained to Bronson Alcott that Thoreau's action was "mean and skulking, and in bad taste"; but Alcott, in reply, defended it as a good example of "dignified noncompliance with the injunction of civil powers." Emerson then sputtered in his journal: "The State is a poor, good beast who means the best: it means friendly. A poor cow who does well by you,—do not grudge it its hay. . . . As long as the state means you well, do not refuse your pistareen. You have a tottering cause: ninety parts of the pistareen it will spend for what you think also good: ten parts for mischief. . . . In the particular, it is worth considering that refusing payment of the state tax does not reach the evil so nearly as many other methods within your reach. . . . The prison is one step to suicide." And when Emerson next met Thoreau, he asked him why he had gone to jail, only to have Thoreau aptly reply, "Why did you not?" Emerson, on further thought, finally admitted in his journal that Thoreau's position was at least stronger than the Abolitionists who denounce the war and yet pay the tax.

As for Sam Staples, his relations with Thoreau continued as amiable as ever. There is a legend that Alcott once, when pestered by Staples for his taxes, picked all the potato bugs off his own vines and dumped them into Staples' garden in retaliation. But Thoreau carried no such grudge. In later years he often hired Staples as his assistant when he was surveying. And Staples, in his turn, often boasted that Thoreau was his most distinguished prisoner.

So many of Thoreau's townsmen expressed a curiosity about his actions and wanted to know the rationale for his trying to go to jail that Thoreau finally wrote out an explanation and delivered it as a lecture on "the relation of the individual to the State" at the Concord Lyceum on January 26, 1848. He found an attentive audience, and Bronson Alcott, at least, "took great pleasure" in the lecture. Three weeks later, by request, he gave the same lecture again so others of his townsmen could hear.

In the spring of 1849 Elizabeth Peabody suddenly wrote to ask Thoreau for permission to publish that lecture. She was establishing a new periodical to be called *Aesthetic Papers* to carry along the Transcendentalist message where *The Dial* had dropped it, and wanted to include his lecture in the first (and what later turned out to be the only) issue. Thoreau at the moment was busy correcting proofs of his first book and replied that he hardly had time left for bodily exercise, let alone copying out an old lecture. Nonetheless he promised to send the manuscript along within a week, but he cautioned her that it was offered for use in her first volume only. He had had enough of delaying actions on the part of editors.

Miss Peabody, however, kept her word. Six weeks later, on May 14, 1849, she published her magazine containing pieces by Emerson and Hawthorne along with Thoreau's essay, now entitled "Resistance to Civil Government." (It did not receive its more widely known title of "Civil Disobedience" until it was collected into his *Yankee in Canada, with Anti-Slavery and Reform Papers* in 1866, four years after his death.)

At the time of its publication, however, the essay produced scarcely a ripple. Although *Aesthetic Papers* was noticed here and there, the reviewers generally ignored Thoreau's contribution. They were more interested in the essays by the better-known Emerson and Hawthorne in the same issue. The one exception was a review by Sophia Dobson Collet in the *People's Review* in London, England. She quoted several of the meatiest paragraphs and prefaced them with the comment that "as it is not likely to be much known in England, we give the following extracts, premising that it ought to be read as a whole to be thoroughly appreciated." But except for Miss Collet's comment, the essay was ignored.

[II]

THE central points of Thoreau's essay are these:

(1) There is a "higher law" than the law of one's land. That is the law of the conscience, the "inner voice," the "over-soul"—call it what you will.

(2) On those rare occasions when this "higher law" and the law of the land come in conflict, it is one's duty to obey that "higher law" and deliberately violate the law of the land.

(3) If one deliberately violates the law of the land, he must be willing to take the full consequences of that action, even to the point of going to jail.

(4) However, going to jail is not necessarily the nega-

tive act it might seem, for it will serve to draw the attention of men of good will to the evil law and thus help to bring about its repeal. Or, if enough men go to jail, their acts will serve to clog the machinery of the state and thus make the evil law unenforceable.

These theories are not original with Thoreau. Socrates in drinking the cup of hemlock and Antigone in sprinkling dust on the body of Polyneices were both committing acts of civil disobedience. Boethius many centuries ago expounded the philosophy in western culture and Mencius in eastern. But the important fact is that it was Thoreau who popularized the idea, though it was half a century after the essay appeared in print before anyone paid any serious attention to it.

About 1900 the Russian novelist and philosopher Count Leo Tolstoy somewhere, somehow, ran across the essay and was struck with its implications concerning his own attempts to better the conditions of the Russian serfs under Czarist domination. But so far as I have been able to find out, the only direct action he ever took with Thoreau's ideas was to write a letter to the *North American Review* asking the American people why they did not pay more attention to the voice of Thoreau than to that of their financial and industrial millionaires and their successful generals and admirals.

True credit for the rediscovery of Thoreau's "Civil Disobedience" should go to a young Hindu law student by the name of Mohandas K. Gandhi who was studying at Oxford University in England about 1900. Gandhi, because of his religion, was a vegetarian. Having difficulty finding food proper to his diet on the university campus, he quite naturally got in touch with some of the English vegetarians—one Henry Stephens Salt in particular. Salt was, by chance, the author of an excellent biography of Thoreau and the editor of several collections of Thoreau's works. Gandhi caught some of Salt's enthusiasm for Thoreau and began to read whatever of his works he could lay hold of. After his graduation from Oxford, Gandhi established himself as a lawyer in South Africa, devoting himself primarily to the defense of violators of the discriminatory laws passed against the members of his own race. To unite the Indian residents of South Africa he established a newspaper entitled *Indian Opinion*. And therein, in the issue of October 26, 1907, he printed Thoreau's "Civil Disobedience," later reprinting it in pamphlet form for wider distribution. He accompanied the essay with editorials advocating the use of civil disobedience against the offensive legislation. He offered prizes for student essays on the most effective methods of passive resistance. And he led direct action against the laws, deliberately violating them to bring about mass arrest. Progress was at first slow, but the movement gradually gained momentum, and eventually the government was forced to choose between enforcing the laws and glutting the jails with hundreds and even thousands of violators. The laws were one by one repealed or became dead letters. Civil disobedience had triumphed.

Word of the effectiveness of Gandhi's Thoreauvian methods soon spread to his native land, where a movement to free the country from British domination was getting under way. Gandhi, at the strong request of his native countrymen, returned to India to lead the movement. For thirty years he conducted civil disobedience campaigns the length and breadth of the country. When the British government, wishing to establish a lucrative monopoly, forbade the manufacture of salt, Gandhi led followers to the seashore, there to symbolically violate the law by producing salt through sea-water evaporation a cupful at a time. As he fully expected, he was immediately arrested and jailed. But the government found it had not solved its problem. In the eyes of his countrymen Gandhi had become a martyr to their own cause, and they rushed forward by the hundreds and thousands to join his movement and to duplicate his violation of the law. In prison Gandhi went on a hunger strike protesting what he considered his illegal arrest. As he sank lower and lower, more and more sympathy was aroused for him, not only in India but around the world. Rather than risk having him die on their hands, the government freed him. As soon as he was physically able, he violated the salt law once again and was once again put into prison. It was a cat-and-mouse game, but eventually public opinion forced the government to abandon the law. Gandhi then turned his attention to other unjust laws. The action and the reaction were repeated again and again. To make a long story short, India under Gandhi's leadership and using Thoreau's techniques of civil disobedience eventually won complete freedom in 1945.

Gandhi directed his techniques not only against unjust governmental laws but also against equally unjust religious codes.

The social structure of Hinduism was based upon a caste system. The lowest group, but the largest numerically, was the so-called Untouchables. Over and over again they found the religious codes turned against them. Let us take a single striking example. The only source of water for many Indian villages was a single well. Since the upper-caste Hindus used the well, the lower-caste Untouchables were forbidden to go near it. They were forced to resort to the open streams and pools. Because of the vast overpopulation of India, all of these sources of water were badly polluted. The Untouchables quite understandably died off like the proverbial flies. When Gandhi found that pleas as to the inhumanity of the religious codes went unheeded, he led the Untouchables to the wells and joined them in filling jars of water. Civil police were called in to enforce the religious laws, and the violators were at first attacked unmercifully. When local police, sickened by the violence used on the passive resisters, refused to enforce the laws, special military police recruited from a notoriously bloodthirsty tribe on the Himalayan border were brought in. But they too eventually found their sympathies won by the martyrdom of the Untouchables and refused to continue their violence. The laws became unenforceable and the Untouchables won their right to use the village wells. Once again Gandhi's Thoreauvian civil disobedience had won.

Some years ago Roger Baldwin, then the director of the American Civil Liberties Union, told me that he once took a long train journey with Gandhi. When Gandhi learned that Mr. Baldwin had been born and brought up in Massachusetts near Thoreau's Concord, he plied him with questions about Thoreau's life and showed him that he was carrying a copy of "Civil Disobedience" in his luggage. He said he never went anywhere—not even to jail—without a copy of the pamphlet because it epitomized the whole spirit of his life.

But we need not confine ourselves to India. "Civil Disobedience" has had a world-wide influence. Let us turn to Denmark for another example. Henry David Thoreau is virtually a folk-hero in Denmark today. Why? Because "Civil Disobedience" was used as a manual of arms by the resistance movement against the Nazi invasion during World War II. It was circulated surreptitiously throughout the war years among the Danes as a means of encouraging them to further acts of resistance. What was the result? Well, let me give a few examples. When the Nazis invoked a law requiring all Jews to wear a large six-pointed yellow star on the back of each article of clothing—the obvious purpose being to single out the Jews for further persecution—virtually every citizen in Denmark, Jew or Gentile, including even King Christian, appeared in the streets wearing the yellow star. The law was thus nullified.

When the King took part in numerous such actions, the Nazis felt obliged to retaliate. But they did not dare to execute or even to arrest the King. They took what they thought was the easiest way out by confining the King to his palace and announcing simply that he was ill. But the Danish people quickly caught on, and citizens from all over the country decided to "say it with flowers." Going to their local florists, they ordered bouquets to be sent to the King—what could seemingly be more harmless? But what was the result? Every road leading into Copenhagen, the capital city, and every street within the city was soon blocked with florists delivering flowers to the King. Traffic could not move. Business could not be conducted. The entire city came to a standstill. Yet people obviously could not be punished for sending flowers. The Nazis were forced to announce that the King had suddenly miraculously recovered and to give him complete freedom of his country for the rest of the years of the invasion. These are only two of many examples of the influence of Thoreau's "Civil Disobedience" in Denmark, but they give some idea of why the Nazis thought the Danes to be the most recalcitrant of all their subjects during the war.

But now let us return to the United States. Has "Civil Disobedience" had any influence here? First you may be surprised to learn of the amount of official resistance there has been to the essay in this our democratic country. Upton Sinclair, the novelist; Norman Thomas, the perennial candidate of the Socialist Party; and Emma Goldman, the anarchist editor of *Mother Earth*, have each been arrested for reading Thoreau's essay from the public platform—Sinclair during a labor strike in California in the early 1930's; Thomas during a protest against the machine rule of Frank ("I am the law") Hague of Jersey City in the late 1930's; and Emma Goldman during protest rallies against the conscription act of 1917. Or again, in the 1930's, the entire edition of one issue of *Heresia*, an Italian-language newspaper in New York City, was confiscated and destroyed by the New York City police because it included a translation of "Civil Disobedience"—this despite the fact that at that very time anyone could go into any bookstore in New York City and purchase an edition of "Civil Disobedience" in English without the least difficulty. To cite still another example of official resistance, when, in the mid-1950's, the United States Information Service included as a standard book in all their libraries around the world a textbook of American literature which reprinted Thoreau's "Civil Disobedience," the late Senator Joseph McCarthy of Wisconsin succeeded in having that book removed from the shelves of each of those libraries—specifically because of the Thoreau essay.

But despite the occasional official opposition—and I in all fairness must stress that the opposition has only been very, very occasional—"Civil Disobedience" has had a continuing influence in this country. I have never been able to discover a direct connection between Thoreau's essay and the famous sit-down strikes led by the C.I.O. during the depression years, but certainly it would be difficult to discover any more practical application of the ideas that Thoreau advocated than those were.

For many years the pacifist movement in this country (and incidentally in England, France, and South America, too), although very small and comparatively uninfluential, has stimulated the publication and distribution of Thoreau's essay. I have in my files numerous editions of "Civil Disobedience" printed by such groups. Many of the conscientious objectors who were imprisoned during World War II quoted Thoreau's essay in defense of their actions. And I know of at least one who took a copy of "Civil Disobedience" to prison with him.

I understand that there is a small group of pacifists who even now each year file a copy of "Civil Disobedience" in lieu of an income tax report, implying by the action that they refuse to underwrite our military budget. I might add that I understand in such cases the Federal Income Tax Bureau, acting as did Thoreau's Aunt Maria, steps in and pays the tax—but with the significant difference that the Income Tax Bureau then confiscates that sum out of the individual's bank account or salary. But the objectors feel that at least the protest has been made. A few years ago when a number of pacifists were protesting the construction of nuclear submarines at New London, Connecticut, they conducted their protest in a rowboat named "Henry D. Thoreau."

A more striking example of Thoreau's influence in our country today however is that of the antisegregation movement throughout the South. The refusal of Negroes to ride segregated buses in Montgomery, Alabama; the boycotting by Negroes of segregated stores in Albany, Georgia; the kneel-ins of Negroes in the white churches of Nashville, Tennessee; the "Freedom" riders in Alabama and Mississippi—each and every one of these is a very specific example of the influence of Thoreau. And let me cite as proof of that, the words of two of the outstanding leaders of the movement. First, the Rev. James Robinson, former pastor of the Church of the Master in Harlem, now director of "Operation Crossroads" (the International Voluntary Work Camps) for the United States in Africa, and one of the most influential Negroes in this country, said in an article on "Civil Disobedience" twenty years ago, that was addressed to the group who later founded CORE (the Committee on Racial Equality):

> Thoreau's Civil Disobedience was not used much by the Abolitionists for whom it was written; probably no one before Gandhi realized its significance for a new type of social movement based upon group discipline and personal conscience. As one reads this essay, it is impossible not to notice that almost every sentence is loaded with meaning for us today. . . . Substitute the economic, political, and social persecution of American Negroes today where Thoreau condemns Negro slavery—and you will scarcely find half a dozen sentences in the entire essay which you cannot apply to your own actions in the present crisis.

I have no doubt but his article led in part at least to the establishment of CORE.

And second, Rev. Martin Luther King, who is universally recognized as the leader of the current struggles for human rights in the South today, tells us in his autobiography, *Stride Toward Freedom*:

> When I went to Atlanta's Morehouse College as a freshman in 1944 my concern for racial and economic

justice was already substantial. During my student days
at Morehouse I read Thoreau's "Essay on Civil Disobedience" for the first time. Fascinated by the idea of refusing to cooperate with an evil system, I was so deeply
moved that I reread the work several times. This was
my first intellectual contact with the theory of nonviolent
resistance.

And then, speaking of the boycott he organized against segregated buses in Montgomery, Alabama, he says:

At this point I began to think about Thoreau's "Essay
on Civil Disobedience." I remembered how, as a college
student, I had been moved when I first read this work.
I became convinced that what we were preparing to do
in Montgomery was related to what Thoreau had expressed. We were simply saying to the white community,
"We can no longer lend our cooperation to an evil system."

Something began to say to me, "He who passively accepts evil is as much involved in it as he who helps to
perpetuate it. He who accepts evil without protesting
against it is really cooperating with it." When oppressed
people willingly accept their oppression they only serve
to give the oppressor a convenient justification for his
acts. Often the oppressor goes along unaware of the evil
involved in his oppression so long as the oppressed accepts it. So in order to be true to one's conscience and
true to God, a righteous man has no alternative but to
refuse to cooperate with an evil system. This I felt was
the nature of our action. From this moment on I conceived of our movement as an act of massive non-co-
operation.

Unquestionably, then, Thoreau's century-old essay has had
and is having a powerful influence on the fight for Negro
rights in our country today . . . an influence as profound as
it had in South Africa fifty years ago or India of thirty years
ago or Denmark of twenty years ago. Its influence has traveled around the world and now has returned home.

No stronger evidence is needed that the civil disobedience
that Thoreau advocated has become a part of the American
way of life than the opposition to the war in Vietnam. The

widespread appearance of protesters from the college campus to the New York Stock Exchange, along the major avenues of cities and at major industrial and military sites, at the White House and the Pentagon—as well as the public burning of draft cards by young men—all attest to the fact that, though it took a century, the American people have become aware of the usefulness and validity of Thoreau's theory.

A NOTE ON THE TEXT

Thoreau's "Civil Disobedience" exists in two slightly differing versions—that entitled "Resistance to Civil Government," which was first published in Elizabeth Peabody's *Aesthetic Papers* in the spring of 1849; and that entitled "Civil Disobedience," which was first published in his *A Yankee in Canada, with Anti-Slavery and Reform Papers* (Boston: Ticknor & Fields, 1866), four years after his death. Except for numerous (but trivial) differences in capitalization and punctuation—which were probably editorial rather than authorial changes—they vary only in a few sentences. I have chosen the 1866 version as my text on the assumption that it was based on a corrected copy made by Thoreau, but I have indicated in my annotations all additions and deletions of words from the 1849 text.

I am grateful to Alfred A. Knopf, Inc., for permission to include in my introduction excerpts from my biography *The Days of Henry Thoreau* (New York, 1965) and to J. Golden Taylor and the Utah State University Press for permission to include excerpts from my "The Influence of Civil Disobedience" published in Professor Taylor's *The Western Thoreau Centenary* (Utah State University Press Monograph Series, X, 1963).

CIVIL DISOBEDIENCE[1]

I HEARTILY accept the motto,[2]—"That government is best which governs least"; and I should like to see it acted up to more rapidly and systematically. Carried out, it finally amounts to this, which also I believe,—"That government is best which governs not at all"; and when men are prepared for it, that will be the kind of government which they will have. Government is at best but an expedient; but most governments are usually, and all governments are sometimes, inexpedient. The objections which have been brought against a standing army, and they are many and weighty, and deserve to prevail, may also at last be brought against a standing government. The standing army is only an arm of the standing government. The government itself, which is only the mode which the people have chosen to execute their will, is equally liable to be abused and perverted before the people can act through it. Witness the present Mexican war,[3] the work of comparatively a few individuals using the standing government as their tool; for, in the outset, the people would not have consented to this measure.

This American government,—what is it but a tradition, though a recent one, endeavoring to transmit itself unimpaired to posterity, but each instant losing some of its integrity? It has not the vitality and force of a single living man; for a single man can bend it to his will. It is a sort of wooden gun to the people themselves.[4] But it is not the less necessary for this; for the people must have some complicated machinery or other, and hear its din, to satisfy that idea of government which they have. Governments show thus how successfully men can be imposed on, even impose on themselves, for their own advantage. It is excellent, we must all allow. Yet this government never of itself furthered any enterprise, but by the alacrity with which it got out of its way. *It* does not keep the country free. *It* does not settle the West.

343

It does not educate. The character inherent in the American people has done all that has been accomplished; and it would have done somewhat more, if the government had not sometimes got in its way. For government is an expedient by which men would fain succeed in letting one another alone; and, as has been said, when it is most expedient, the governed are most let alone by it. Trade and commerce, if they were not made of India-rubber, would never manage to bounce over the obstacles which legislators are continually putting in their way; and, if one were to judge these men wholly by the effects of their actions and not partly by their intentions, they would deserve to be classed and punished with those mischievous persons who put obstructions on the railroads.

But, to speak practically and as a citizen, unlike those who call themselves no-government men,⁵ I ask for, not at once no government, but *at once* a better government. Let every man make known what kind of government would command his respect, and that will be one step toward obtaining it.

After all, the practical reason why, when the power is once in the hands of the people, a majority are permitted, and for a long period continue, to rule, is not because they are most likely to be in the right, nor because this seems fairest to the minority, but because they are physically the strongest. But a government in which the majority rule in all cases cannot be based on justice, even as far as men understand it. Can there not be a government in which majorities do not virtually decide right and wrong, but conscience?—in which majorities decide only those questions to which the rule of expediency is applicable? Must the citizen ever for a moment, or in the least degree, resign his conscience to the legislator? Why has every man a conscience, then? I think that we should be men first, and subjects afterward. It is not desirable to cultivate a respect for the law, so much as for the right. The only obligation which I have a right to assume, is to do at any time what I think right. It is truly enough said, that a corporation has no conscience;⁶ but a corporation of conscientious men is a corporation *with* a conscience. Law never made men a whit more just; and, by means of their respect for it, even the well-disposed are daily made the agents of injustice. A common and natural result of an undue respect for law is, that you may see a file of soldiers, colonel, captain,

corporal, privates, powder-monkeys,[7] and all, marching in admirable order over hill and dale to the wars, against their
wills, ay, against their common sense and consciences, which
makes it very steep marching indeed, and produces a palpitation of the heart. They have no doubt that it is a damnable
business in which they are concerned; they are all peaceably
inclined. Now, what are they? Men at all? or small movable
forts and magazines, at the service of some unscrupulous
man in power? Visit the Navy-Yard, and behold a marine,
such a man as an American government can make, or such as
it can make a man with its black arts,—a mere shadow and
reminiscence of humanity, a man laid out alive and standing,
and already, as one may say, buried under arms with funeral
accompaniments, though it may be,—

> "Not a drum was heard, not a funeral note,
>   As his corse to the rampart we hurried;
> Not a soldier discharged his farewell shot
>   O'er the grave where our hero we buried." [8]

The mass of men serve the state thus, not as men mainly,
but as machines, with their bodies. They are the standing
army, and the militia, jailers, constables, posse comitatus,[9] &c.
In most cases there is no free exercise whatever of the judgment or of the moral sense; but they put themselves on a level
with wood and earth and stones; and wooden men can perhaps be manufactured that will serve the purpose as well.
Such command no more respect than men of straw or a lump
of dirt. They have the same sort of worth only as horses and
dogs. Yet such as these even are commonly esteemed good
citizens. Others,—as most legislators, politicians, lawyers,
ministers, and office-holders,—serve the state chiefly with their
heads; and, as they rarely make any moral distinctions, they
are as likely to serve the Devil, without *intending* it, as God.
A very few, as heroes, patriots, martyrs, reformers in the great
sense, and *men*, serve the state with their consciences also,
and so necessarily resist it for the most part; and they are
commonly treated as enemies by it. A wise man will only be
useful as a man, and will not submit to be "clay," and "stop
a hole to keep the wind away," [10] but leave that office to his
dust at least:—

"I am too high-born to be propertied,
To be a secondary at control,
Or useful serving-man and instrument
To any sovereign state throughout the world." [11]

He who gives himself entirely to his fellow-men appears to them useless and selfish; but he who gives himself partially to them is pronounced a benefactor and philanthropist.

How does it become a man to behave toward this American government to-day? I answer, that he cannot without disgrace be associated with it. I cannot for an instant recognize that political organization as *my* government which is the *slave's* government also.

All men recognize the right of revolution; that is, the right to refuse allegiance to, and to resist, the government, when its tyranny or its inefficiency are great and unendurable. But almost all say that such is not the case now. But such was the case, they think, in the Revolution of '75.[12] If one were to tell me that this was a bad government because it taxed certain foreign commodities brought to its ports, it is most probable that I should not make an ado about it, for I can do without them. All machines have their friction; and possibly this does enough good to counterbalance the evil. At any rate, it is a great evil to make a stir about it. But when the friction comes to have its machine, and oppression and robbery are organized, I say, let us not have such a machine any longer. In other words, when a sixth of the population of a nation which has undertaken to be the refuge of liberty are slaves, and a whole country is unjustly overrun and conquered by a foreign army, and subjected to military law, I think that it is not too soon for honest men to rebel and revolutionize. What makes this duty the more urgent is the fact, that the country so overrun is not our own, but ours is the invading army.

Paley,[13] a common authority with many on moral questions, in his chapter on the "Duty of Submission to Civil Government," resolves all civil obligation into expediency; and he proceeds to say, "that so long as the interest of the whole society requires it, that is, so long as the established government cannot be resisted or changed without public inconveniency, it is the will of God that the established government be obeyed, and no longer. . . . This principle being ad-

mitted, the justice of every particular case of resistance is reduced to a computation of the quantity of the danger and
grievance on the one side, and of the probability and expense
of redressing it on the other." Of this, he says, every man
shall judge for himself. But Paley appears never to have
contemplated those cases to which the rule of expediency does
not apply, in which a people, as well as an individual, must
do justice, cost what it may. If I have unjustly wrested a plank
from a drowning man, I must restore it to him though I
drown myself.[14] This, according to Paley, would be inconvenient. But he that would save his life, in such a case, shall
lose it.[15] This people must cease to hold slaves, and to make
war on Mexico, though it cost them their existence as a
people.

In their practice, nations agree with Paley; but does any
one think that Massachusetts does exactly what is right at the
present crisis?

"A drab of state, a cloth-o'-silver slut,
  To have her train borne up, and her soul trail in the dirt." [16]

Practically speaking, the opponents to a reform in Massachusetts are not a hundred thousand politicians at the South,
but a hundred thousand merchants and farmers here,[17] who
are more interested in commerce and agriculture than they
are in humanity, and are not prepared to do justice to the
slave and to Mexico, *cost what it may.* I quarrel not with far-
off foes, but with those who, near at home, co-operate with,
and do the bidding of, those far away, and without whom
the latter would be harmless. We are accustomed to say, that
the mass of men are unprepared; but improvement is slow,
because the few are not materially wiser or better than the
many. It is not so important that many should be as good as
you, as that there be some absolute goodness somewhere; for
that will leaven the whole lump.[18] There are thousands who
are *in opinion* opposed to slavery and to the war, who yet in
effect do nothing to put an end to them; who, esteeming themselves children of Washington and Franklin, sit down with
their hands in their pockets, and say that they know not what
to do, and do nothing; who even postpone the question of
freedom to the question of free-trade, and quietly read the
prices-current along with the latest advices from Mexico, after

dinner, and, it may be, fall asleep over them both. What is the price-current of an honest man and patriot to-day? They hesitate, and they regret, and sometimes they petition; but they do nothing in earnest and with effect. They will wait, well disposed, for others to remedy the evil, that they may no longer have it to regret. At most, they give only a cheap vote, and a feeble countenance and God-speed, to the right, as it goes by them. There are nine hundred and ninety-nine patrons of virtue to one virtuous man. But it is easier to deal with the real possessor of a thing than with the temporary guardian of it.

All voting is a sort of gaming, like checkers or backgammon, with a slight moral tinge to it, a playing with right and wrong, with moral questions; and betting naturally accompanies it. The character of the voters is not staked. I cast my vote, perchance, as I think right; but I am not vitally concerned that that right should prevail. I am willing to leave it to the majority. Its obligation, therefore, never exceeds that of expediency. Even voting *for the right* is *doing* nothing for it. It is only expressing to men feebly your desire that it should prevail. A wise man will not leave the right to the mercy of chance, nor wish it to prevail through the power of the majority. There is but little virtue in the action of masses of men. When the majority shall at length vote for the abolition of slavery, it will be because they are indifferent to slavery, or because there is but little slavery left to be abolished by their vote. *They* will then be the only slaves. Only *his* vote can hasten the abolition of slavery who asserts his own freedom by his vote.

I hear of a convention to be held at Baltimore,[19] or elsewhere, for the selection of a candidate for the Presidency, made up chiefly of editors, and men who are politicians by profession; but I think, what is it to any independent, intelligent, and respectable man what decision they may come to? Shall we not have the advantage of his wisdom and honesty, nevertheless? Can we not count upon some independent votes? Are there not many individuals in the country who do not attend conventions? But no: I find that the respectable man, so called, has immediately drifted from his position, and despairs of his country, when his country has more reason to despair of him. He forthwith adopts one of the candidates thus selected as the only *available* one, thus proving that he is himself *available* for any purposes of the demagogue. His vote is of no more worth than that of any unprincipled foreigner or hireling native, who may have been bought. O for a man who is a *man*, and, as my neighbor says, has a bone in his back which you cannot pass your hand through! Our statistics are at fault: the population has been returned too large. How many *men* are there to a square thousand miles in this country? Hardly one. Does not America offer any inducement for men to settle here? The American has dwindled into an Odd Fellow,[20]—one who may be known by the development of his organ of gregariousness, and a manifest lack of intellect and cheerful self-reliance;[21] whose first and chief concern, on coming into the world, is to see that the Almshouses are in good repair; and, before yet he has lawfully donned the virile garb,[22] to collect a fund for the support of the widows and orphans that may be; who, in short, ventures to live only by the aid of the Mutual Insurance Company, which has promised to bury him decently.

It is not a man's duty, as a matter of course, to devote himself to the eradication of any, even the most enormous wrong; he may still properly have other concerns to engage him; but it is his duty, at least, to wash his hands of it, and, if he gives it no thought longer, not to give it practically his support. If I devote myself to other pursuits and contemplations, I must first see, at least, that I do not pursue them sitting upon another man's shoulders. I must get off him first, that he may pursue his contemplations too. See what gross inconsistency is tolerated. I have heard some of my townsmen say, "I should like to have them order me out to help put down an insurrection of the slaves, or to march to Mexico;—see if I would go"; and yet these very men have each, directly by their allegiance, and so indirectly, at least, by their money, furnished a substitute. The soldier is applauded who refuses to serve in an unjust war by those who do not refuse to sustain the unjust government which makes the war; is applauded by those whose own act and authority he disregards and sets at naught; as if the State were penitent to that degree that it hired one to scourge it while it sinned, but not to that degree that it left off sinning for a moment. Thus, under the name of Order and Civil Government, we are all made at last to pay homage to and support our own meanness. After the first blush of sin comes its indifference; and from immoral it becomes, as it were, *un*moral, and not quite unnecessary to that life which we have made.

The broadest and most prevalent error requires the most disinterested virtue to sustain it. The slight reproach to which the virtue of patriotism is commonly liable, the noble are most likely to incur. Those who, while they disapprove of the character and measures of a government, yield to it their allegiance and support, are undoubtedly its most conscientious supporters, and so frequently the most serious obstacles to reform. Some are petitioning[23] the State to dissolve the Union, to disregard the requisitions of the President. Why do they not dissolve it themselves,—the union between themselves and the State,—and refuse to pay their quota into its treasury? Do not they stand in the same relation to the State, that the State does to the Union? And have not the same reasons prevented the State from resisting the Union, which have prevented them from resisting the State?

How can a man be satisfied to entertain an opinion merely, and enjoy *it?* Is there any enjoyment in it, if his opinion is that he is aggrieved? If you are cheated out of a single dollar by your neighbor, you do not rest satisfied with knowing that you are cheated, or with saying that you are cheated, or even with petitioning him to pay you your due; but you take effectual steps at once to obtain the full amount, and see that you are never cheated again. Action from principle, the perception and the performance of right, changes things and relations; it is essentially revolutionary, and does not consist wholly with anything which was. It not only divides states and churches, it divides families; ay, it divides the *individual*, separating the diabolical in him from the divine.

Unjust laws exist: shall we be content to obey them, or shall we endeavor to amend them, and obey them until we have succeeded, or shall we transgress them at once? Men generally, under such a government as this, think that they ought to wait until they have persuaded the majority to alter them. They think that, if they should resist, the remedy would be worse than the evil. But it is the fault of the government itself that the remedy *is* worse than the evil. *It* makes it worse. Why is it not more apt to anticipate and provide for reform? Why does it not cherish its wise minority? Why does it cry and resist before it is hurt? Why does it not encourage its citizens to be on the alert to point out its faults, and *do* better than it would have them? Why does it always crucify Christ, and excommunicate Copernicus[24] and Luther,[25] and pronounce Washington and Franklin[26] rebels?

One would think, that a deliberate and practical denial of its authority was the only offence never contemplated by government; else, why has it not assigned its definite, its suitable and proportionate penalty? If a man who has no property refuses but once to earn nine shillings for the State, he is put in prison for a period unlimited by any law that I know, and determined only by the discretion of those who placed him there; but if he should steal ninety times nine shillings from the State, he is soon permitted to go at large again.

If the injustice is part of the necessary friction of the machine of government, let it go, let it go: perchance it will wear smooth,—certainly the machine will wear out. If the injustice has a spring, or a pulley, or a rope, or a crank, exclusively for itself, then perhaps you may consider whether the remedy will not be worse than the evil; but if it is of such a nature that it requires you to be the agent of injustice to another, then, I say, break the law. Let your life be a counter friction to stop the machine. What I have to do is to see, at any rate, that I do not lend myself to the wrong which I condemn.

As for adopting the ways which the State has provided for remedying the evil, I know not of such ways. They take too much time, and a man's life will be gone. I have other affairs to attend to. I came into this world, not chiefly to make this a good place to live in, but to live in it, be it good or bad. A man has not everything to do, but something; and because he cannot do *everything*, it is not necessary that he should do *something* wrong. It is not my business to be petitioning the Governor or the Legislature any more than it is theirs to petition me; and, if they should not hear my petition, what should I do then? But in this case the State has provided no way: its very Constitution is the evil. This may seem to be harsh and stubborn and unconciliatory; but it is to treat with the utmost kindness and consideration the only spirit that can appreciate or deserves it. So is all change for the better, like birth and death, which convulse the body.

I do not hesitate to say, that those who call themselves Abolitionists should at once effectually withdraw their support, both in person and property, from the government of Massachusetts, and not wait till they constitute a majority of one,

before they suffer the right to prevail through them. I think
that it is enough if they have God on their side, without waiting for that other one. Moreover, any man more right than
his neighbors constitutes a majority of one already."[27]

I meet this American government, or its representative, the
State government, directly, and face to face, once a year—no
more—in the person of its tax-gatherer; this is the only mode
in which a man situated as I am necessarily meets it; and it
then says distinctly, Recognize me; and the simplest, the most
effectual, and, in the present posture of affairs, the indis-
pensablest mode of treating with it on this head, of expressing
your little satisfaction with and love for it, is to deny it then.
My civil neighbor, the tax-gatherer, is the very man I have
to deal with,—for it is, after all, with men and not with parch-
ment that I quarrel,—and he has voluntarily chosen to be an
agent of the government. How shall he ever know well what
he is and does as an officer of the government, or as a man,
until he is obliged to consider whether he shall treat me, his
neighbor, for whom he has respect, as a neighbor and well-
disposed man, or a maniac and disturber of the peace, and see
if he can get over this obstruction to his neighborliness without a ruder and more impetuous thought or speech corresponding with his action. I know this well, that if one thousand, if one hundred, if ten men whom I could name,—if ten
honest men only,—ay, if *one* HONEST man, in this State of
Massachusetts, *ceasing to hold slaves,* were actually to withdraw from this copartnership, and be locked up in the county
jail therefor, it would be the abolition of slavery in America.
For it matters not how small the beginning may seem to be:
what is once well done is done forever. But we love better
to talk about it: that we say is our mission. Reform keeps
many scores of newspapers in its service, but not one man. If
my esteemed neighbor, the State's ambassador,[28] who will devote his days to the settlement of the question of human
rights in the Council Chamber, instead of being threatened
with the prisons of Carolina, were to sit down the prisoner of
Massachusetts, that State which is so anxious to foist the sin
of slavery upon her sister,—though at present she can discover only an act of inhospitality to be the ground of a quarrel
with her,—the Legislature would not wholly waive the subject the following winter.

Under a government which imprisons any unjustly, the true

place for a just man is also a prison. The proper place to-day, the only place which Massachusetts has provided for her freer and less desponding spirits, is in her prisons, to be put out and looked out of the State by her own act, as they have already put themselves out by their principles. It is there that the fugitive slave, and the Mexican prisoner on parole, and the Indian[29] come to plead the wrongs of his race, should find them; on that separate, but more free and honorable ground, where the State places those who are not *with* her, but *against* her,—the only house in a slave State in which a free man can abide with honor. If any think that their influence would be lost there, and their voices no longer afflict the ear of the State, that they would not be as an enemy within its walls, they do not know by how much truth is stronger than error, nor how much more eloquently and effectively he can combat injustice who has experienced a little in his own person. Cast your whole vote, not a strip of paper merely, but your whole influence. A minority is powerless while it conforms to the majority; it is not even a minority then; but it is irresistible when it clogs by its whole weight. If the alternative is to keep all just men in prison, or give up war and slavery, the State will not hesitate which to choose. If a thousand men were not to pay their tax-bills this year, that would not be a violent and bloody measure, as it would be to pay them, and enable the State to commit violence and shed innocent blood. This is, in fact, the definition of a peaceable revolution, if any such is possible. If the tax-gatherer, or any other public officer, asks me, as one has done, "But what shall I do?" my answer is, "If you really wish to do anything, resign your office." When the subject has refused allegiance, and the officer has resigned his office, then the revolution is accomplished. But even suppose blood should flow. Is there not a sort of blood shed when the conscience is wounded? Through this wound a man's real manhood and immortality flow out, and he bleeds to an everlasting death. I see this blood flowing now.

I have contemplated the imprisonment of the offender, rather than the seizure of his goods,—though both will serve the same purpose,—because they who assert the purest right, and consequently are most dangerous to a corrupt State, commonly have not spent much time in accumulating property. To such the State renders comparatively small service, and a slight tax is wont to appear exorbitant, particularly if they are obliged to earn it by special labor with their hands. If there were one who lived wholly without the use of money,[30] the State itself would hesitate to demand it of him. But the rich man,—not to make any invidious comparison,—is always sold to the institution which makes him rich. Absolutely speaking, the more money, the less virtue; for money comes between a man and his objects, and obtains them for him; and it was certainly no great virtue to obtain it. It puts to rest many questions which he would otherwise be taxed to answer; while the only new question which it puts is the hard but superfluous one, how to spend it. Thus his moral ground is taken from under his feet. The opportunities of living are diminished in proportion as what are called the "means" are increased. The best thing a man can do for his culture when he is rich is to endeavor to carry out those schemes which he entertained when he was poor. Christ answered the Herodians according to their condition. "Show me the tribute-money," said he;—and one took a penny out of his pocket;—if you use money which has the image of Caesar on it, and which he has made current and valuable, that is, *if you are men of the State,* and gladly enjoy the advantages of Caesar's government, then pay him back some of his own when he demands it; "Render therefore to Caesar that which is Caesar's, and to God those things which are God's," [31]—leaving them no wiser than before as to which was which; for they did not wish to know.

When I converse with the freest of my neighbors, I perceive that, whatever they may say about the magnitude and seriousness of the question, and their regard for the public tranquillity, the long and the short of the matter is, that they cannot spare the protection of the existing government, and they dread the consequences to their property and families of disobedience to it.[32] For my own part, I should not like to think that I ever rely on the protection of the State. But, if I deny the authority of the State when it presents its tax-bill, it will soon take and waste all my property, and so harass me and my children without end. This is hard. This makes it impossible for a man to live honestly, and at the same time comfortably, in outward respects. It will not be worth the while to accumulate property; that would be sure to go again. You must hire or squat somewhere, and raise but a small crop, and eat that soon. You must live within yourself, and depend upon yourself always tucked up and ready for a start, and not have many affairs. A man may grow rich in Turkey even, if he will be in all respects a good subject of the Turkish government. Confucius said: "If a state is governed by the principles of reason, poverty and misery are subjects of shame; if a state is not governed by the principles of reason, riches and honors are the subjects of shame." [33] No; until I want the protection of Massachusetts to be extended to me in some distant Southern port, where my liberty is endangered, or until I am bent solely on building up an estate at home by peaceful enterprise, I can afford to refuse allegiance to Massachusetts, and her right to my property and life. It costs me less in every sense to incur the penalty of disobedience to the State, than it would to obey. I should feel as if I were worth less in that case.

Some years ago, the State met me in behalf of the Church,[34] and commanded me to pay a certain sum toward the support of a clergyman whose preaching my father attended, but never I myself. "Pay," it said, "or be locked up in the jail." I declined to pay. But, unfortunately, another man saw fit to pay it. I did not see why the schoolmaster should be taxed to support the priest, and not the priest the schoolmaster; for I was not the State's schoolmaster, but I supported myself by voluntary subscription. I did not see why the lyceum[35] should not present its tax-bill, and have the State to back its demand, as well as the Church. However, at the request of the selectmen, I condescended to make some such statement as this in writing:—"Know all men by these presents, that I, Henry Thoreau, do not wish to be regarded as a member of any incorporated society which I have not joined." This I gave to the town clerk; and he has it. The State, having thus learned that I did not wish to be regarded as a member of that church, has never made a like demand on me since; though it said that it must adhere to its original presumption that time. If I had known how to name them, I should then have signed off in detail from all the societies which I never signed on to; but I did not know where to find a complete list.

I have paid no poll-tax for six years. I was put into a jail once on this account, for one night;[36] and, as I stood considering the walls of solid stone,[37] two or three feet thick, the door of wood and iron, a foot thick, and the iron grating which strained the light, I could not help being struck with the foolishness of that institution which treated me as if I were mere flesh and blood and bones, to be locked up. I wondered that it should have concluded at length that this was the best use it could put me to, and had never thought to avail itself of my services in some way. I saw that, if there was a wall of stone between me and my townsmen, there was a still more difficult one to climb or break through, before they could get to be as free as I was. I did not for a moment feel confined, and the walls seemed a great waste of stone and mortar. I felt as if I alone of all my townsmen had paid my tax. They plainly did not know how to treat me, but behaved like persons who are underbred. In every threat and in every compliment there was a blunder; for they thought that my chief desire was to stand the other side of that stone wall. I could not but smile to see how industriously they locked the door on my meditations, which followed them out again without let or hindrance, and *they* were really all that was dangerous. As they could not reach me, they had resolved to punish my body; just as boys, if they cannot come at some person against whom they have a spite, will abuse his dog. I saw that the State was half-witted, that it was timid as a lone woman with her silver spoons, and that it did not know its friends from its foes, and I lost all my remaining respect for it, and pitied it.

Thus the State never intentionally confronts a man's sense, intellectual or moral, but only his body, his senses. It is not armed with superior wit or honesty, but with superior physical strength. I was not born to be forced. I will breathe after my own fashion. Let us see who is the strongest. What force has a multitude? They only can force me who obey a higher law[38] than I. They force me to become like themselves. I do not hear of *men* being *forced* to live this way or that by masses of men. What sort of life were that to live? When I meet a government which says to me, "Your money or your life," why should I be in haste to give it my money? It may be in a great strait, and not know what to do: I cannot help that. It must help itself; do as I do. It is not worth the while to snivel about it. I am not responsible for the successful working of the machinery of society. I am not the son of the engineer. I perceive that, when an acorn and a chestnut fall side by side, the one does not remain inert to make way for the other, but both obey their own laws, and spring and grow and flourish as best they can, till one, perchance, overshadows and destroys the other. If a plant cannot live according to its nature, it dies; and so a man.

The night in prison was novel and interesting enough. The prisoners in their shirt-sleeves were enjoying a chat and the evening air in the doorway, when I entered. But the jailer[39] said, "Come, boys, it is time to lock up"; and so they dispersed, and I heard the sound of their steps returning into the hollow apartments. My room-mate was introduced to me by the jailer, as "a first-rate fellow and a clever man." When the door was locked, he showed me where to hang my hat, and how he managed matters there. The rooms were whitewashed once a month; and this one, at least, was the whitest, most simply furnished, and probably the neatest apartment in the town. He naturally wanted to know where I came from, and what brought me there; and, when I had told him, I asked him in my turn how he came there, presuming him to be an honest man, of course; and, as the world goes, I believe he was. "Why," said he, "they accuse me of burning a barn; but I never did it." As near as I could discover, he had probably gone to bed in a barn when drunk, and smoked his pipe there; and so a barn was burnt. He had the reputation of being a clever man, had been there some three months waiting for his trial[40] to come on, and would have to wait as much longer; but he was quite domesticated and contented, since he got his board for nothing, and thought that he was well treated.

He occupied one window, and I the other; and I saw, that, if one stayed there long, his principal business would be to look out the window. I had soon read all the tracts that were left there, and examined where former prisoners had broken out, and where a grate had been sawed off, and heard the history of the various occupants of that room; for I found that even here there was a history and a gossip which never circulated beyond the walls of the jail. Probably this is the only house in the town where verses are composed, which are afterward printed in a circular form, but not published. I was shown quite a long list of verses which were composed by some young men who had been detected in an attempt to escape, who avenged themselves by singing them.

I pumped my fellow-prisoner as dry as I could, for fear I should never see him again; but at length he showed me which was my bed, and left me to blow out the lamp.

It was like travelling into a far country, such as I had never expected to behold, to lie there for one night. It seemed to me that I never had heard the town-clock strike before, nor the evening sounds of the village; for we slept with the windows open, which were inside the grating. It was to see my native village in the light of the Middle Ages, and our Concord was turned into a Rhine stream, and visions of knights and castles passed before me. They were the voices of old burghers that I heard in the streets. I was an involuntary spectator and auditor of whatever was done and said in the kitchen of the adjacent village-inn,[41]—a wholly new and rare experience to me. It was a closer view of my native town. I was fairly inside of it. I never had seen its institutions before. This is one of its peculiar institutions; for it is a shire town.[42] I began to comprehend what its inhabitants were about.

In the morning, our breakfasts were put through the hole in the door, in small oblong-square tin pans, made to fit, and holding a pint of chocolate, with brown bread, and an iron spoon. When they called for the vessels again, I was green enough to return what bread I had left; but my comrade seized it, and said that I should lay up for lunch or dinner. Soon after he was let out to work at haying in a neighboring field, whither he went every day, and would not be back till noon; so he bade me good-day, saying that he doubted if he should see me again.

When I came out of prison,—for some one[43] interfered, and paid that tax,—I did not perceive that great changes had taken place on the common, such as he observed who went in a youth, and emerged a tottering and gray-headed man; and yet a change had to my eyes come over the scene,—the town, and State, and country,—greater than any that mere time could effect. I saw yet more distinctly the State in which I lived. I saw to what extent the people among whom I lived could be trusted as good neighbors and friends; that their friendship was for summer weather only;[44] that they did not greatly propose to do right; that they were a distinct race from me by their prejudices and superstitions, as the Chinamen and Malays are; that, in their sacrifices to humanity, they ran no risks, not even to their property; that, after all, they were not so noble but they treated the thief as he had treated them, and hoped, by a certain outward observance and a few prayers, and by walking in a particular straight though useless path[45] from time to time, to save their souls. This may be to judge my neighbors harshly; for I believe that many of them are not aware that they have such an institution as the jail in their village.

It was formerly the custom in our village, when a poor debtor came out of jail, for his acquaintances to salute him, looking through their fingers, which were crossed to represent the grating of a jail window, "How do ye do?" My neighbors did not thus salute me, but first looked at me, and then at one another, as if I had returned from a long journey.[46] I was put into jail as I was going to the shoemaker's to get a shoe which was mended. When I was let out the next morning, I proceeded to finish my errand, and having put on my mended shoe, joined a huckleberry party, who were impatient to put themselves under my conduct; and in half an hour,—for the horse was soon tackled,—was in the midst of a huckleberry field, on one of our highest hills, two miles off, and then the State was nowhere to be seen.

This is the whole history of "My Prisons." [47]

I have never declined paying the highway tax, because I am as desirous of being a good neighbor as I am of being a bad subject; and, as for supporting schools, I am doing my part to educate my fellow-countrymen now. It is for no particular item in the tax-bill that I refuse to pay it. I simply wish to refuse allegiance to the State, to withdraw and stand aloof from it effectually. I do not care to trace the course of my dollar, if I could, till it buys a man or a musket to shoot one with,—the dollar is innocent,—but I am concerned to trace the effects of my allegiance. In fact, I quietly declare war with the State, after my fashion, though I will still make what use and get what advantage of her I can, as is usual in such cases.

If others pay the tax which is demanded of me, from a sympathy with the State, they do but what they have already done in their own case, or rather they abet injustice to a greater extent than the State requires. If they pay the tax from a mistaken interest in the individual taxed, to save his property, or prevent his going to jail, it is because they have not considered wisely how far they let their private feelings interfere with the public good.

This, then, is my position at present. But one cannot be too much on his guard in such a case, lest his action be biassed by obstinacy, or an undue regard for the opinions of men. Let him see that he does only what belongs to himself and to the hour.

I think sometimes, Why, this people mean well; they are only ignorant; they would do better if they knew how: why give your neighbors this pain to treat you as they are not inclined to? But I think again, this is no reason why I should do as they do, or permit others to suffer much greater pain of a different kind. Again, I sometimes say to myself, When many millions of men, without heat, without ill will, without personal feeling of any kind, demand of you a few shillings only, without the possibility, such is their constitution, of retracting or altering their present demand, and without the possibility, on your side, of appeal to any other millions, why expose yourself to this overwhelming brute force? You do not resist cold and hunger, the winds and the waves, thus obstinately; you quietly submit to a thousand similar necessities. You do not put your head into the fire. But just in proportion as I regard this as not wholly a brute force, but partly a human force, and consider that I have relations to those millions as to so many millions of men, and not of mere brute or inanimate things, I see that appeal is possible, first and instantaneously, from them to the Maker of them, and, secondly, from them to themselves. But, if I put my head deliberately into the fire, there is no appeal to fire or to the Maker of fire, and I have only myself to blame. If I could convince myself that I have any right to be satisfied with men as they are, and to treat them accordingly, and not according, in some respects, to my requisitions and expectations of what they and I ought to be, then, like a good Mussulman[48] and fatalist, I should endeavor to be satisfied with things as they are, and say it is the will of God. And, above all, there is this difference between resisting this and a purely brute or natural force, that I can resist this with some effect; but I cannot expect, like Orpheus,[49] to change the nature of the rocks and trees and beasts.

I do not wish to quarrel with any man or nation. I do not wish to split hairs, to make fine distinctions, or set myself up as better than my neighbors. I seek rather, I may say, even an excuse for conforming to the laws of the land. I am but too ready to conform to them. Indeed, I have reason to suspect myself on this head; and each year, as the tax-gatherer comes round, I find myself disposed to review the acts and position of the general and State governments, and the spirit of the people, to discover a pretext for conformity.

> "We must affect our country as our parents;
>   And if at any time we alienate
>   Our love or industry from doing it honor,
>   We must respect effects and teach the soul
>   Matter of conscience and religion,
>   And not desire of rule or benefit." [50]

I believe that the State will soon be able to take all my work of this sort out of my hands, and then I shall be no better a patriot than my fellow-countrymen. Seen from a lower point of view, the Constitution, with all its faults, is very good; the law and the courts are very respectable; even this State and this American government are, in many respects, very admirable and rare things, to be thankful for, such as a great many have described them; but seen from a point of view a little higher, they are what I have described them; seen from a higher still, and the highest, who shall say what they are, or that they are worth looking at or thinking of at all?

However, the government does not concern me much, and I shall bestow the fewest possible thoughts on it. It is not many moments that I live under a government, even in this world. If a man is thought-free, fancy-free, imagination-free, that which *is not* never for a long time appearing *to be* to him, unwise rulers or reformers cannot fatally interrupt him.

I know that most men think differently from myself; but those whose lives are by profession devoted to the study of these or kindred subjects, content me as little as any. Statesmen and legislators, standing so completely within the institution, never distinctly and nakedly behold it. They speak of moving society, but have no resting-place without it. They may be men of a certain experience and discrimination, and have no doubt invented ingenious and even useful systems, for which we sincerely thank them; but all their wit and usefulness lie within certain not very wide limits. They are wont to forget that the world is not governed by policy and expediency. Webster[51] never goes behind government, and so cannot speak with authority about it. His words are wisdom to those legislators who contemplate no essential reform in the existing government; but for thinkers, and those who legislate for all time, he never once glances at the subject. I know of those whose serene and wise speculations on this theme would soon reveal the limits of his mind's range and hospitality. Yet, compared with the cheap professions of most reformers, and the still cheaper wisdom and eloquence of politicians in general, his are almost the only sensible and valuable words, and we thank Heaven for him. Comparatively, he is always strong, original, and, above all, practical. Still his quality is not wisdom, but prudence. The lawyer's truth is not Truth, but consistency, or a consistent expediency. Truth is always in harmony with herself, and is not concerned chiefly to reveal the justice that may consist with wrong-doing. He well deserves to be called, as he has been called, the Defender of the Constitution. There are really no blows to be given by him but defensive ones. He is not a leader, but a follower. His leaders are the men of '87.[52] "I have never made an effort," he says, "and never propose to make an effort; I have never countenanced an effort, and never mean to countenance an effort, to disturb the arrangement as originally made, by which the various States came into the Union." [53] Still thinking of the sanction which the Constitution gives to slavery, he says, "Because it was a part of the original compact,—let it stand." Notwithstanding his special acuteness and ability, he is unable to take a fact out of its merely political relations, and behold it as it lies absolutely to be disposed of by the intellect,—what, for instance, it behooves a man to do here in America to-day with regard to slavery, but ventures, or is driven, to make some such desperate answer as the following, while professing to speak absolutely, and as a private man,—from which what new and singular code of social duties might be inferred? "The manner," says he, "in which the governments of those States where slavery exists are to regulate it, is for their own consideration, under their responsibility to their constituents, to the general laws of propriety, humanity, and justice, and to God. Associations formed elsewhere, springing from a feeling of humanity, or any other cause, have nothing whatever to do with it. They have never received any encouragement from me, and they never will." * 54

They who know of no purer sources of truth, who have traced up its stream no higher, stand, and wisely stand, by the Bible and the Constitution, and drink at it there with reverence and humility; but they who behold where it comes trickling into this lake or that pool, gird up their loins once more,55 and continue their pilgrimage toward its fountain-head.

No man with a genius for legislation has appeared in America. They are rare in the history of the world. There are orators, politicians, and eloquent men, by the thousand; but the speaker has not yet opened his mouth to speak, who is capable of settling the much-vexed questions of the day. We love eloquence for its own sake, and not for any truth which it may utter, or any heroism it may inspire. Our legislators have not yet learned the comparative value of free-trade and of freedom, of union, and of rectitude, to a nation. They have no genius or talent for comparatively humble questions of taxation and finance, commerce and manufactures and agriculture. If we were left solely to the wordy wit of legislators in Congress for our guidance, uncorrected by the seasonable experience and the effectual complaints of the people, America would not long retain her rank among the nations. For eighteen hundred years, though perchance I have no right to say it, the New Testament has been written; yet where is the legislator who has wisdom and practical talent enough to avail himself of the light which it sheds on the science of legislation?

The authority of government, even such as I am willing to submit to,—for I will cheerfully obey those who know and can do better than I, and in many things even those who neither know nor can do so well,—is still an impure one: to be strictly just, it must have the sanction and consent of the governed. It can have no pure right over my person and property but what I concede to it. The progress from an absolute to a limited monarchy, from a limited monarchy to a democracy, is a progress toward a true respect for the individual. Even the Chinese philosopher was wise enough to regard the individual

---

* These extracts have been inserted since the Lecture was read. [Thoreau's Footnote.]

as the basis of the empire.[56] Is a democracy, such as we know it, the last improvement possible in government? Is it not possible to take a step further towards recognizing and organizing the rights of man? There will never be a really free and enlightened State, until the State comes to recognize the individual as a higher and independent power, from which all its own power and authority are derived, and treats him accordingly. I please myself with imagining a State at last which can afford to be just to all men, and to treat the individual with respect as a neighbor; which even would not think it inconsistent with its own repose, if a few were to live aloof from it, not meddling with it, nor embraced by it, who fulfilled all the duties of neighbors and fellow-men. A State which bore this kind of fruit, and suffered it to drop off as fast as it ripened, would prepare the way for a still more perfect and glorious State, which also I have imagined, but not yet anywhere seen.[57]

NOTES

1. When Thoreau first delivered the essay as a lecture before the Concord Lyceum on January 26, 1848, he entitled it "On the Relation of the Individual to the State." When it was first printed, in Elizabeth Peabody's *Aesthetic Papers* in May, 1849, it was entitled "Resistance to Civil Government." It did not receive its present title of "Civil Disobedience" until it was published in Thoreau's *A Yankee in Canada, with Anti-Slavery and Reform Papers* in 1866, four years after his death. Professor Tokihiko Yamasaki of Osaka City University has pointed out to me the pun in the title—not only does it imply disobedience of civil authority, but also a civil (*i.e.*, a courteous) form of disobedience.

2. The motto is not from Thomas Jefferson, as many have supposed, but is rather from the masthead of the *Democratic Review*, a periodical to which Thoreau several times contributed articles. (Lee A. Pederson, "Thoreau's Source of the Motto in 'Civil Disobedience,'" *TSB*, 67.)

3. The war with Mexico was not declared until 1846, whereas Thoreau had refused to pay his tax as early as 1843. In citing the war, he was simply taking advantage of the fact that the war was a particularly unpopular one in the North. (John C. Broderick, "Thoreau, Alcott, and the Poll Tax," *SP*, LIII, 1956, 612-26.)

4. The *Aesthetic Papers* version at this point adds: "and, if ever they should use it in earnest as a real one against each other, it will surely split."

5. The 1840's, when "Civil Disobedience" was written, was a period of intense interest in social reform in the United States, which included a number of philosophical anarchists who advocated the dissolution of all government.

6. Thoreau is apparently thinking of Sir Edward Coke's "Corporations . . . have no souls" from his *Case of Sutton's Hospital.*

7. Those who transport gunpowder from the magazines to the guns during battle.

8. Charles Wolfe (1791-1823), "Burial of Sir John Moore at Corunna."

9. The entire body of inhabitants who may be summoned by the police in the event of a riot.

10. "Imperious Caesar, dead and turn'd to clay, Might stop a hole to keep the wind away."—Shakespeare, *Hamlet*, V. i. 236-37.

11. Shakespeare, *King John*, V. ii. 79-82.

12. The American Revolution, which began in Concord on April 19, 1775.

13. William Paley (1743-1805). *Moral and Political Philosophy*, VI. ii.

14. "If a fool should snatch a plank from a wreck, shall a wise man wrest it from him if he is able?"—Cicero, *De officiis*, III. xxiii.

15. "Whosoever will save his life shall lose it."—Matt. x: 39.

16. Cyril Tourneur, *The Revengers Tragaedie* (1608), IV. iv.

17. Much of the resistance against the abolition of slavery at the time came from Northerners who feared that such a move would damage the economy of the nation and cut their own profits.

18. "Know ye not that a little leaven leaventh the whole lump?" —I Cor. v. 6.

19. The Democratic Party held its 1848 convention in Baltimore. Trying to walk the fence between North and South, they avoided any discussion of slavery.

20. The Independent Order of Odd Fellows is a secret fraternal order which still exists throughout the United States.

21. An allusion to Ralph Waldo Emerson's famous essay of that name.

22. Roman boys assumed the *toga virilis* upon attaining puberty.

23. Some of the more radical Abolitionists, believing that it would be impossible ever to force the abolition of slavery through Congress, advocated the Northern states' withdrawal from the Union rather than obedience to laws which endorsed slavery.

24. Nicolaus Copernicus (1473-1543) escaped excommunication for the dissertation on the solar system only because he was on his deathbed when it was published.

25. Martin Luther (1483-1546) was excommunicated by Pope Leo X in 1520.

26. Washington and Franklin were, of course, leaders of the American Revolution against British authority.

27. *Cf.*, "A Man with God is always in the majority"—John Knox (1505-72).

28. Samuel Hoar (1778-1856), Thoreau's neighbor and father of his close friend Edward Hoar, was sent to South Carolina by the Commonwealth of Massachusetts in 1844 to protest the arrest of

Negro seamen on Massachusetts ships in South Carolina waters. He was forcibly evicted from the state by action of its legislature.

29. Thoreau was one of the few in his day to protest the ruthless treatment of the American Indian.

30. Edward Palmer, one of Thoreau's contemporaries, renounced the use of money entirely, and tried to pay his living costs with copies of the *Herald of Holiness*, a little paper he printed on New York's Bowery.

31. Matt. xxii: 19-21.

32. The word order of this sentence has been slightly changed from that of the *Aesthetic Papers* version.

33. *The Analects*, VIII, xiii.

34. In Thoreau's day, the church taxed each member of its congregation, and the taxes were billed and collected by the town officials. The First Parish Church (Unitarian) of Concord assumed that since Thoreau's parents attended the church, he himself wished to be considered a member and accordingly had him sent a tax bill in 1840. Because of his protest the bill was never sent again.

35. The lyceum movement sponsored lecture series in many American towns in the period from 1830 to the Civil War. Thoreau not only lectured frequently from their platform both in Concord and elsewhere, but was for a time curator of the Concord Lyceum.

36. It is not certain now just what night Thoreau did spend in the Concord jail, but it was probably either the 23rd or 24th of July, 1846.

37. The Concord jail was not a small-town lockup, but the Middlesex County Jail, a massive granite structure three stories high.

38. A favorite phrase with the Transcendentalists, referring to one's conscience or "the voice of God within." Thoreau had a chapter by this title in *Walden*.

39. The local jailer, constable, and tax collector at the time was Sam Staples, a personal friend of Thoreau. In later years Thoreau often hired Staples as an assistant when he did surveying.

40. Thoreau later learned that his cellmate was acquitted when he came up for trial.

41. The Middlesex Hotel, no longer extant.

42. At that time Concord shared with Cambridge the honor of being county seat of Middlesex County.

43. Although the person who paid Thoreau's tax has never been positively identified, it is generally agreed that it was probably his Aunt Maria Thoreau.

44. "Like summer friends, Flies of estate and sunshine"—George Herbert, *The Answer*.

45. Thoreau was obviously thinking of the many Biblical references (such as Heb. xii: 13) to a "straight path" through life.

46. Young Georgie Bartlett of Concord has said that he thought from the excitement stirred up over Thoreau's jailing he was seeing a Siberian exile or John Bunyan himself. (Walter Harding, *The Days of Henry Thoreau*, New York: Knopf, 1965, p. 205.)

47. Silvio Pellico (1789–1854), the Italian revolutionary, wrote an autobiography with this title that was popular in the 1840's.

48. *I.e.*, a Mohammedan.

49. Orpheus, son of the Muse Calliope, according to Greek mythology, played his lyre with such a masterly hand that rivers ceased to flow, beasts forgot their wildness, and even the mountains were moved to listen.

50. George Peele, *The Battle of Alcazar* (1588–89), II. ii. Thoreau has slightly reworded and modernized the text and, as John T. Onuska, Jr. has pointed out (*New York Times Book Review*, February 6, 1966, p. 47), has wrenched its meaning from its original context. These lines were not included in the *Aesthetic Papers* version.

51. Daniel Webster (1782-1852), famed Massachusetts senator.

52. *I.e.*, those who framed the American Constitution.

53. Speech on the Texas question, delivered by Webster on December 22, 1845. *Writings*, IX, 57.

54. Speech on the bill to exclude slavery from the territories, delivered by Webster on August 12, 1848. *Writings*, X, 38.

55. "Let your loins be girded about."—Luke xii: 35.

56. Confucius. This sentence was not included in the *Aesthetic Papers* version.

57. Note that this essay, like all of Thoreau's, ends on an essentially optimistic note.

LIST OF ABBREVIATIONS USED IN NOTES

AL	American Literature
ALLEN	*Henry David Thoreau, Walden,* edited by Francis H. Allen (Boston, 1910)
BPLQ	Boston Public Library Quarterly
CRAWFORD	*Henry David Thoreau: Representative Selections,* edited by Bartholow V. Crawford (New York, 1934)
DAE	Dictionary of American English
MLN	Modern Language Notes
NED	New English Dictionary
NEQ	New England Quarterly
SP	Studies in Philology
TSB	Thoreau Society Bulletin
UTSE	University of Texas Studies in English

All references to Thoreau's *writings* are to the first six volumes of the Manuscript (or Walden) Edition (Boston, 1906); and to Thoreau's *Journal,* to the last fourteen volumes (numbered separately) of that same edition.

BIBLIOGRAPHY

For a general evaluation of Thoreau's life, works, sources, ideas, and fame, see Walter Harding, *A Thoreau Handbook* (New York: New York University Press, 1959); a listing and analysis of the major works on *Walden* will be found on pp. 60-65 and 91-93, therein.

The definitive study of the *Walden* manuscripts is J. Lyndon Shanley, *The Making of Walden* (Chicago, Ill.: University of Chicago Press, 1957).

For a complete concordance of *Walden*, see J. Stephen Sherwin and Richard C. Reynolds, *A Word Index to Walden with Textual Notes* (Charlottesville, Va.: University of Virginia Press, 1960).

For a description of the various editions of *Walden*, see Walter Harding, *A Centennial Check-List of the Editions of Henry David Thoreau's Walden* (Charlottesville, Va.: University of Virginia Press, 1954).

There is no fully satisfactory biography of Thoreau available. Most detailed and complete is Henry Seidel Canby, *Thoreau* (Boston: Houghton Mifflin, 1939). For a more sympathetic approach to Thoreau's philosophy, see Henry Salt, *The Life of Henry D. Thoreau* (London, 1890). Walter Harding, *Thoreau: Man of Concord* (New York: Holt, Rinehart & Winston, 1960), anthologizes more than a hundred different reminiscences of Thoreau by his friends and contemporaries.

Twenty-four of the major critical articles on Thoreau are anthologized in Walter Harding, *Thoreau: A Century of Criticism* (Dallas, Tex.: Southern Methodist University Press, 1954).

The standard edition of Thoreau's works is the twenty-volume Manuscript (or Walden) Edition published by Houghton Mifflin in 1906.